THE DAIRY BOOK OF

BRITISH FOOD

THE DAIRY BOOK OF

BRITISH FOOD

OVER 400 RECIPES FOR EVERY OCCASION

Published by Ebury Press
Division of The National Magazine Company Ltd
Colquhoun House, 27–37 Broadwick Street,
London W1V 1FR
On behalf of the Milk Marketing Board
And distributed by The Dairy Industry

First impression 1988

ISBN 0 85223 735 9

EDITORIAL DIRECTION:	Yvonne McFarlane
ART DIRECTION:	Frank Phillips
EDITORS:	Helen Dore
	Ann Wilson
	Beverly Le Blanc
EDITORIAL ASSISTANT:	Rachel Gosling
TEXT:	Elizabeth Martyn
	Cassandra Kent
SENIOR HOME ECONOMIST:	Susanna Tee
DESIGNER:	Grahame Dudley
FOOD PHOTOGRAPHY BY	James Murphy
	Laurie Evans
	Grant Symon
STYLISTS:	Cathy Sinker
	Lesley Richardson
	Gina Carminati
FOOD PREPARED FOR	
PHOTOGRAPHY BY	Jacki Baxter
	Allyson Birch
	Maxine Clark
	Sue Philpot
	Janet Smith
ILLUSTRATIONS BY	Susan Robertson
	Gill Tomblin

THE PUBLISHERS WOULD ALSO LIKE TO THANK
THE DAIRY PRODUCE ADVISORY SERVICE,
MILK MARKETING BOARD, FOR THEIR HELP
IN COMPILING THE RECIPES

Computerset by MFK Typesetting Ltd, Hitchin, Herts.
Printed and bound by Jarrold and Sons Ltd, Norwich

CONTENTS

H.R.H. The Duchess of Kent

YORK HOUSE
ST. JAMES'S PALACE
LONDON S.W.1

I congratulate the Milk Marketing Board on making
such a positive contribution to British Food and
Farming Year 1989 through the publication of this
splendid new book featuring the best of British food
and cookery.

The Year will provide a marvellous opportunity for
our food and farming industry to tell the British
public more about its work and contribution to the
success of our Country.

This book will help to improve still further the
standards of British cooking and add greatly to the
enjoyment of eating imaginatively-prepared
home-produced food.

Katharine

A Taste of the Regions

The West Country

Avon, Cornwall, Devon, Dorset, Gloucestershire, Somerset, Wiltshire.

The mild climate and long coastline make this region not just a holiday-makers' paradise but the source of many delectable foods. Tender young vegetables and fruits, fine fish and shellfish, refreshing ciders and, above all, superb cream and cheeses are typical West Country temptations.

Merthyr Tydfil

Tewkesbury
Cheltenham
Forest of Deanester
GLOUCESTER HILLS
elvers
COTSWOLD
Oxford

Sharpness
lampreys

Newport
Wildfowl
Slimbridge
Sally Lunns
Swindon
Avebury
Marlborough

Bristol
Bath Buns
AVON
Bath

Silbury Hill
Savernake Forest
cèpes

CHANNEL
Minehead
Cheddar Gorge
Bath Olivers
Frome
WILTSHIRE

Lynton
Dunster
Wells
Yogurt
Stonehenge

XMOOR
Caerphilly
Honey
Salisbury

SOMERSET

withies
Glastonbury Tor
Sedgemoor

DORSET

Taunton
Scrumpy
Yeovil

Tarr Steps
Lace
Goats' Cheese
Honiton

Cerne Abbas Giant
Poole Pottery

Exeter
Fossils
Montacute House
Blue Vinney
Corfe Castle
Poole
Bournemouth

Lyme Regis
Chesil Beach
Weymouth

Torquay
The Cob

Brixham
Turbot
Red Mullet
Grey Mullet

Scallops

K·C

The land of the West Country is so fertile that
it spills over with a wealth of good produce.
Add to this the fact that the area enjoys the
mildest climate in England and it's not hard
to see why there's so much agricultural activity. To sum
up the food story of this generous region, think of cream
teas, cooling ciders, ripe strawberries and mellow
cheeses. Many people have sampled these West
Country delights on family holidays, and will have
travelled through the lush pastures past gently grazing
cattle on their way to the glorious beaches of Devon and
Cornwall.

The seas are warmed by the Gulf Stream, another
plus for holiday-makers, and the occupation of fishing
goes back for centuries. There are many bustling ports,
busy handling the vast quantity of fish and shellfish that
are landed here.

Spring arrives early in the West, ripening fruit and
vegetables well before they are ready elsewhere. Apple
orchards abound, filled with fruit to make the famous
cider, and everywhere there are grassy fields supporting
the dairy herds, which have made the production of
cream and cheese such a popular part of the farmer's
livelihood. Pig farming is also traditional, especially in
Wiltshire. Crops tend to come second to livestock,
although wheat, barley and oats are grown in
Gloucestershire.

Moving away from the countryside, the elegant
towns of Bath and Bristol have each made a
contribution to West Country eating. Bath has given its
name to several local goodies, mentioned later in this
chapter, and Bristol, which as a port was once second
only to London, used to trade in food and drink from all
over the world.

FAMOUS DAIRYING

All the breeds of cattle raised on the rich green grazing
of the West Country give milk with a high butterfat
content, perfect for making the cream, cheese and
butter for which the region is justly renowned. No visit
here would be complete without a traditional cream tea
– a plate heaped high with fresh scones or splits, lavishly
spread with strawberry jam and, of course, clotted
cream. This type of cream is one of the best-known
regional products and, as it both keeps and travels well,
is often brought or posted home as a souvenir by the
tourists who throng to this part of the country every
summer.

Clotted cream is widely made in Cornwall and
Devon, and some also comes out of Dorset. A handful
of farms make it by the traditional method, but most
producers use automatic separators and more up-to-date
equipment. The basic idea is simple: double cream is

heated, held at a high temperature for up to 40 minutes, and then cooled. The clotted cream that forms has a yellowish colour, wrinkled appearance, distinctive flavour and a very thick, grainy texture. Cream, clotted or otherwise, features in many West Country recipes (try Pork Fillet in Mustard Cream Sauce, see recipe, page 141). Luscious ice creams are another dairy product that is being more widely made.

It is, however, cheese for which the West Country is truly celebrated. The best-known variety of all must be Cheddar, which originated in Somerset and is now the most widely made cheese in the world. Its history dates back over the centuries – it was already highly thought of in the time of Henry II and has been prized ever since. English Farmhouse Cheddar is made by traditional methods. The milk will have been produced on the maker's farm, although by agreement milk from other local farms can also be used. The cheese is allowed to mature for at least six months and is carefully graded, with only the best being selected for its rich, mellow flavour. Cheddar comes with many different flavouring variations; you can also choose between mild and mature, depending on strength of flavour preferred.

Gloucestershire cheeses have an equally long history. They were originally made from the milk of the now rare Gloucester cattle, and came in two sizes. Double Gloucester is disc-shaped and, at 5 inches thick, was twice the depth of Single Gloucester, which is very hard to find these days. The two cheeses also differed in colour and flavour. Gloucester cheese was originally made with a tough rind, which enabled it to withstand the annual cheese-rolling ceremonies. These still take place, although today the cheese is wrapped in hessian to help it stand up to its downhill journey (see Food Fairs and Festivals, page 17).

A cheese with a somewhat shorter history is Lymeswold, which has quickly become popular since its launch in 1982 as the first new, natural English cheese for centuries.

Blue Vinney, a hard, white, blue-veined cheese, is an interesting variety that is well worth seeking out, although it is hard to track down. It was made only in

WEST COUNTRY CHEESES

Whether you are putting together an English cheeseboard or looking for a well-flavoured cheese for cooking, the West Country has something to offer. The most popular and famous of these cheeses are widely available at supermarkets, while others, made on a smaller scale, are stocked by delicatessens or specialist cheese shops.

CHEDDAR

A hard, golden yellow, firm cheese. Sweet and mild when young, stronger when mature. An excellent cheeseboard choice, and also good for cooking. Comes with added flavourings such as smoky paprika (Applewood and Charnwood); beer and garlic (Ilchester); chives (Cheviot) and several others.

DOUBLE GLOUCESTER

Golden straw-colour with a good mellow flavour. Melts beautifully, so ideal for cooking and toasting.

CURWORTHY

A semi-hard cheese made in Devon. A creamy buttery taste, develops a fuller flavour when matured. Good for cheeseboards.

CORNISH YARG

Full-flavoured and creamy, with a coating of nettle leaves.

DEVON GARLAND

A Jersey milk, semi-soft cheese that has a band of herbs running through it.

DOUBLE GLOUCESTER

CORNISH YARG

CURWORTHY

CHEDDAR

DEVON GARLAND

Dorset, from partly skimmed cows' milk, and local rumour claimed that the blue veining came from the mould of horses' leather tack. One farm in the area is now making Blue Vinney again, by more acceptable methods, so snap some up if you should come across it. However, you may have more luck in the search for Dorset Blue, which is similar but made from full-fat milk.

Many other cheeses originate from this part of the country. Look out for Cornish Yarg, Curworthy, Devon Garland, all delicious in their own ways (see fact panel for more details). And there are tasty goat and sheep cheeses emerging from the West too.

MORE-ISH BAKES AND CAKES

Probably the best-known bake of the West Country is the Cornish pasty, a portable meal originally made for farmers and miners to take to work. A good one has chunks of meat, not mince, plus potatoes and onions, inside a crisp pastry overcoat. But sometimes pasties don't live up to these high ideals – there is even a legend that the Devil refused to cross the Tamar into Cornwall because he had heard that the Cornish would put anything into their pasties!

Lots of lovely cakes come from these parts, including fruit cakes and honey cakes. The flowers of the countryside provide the perfect feeding ground for bees, and one of the monks at Buckfast Abbey maintains over 300 colonies in Devon and Cornwall, and sells the

honey in the Abbey shop. The colour and texture differ according to where the bees have gathered the nectar.

Ginger and spice feature strongly among the flavourings – they used to arrive at the ports from strange foreign places, and were pounced on by local cooks to add interest to their recipes. Saffron, although now quite hard to come by, was a popular if expensive flavouring and colouring ingredient. Apples, of course, crop up in cakes and puddings (try Somerset Apple Cake and Cider Cake, recipes, pages 265 and 266), and another favourite, Lardy Cake (recipe, page 292), also comes from the region. Devon Flats are a very more-ish biscuit, made with clotted cream (recipe, page 278). There are plenty of different flours for home-bakers to choose from, as several mills in the south-west produce organic and stone-ground varieties.

The spa town of Bath is known for three baked delicacies. Bath buns are made from a rich, yeasty mixture; they are beautifully yellow inside and are topped with crushed lump sugar. The Pump Room still serves them for tea. Dr W. Oliver, who founded the Bath Mineral Water Hospital, performed another great service when he invented the Bath Oliver biscuit as part of the simple diet required by those taking the waters for their health. These crisp crackers are still made today, and are the ideal accompaniment to a chunk of Cheddar cheese. Look for the portrait of their originator, imprinted on one side of each biscuit. Thirdly, from Bath, comes Sally Lunn, a round, light, yeast cake. There are various legends attached to the name, but whether Sally Lunn was really an 18th-century street seller will never be known. Again, you can buy the cakes in the town, and apparently the best way to eat them is split and filled with whipped, sweetened cream.

FISH AND SHELLFISH GALORE

Cornish coasts face two seas, and consequently the fleets bring home a wide variety of fine-quality fish. Pilchards were formerly the biggest catch, but mysteriously disappeared earlier this century and have now been replaced by huge hauls of mackerel. Pilchards still turn up occasionally but in unpredictable quantities. They were traditionally used to make the delightfully named Stargazey Pie, in which the heads of the fish are left poking out through the pastry crust, to gaze at the stars.

Newlyn and Falmouth are the big ports in Cornwall, where monkfish, sole, hake, skate and many other varieties are landed. Fishing is big business in Devon

BELOW
Lobster pots line the harbour at Boscastle, Cornwall. This baited pot or 'creel' is the most common way of catching them. Lobsters are ideal for special occasions – allow two servings per average-sized lobster.

OILY FISH

A lot of oily fish are caught and brought into western ports. These varieties tend to be excellent value for money and, as well as being full of flavour, they are exceptionally nutritious. You'll find some tempting fish recipes on pages 184 to 204.

PILCHARDS

Rarely available fresh and usually only found locally to fishing port. Most are exported or canned. A strong, oily flavour, best enjoyed grilled or fried whole. Best between November and February.

HERRING

A streamlined fish, with a steely-blue back and silvery belly. At their best from July to February. Braise, bake, fry or grill. Also available smoked or kippered, and as rollmops in vinegar.

MACKEREL

Larger than herring, with a pattern of dark zigzags on the back and a silver belly. Firm, well-flavoured flesh. Cook as for herring, or can be soused in vinegar. In season all year round. Also available smoked.

SPRATS

A smaller member of the herring family (but not a young herring). Has a bluish-green back and silvery sides and belly. In season October to March. Bake, fry or grill. Also available smoked.

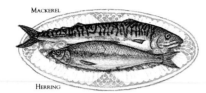

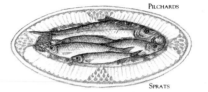

RIGHT
A fisherman lands a basketful of crabs. Fishmongers sell them live, boiled or dressed. Crabs provide two types of meat: white (legs and claws) and brown (the body meat), which is stronger in flavour with a creamier texture. Both are delicious.

OPPOSITE TOP
Small, hardy breeds of sheep, such as the Welsh Mountain, can survive the harsh winter conditions on Dartmoor in Devon. The animals are good foragers, and can live through the coldest weather without needing extra fodder.

OPPOSITE BELOW
Feeding time for these Gloucester Old Spot piglets, which are allowed to roam freely in orchards as they fatten. Each sow produces two litters per year.

too, and trawlers out of Brixham and Plymouth catch about 10 per cent of the total English haul. Dover sole are common, despite their name, and turbot, brill, dabs, conger eel and red and grey mullet also feature among the catch. You'll find interesting recipe ideas for fish between pages 184 and 204.

A great deal of this fish is exported or sent up to London. But some is sold fresh locally, and more finds its way into West Country smokeries, which produce smoked mackerel, kippers and bloaters. Fish for smoking has to be in tip-top condition, with a high oil content to make sure that the finished product is still deliciously moist. Most mackerel is hot-smoked, which means that no further cooking is needed and it can be eaten cold, just as it is. Alternatively, you can use it in recipes such as Smoked Mackerel Soufflé (page 196). Cold-smoked mackerel has a mavellous succulent flavour but needs to be cooked, or served cut in wafer-thin slices, like smoked salmon.

The waters of the West are well stocked with shellfish, and spider crabs, crayfish, scallops and lobsters are all considered local delicacies (you'll find recipes for crab and lobster on page 202). The crabs in Cornwall are larger than those caught in East Anglia, but the two areas both claim that *their* crabs have the finest flavour! Besides these luxurious treats, the everyday favourites – cockles, winkles, prawns and mussels – also thrive in these seas. There are oyster beds too, in Devon and Cornwall, producing both Native and Pacific oysters.

Freshwater fish, especially salmon and trout, from rivers such as the Dart, Exe and Tamar, feature on the menus of local restaurants and are frequently served cooked with cider or cream. Fish farms have sprung up here as they have elsewhere in the country. As well as trout and salmon, some enterprising fish farmers are producing more unusual fish, including pike, grayling and carp. Shellfish are also farmed on a small scale and oysters, crayfish and mussels are all commercially grown. Again, many of these fish end up in the smokeries or are made into fish products such as pâté and mousses.

Gloucestershire is well known for Severn salmon, and perhaps less famed for its elvers. The salmon are thought to have a fine flavour and are caught in May, by skilled fishermen using either traditional 'lave nets' or basket traps. Elvers, or baby eels, swim thousands of miles from the Sargasso Sea to come swarming up the Severn, and have been much relished for centuries. You're not likely to find them on the fishmonger's slab, however, and probably the only way to taste them is to join in the annual elver eating contests (see Food Fairs and Festivals, page 17).

PRIME MEAT

Pork is the prime meat of the West and is produced mainly in Wiltshire, which has been famous for pig farming for centuries. This is the county to visit for traditional sausages and faggots, and the hams and bacon are also well worth trying. The 'Wiltshire cure' produces sweet-flavoured, mild bacon, smoked or unsmoked. And Bradenham hams are a great treat, and are still prepared to a special, secret recipe. Soaked in juniper-flavoured molasses before smoking, they have a

black, shiny outer coating which is unmistakable. Another West Country pork speciality is Bath chaps, which are the cured cheeks of the pig. Originally they came from a breed called the Gloucestershire Old Spot, an attractive dappled creature which has fortunately been saved from dying out completely. The pigs were fed on windfalls from the many apple orchards, which was said to give the flesh a particularly sweet flavour.

Plump, tender chickens and turkeys are bred all over the region, with ducks found particularly in Wiltshire, and the more unusual guinea fowl being reared in Somerset. If cooked carefully (see page 172 for roasting details) these birds compare well with the more costly pheasant. There is, of course, a wide variety of wild game to be found on the moors of Wiltshire, Devon and Cornwall, including rabbit and duck.

There is no shortage of cattle or sheep in these parts, and both Devon and Dorset produce good beef and excellent lamb. Cornwall, with its harsher landscape, has less of a tradition of livestock rearing and used, in the past, to rely mainly on the hardy goat for meat. However, the county does produce early lambs which have a superb flavour.

WEST COUNTRY CIDER

Traditionally, cider from this part of the country is made from cider apples, rather than the culinary and dessert varieties used in other regions. This gives farmhouse ciders their distinctive dryness.

FARMHOUSE CIDERS

From bone dry to reasonably sweet, many types of cider are brewed by small producers and sold locally 'over the gate'. These farmers tend to use the cider apples known as bittersharps and bittersweets to get the flavour they want.

Production is simple: the apples are pulped and allowed to ferment naturally in barrels. Different fruits might be blended or the cider may be made from one variety only.

These ciders vary widely in quality and can be excellent. They are only available locally, and it is wisest to try before you buy.

COMMERCIALLY PRODUCED CIDERS

Two of the country's largest cider producers are in the West Country and make a range of ciders of a consistent standard and flavour. Again, special cider apples are widely used. The drink is aged in oak vats and then carefully blended.

Types available include still, dry ciders, which are fairly strong; sweet, sparkling bottled ciders; and still, mellow, dryish ciders, which are almost like wine.

Blossom time in a cider apple orchard. The trees are planted close together and kept well pruned. Fertile valleys are ideal for apples, as they provide shelter from the frosts and winds that can damage the flowers and threaten the fruit crop.

YOUNG AND TENDER FRUIT AND VEG

The fertile land and well-warmed climate, with its regular rainfall, make the West Country ideal for growing vegetables. In fact the unusual warmth of these southerly parts means that crops are ripe well before those grown further north. In Cornwall, farmers can start planting potatoes in February, a month earlier than in less sheltered places. The very first crop is ready by May and these young early potatoes and other vegetables, such as peas and broad beans, have a tenderness and delicacy of flavour that is unbeatable. Other staple main-crop vegetables, such as carrots, Brussels sprouts and onions, also grow well. A scattering of herb farms, some salads and asparagus, and sizeable crops of sweet peppers, cauliflower and turnips complete the vegetable picture in the West.

Early strawberries from the Tamar valley are another great delicacy, and Cornwall also grows gooseberries, no doubt in order to cook one of the county's best traditional dishes, Baked Mackerel with Gooseberry Sauce (recipe, page 195). However, this is not really a great area for soft fruit, as the climate in Dorset and Devon is too wet to guarantee a good harvest, although strawberries are produced under intensive market gardening methods in Somerset, and in Gloucestershire they grow apricots, cherries and plums.

But it is apples, apples and more apples in the West Country, reflected deliciously in regional recipes like Somerset Apple Cake or Pork Fillet in Mustard Cream Sauce (recipes, pages 265 and 141). Apple orchards

FOOD FAIRS AND FESTIVALS

JANUARY

Wassailing the Apple Trees, Carhampton, Somerset: annual festival of toasting the orchard to bring a good crop.

EASTERTIDE

Easter Monday. Elver Eating Contest, Frampton on Severn, Gloucestershire.
Easter Tuesday. Distribution of Twopenny Starvers, St Michael on the Mount Without, Bristol: buns are distributed to the young and old of the parish in a ceremony dating from 1739.

APRIL

Wimborne Horticultural Society Spring Show, Allendale Community Centre, Hanham Road, Wimborne, Dorset: spring flowers and produce, cookery, handicrafts.

MAY

Cheese Rolling Ceremony, Randwick, Gloucestershire, and Cooper's Hill, Brockworth, Gloucestershire (held on Whit Monday): large Double Gloucester cheeses are rolled downhill; originally carried out to protect grazing rights.
Devon County Show, County Showground, Exhibition Way, Whipton, Exeter, Devon: agricultural show.
Royal Bath and West Show, Showground, Shepton Mallet, Somerset: includes British Farm Food Fair, crafts, conservation, forestry.

JUNE

Royal Cornwall Agricultural Show, Wadebridge: livestock, crops and flowers.

JULY

Stithians Show, Playing Fields, Stithians, Truro, Cornwall: horses, cattle, goats, dogs, chickens, horticulture.

AUGUST

Harvest Home. Procession at East Brent, Somerset: church service, followed by procession of women carrying plum puddings; a huge loaf and 100 lb cheese are carried through the streets.

OCTOBER

Taunton Annual Illuminated Carnival and Cider-Barrel Rolling Race, Taunton, Somerset: carnival procession and race between teams pushing wooden cider barrels.

NOVEMBER

Great Western Beer Festival, Bristol Exhibition Centre, Canon's Road, Bristol, Avon: over 200 real ales and ciders, plus food and entertainments.

flourish all over the region. In the main, the apples are grown for cider-making (see Cider Fact Panel, opposite).

DRINKS FOR SIPPING AND SLURPING

Cider, in all styles and strengths, is the hallmark of West Country drinking. From farmhouse, scrumpy-type brews, to dry, smooth ciders, there is something to suit every taste. Some beer is also brewed in the region.

Wine-making is a growing venture in the West Country, even though the climate is not quite as suitable as it is in drier parts of the country. But there are commercial vineyards in Avon, Somerset, Wiltshire, Devon and Cornwall, producing a range of white wines. Many vineyards are experimenting with different grape varieties, but it is too soon yet to say how successful these will be.

Devon is home to the manufacturers of a rich cream liqueur, which combines local cream with brandy and whisky to make a sumptuous after-dinner drink. Another company in the area produces a range of fruit liqueurs, including raspberry, strawberry and blackcurrant. And in Somerset, they are distilling their cider to make an apple wine and have plans to launch an apple brandy in the near future. Plymouth has its very own gin distillery, where Plymouth gin has been made since 1793, and mead, an alcoholic drink made from fermented honey, is produced on a small scale.

Part-time pickers gather the harvest into baskets, to be taken for pressing. Cider apples are left on the trees until they start to fall, as the autumn sunshine helps the fruit to build up a high sugar content, vital for the strength and flavour of the cider.

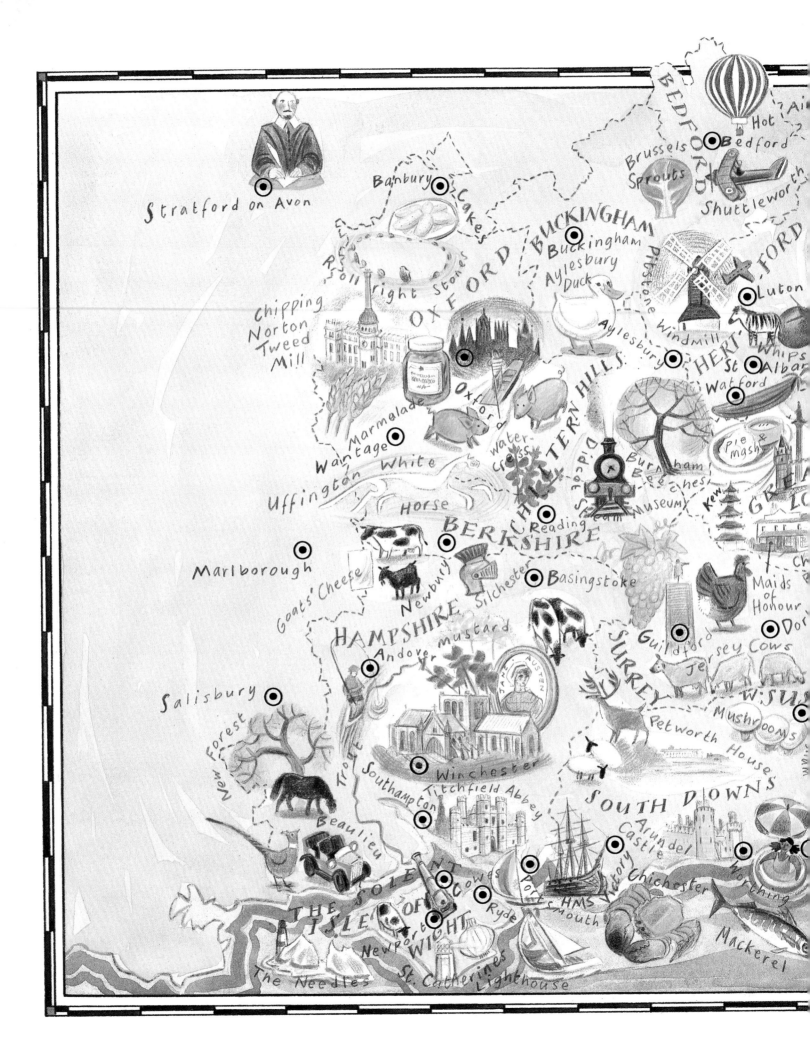

Stratford on Avon

Banbury

Cakes

Roll right Stones

BEDFORD

Hot Air

Bedford

Brussels
Sprouts

Shuttleworth

BUCKINGHAM

Buckingham

Aylesbury
Duck

Pitstone

Aylesbury Windmill

Luton

Chipping
Norton
Tweed
Mill

Oxford

Marmalade

Wantage

OXFORD

water-
cress

Didcot

HERT

St
Albans

Whips

Watford

CHILTERN HILLS

Burnham
Bee ches

Steam Museum

Pie mash

Kew

GR
LO

Uffington White

Horse

Reading

BERKSHIRE

Marlborough

Goats' Cheese

Newbury

Silchester

Basingstoke

Maids
of
Honour

Dor

Jersey Cows

HAMPSHIRE

Andover

mustard

SURREY

Guildford

W. SU

Salisbury

New Forest

Trout

Southampton

Winchester

Titchfield Abbey

JANE AUSTEN

Petworth House

Mushrooms

SOUTH DOWNS

Arundel
Castle

Chichester

Worthing

Beaulieu

THE SOLENT

ISLE of

Cowes

Ryde

Dor

Victory

HMS mouth

Mackerel

Newport

WIGHT

The Needles

St. Catherines Lighthouse

A TASTE OF THE REGIONS

THE SOUTH-EAST

BEDFORD, BUCKINGHAM, OXFORD, BERKSHIRE, HAMPSHIRE, ISLE OF WIGHT, WEST SUSSEX, EAST SUSSEX, KENT, SURREY, GREATER LONDON, HERTFORD.

Orchards in blossom, roadside stalls laden with glowing fruit, sheep and cattle grazing contentedly, fields of grain – such are the sights that open up from London. Rich farmlands stretch down to the coast, encompassing the Garden of England and making a cornucopia filled with soft fruits, vegetables, seafoods, meat, milk and other good things.

ENGLISH WINES

Most are white, and range
from dry to medium sweet.
They are similar to
German Hock or Moselles
in style and the best have a
good crisp acidity, a fresh
taste and a deeper flavour
than their continental
counterparts. Delicious
with fish, light meats, or as
an aperitif.

*These labels illustrate just a few
of the many English wines
available. Look out for them in
your supermarket or off-licence,
or pay a visit to your local
vineyard – most welcome
visitors.*

A kind climate, enough rain to keep the crops
watered and a fertile soil – all these bonuses
are enjoyed by farmers in the South-East.
Farming of all types goes on here. Cereals,
such as wheat, barley and oats, and root vegetables are
grown, but the area is most famous for market
gardening, with the Kent and Sussex Weald especially
producing large amounts of fruit and vegetables.
Relative newcomers to the scene are grape vines,
rapidly becoming more widespread as the fine ancient
tradition of English wine-making is revived.

As well as producing top-quality crops, the land is
ideal for raising cattle and sheep, while the fishing
industry is still important around parts of the south-east
coast.

In the heart of the region is London. The days are
long gone when London produced some of its own food.
Everything has to be brought in. Billingsgate,
Smithfield and Covent Garden, major centres of food
distribution, are still here. But no crops are grown near
London, no animals reared. Even the Home Counties
have lost some of their farming tradition, as they have
been gradually swallowed up by the capital. You can buy
food of every possible type and nationality in London's
markets and specialist shops, and you can sample the
cuisines of the world in the city's numerous restaurants.
It's the place to visit for traditional dishes like jellied
eels or boiled beef and carrots, or for exotic ethnic food
from far-flung countries like India, Africa, Mexico,
China and Thailand, to name just a few.

But travel just that bit further towards the south coast
and you reach the fertile acres and overflowing market
gardens from which the rest of Britain gains tender
lamb, fine fruit, superb shellfish and much more.

SUCCULENT PASTURES

Herds of dairy cattle are a common sight in the fields of
the South-East. By far the most are found in
Hampshire, where the lush pastures make ideal fodder.

Cutting the barley by
combine harvester. The
relatively dry late summer and
autumn in these parts means
there's less chance of the crops
being ruined by rain.

There are sizeable dairy herds, too, on the Isle of Wight and in Berkshire, Sussex and Kent. The number of cows kept for milk in Greater London, where until the mid-19th century large herds grazed on Clapham Common and Hampstead Heath, has diminished to almost nothing. Nowadays, London gets all its milk from the surrounding counties and 169 million gallons are brought into the capital every year.

The South-East has no tradition of cheese-making. Some new cheeses are being created as part of the national revival of interest in the farmhouse cheeses, but none of these is widely obtainable. Oxford cheese is a Cheddar type, available plain or smoked, which has recently been re-introduced. There is only one producer, but you should be able to find Oxford cheese in specialist delicatessens countrywide.

Other small-scale enterprises in the South-East include many dairy sheep and goat farms, producing milk, yogurt and cheeses. Look out for these delicacies if you are in the area. Loseley Park Farm near Guildford in Surrey use the milk of their pedigree Jerseys to make a range of natural, additive-free dairy products and these are widely found in wholefood shops in the south of England.

FLOURISHING FRUIT

Its warm, moist climate and rich soil make the Kent Weald exceptionally fertile. Fruit and vegetables thrive here in the Garden of England, as they have since the 16th century. But fruit was flourishing in this area long before then. Cherries first came to England with the Romans and still turn the orchards of the South-East into a mass of blossom every spring, even though far fewer cherry orchards exist than 30 or 40 years ago. The numbers have dwindled because the trees are tall and the crops had to be harvested from ladders – a costly and time-consuming business. However, small trees are gradually being introduced which make mechanised gathering possible.

Several varieties of sweet cherry are grown in Kent. You'll see many different types in the shops and it's worth buying them as they arrive. The picking period in any orchard is only about a week, so the supplies to the markets are constantly changing. If you want to cook cherries in a savoury dish, like Lamb with Cherries (see recipe, page 116), look out for red-skinned, sour types. Morellos are also a good choice – they have dark skin and flesh, and are also used for canning, bottling and making cherry brandy.

Apples are the other major fruit crop of Kent, the trees laden with more of that breathtaking spring blossom. Cox's Orange Pippins, one of Britain's favourite apples, were first grown in the South-East, and many other eaters, cookers, especially Bramley's, and cider apples are cultivated here.

Conference pears are frequently planted alongside dessert apple orchards. Also widely grown are Doyenne du Comice, which has a melting, fragrant flesh, and Williams' Bon Chrétien, a juicy sweet pear, often used

DESSERT APPLES

Numerous varieties of apple are grown and those listed here and overleaf are just a few of the types most widely available. Choose unblemished fruit without bruises, buy little and often, and store in a cool place, not in a bowl in a warm room. Many dessert apples can also be used successfully for cooking.

Cox's Orange Pippin
Crisp, juicy and very aromatic. (October to May.)

Ida Red
Succulent and crisp with white, juicy fresh. (November to March.)

Discovery
Firm, white and juicy. Fairly sweet. (August to September.)

Egremont Russet
Small and crisp with a distinctive nutty flavour. (October to December.)

Cox's Orange Pippins, fresh from the tree in a Sussex orchard, waiting to be graded according to size and skin quality before going to market. The picker, who has just emptied her fruit into the central collecting point, would belong to the team of extra casual labour taken on every year for the harvest.

Worcester Pearmain
Sweet, with crisp white flesh.
Eat when really ripe.
(September to October.)

Spartan
Firm, crisp and juicy. Refreshing
flavour. (November to March.)

Laxton Superb
Very sweet and juicy with firm
flesh. (November to April.)

ABOVE
The Georgian shop-front of
one of the most celebrated
cheesemongers in the country
– Paxton & Whitfield, in
central London's exclusive
Jermyn Street. The store
stocks over 50 varieties of
English cheeses, as well as
English hams.

RIGHT
English's Oyster Bar in
Brighton has been serving
delicious fresh shellfish to
satisfied customers for 150
years from premises in the
charming olde worlde area of
the town, known as The
Lanes.

for canning. South Buckinghamshire is known for its
plums and damsons, while Victoria plums from Kent
also make excellent eating.

As well as acres of fruit trees, the South-East boasts
bushels of soft fruit – much of it on offer at pick-your-
own farms. Black- and redcurrants, gooseberries,
raspberries and strawberries make a brightly coloured
display throughout the summer.

A WEALTH OF FRESH VEGETABLES

No market gardening area would be complete without
plentiful vegetables, and salads galore are grown in the
South-East, as well as broccoli, beans, cauliflower and
almost every other vegetable you care to name. Some
counties have specialities: Brussels sprouts are big news
in Bedfordshire, Sussex has a large number of
mushroom farms and Hampshire grows most of Britain's
native watercress. Its deliciously tangy flavour is good
for enlivening a dish like Warm Watercress, Potato and
Bacon Salad (see recipe, page 89).

That deliciously aromatic member of the lily family,
garlic, is produced on a small scale in the UK, mostly on
the Isle of Wight. As well as adding flavour to recipes,
garlic is said to have many medicinal properties, not to
mention being useful for warding off evil spirits.

Kentish cob nuts, sometimes called Lambert's
Filberts, were first grown by Mr Lambert in about 1830.
They are a variety of hazelnut which has pleasant, sweet
flesh. The crop is smaller now than in the past but you
should still be able to find Kentish cobs in the shops
during October.

GOOD GRAZING

Most farms in the South-East are mixed, and sheep are
kept on more than half of them, as they are happy to

graze on pasture which is unsuitable for cattle. The ewes
are mainly cross breeds, bought from upland farms.
They are crossed again with good meat breeds to
produce hardy lambs with the best characteristics of
both types. The Suffolk sheep, a hornless creature, with
a black, bare face and legs and a long body, is probably
most commonly used as a sire in the South-East.

Pure breeds are used only when their special
characteristics make them ideal for a particular area.
One famous pure breed is the Romney Marsh, which
feeds on the salty pastures that border Sussex and Kent,
and is robust enough to withstand the winds that sweep
across the grazing grounds from the Channel.

Sheep normally produce lambs once a year, usually in
the early spring, always a busy time for sheep farmers.
The young start nibbling grass at about three to four
weeks old and are fully weaned by mid-summer. Lambs
sold for meat are under a year old, and English lamb is
reckoned to be at its best from August to November.

Cattle also do well in the South-East and although many belong to dairy herds, beef production is also important. The two types of farming are closely interlinked. Some of the calves born to the dairy herd are kept to supplement the milk-producers, others are used for breeding and the remainder are reared for meat.

Sussex cattle – which are large and reddish-brown – are a breed commonly found in the area. But once again, they are cross bred in order to combine the good qualities of beef bulls and dairy cows.

Poultry and turkeys are important in the South-East, where almost half the 13 million chickens kept are for egg production, the rest being reared for the table. Surrey has been famous for capons and chickens for centuries, since they were bred for the royal table at Hampton Court. The Aylesbury duck, a large, plump, white species, originated in Buckinghamshire, but the pure breed has now almost disappeared.

Pig farms are scattered throughout the South-East, mainly in Kent and Hampshire, and there's good game to be had, with venison from the New Forest as well as excellent pheasant, partridge, quail and hare.

RICH IN SHELLFISH

The long coastline of Sussex and Kent has made fishing an important part of life in those counties for centuries. However, the inshore fishing industry has gradually decreased over the years, especially in Kent. Dover, the port once renowned for the superb sole that was landed there and sent to London, now has no fishing boats. The fishing tradition does continue in Sussex, with sea bass, conger eel, and red and grey mullet all found among the catch. A growing number of small manufacturers are setting up business near the coast, producing a variety of smoked seafoods.

Shellfish are plentiful all round the south coast. Fine lobsters are caught in pots from May to October, and shrimps, scallops, clams, whelks and superb crabs are also found in these waters.

Good-quality, well-fattened oysters are farmed in quantity in the Solent and in smaller numbers at Whitstable. Two main varieties are produced – the Flat oyster and the Pacific oyster – both of which are at their most delicious eaten raw with a squeeze of lemon and some bread and butter, although they can also be cooked (Oyster Loaves, page 201). The old 'R in the month' method of telling when oysters are in season still holds good, so look for them from September to April.

Oysters have had a rather chequered history. From being cheap and plentiful up until the start of the 19th century, they then became far scarcer and more of a luxury, because overfishing had severely depleted the oyster beds. The industry has been revived but the stocks are always at risk from disease, bad weather and predatory sea creatures.

From a food that used to be cheap and is now a luxury, to one that used to be pricy and is now much more affordable. Rainbow trout are farmed extensively all over the South-East and because the methods are so efficient, trout is more widely available – and therefore cheaper – than ever before. Farms spring up wherever there is a good supply of clean cool water and many of them welcome visitors. The trout are fed on a high-protein diet and grow rapidly, producing a good weight of sweet, succulent flesh for their size.

If you're lucky, you may find 'wild' trout from Sussex, or from the River Test in Hampshire, although these tend to be consumed close to where they are caught. Other freshwater fish, such as pike and zander, a relative of perch, are farmed to a small extent in the South-East, but may be hard to come by outside the local area.

London is home to Billingsgate, the famous fish market, where much of the British catch ends up. Although now moved from its former site in the City of London to the Docklands, the market continues to ply its trade as it has done for centuries. Most fish is sent directly by road from the ports and arrives in the early hours of the morning, to be rushed to fishmongers all over the country while it is still fresh.

WARM FROM THE OVEN

The streets of London no longer resound to the cries of traders ringing their bells as they walk along with a tray of fresh crumpets or muffins for sale on their heads. Such picturesque scenes disappeared in the 1930s, but we can still buy those wonderfully comforting foods, or even make them at home (see recipe, page 297).

Chelsea buns are another London delicacy, which fortunately has survived (see recipe, page 295). They were originally sold from the Old Chelsea Bun House in Pimlico, destroyed in 1839. King George III was a regular customer.

Kentish Maids were keen on baking and many traditional recipes exist, although few are made commercially. Huffkins (see recipe, page 287) have a long history, and although you won't see them in the shops, they are easy to make yourself. For an authentic Kentish touch, fill the hole in the centre of each huffkin with hot cherries and serve as a dessert. Not surprisingly,

Fly-fishing on the River Test, Hampshire. The most likely catch is brown trout, which can weigh as much as 5 kg (11 lb). However, smaller fish, although less impressive, make better eating, as they are more tender.

recipes featuring cherries and apples are common in
Kent. Ripe Tart (see recipe, page 241) is a more-ish
cherry flan, and Apple and Hazelnut Layer (see recipe,
page 258) uses two of the country's best-known products.

Banbury cakes, shown opposite, can still be bought
in the town of Banbury, Oxfordshire, which is also
famous for the Cross mentioned in the nursery rhyme
'Ride a Cock Horse'. A Victorian replacement of the
original Cross still stands. Another sweet speciality
from Oxford is Frank Cooper's Oxford Marmalade. This
essential part of the British gentleman's breakfast was
first made in 1874 by Sarah Cooper. Her husband was so
delighted with the result that he packaged the
marmalade in earthenware jars and sold it in his grocery
shop. Its success soon led to the full-scale production of
this mouthwatering, coarse-cut confection.

DRINKS NEW AND OLD

The English wine industry has seen an amazing upsurge
in the last 20 years. Although wine-making has gone on
here since the time of the Romans, it was an activity
mainly confined to the monasteries and more or less
disappeared when they were dissolved by Henry VIII.
Interest in wine-making revived in the late 1940s and
now there are over 1000 growers, many of them in the
South-East.

Vines need a south-facing slope with well-drained
soil to thrive, and are at the mercy of the climate. Frost
kills the buds, high winds break down the vines, and if
there's not enough sun, the grapes won't ripen properly.

FOOD FAIRS AND FESTIVALS

JANUARY

Wassailing the Apple Trees, Gill Orchard, Henfield, West Sussex: annual ritual of toasting the orchard to bring a good crop.

MARCH/APRIL

CAMRA London Drinker Beer Festival, Bidborough Street, London WC2.

EASTERTIDE

Shrove Tuesday: Pancake Race, Olney, Buckinghamshire: race, run since 1445, of local women who dash from the market place to the church tossing pancakes as they go.

Good Friday: Easter Bun Ceremony, The Widow's Son Inn, 75 Devons Road, Bromley-by-Bow, London E3: a sailor adds a bun to those already hanging from the inn's ceiling, to commemorate the poor widow who baked a bun for her only son, who was expected home from sea and never returned.

Good Friday: Butterworth Charity, St Bartholomew-the-Great, London EC1: hot cross buns and coins are presented to the 'poor widows of the parish' after the 11.00 service.

Rogation Day: Blessing of the Nets and Mackerel, on the beach opposite the Old Ship Hotel, Brighton, East Sussex; also at Hastings.

MAY

Festival of English Wines, Leeds Castle, Maidstone, Kent.

Greenwich Real Ale Festival, Greenwich Town Hall, London.

Hertfordshire Show, Showground, Friars Wash, Redbourn, Hertfordshire: agricultural show with show jumping.

Surrey County Show, Stoke Park, Guildford, Surrey: agricultural show with sheepdog display, vintage farm machinery, heavy horses and other attractions.

JUNE

Annual South of England Show, Ardingly, West Sussex: livestock.

JULY

Blessing the Sea Ceremony, Margate and Whitstable: ceremony dating back to Saxon times, held as near to St James's Day as high tide permits.

Kent County Show, Detling, Maidstone, Kent: livestock and produce.

Rare Breeds Show, Weald and Downland Open Air Museum, Singleton, Chichester, West Sussex.

Whitstable Oyster Festival: celebration of oyster harvest, held towards end of month.

SEPTEMBER

English Wine Festival and Regional Food Fair, The English Wine Centre, Alfriston, East Sussex.

DECEMBER

Royal Smithfield Show, Earl's Court Exhibition Centre, Warwick Road, London SW5: major event in farming calendar, with livestock and exhibition of machinery.

Despite these problems, English wine growers have experimented with different grapes and found that there are several types, mainly German, which can cope with our uncertain climate. If you happen to be visiting the South-East, remember that many vineyards are happy to show you around and let you sample their products.

Although most English wine is sold 'over the farm gate', many brands are starting to appear in shops further afield. EEC regulations mean that all English wines have to bear the words 'Table Wine' on the label. However, the English Vineyards Association have introduced a Seal of Quality, so look out for that when buying. Don't confuse *English* wines, made in England from grapes grown here, with *British* wines, made from grapes and concentrates imported from Europe.

When you're shopping for wines, keep an eye out for the growing range of English country wines, made not from grapes but from apples, redcurrants, gooseberries, elderflowers and berries and other old-fashioned ingredients – delicious, and well worth trying.

Hops have been an important crop in Kent for centuries and although less widespread now, fields of hop cones and oast houses are still a familiar part of the Kent countryside. Families from London's East End used to make an annual holiday of hop-picking, but the operation is now mechanised. Hops were originally grown as a vegetable and weren't used in brewing until the 16th century. After harvesting, they are placed in the oast houses to dry out over slow-burning fires, before being sent to breweries around the country. Beers brewed in Kent tend to have a strong hoppy flavour, which can be something of an acquired taste.

The vast crops of fruit produced every year in Kent have other delicious alcoholic spin-offs. Cider is made from local apples, and Morello cherries are used to make delectable cherry brandy. The slight hint of almonds in the flavour comes from the crushed cherry stones which are added to the pulped fruit.

Some beer is brewed around London, which has independent breweries at Wandsworth and Chiswick. London Dry Gin is another tipple associated with the capital and the recipe, based on juniper berries and various herbs, has been the same for 200 years.

And if you're starting to feel the effects of all this booze, try a glass of refreshing mineral water from the Hertfordshire Chilterns. The water is exceptionally pure, having permeated slowly through the chalk hills.

Penshurst vineyards in Kent were first planted in 1972, and now cover 12 acres. Each acre produces roughly three tons of grapes – enough to make 3,000 bottles of English wine.

A TASTE OF THE REGIONS

WALES

CLWYD, DYFED, GWYNEDD, POWYS, GWENT, WEST GLAMORGAN, MID GLAMORGAN, SOUTH GLAMORGAN.

Sweet, tender lamb from the mountains; oats, wheat and barley; soft fruits in the warmer south; fish of all types, from cockles to sea trout; creamy milk and butter; carrots, cabbage and early potatoes. These are the good things of Wales, a country where the cooking is simple and wholesome.

Puffin Island

Bangor

Caernarfon

GWYNEDD

CLWYD

Trout

Chester

Wrexham

Ffestiniog

Butter

Cheese

Little Moreton Hall

Stoke

Stafford

Snowdon

Harlech

River Dove

Powis Castle

Welshpool

Shrewsbury

Ironbridge

Wolverhampton

MOUNTAINS

Salmon

CAMBRIAN

Aberystwyth

Welsh Mountain Sheep

Builth Wells

Sgwd-yr-Eira Waterfall

River Teifi

Cheese

POWYS

Hereford

Monmouth

Laver BRECON BEACONS

Merthyr Tydfil

GLAMORGAN

Rhondda

Caerphilly

Tintern Abbey

Newport

GWENT

Swansea

Cardiff

Bristol

A land of breathtaking scenery, with its own lilting language, Wales possesses a terrain that has always presented a challenge to farmers. Those in the north, where the rugged mountains will support little other than oats and sheep, had to scrape a living from the land. In the more affluent south, where the landscape as well as the climate is kinder, the story is different. In the rolling hills dairy and beef cattle do well and it is possible to grow soft fruit, vegetables and crops of wheat and barley, the last of which is mainly used for fattening beef herds. In the warmest parts of the south, there are even vineyards.

Milk, butter, cream and cheese all feature in Welsh cooking. Lamb is popular and so are oats, which appear in many guises. Fishing from the long coastline has had its heyday and the industry which formerly stretched right along the coast is now concentrated in the south. Attempts are being made to revive the shellfish beds in the north, although this is inevitably a gradual process. Clear rivers and deep mountain lakes provide excellent freshwater fish.

The cooking of Wales is that of a region where the living has often been less than easy. People who laboured hard on the land or in the mines and factories concentrated in the industrial south needed sustaining but uncomplicated food that could be quickly prepared at the end of a long day. The thrifty housewife was ingenious in her use of such ingredients as were available, providing nourishing soups and stews as well as mouthwatering home-baking.

CREAMY MILK, SALTY BUTTER

The pastoral country of south Wales, warmed by breezes from the Gulf Stream, and with a high rainfall, has always supported large dairy herds. Even in the mountainous north the dairy tradition exists, and some herds are kept on the lower slopes of the uplands. The country as a whole produces around 1500 million litres of milk a year. Much of the liquid milk goes to London, and the rest is used for cheese, cream, yogurt, ice cream, butter and buttermilk.

Herefords were formerly the predominant breed but these days the Welsh Black is also favoured. Hardy, and mainly concentrated in the north, this is a beef cattle that can provide good-quality milk as well.

Welsh butter is known for its saltiness. The size of a herd of cattle used to be a status symbol among farmers, so few animals were killed off for beef and the dairy herd gradually grew and grew. This naturally led to surpluses of dairy products, including butter, which had then to be well salted in order to preserve it. It is still a salty butter, with a rich, creamy texture, and is delicious spread on scones or teabreads. But if you use it in cooking, you won't need to add much extra salt.

Friesian cattle are immediately recognisable by their black and white markings, and produce about 85% of British milk. The breed comes originally from Holland, but has been developed in various ways in different parts of the world.

A view down into the fields shows a pleasing pattern of straw gathered together and left to dry after the harvest is finished.

The Welsh Black cow is bred mainly for beef. It feeds on grass in the summer, and on hay or silage during the winter. The cattle can be kept on the uplands, which are unsuitable for growing crops.

CHEESES, NEW AND OLD

Caerphilly, a mild, young, salty cheese, which was a favourite lunchtime snack for miners, is probably the best-known cheese of Welsh origins. However, most Caerphilly is now made in the West Country, although a handful of farms in Wales are producing it again, some by totally traditional methods. Welsh creameries instead turn out excellent Red Leicester, Cheddar and Cheshire varieties.

In the past Wales had several home-grown cheeses, which feature in the history books. Although these have disappeared, many new farm cheeses are being produced, but all, so far, on a small, fairly local scale. Llangloffan, for instance, is a creamy, semi-hard cheese which is available plain or flavoured with garlic; Caws Fferm Teifi is made by methods which are 500 years old and is similar in style to Dutch Gouda; and Llanboidy is a hard, full-fat cheese made from the milk of the rare breed of Red Poll cattle. And there are numerous other delicious Welsh cheeses.

Herds of dairy goats and, to a lesser extent, sheep are widespread in Wales and many different sorts of cheese are made from their milk. The traditional cooking of Wales leans heavily on dairy products and cheese crops up in two simple but delicious dishes. Glamorgan sausages, despite their name, contain no meat but are made of cheese, breadcrumbs, herbs and chopped onion or leek, mixed together, formed into sausage shapes, fried and eaten with potatoes (see recipe, page 100). They used to be made with the firm white cheese of Glamorgan, now no longer produced. Welsh rabbit (or rarebit) is a traditional dish that has been adopted nationwide. There are several ways to make it, from simply toasting a slice of cheese on a piece of bread to making a smooth, creamy cheese mixture, perhaps incorporating cream, butter or ale, pouring it on to toast and browning the top under the grill.

SWEET MOUNTAIN SHEEP

The mountains of the north spell sheep, which are the creatures best able to withstand the exposure to wind, rain and cold. The main breed is the Welsh Mountain, which is found throughout Wales. These sheep are the smallest commonly reared in Britain and have smooth

With the increasing interest in self-sufficiency the demand for goats' products such as milk, cheese and yogurt is growing steadily. More than 75,000 goats are kept in Britain, over half of them in herds numbering five or less.

A flock of sheep wends its way home at sunset in the Brecon Beacons. There are well over 3½ million breeding ewes in Wales, and in a year, an efficient upland farm could produce 120 lambs from every 100 ewes.

faces, bright, prominent eyes, small ears and slim, wool-free legs. The rams have curled horns. They are hardy, stocky animals, well suited to mountain life, and produce very fine, soft wool as well as marvellous meat.

Welsh lamb is available nationwide, and a new scheme of marking it clearly has recently been introduced, so it should be easy for shoppers to recognise. The meat is tender and lean, with a rich delicate flavour, which may have a hint of herbs if the flocks have been grazing on the patches of wild thyme and rosemary that grow in the mountains. As Welsh honey tends to have a similarly herby flavour, the two work very successfully together in recipes (see, for example, page 115). Cider and rosemary are other ingredients commonly used to enhance the flavour of the delicious meat.

Hill farmers aim to produce lambs no earlier than April, when the weather starts to improve and the grass begins to sprout again. Most female lambs are kept on the hills to replace older or barren ewes, which are sold to upland farmers to be kept in less harsh conditions. Male lambs are sent to market for meat.

Although the ubiquitous Welsh Mountain sheep predominates, there are also several breeds of sheep which are restricted to local areas, for instance, two of the Welsh upland breeds are the black-faced Clun Forest and the Kerry Hill, which has a white face with black markings. They are less hardy than hill sheep. Beef cattle, which are a natural spin-off from dairy farming, are found wherever milk is produced. But in many lowland parts of South Wales, flocks of sheep have gradually replaced the herds of cattle.

Many traditional Welsh recipes feature lamb. Mutton hams were made by shepherds, who cured the hind leg of a sheep at home, using salt, sugar and spices, then hung the joint in the chimney to smoke. Lamb and mutton pies were a familiar part of the hiring and livestock fairs that were held throughout Wales. Sometimes the minced meat would be mixed with leek or topped with rowanberry jelly. Cawl was a staple dish using scraps of lamb or bacon and vegetables, cooked together in a broth. The liquid might be served separately, or the whole dish eaten together from a bowl with a special spoon.

Most people probably enjoyed a taste of sweet Welsh lamb only on highdays and holidays. As in so many other parts of the country, the poorer people's staple fare was pork, from the pig kept at the bottom of the garden. Commercial pig farming has declined in Wales in recent years, although it is still carried out in some areas. Poultry farming, particularly of turkeys, is another industry that has faced problems, although it is now being gradually revived.

Salt duck is a peculiarly Welsh way to treat duckling, which is rubbed thoroughly with salt and left for a day or two before cooking. This results in tender meat with a delicious flavour that is not too salty.

GATHERED FROM THE SANDS

Fine salmon are caught in the rivers Teifi, Tywi and Taf in west Wales, where occasionally you will still see coracles, the traditional fisherman's craft. They are light boats, made by stretching hide or canvas over a willow framework. The fishermen went out in pairs in their coracles and caught the fish in nets from the boats. Salmon are also caught in the Severn estuary in special baskets, the design of which has remained the same for centuries. Some of this salmon is smoked in Wales.

The lakes and rivers also provide homes for sea trout, called sewin, brown trout, grayling and red-bellied char, although this last is something of a rarity. A popular way to eat trout, and other fish, is to wrap it in bacon rashers and bake it, or fry it in bacon fat.

Cockles are gleaned from the sands around the beautiful Gower peninsula, and also from some beaches in north Wales. They are mostly gathered by hand, a back-breaking job which can only be done at low tide. Donkeys and ponies are still used to take the wooden carts down to the cockle beds. Some of the fish are cooked and removed from the shells before being sold but many are sold live and can be seen in great heaps on the market stalls of Swansea and Cardiff.

If you buy some or are lucky enough to find fresh cockles elsewhere, wash them well and boil them until the shells open.

Swansea, in common with many other coastal towns of Wales, was once a busy fishing port but now only small catches of cod, sole and hake are landed there. Other sea fish caught off Wales include mullet, bass, plaice and flounder. Herrings and mackerel have been fished at Aberystwyth since medieval times, and were important at many other ports, but today the fishing industry has declined. However, the oyster and mussel beds along the Menai Straits are being revived and now produce good crops. Cardigan Bay is being gradually restocked with lobsters, after overfishing had led to restrictions being placed on the catch. Scallops, clams and crabs are also caught off the Welsh coast.

ABOVE
This fearsome creature was caught off Pembrokeshire. It takes seven years for a lobster to reach marketable size.

BELOW LEFT
Gather Gower cockles to eat at home, and you're limited to a saucepanful. More than that, and a licence is needed.

BELOW RIGHT
Ponies and traps are still used in Wales to transport the cockles from the seashore.

A food from the sea which is considered a great delicacy in Wales is laver, an edible seaweed, gathered from the rocks. The seaweed is processed commercially into laverbread, a gelatinous purée. It can be eaten coated with oatmeal and fried with bacon, or made into laver sauce to eat with fish or mutton.

PICK YOUR OWN IN THE SOUTH

Fruit and vegetable growing does not lend itself to such a hilly landscape but there are places where horticulture is well established. Carrots, potatoes, peas, cabbage and

cauliflower are all grown, with some salads and courgettes produced under glass. Early potatoes are an important crop in Gwynedd, on the Gower peninsula and in Pembrokeshire, now part of Dyfed, although here the rich soils have been depleted by intensive farming and now depend heavily on fertilisers.

Pick-your-own farms flourish in the warmer, flatter south, particularly in Gwent and Glamorgan. Soft fruits, including strawberries, raspberries, red- and blackcurrants, gooseberries, loganberries and blackberries are all on offer, along with tender vegetables such as French and broad beans, sweetcorn and many others. The leek, national symbol of Wales, is not widely grown in the region, but the custom of wearing a leek on 1 March, St David's Day, still survives. It is said to date back to the 7th century when, during a battle against the Saxons, the Welsh troops wore leeks in their helmets to distinguish them from the enemy.

FRESH FROM THE GRIDDLE

Here, as in the north of England and Scotland, oats were the most readily available cereal, widely grown because they are not averse to the cool and wet climate. The village mill also provided wheat and barley flours, and some of these watermills are now being brought back into service to produce nourishing, stone-ground flours.

Tea was always a much-loved meal in Wales, although working families could not indulge in it every day. A lot of the cooking in a Welsh cottage was done on a well-greased griddle, or bakestone, set above the hearth. All kinds of baked goods, including bread, tarts and fruit turnovers, could be produced on the bakestone by a skilled cook, who could even transform her griddle into a primitive oven by inverting a metal pot over it.

Welsh oatcakes are similar to Scottish ones, but thinner, while their pancakes, or *crempog,* are made with buttermilk, then well buttered and stacked up in piles, which are sliced down into portions. They can also be layered with a variety of fillings, sweet or savoury. Welsh cakes are another type of firm griddle cake, served sprinkled with sugar and with a dab of butter in the centre. They are at their best when fresh, although many households still store away a supply to offer to visitors. Traditionally, they were served at inns to weary travellers, while they waited for their supper.

Also on the tea table you might find scones and pikelets, and perhaps a loaf of bara brith, a spicy, speckled fruit bread, best served sliced and spread with Welsh butter. Many cakes are agreeably spicy, with cinnamon and caraway seeds being favourite flavourings.

PURE SPRING WATERS

The influence of the Methodist Church and the temperance movement made a strong mark on Welsh drinking habits and relatively little alcohol is produced. There are a few independent breweries, and mead, from fermented Welsh honey, is made on a small scale. One company in Powys produces a herb-flavoured Welsh whisky and a cream liqueur flavoured with honey. The

---

ABOVE

Laver is an edible seaweed packed with minerals and vitamins. The locals eat it as a savoury snack, simply fried or boiled to a purée and spread on slices of fried bread.

RIGHT

A mechanical spinner is used to bring these Pembrokeshire early potatoes to the surface of the ground, then they are gathered up and bagged by hand. The earlier the crop is picked, the lighter the yield – but the higher the price that can be fetched.

------ EARLY POTATOES ------

The mild coastal slopes of Pembrokeshire rival those of Cornwall and Kent in the race to bring the first of the early potatoes to the markets at the end of May.

Delicately flavoured, these 'first earlies', available until mid-August, are ideal for salads and simple summer dishes, such as Cauliflower and Potato Bake on page 222.

Buy little and often and handle gently to avoid bruising. Scrub or scrape gently before cooking or cook in skins in lightly salted boiling water flavoured with a sprig of fresh mint.

Here are the main varieties of first earlies from Pembrokeshire:

HOME GUARD	ARRAN COMET
Creamy white flesh, more floury than other earlies. Particularly good boiled, served with plenty of butter.	*Very creamy flesh, less waxy than Ulster Sceptre but still firm and can be cooked in the same way.*

ULSTER SCEPTRE

DUTCH PREMIERE

ARRAN COMET

HOME GUARD

ULSTER SCEPTRE	DUTCH PREMIERE
Excellent cooking quality and firm waxy texture that does not crumble or break when boiled. Also good in salads or chipped.	*A newcomer to the British scene which is gaining popularity. Pale-yellow flesh, good flavour particularly suitable for chips.*

FOOD FAIRS AND FESTIVALS

APRIL

Llyn Agricultural Show, Botacho Wyn, Nefyn, Pwllheli, Gwynedd: agricultural show with cattle, sheep, goats, poultry, etc.

MAY

Montgomeryshire Agricultural Show, Feggy Leasone, Welshpool: livestock, ring events and stands.

JUNE

Aberystwyth Agricultural Show, Tanycastell Park, Rhydyfelin, Aberystwyth, Dyfed.

JULY

Abergavenny and Border Counties Annual Exhibition: horses, sheep, cattle, horticulture.
Bridgend Show, Waterton, Bridgend: cattle, show jumping, etc.
Royal Welsh Show, Llanelwedd, Builth Wells; livestock.

AUGUST

Anglesey Agricultural Show, Mona nr. Llangefni, Anglesey: livestock and horticulture.
Chepstow Agricultural Show, Chepstow Racecourse, Chepstow, Gwent: livestock, horticulture and crafts.
The North Wales Show, Vaynol Estate, Portdinorwic, Gwynedd: agricultural show including cattle, horses, goats and dogs.
Pembrokeshire County Show,

Showground, Withybush, Haverfordwest, Dyfed: livestock, horticulture, trade stands and fair.
United Counties Agricultural and Hunters Society Show, Showground, Nantyci, Dyfed: livestock and horticulture.
Vale of Glamorgan Agricultural Show, Penllyne Castle, Cowbridge, South Glamorgan: livestock and horticulture.

south-facing coastal slopes of Glamorgan have a long history of viniculture; grapes have been grown there for wine since medieval times. Today, a sprinkling of vineyards in Glamorgan and Dyfed produce crisp, dry white wines from German grape varieties.

Filtering down through the hills and mountains of Wales come pure waters, several of which are bottled commercially. Carmarthen water comes from Prysg spring in the Teify valley and is available still or sparkling. Decantae is an extremely pure mineral water, very low in metals and salts, which is bottled at source on Trofarth farm in the foothills of Snowdonia. And Brecon Natural Mineral Water comes from the village of Trap in Brecon Beacons National Park. The carbonated version comes from Carreg spring, while the still water issues from the spring of St David.

Rugged mountains and regular rainfall can cause problems for farmers in the Dovey Valley. But the beauty of the scenery is a great compensation.

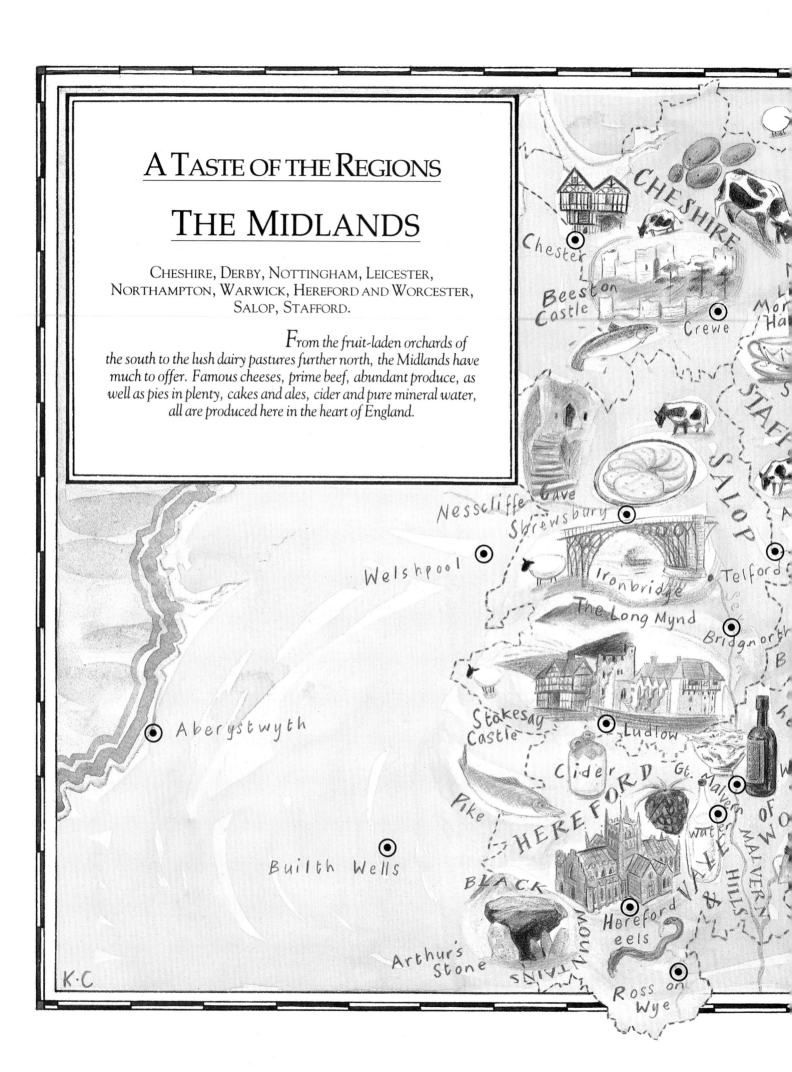

A TASTE OF THE REGIONS

THE MIDLANDS

CHESHIRE, DERBY, NOTTINGHAM, LEICESTER, NORTHAMPTON, WARWICK, HEREFORD AND WORCESTER, SALOP, STAFFORD.

From the fruit-laden orchards of the south to the lush dairy pastures further north, the Midlands have much to offer. Famous cheeses, prime beef, abundant produce, as well as pies in plenty, cakes and ales, cider and pure mineral water, all are produced here in the heart of England.

CHESHIRE

Chester

Beeston
Castle

Crewe

Mor...
Ha...

STAFF...

SALOP

Cave

Nesscliffe

Shrewsbury

Welshpool

Ironbridge

Telford

The Long Mynd

Bridgnorth

Stakesay
Castle

Ludlow

Abergystwyth

Cider

Gt. Malvern

Pike

water

HEREFORD

VALE

MALVERN HILLS

OF WO...

Builth Wells

BLACK

Hereford
eels

Arthur's
Stone

MOUNTAINS

Ross on
Wye

K·C

PEAK DISTRICT

Clumber
Spaniels

Clumber
Park

Bramleys Seedlings

Trent

Buxton

DERBY

Chesterfield

NOTTINGHAM

Sherwood Forest

Newark

Bakewell

Chatsworth

Puddings

Blandy
Snaps

Gingerbread

Belvoir
Castle

Ashbourne

Derby

Mineral
Water

Nottingham
Goose
Fair

Grantham

Burton on
Trent

Bromley
Dance

Ashby
de la
Zouch

Stilton

Loughborough

Melton Mowbray

Hare

LEICESTER

WEST

Wolverhampton

MIDLANDS

Lichfield

Rabbit

Leicester

Harringworth
Viaduct

gham

Foxton
Locks

Corby

Kirby Hall

Coventry

Avon

Kettering

SHAKE-
SPEARE

Stratford upon Avon

WARWICK

Northampton

Goats Milk
cheese

Warwick

NORTHAMPTON

Bedford

Broadway

on Tower

Although the Midlands are often thought of as a purely industrial area, they do in fact make a big contribution to the nation's food. Besides some of Britain's major manufacturing centres, this region includes some of the richest agricultural land in the country. From the beautiful orchards of the Vale of Evesham in the south to the lush dairy pastures of Cheshire in the north, there is plenty of farming activity.

To start in the south, Hereford & Worcester has rich, red soil which supports extensive market gardens as well as allowing fruit orchards to thrive. Hops, apples, pears and plums as well as soft fruits, many types of vegetables and fine asparagus overflow from this area. Locally named Hereford cattle are known all over the country and produce some of the best of British beef.

Moving east and north, the Shires are famed as riding and hunting country, with large rolling fields which support cattle and some sheep as well as barley, wheat and other crops.

Travel further north to Cheshire and Derbyshire and both soil and climate are less suitable for fruit. Nevertheless these are fertile areas, which benefit from being in the warmer west. Cheshire has gently rolling countryside with a mixture of grass, arable, heath and mixed farming. The heart of the county is strongly agricultural, with potatoes and milk being the main products. Cheshire is also known for its salt, which for hundreds of years was an important industry here. Derbyshire is the big sheep-rearing county of the Midlands.

FINE, FLAVOURSOME CHEESES

Dairy cattle graze the rich grass throughout the area, which is one of the biggest milk-producing regions in the country. Every county has some dairy farming, but by far the most cattle are found in the more westerly counties of Shropshire, Staffordshire, Cheshire and Derbyshire, where the warm, wet climate is perfect for producing succulent pasture.

Much of the milk that flows annually from the Midlands is sent for bottling. A proportion is processed for cream – double, single and whipping – and then, of course, there is cheese-making.

It is hardly surprising that with such an abundance of creamy milk available, the Midlands have seen the birth of many traditional cheeses. The most famous of all has to be Stilton, sometimes called King of Cheeses. It is the only British cheese that has its name registered as a trademark, which means that it can only be produced from British milk in the three counties of Derbyshire, Leicestershire and Nottinghamshire.

A Stilton cheese takes about four months to produce

and needs careful attention during that time as each individual cheese develops at its own rate. Mass-production would be impossible, because the cheeses need so much tender loving care to produce perfect results. Stilton was first made 300 years ago by a Mrs Paulet of Leicestershire, who received the recipe from a Lady Beaumont's housekeeper. Mrs Paulet sold her cheeses to her brother-in-law, keeper of the Bell Inn at Stilton (now in Cambridgeshire). The inn was on the main London–York road, and as passing travellers soon developed a fancy for the cheese, so its reputation spread. Eventually Midlands farmers began to make it, and now the cheese is produced by a handful of dairies who belong to the Stilton Cheese Makers' Association.

Stilton may be the most famous, but many other fine cheeses come from the Midlands. Red Leicester was produced from the surplus milk left when Stiltons had been made. Its reddish colour originally came from carrot or beetroot juice added to the milk, but now a natural vegetable colouring called annatto is used. Leicester was originally made on small farms throughout the county and became popular in London during Victorian times.

Cheshire, white and red, is the oldest British cheese and gets a mention in the Domesday Book. It takes only a few hours to make and ripens in four to eight weeks. The blue version matures for longer and has a particularly good flavour.

Derby and Sage Derby are less common than some of the others, but worth seeking out. The more mature the cheese, the better the flavour. The texture is close and flaky, the flavour mild. Sage Derby gets its distinctive herbiness from sage added during processing.

Blue Shropshire is actually made in Leicestershire by a similar method to Stilton. The cheese is also blue-veined, but with an orange colour.

Colwick is a soft cheese with a mildly sour flavour. It was traditionally sold at the Nottingham Goose Fair and has only been revived fairly recently. And goat's milk cheeses and other products are being produced more and more widely, especially around the Northamptonshire area.

ALL SORTS OF FRUIT AND VEG

Worcestershire's Vale of Evesham enjoys a warm, moist climate and boasts rich, heavy soil, which is ideal for growing fruit trees. In spring, so many trees are in flower that motorists can follow the specially signposted 'Blossom Trail' that wends its way past flower-festooned orchards. Many farms specialise, growing only one or two types of fruit, although they may produce several varieties of each type. A farmer might, for instance, grow four or five varieties of eating apples, two cookers, and a couple of varieties of plum, all chosen with an eye to spreading cropping carefully through the season. In this way best use can be made of costly storage facilities.

Many types of eating apples are grown, as well as apples for cider. Bramley's Seedlings, the famous cooking apple, are widely found in Midlands orchards and were first raised at the minster town of Southwell, Nottinghamshire, in the early 19th century. The original tree, which grew from a pip planted in the garden of Matthew Bramley's cottage, apparently still survives.

Heavily laden boughs of fruit are a common sight in the orchards of Evesham. Apples mature slowly through the summer, and gradually develop their true, full flavour.

THE ENGLISH CHEESE QUALITY MARK

Look for this symbol when you buy your cheese. Only cheeses which are produced by a registered cheesemaker, and which have been regularly checked for flavour, body and texture by an English Country Cheese Council Inspector are entitled to bear this symbol. It's your guarantee of quality.

TRADITIONAL HARD CHEESES FROM THE MIDLANDS

Although many cheeses are made here, three stand out above the rest for their excellent flavour, long history and versatility. All can be savoured on their own with biscuits or celery and perhaps a glass of port, or they can be used successfully in many different types of recipe.

BLUE STILTON

A smooth, close-textured, creamy-white cheese with a network of blue veins which become more strongly marked as the cheese matures, and a dry, wrinkled, greyish-brown coat. It has a rich, tangy flavour, and makes an excellent dessert cheese. White Stilton is also available.

RED LEICESTER

A flaky, semi-hard cheese, with a grainy texture and a clean, fresh, medium-strong flavour. The colour varies from rich russet to a darker red and the cheese is made in flat cartwheels. It melts well and is ideal for toasting.

CHESHIRE

A rich cheese with a mellow, salty flavour and a crumbly texture. The red or white varieties are easy to find, and there is also a blue-veined version of the red cheese.

CHOOSING CHEESES

★ If possible, taste before you buy, and take time to decide.

★ Avoid cheeses that have cracks or a dark, shiny surface around the cut edges.

★ Buy small amounts. Keep in a larder or the fridge salad drawer, wrapped in foil.

Stalls laden with cabbages, leeks, cauliflowers, turnips and other fresh fruit and vegetables line the street of the old market town of Oakham in Leicestershire for its Wednesday open air market.

SOFT FRUITS

Soft fruits are only around for a short season, so don't hesitate when you see them. If there's a glut you might be lucky and pick up a bargain which can be used to make jam, or stored in the freezer to be enjoyed later in the year.

BLACKBERRIES

Look for firm, dry berries which are completely black. Use on the same day. Eat them raw, or use in cooking or for jam or wine. They are good combined with apples. They freeze well. (Late July to late September.)

BLACKBERRIES

GOOSEBERRIES

GOOSEBERRIES

Choose firm, unblemished fruit. Early gooseberries are small, hard and very green and sour, suitable only for cooking. Dessert gooseberries arrive later in the season. They are larger, softer, paler in colour and sweeter. They keep well in the fridge and freeze well, too. (Late May to August.)

CURRANTS

Black, red and white currants should be firm, glossy and clean, with few withered or unripe berries or empty sprigs. They will keep in the fridge for up to 10 days. Eat raw, use in cooking, for jams, jellies or sauces. They can be frozen. (July to August.)

CURRANTS

Plums also come into their own here. The Pershore Yellow Egg, an excellent plum for cooking and jam-making, was first discovered in 1822, growing wild in the woods near the little market town of Pershore. It was farmed commercially on a large scale at one time, but fewer plums are grown now than in the past and much of the acreage is planted with the more popular Victoria. However, Pershore Yellow Egg has by no means disappeared completely, so look out for it in late August.

Soft fruits and berries of all kinds flourish in the Vale, and pick-your-own farms and roadside farm stalls offering strawberries, raspberries and many other fruits and vegetables are found everywhere. Gooseberries are cultivated keenly all over the Midlands, as well as further north. Pears are grown in Hereford & Worcester, mainly for perry (see 'Cider-making and Brewing', page 41), although they prefer a richer, wetter soil than apples and, as they flower earlier, are more vulnerable to frost.

Some farmers are specialising in interesting new crops such as alpine strawberries, kohlrabi and fennel. Herb farms are springing up throughout the Midlands to cater for the renewed interest in the subtle flavours herbs bring to many dishes. Many types are grown, often under glass, which helps to prolong the season as well as protecting more delicate varieties from the weather.

Travel through Leicestershire and you'll see field upon field of Brussels sprouts, one of the nation's favourite vegetables. Root vegetables – potatoes, parsnips and turnips – are grown, as well as peas and cabbage. And, back in the Vale of Evesham, salads, runner beans and many other vegetables are farmed intensively.

Perhaps the Vale's most famous vegetable is asparagus. The stalks are thin and delicate and the flavour is excellent. Asparagus was brought here by the Romans, although it has only been cultivated commercially for 80 years. It has a short season – just six weeks – although the plants occupy the ground for the whole year, not just their own season. Harvesting has to be done by hand and, although the crop fetches a good price, many producers have decided to use the land more economically. But even if the crop may be dwindling, the custom of celebrating the harvest with a feast of asparagus continues in some local pubs.

FIRST-CLASS BEEF

Hereford cattle, with their characteristic white markings on the face and reddish coats, are one of the best-known breeds in Britain and are extensively reared in their home county of Hereford & Worcester. The breed is a cross between the British Red Longhorn and cattle introduced from the Low Countries in the 17th century.

Beef was not always the tender, juicy meat we enjoy today. Until the 18th century, cattle were smaller and tougher than they are now, and it took the work of a Leicestershire man, Robert Bakewell, in improving breeds, to bring them up to the standard we expect today. Beef cattle nowadays have a high ratio of meat to bone. They grow faster than their forebears, and are ready for market younger, so providing more tender meat. Herefords mature early. They thrive on grass and don't need much cereal feed. And the meat, if properly hung, has first-class flavour and texture.

There are sheep in Hereford & Worcester too, and

Serried ranks of redcurrants, raspberries and strawberries are grown in orderly rows on this Herefordshire pick-your-own fruit farm. The characteristic red sandstone soil of the area can be clearly seen.

also in Northamptonshire and Derbyshire, where a large part of the county's farmland is given over to sheep rearing. However, with these exceptions, sheep farming is not as important in the Midlands as in other parts of the country.

In spite of having such good-quality beef on the doorstep, most butchers' shops in the Midlands concentrate first and foremost on pork products. Throughout the Shires the butchers' windows are full of black puddings, polony, home-cured bacon and hams, sausages, faggots, brawns and, last but by no means least, pork pies. The town of Melton Mowbray, in the heart of Leicestershire's fox-hunting country, is famous for its pork pies. Originally they were eaten after the hunt – or even for breakfast, before it. The bulbous pies have a crisp, hot-water crust and a mouthwatering filling of roughly chopped pork (see recipe, page 148). Commercial production has gone on in Melton Mowbray since the mid-19th century. However, several other manufacturers produce the pies elsewhere, so wherever you live, they should be available.

The rolling, wooded countryside of the Shires provides cover for all sorts of game – pheasant, rabbit and hare amongst others. And to add spice and savour

A window crowded with good things, in this traditional shop in Upton-upon-Severn. Home-cured hams hang at the back of the display.

to all things meaty is Worcestershire Sauce, developed almost by accident in the 1830s by two chemists, Mr Lea and Mr Perrins, from a recipe brought back from India by the Governor of Bengal. The exact ingredients and the length of time needed for the sauce to mature in oak barrels are still secret. As well as enhancing casseroles and soups, a dash of the sauce added to tomato juice makes a good hangover cure.

CIDER-MAKING AND BREWING

Hereford & Worcester is second only to Kent as a major

The Nottingham Goose Fair is held every October, but has changed immensely since it started in the 13th century, when hundreds of geese were brought here from miles around to be sold and herded down to London, in time for the Christmas feast.

hop-growing region and the heady, yeasty scent of hops fills the lanes during early autumn. But there are surprisingly few breweries in the area. Instead the main drinks found here are cider and perry, made from fermented pear juice. Both are produced commercially but perry is less widely available than cider. It has a pleasant, mellow flavour, which is not at all sharp.

There are many varieties of apple and pear suitable for making into these delicious alcoholic drinks, and most of them are grown in the surrounding areas. Some farmers make single-variety ciders and perries, mainly for their own use or to sell over the gate, but most of the drinks sold commercially are made with a blend of juices from different varieties.

The abundant fruits of Hereford & Worcester are also used to make concentrated fruit juices. These contain no preservatives, sweeteners, colouring or water, and have a delicious full flavour and aroma. The emphasis is very much on apple and flavours include pure apple – made from Cox's and Russets – as well as apple with blackcurrant, blackberry or plum.

Burton-on-Trent, in Staffordshire, is a town once famous for brewing, but now there are only five breweries left, one of which is a working museum. IPA, found on draught in pubs all over the country, derives from the pale ales once brewed at Burton-on-Trent. Burton pale ales were prized for their brightness and clarity, which came from the natural spring water used in their production. In the 1820s Burton brewed an even paler, hoppier ale for export to India; India Pale Ale (IPA) was so popular that it has been made ever since. Bottled bitters are usually called pale or light ales.

Mild ale is drunk widely in the Midlands, where it is still very popular. Some breweries in the region also produce stout, derived from porter, a dark, well-matured beer which dominated the British beer scene until the late 1800s, when it was superseded by bitter. Real ale brewing is also carried on in many Midlands breweries, and the region has seen the revival of the old custom that was once common in pubs throughout the land – that of home-brewing beer.

NATURAL WATERS
FROM THE MIDLANDS

Cool spring water makes a
refreshing drink, and more
and more people are
turning to it for health
reasons, as it has no
artificial additives and is
totally pure. Drink it just
as it comes, or use
sparkling waters as mixers
with white wine, spirits or
fruit juices.

MALVERN WATER

*Rises at Primeswell Spring in the
Malvern Hills where the granite
slopes meet the impervious rocks
of the valley. Designated a
'natural mineral water' by the
EEC. Available still or
sparkling.*

BUXTON SPRING
WATER

*Takes over 20 years to permeate
through limestone and volcanic
lava in the High Peak District of
Derbyshire. Emerges at a
temperature of 81°F from St
Ann's Well in the centre of
Buxton. Available still or
sparkling.*

ASHBOURNE
WATER

*Another natural spring water
from the Peak District. Comes
from an underground source in
beautiful Dovedale, above the
town of Ashbourne. Available
still or sparkling.*

The fine spring waters of the Midlands led to the
development of spas, where people travelled for health
reasons to 'take the water'. Spa towns like Buxton and
Malvern boomed in Victorian times and still produce
large quantities of bottled water every year.

The English wine industry, although centred in the
South-East, is also suited to the soil and climate of the
southern and western Midlands counties, especially
Hereford & Worcester. Some good wines are produced
in the region but wine-making is not yet as important
here as elsewhere in Britain.

DELICIOUS BAKING

Oats were the main cereal grown in Derbyshire during
the 18th and 19th centuries, and local shops still sell
oatcakes as a reminder of those times, although today's
main arable crops are barley and winter wheat. Shops
selling oatcakes also proliferate in the north of
Staffordshire, where oatcakes are considered a local
delicacy, much missed by those who move away from
the area. The same shops often sell pikelets and
crumpets too.

Midlands oatcakes are quite different from the
Scottish variety, being rather like thick pancakes but
made with yeast and fine oatmeal and cooked on a hot
griddle. They can be eaten for breakfast with eggs and
bacon, or enjoyed at tea-time, spread with butter and
honey.

Bakewell puddings – not to be confused with
Bakewell tarts, which locals claim are distinctly inferior
– also come from Derbyshire. They were first made by
accident at an inn in the town of Bakewell, around
1860. The cook's simple mistake with the recipe
created such an appetising result that the puddings were
soon being made for sale. They are still produced by
hand – but if you can't get to the Old Original Bakewell
Pudding Shop to buy one for yourself, there's a recipe on
page 241.

Little cheesecakes were made in Northamptonshire

FOOD FAIRS AND FESTIVALS

EASTER MONDAY

Hallaton Hare Pie Scrambling and Bottle Kicking: a contest of ancient origins between the Leicestershire villages of Hallaton and Medbourne. Pieces of a hare pie are emptied from a sack on to Hare Pie Bank and the onlookers scramble for them. There is then a bottle-kicking contest, when teams from each village try to get their own bottle down the hill across the brook. Anyone can join in, but the proceedings are extremely boisterous.

JUNE

Country Heritage Fair, Shugborough, Milford, nr Stafford: incorporates Midlands Country Rare Breeds Show, plus country crafts and vintage tractors.
Three Counties Show, Malvern, Worcestershire: agricultural show for Gloucestershire, Herefordshire and Worcestershire.
Wine Festival, Royal Hotel, Kettering, Northamptonshire: held annually towards the end of June.

JULY

Royal Show, National Agricultural Centre, Stoneleigh, Kenilworth, Warwickshire.
Nantwich Show, Dorfold Park, Nantwich: one-day agricultural and horticultural show.

AUGUST

Bakewell Show, Derbyshire: two-day agricultural show, featuring livestock and horticultural contests, plus many other attractions.
Madresfield Agricultural Show, Madresfield, Malvern: livestock, horse events, stands and rabbit show.
Three Counties Show, National Agricultural Centre Showground, Stoneleigh, Kenilworth, Warwickshire.

SEPTEMBER

Goat and Smallholders' Show, National Agricultural Centre, Stoneleigh, Kenilworth, Warwickshire: goat show, bee- and rabbit-keeping, organic farming and trade exhibits.
Rare Breeds Survival Trust Show, National Agricultural Centre, Stoneleigh, Kenilworth, Warwickshire: rare breeds of livestock.

OCTOBER

Nottingham Goose Fair: historic fair but today the geese have been replaced by a three-day funfair with side-shows, rides and amusements.

OPPOSITE
A drinking fountain guarded by the statue of St Ann, where passers-by can taste the waters from Buxton spring. The water falls as rain on the hills surrounding the town, and is purified as it filters through the rocks before emerging here.

LEFT
A selection of pastries, with Bakewell Puddings taking pride of place in the window. At 'The Old Original Bakewell Pudding Shop', Bakewell Puddings (which are never called 'tarts' here) are freshly made each day to a secret recipe.

to be eaten at sheep-shearing time, and the town of Shrewsbury in Shropshire has given its name to the large, flat, crisp biscuits that have been baked there for over three centuries. They were originally flavoured with caraway seeds, and sometimes made with currants (see recipe, page 275).

Brandy snaps and gingerbread were sold at fairs all over the Midlands, as well as in the North. And a traditional speciality, still available, is Melton Hunt Cake, which claims to have been 'supplied to the Nobility, Clergy and Gentlemen of the Melton Hunt for over 100 years'. It is a rich fruit cake, liberally laced with rum, and a slice was taken with a glass of sherry by the members of the Hunt while mounted on horseback waiting for the chase to start.

FISH FROM RIVERS AND LAKES

With no coastline to speak of, except for the mouths of the Dee and the Mersey in Cheshire, the Midlands have to rely on other areas for supplies of sea fish. However, there is superb freshwater fish to be had. Salmon are found in the Dee and also in the Wye, where the fish are said to be particularly succulent. Pike, eels and grayling are also caught in Hereford & Worcester. The River Dove in Derbyshire has pure waters which have been renowned for centuries for their valuable fishing. Grayling can still be caught here. Rutland Water in Leicestershire is a large man-made lake with a stock of excellent trout to tempt local fishermen. There are also a few fish farms scattered through the area.

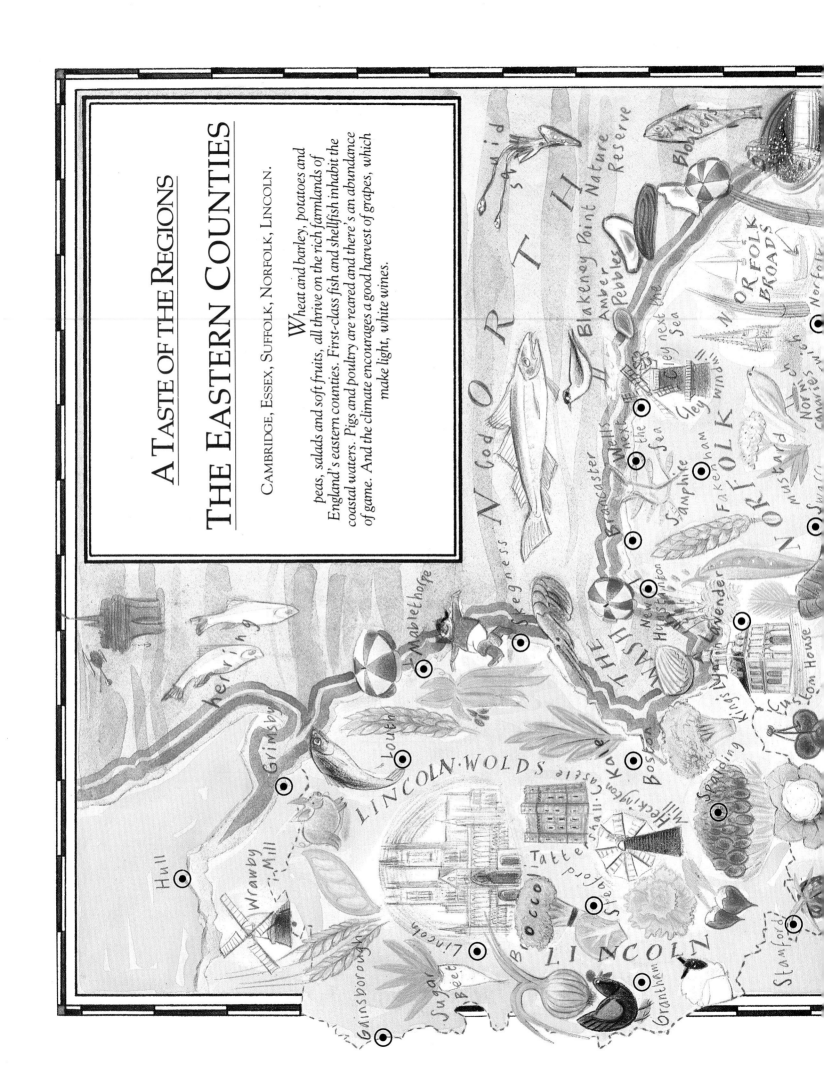

A Taste of the Regions

The Eastern Counties

Cambridge, Essex, Suffolk, Norfolk, Lincoln.

Wheat and barley, potatoes and peas, salads and soft fruits, all thrive on the rich farmlands of England's eastern counties. First-class fish and shellfish inhabit the coastal waters. Pigs and poultry are reared and there's an abundance of game. And the climate encourages a good harvest of grapes, which make light, white wines.

NORTH Sea

Blakeney Point Nature Reserve

Amber Pebbles

Blakeney

NORFOLK BROADS

Cley next the Sea

Cley

Wells next the Sea

Brancaster

Samphire

Fakenham

Norwich

NORFOLK

mustard

New Hunstanton

Lavender

King's Lynn

Custom House

THE WASH

Boston

Kale

Skegness

Mablethorpe

Louth

LINCOLN·WOLDS

Heckington Mill

Tattershall Castle

Spalding

Hull

Grimsby

herring

Wrawby Mill

Gainsborough

Sugar Beet

Lincoln

Boccio

Spelds

LINCOLN

Stamford

Grantham

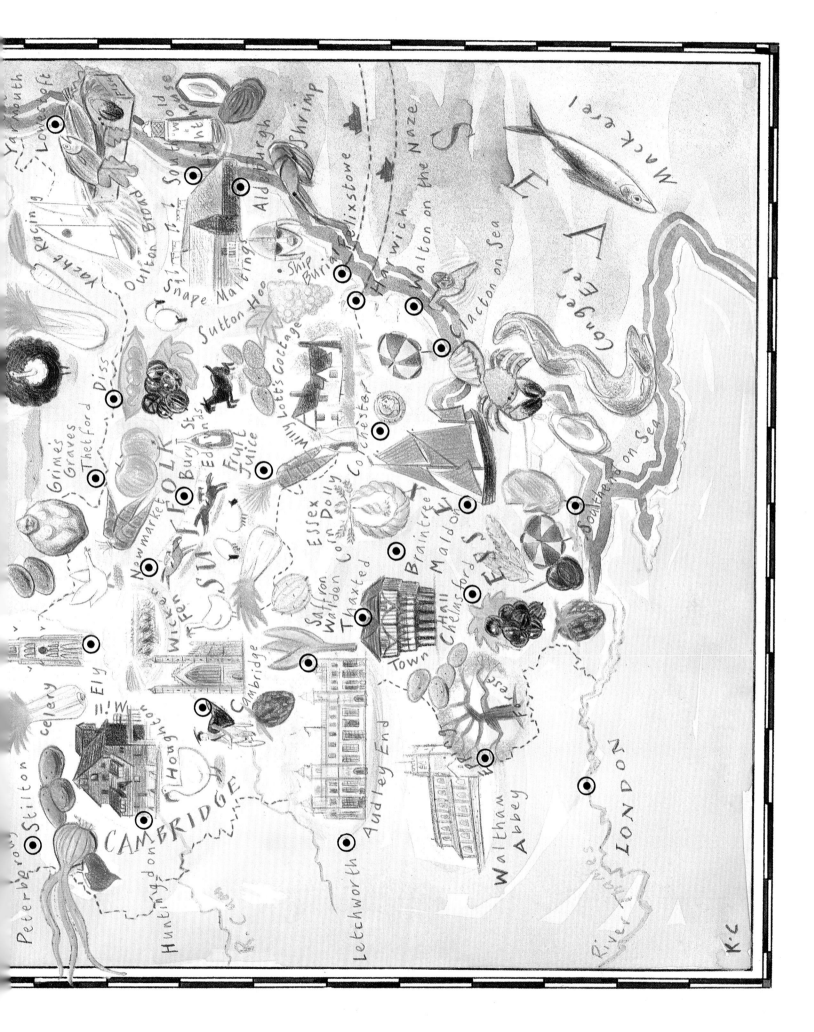

The countryside of the eastern counties has a beauty all of its own. The sight of the Fens or the Broads, stretching away as far as the eye can see towards the glittering horizon, is unforgettable. The Suffolk and Essex landscapes are rounder and less flat. True, it can be windy in the east, especially near the coast, and hence the many windmills still to be seen, although few are working now. But even if the winters tend to be chilly, the summers are drier and often warmer than elsewhere.

The eastern counties are the arable farmlands of Britain. Although the soils vary from county to county – rich and peaty in the fenlands, sandier near the coasts, with belts of heathland and forest throughout – the crops grown are similar. Wheat and barley, oil-seed rape and sugar beet stretch for miles across broad, fertile fields. The grains are used for milling, baking, brewing, animal feed and export. Rape, with its vivid yellow flowers, is a relatively new crop, used in the production of vegetable oils and animal feeds.

Horticulture is vital too, and the eastern counties go a long way towards keeping the nation's salad bowls and vegetable racks filled. All the staple vegetables are grown here, including main crop potatoes, other roots and brassicas, particularly cauliflowers. There are many processing and packaging plants in the region, the products of which find their way to all parts of the country in the form of frozen peas, canned carrots and suchlike. Fruit is also important, with big soft fruit farms and plenty of orchard fruits.

The wool industry no longer thrives in Suffolk as it did centuries ago. Cattle and sheep are farmed, but pigs and poultry are more important. And then, of course, there's the sea. Stretching from the Thames Estuary in Essex, round the bulging coastline of Suffolk and Norfolk, and up to the Wash, the waters are thronging with fish and shellfish.

KEEPING THE BALANCE

The soil of the eastern counties, coupled with the climate, which is relatively dry compared to that of the westerly grasslands, means that this is first and foremost arable land and not a major centre for milk production. However, cattle herds do have a part to play in the

Straw, left behind when the wheat has been harvested, is a valuable litter for livestock. Bales like these stand in fields all over the eastern counties in late August/early September, waiting to be taken to the farmer's barn for storage.

farming 'balance' of the region, which supports dairy and beef breeding herds totalling around 100,000 animals. And indirectly the eastern counties play a crucial role in milk production throughout the UK, as they grow massive amounts of the cereals used for cattle food.

In past years, dairy production has been more important here than it is today, particularly in Suffolk and Essex. But no famous cheeses come from this area. Daniel Defoe, writing in the early 18th century, remarked that Suffolk was famous for 'the best butter and perhaps the worst cheese in England'. This cheese was made from skimmed milk and sold to the poor in London. However, some enterprising sheep and goat farmers are starting to supply milk, cheese and yogurt from their livestock.

TEEMING WATERS

Historically, the ports of Great Yarmouth and Lowestoft thrived on the herring industry for centuries. Sadly, the story is the same here as in other parts of the country, where ecological factors, including over-fishing, have led to the decline of the industry. The little fleets of colourful fishing boats have largely disappeared and in their place are the huge refrigeration vessels, many from foreign countries, which freeze down the catch while still at sea.

ABOVE
There are pockets of dairying and some beef production amongst the flat and fertile expanses of the east of England that are perfect for arable farming.

LEFT
Windmills stand all around the east coast as reminders of the importance of grain to the local farming economy. Once vital in the grinding of grain to produce flour, this impressive building dominates the scene in the village of Cley, Norfolk.

However, the tradition of making smoked herring products – red herrings, bloaters and kippers – has revived to a certain extent. Herrings preserved as 'reds' were essential in the days before refrigeration, but although still produced they are not as popular as they once were. The fish are cured in brine and then smoked for up to six weeks until rock-hard. They have a strong, salty flavour, sometimes likened to ham, and can be soaked before cooking or grilled without soaking. As they keep so well, many are exported to hot countries where storage of fish is a problem.

Bloaters are a different, and very delicious, proposition. They have a short soaking in brine and are slowly smoked over oak, ungutted, for 24 hours. The flavour is mild but slightly gamey, and the flesh pale and tender. The best way to serve them is simply grilled with butter.

Reasonable catches of fish such as plaice, sole, turbot, cod, haddock and skate are landed at ports along the coast, Lowestoft being the largest. Much of this fish is processed and frozen. Sprats, a small and tasty relation of the herring, are always cheap and can sometimes be bought on the beach, straight from the boats at the Suffolk villages of Aldeburgh, Southwold and Dunwich.

Shellfish, too, thrive in eastern waters. Pacific oysters are farmed in the North, for instance at Brancaster or Morston in Norfolk, while in Essex are found the native flat oysters. Sadly, the Colchester oyster beds in Essex, which have the reputation of producing some of the finest oysters in the country, have declined in recent years. However, some oysters are still produced, and there is hope that the crop will revitalise in time.

It's not all a tale of gloom. Pink and brown shrimps, both large and small, are caught in abundance all round the coast. Many fishing villages have developed a speciality over the years. Cromer, in Norfolk, is famous for its crabs. These are smaller than those fished elsewhere, but heavy for their size and packed with meat. The tiny crab boats ply dangerous waters, full of

hidden rocks and dangerous tides, to bring home the catch. The crab pots are checked daily, so there is always a fresh supply. Lobsters are caught off the same coast.

Mussels are a cheap, plentiful shellfish which can be used in all sorts of delicious recipes, such as Mussels and Clams with Tomatoes (see recipe, page 204), and they are in season throughout the winter. There are mussel beds all round the East Anglian coast, especially off north Norfolk, and Lincolnshire also benefits from the clean waters of the Wash to produce sweet, plump mussels.

Cockles and whelks are found in great quantities in Norfolk. Stiffkey (pronounced Stookey) is known for 'Stookey Blues', large cockles with grey-blue shells, which are raked out of the sand flats at low tide, using short-handled rakes. They are usually sold boiled and are best eaten well-seasoned with pepper and vinegar. Another north Norfolk village, Wells-next-the-Sea, produces no less than 80 per cent of the nation's whelks, which are caught by fishermen who go miles out to sea and fish with pots baited with herring. Whelks from Wells are commonly found as far afield as London and the Midlands.

Freshwater eels are caught in the Norfolk Broads using traps, but most are exported. Other freshwater fish, such as pike and zander, are found in the county's rivers.

Still on the subject of the sea, samphire is an edible plant which is commonly found around the East Anglian coast and can sometimes be bought on fish stalls in the area. It is fleshy and succulent, and should be eaten lightly boiled and tossed in melted butter.

PICKED FOR PROCESSING

More than a third of the country's entire vegetable crop comes from the eastern counties, including a third of all the peas, half the onions and two-thirds of all the carrots grown. Added to that, a quarter of the soft fruit of England and Wales is grown here, and a fifth of all the orchard fruit. Every county of the region has a special contribution to make to this massive harvest.

The wide, flat fields of Lincolnshire are planted with vegetables as far as the eye can see. There are acres of peas, most of which are destined to be canned or frozen. All the most popular British vegetables are grown here,

SHELLFISH FROM THE EASTERN COUNTIES

OYSTERS

Portuguese and Pacific oysters are the main types harvested off the east coast. Eat raw, with a dash of lemon juice, straight from the shell. If served hot, cook lightly. (September to April.)

COCKLES

Usually white or cream in colour, with a circular shell. Sold cooked, shelled and often preserved in brine or vinegar. (Best April to December.)

WHELKS

A brownish or greyish spiral shell, white flesh. Sold boiled, often from stalls. (Best February to July.)

CRABS

Brown crab is the most common variety. Sold boiled and dressed, with meat removed from shell, or undressed. Choose by weight rather than size. Flesh is white and dark. Can be used in recipes or eaten dressed with mayonnaise in salads. (April to December.)

MUSSELS

Dark blue shells, bright yellow flesh. Sold live. Steam open and serve in or out of shell, with a sauce. (September to February.)

LOBSTERS

Usually sold boiled, in the shell, which turns bright scarlet when cooked. The white flesh can be removed from the shell and used in recipes. (April to November.)

SHRIMPS

Brown and pink shrimps are caught in the Wash. Brown shrimps are greyish-brown and have no pointed 'snout'. Usually sold cooked. Shell before eating or using in recipes. (February to October.)

LEFT
A Lincolnshire pea field, in full flower. The crop is planted successively, so that the peas can be harvested in relays from June through to August. Podded, blanched and frozen within 3 hours, they reach the market almost as fresh as when they were picked.

they specialise in apples, with over 3400 acres of dessert apples alone. There are apples in Norfolk, too, although not the wide range of varieties that were grown as recently as the 1930s. The Norfolk Biffin was a popular variety that has virtually disappeared. It used to be preserved by being pressed flat and dried, and was then eaten as a sweetmeat or used for stewing. But now the orchards are mostly given over to Cox's Orange Pippins and Bramley's Seedlings. Much soft fruit is also grown in the county.

Finally to Essex, home of Tiptree and Elsenham jams, which are made in the centre of soft fruit-growing lands. Strawberry production is particularly important and once again pick-your-own signs are a familiar sight. Plums, cherries and pears are also grown, and many of them end up in cans or as jams and preserves. The Lea Valley has the largest concentration of glasshouses in Britain and over a third of the country's cucumbers are grown here, as well as other salad crops. And out in the fields, broad, runner and French beans, sweetcorn and

To be a successful strawberry picker, you need to know that the best berries are usually found on the outside edge of the strawberry plant. The bulk of each plant's fruit is found hidden beneath the protective leaves. These pick-your-own farms are very popular: it is backbreaking but rewarding work.

including potatoes, cabbage, and onions, which ripen well in the dry climate. Broad and runner beans proliferate and again are used mainly for processing. And the soil and climate are ideal for producing top-quality cauliflowers and spinach.

Next door, in Cambridgeshire, it's still a story of vegetables, but fruit gets a good look in as well. Onions, carrots, peas and potatoes all feature, and the crisp, white celery is justly famous. There are large orchards of apples, both cooking and dessert varieties, as well as pears and plums. Wisbech is the centre for soft fruit and you'll find strawberries, gooseberries, raspberries, red and blackcurrants and much more on sale at roadside stalls and pick-your-own farms.

Norfolk and Suffolk both have long agriculture histories. Again, masses of vegetables are produced, many of them for freezing and canning. Roots such as potatoes, carrots, parsnips and onions do particularly well here. Peas and beans thrive in the dryish climate, as well as salad crops and cabbage, cauliflowers and celery. But perhaps the best-loved East Anglian vegetable is asparagus. The season is frustratingly short, although work is being done to develop strains that give a higher yield. Asparagus comes in several grades and in each one the stalks are fatter, and costlier, than the one before. The grading system starts with Sprue, which has very thin stalks and is relatively cheap, and works its' way up through Choice, Selected and Jumbo, ending with Super Extra Selected, by which time the stalks are so plump that you might only get eight to a kilo!

Fruit has an important role to play as well. In Suffolk

RIGHT
A golden field of oil seed rape, which is widely grown throughout the eastern counties.

many other vegetable varieties fill over 13,000 acres of land.

TALKING TURKEY

Historically, pigs and poultry have played an important part in the economy of the eastern counties. Yes, you will find beef cattle and lambs here. But most farmers prefer to use their land for arable farming and have little to spare for the grassy pastures required by cows and sheep.

Between them, the eastern counties provide a considerable proportion of home-produced pork and bacon. Pigs are prolific creatures and a sow can produce 16 or more piglets a year in two litters. When aged between four and seven months, lighter pigs are sold for pork and heavier pigs for bacon.

Ham and bacon curing is a traditional East Anglian industry. Suffolk sweet-cured hams are renowned, although becoming rarer. They take nearly 10 weeks to cure – a month soaking in brine, then several weeks in a sweet pickling solution of sugars, salt and saltpetre, during which they have to be turned every day. Then they are smoked over an applewood and oak fire to develop their characteristic shiny black skins. The results are handsome to look at and taste marvellous. Another delightful traditional pork dish from the eastern counties is the oddly named Huntingdon Fidget Pie, which makes use of the region's onions and apples as well as bacon (see recipe, page 150).

A curious custom involving bacon has taken place in the Essex town of Great Dunmow every third year on Whit Monday since the 13th century. At the Dunmow Flitch Trial, a flitch, or side of bacon, is given to a local married couple who can prove, to the satisfaction of a jury, that they have not quarrelled or wished they were not married for the whole of the preceding year!

As for poultry, millions of birds are reared, particularly in Suffolk and in Norfolk, which is the national centre for turkey production. Norfolk used to

SALT, MUSTARD AND VINEGAR

Three of the most popular condiments come from the eastern counties. Salt is the essential seasoning for all savoury dishes, as it brings out the flavour, besides adding its own tang. Mustard is the classic accompaniment to roast beef, as well as enhancing many recipes. And without vinegar, fish and chips just wouldn't be the same!

SALT

Maldon Crystal Salt comes from a part of the Essex marshes that has been in production for 700 years. It is crisp and crumbly, with an intense flavour, and has no additives at all. The salty river water is first filtered and then heated so that the water evaporates, leaving behind the pure sea salt.

MUSTARD

In June the fields of East Anglia are golden with mustard, much of which goes to the famous company of Colman's of Norwich for processing. Two types – brown and white – are grown. The seeds are milled and then blended together. Mustard can be bought as a powder or ready made-up. Colman's have a Mustard Shop and Museum in Norwich.

VINEGAR

Cyder vinegar is made by Aspall's in Suffolk from organically grown apples with no additives. The taste is far less harsh than that of malt or spirit vinegar and is thought to be the best for all culinary uses. Red and white wine vinegars are also made by the same firm.

Wild hares inhabit East Anglian farmlands in large numbers. Surprisingly enough, these two young adults, spotted boxing on a spring day, are probably not a pair of males. It's more likely that one is a female, who is fending off the advances of her would-be mate.

be well known for its small, black-plumed turkeys, which could be seen walking to London – a journey that took three months – for the Christmas markets. Since then, other breeds have become standard, although a few local specialist farmers are now rearing the black turkey again. Today there's no need to buy a whole bird except at the festive season, since with turkey joints you can buy just enough for one or two meals (see recipe, page 167). As well as turkeys, chickens and ducks are farmed in great numbers, for meat and eggs, and geese and guinea-fowl are also reared.

Game is plentiful throughout the eastern counties. The countryside, with its fields high with wheat, its marshes, flat watery fens and the Broads, is the perfect habitat for many game birds. Pheasant can be seen

scurrying across the country lanes, and partridge, woodcock, quail and wild duck are also common. Rabbit and hare almost overran parts of East Anglia before farming methods improved enough to control them. Local recipes, like the one for rabbit casserole on page 176, reflect the fact that these animals were a staple part of the local diet for many years.

BEER, CIDER AND WINES

An area so rich in grain is bound to produce first-class beer, which is made from fermented barley as well as hops. There are several independent breweries in the region, all of which have a dedicated local following. Adnams, in the charming Suffolk town of Southwold,

Buckets of berries in Lincolnshire, at the height of the strawberry season. Most are grown outdoors, although strawberries can also be cultivated under glass, or in plastic tunnels.

is perhaps the best known. Its beers are produced by traditional methods and are available outside the county in a limited number of outlets in the east. There are also breweries in Essex and Norfolk with links to the big national groups. Bitter is popular in this part of the country, where a good head of foam is not considered vital to the enjoyment of a pint.

Cyder (spelled with a 'y') is another favourite drink in these parts, and used to be the most common thirst-quencher among farmers and country people. Norfolk and Suffolk cyders were reckoned to be especially good and were made, not from sharp cider apples, as were the ciders of the West Country, but from cooking varieties such as Bramley's Seedling. Aspall, a Suffolk firm which has been making cyder since the 18th century, had a traditional stone-trough mill in use until as recently as 1947, when their last working horse died. The mill was a simple but very efficient device, with the fruit placed in a circular trough below a millstone with a yoke to which the horse was harnessed. As the horse walked round the trough, the stone crushed the apples. Traditional cyder is still made, although by more up-to-date methods, and is a strong, unsparkling drink with a flavour that is not too sweet.

Apples are also used to make fine ciders that are more like apple wines, with a pale colour, delicate flavour and a relatively high alcohol content. Non-alcoholic fruit juices are also produced in a range of flavours, including grape, apple with cherry or strawberry, pear and apple, and apple and carrot.

The great English wine revival has reached the eastern counties, which have become one of the most important grape-growing regions in the country. The climate is good for vines, with relatively sunny summers, a low rainfall and warm, late autumns for ripening the grapes, followed by cold, hard winters during which the vines can rest. The region has a range of soils from sandy clay to chalk and gravel, and this results in wines of very different characters. The wines are white and mostly grown from German grape varieties. They can be of very high quality, with a rich, intense flavour. Vineyards are scattered throughout the

counties of the region, except for Lincolnshire. Many welcome visitors and sell wine on the premises.

FINE CAKES AND GINGERBREAD

Here, as in all parts of the country, home baking has a long tradition. There are many recipes using apples in cakes, puddings and pies. An old recipe for saffron cake from Suffolk is a reminder of the distant time when a huge crop of saffron was grown there. The fields would be blue with crocuses, the dried stamens of which become saffron. It was originally produced for medicine, before being given a culinary use.

Grantham, in Lincolnshire, is famous for its gingerbreads, which are puffed up, crunchy biscuits. A brown and white spiced version of gingerbread came from Diss in Norfolk and there were other local spicy biscuits and cakes which were sold at fairs throughout the region.

Another traditional Norfolk dish was 'swimmers', or dumplings, made from dough and cooked on top of soup or stew. You'll find a recipe for rabbit casserole with dumplings on page 176.

FOOD FAIRS AND FESTIVALS

JUNE

Cakes and Ale ceremony, St Mary's Church, Bury St Edmunds: service held annually since 1482 to commemorate town benefactor, Jankyns Smythe.
Lincoln Wine Festival, The Cornhill, Lincoln: wines from Lincoln's twin town in Germany.
The Royal Norfolk Show, New Costessey, Norwich: county agricultural show.

JULY

East of England Show, Peterborough: livestock show.

SEPTEMBER

Blessing the whitebait catch ceremony, held in Southend, Thorpe Bay and Leigh-on-Sea areas: exact date and venue vary annually.

OCTOBER

Sea-angling Festival, Lowestoft: fishing contests, held over several days.

Berwick upon Tweed

Holy Island

Chillingham Wild Cattle

Bamburgh Castle Alnwick

CHEVIOT HILLS

NORTHUMBERLAND

Ayr

KIELDER WATER

HADRIAN'S NORAN'S WALL

Dumfries

Hexham

Kirkcudbright

Salt Marshes Carlisle

Corby Castle

DURHAM

SOLWAY FIRTH

Castlerigg Circle

Penrith

Workington

Keswick

ULLSWATER

Appleby

High Force

Barnard Castle

Whitehaven

WAST WATER

DERWENT WATER

CUMBRIA

Horse Fair

Scale Force

Windermere

Kendal

Wensleydale Swa...

Manx Cat races

Kendal

NORTH YORK

Castle Rushton

Laxey 'Lady Isabella' water-wheel

Castletown glas

Beatrix Potter

Tripe

Pen-y-ghent

Sol...

ISLE of MAN

Barrow in Furness

Hot Pot

Morecambe

MORECAMBE BAY

Beacon Hill

Haworth

Lancaster

M/c Terrier

IRISH SEA

Plaice

LANCASHIRE

Hebden Bridge

Black pool

Scouse

MERSEYSIDE

M/c Ship Canal

GREATER MANCHESTER

K·C

Liverpool

A TASTE OF THE REGIONS

THE NORTH

NORTHUMBERLAND, TYNE AND WEAR, DURHAM, CLEVELAND, NORTH YORKSHIRE, HUMBERSIDE, SOUTH YORKSHIRE, WEST YORKSHIRE, GREATER MANCHESTER, MERSEYSIDE, LANCASHIRE, CUMBRIA.

Dales and moors, hills and mountains, seas, rivers and deep lakes, the North has miles of truly glorious scenery outside its major industrial centres. And there's a wealth of good food to discover: choice lamb, celebrated cheeses, excellent fish, thirst-quenching beers and mouthwatering home-baked cakes.

Northern cooking is based on dishes suitable for a hard-working community living in a bracing climate. Simple, cheap and tasty meals were designed to satisfy hearty appetites and keep working families well fed for the least possible cost. Ingenious cooks made sure that nothing was wasted and many of their dishes, which always used the best produce available locally, are still enjoyed today.

The North is often thought of as being primarily an industrial area, but once you leave the sprawling conurbations behind, you soon find what a large proportion is rural, encompassing many different types of unspoilt landscape and scenery of great beauty. There's plenty of good grass, to feed the region's numerous flocks of sheep and cattle herds. Hill breeds are used where the terrain becomes steeper and less hospitable. And this emphasis on livestock means farms provide top-quality beef and lamb, as well as plenty of milk to make the famous cheeses for which the North is known.

Much of the land is given over to grazing but some arable farming does go on, especially in the lower-lying areas of the drier north-east. It's not easy to grow fruit and vegetables successfully in a place where the climate is often cold and wet, although Lancashire, which has the advantage of being on the warmer west side of the Pennines, does well with root crops and salads.

The coastline has long played a vital role in the region's economy and fishing is still important. Some of the best kippers in the land are smoked in the North, and the people also claim that their fish and chips are second to none, with light, crispy batter that's unbeatable. On the subject of batter, there is one Northern dish that is cooked every week in thousands of homes across the country – Yorkshire pudding.

Numerous recipes survive for a whole range of traditional baked goodies. Workers, both agricultural and industrial, have for many years marked the end of a hard day with a pint of one of the fine local beers, and the brewing industry still thrives. The North is a huge and varied area, and each part has a distinct character with its own proud traditions of food and drink.

CHOICE CHEESES

Yorkshire, Cumbria and Lancashire between them encompass huge tracts of land and a wide variety of terrain. On the lower fields, cattle are kept in large numbers and almost 2½ million litres of milk a year are produced in the area. That is enough to make a fair quantity of butter and cream, and of course much is also used to produce the delicious cheeses for which the region is famous. The fact panel opposite describes the most famous cheeses and one or two less well-known types which are well worth trying.

Upper Hindhope, in Northumbria's beautiful Cheviot Hills, where the sturdiest breeds of livestock are kept. Stone farmhouses nestle in sheltered spots among the rolling hills.

The Friesian cow, seen here in North Yorkshire, is the most widely kept breed in the country. Friesians are renowned for their high milk yield, and are also good beef cattle.

FARMHOUSE CHEESE

Look for this symbol when buying Farmhouse English Cheddar, Cheshire and Lancashire. These cheeses are still made by traditional methods on the farms where the milk is produced. They have unique qualities of texture and flavour and are independently graded. Only the fine grade Farmhouse English cheese is entitled to bear this mark.

Lancashire is probably the most readily recognised cheese from the North. Try if you can to sample Farmhouse Lancashire, first made in 1913. It is wonderfully buttery and rich, but unfortunately made only by a handful of producers, whose number has dwindled drastically since the Second World War. The production process is laborious but the results well worth the effort. The cheese is made from a mixture of curds from two days' milk, and is salted and cut by hand. It is carefully graded and only superfine and fine grades are sold as farmhouse. Creamery Lancashire, on the other hand, is widely made, using commercial methods, and the curds are from just one day's milk. Lancashire cheese is sometimes referred to locally as 'toaster' because it melts so well and is often labelled 'mild' or 'tasty', depending on strength of flavour. Try Pan Haggerty (see recipe, page 101), a delicious vegetable dish, to see for yourself.

Wensleydale, until the 1920s, always had blue veins. However, these days the white version is more common and the veined cheese is now known as Blue Wensleydale. French monks who founded the great abbeys in the Yorkshire Dales, following the Norman Conquest of 1066, first brought the recipe to this country. The cheese was made at Jervaulx Abbey by the Cistercians, although in those times ewes' milk was used. It wasn't until after the 16th century, when the monasteries were dissolved and production moved to

---

NORTHERN CHEESES

Choose mild Northern cheeses, made from the rich milk of local cattle, for cheeseboards or cooking. Some varieties are widely available, while others might be harder to track down. Try your local specialist cheese shop or delicatessen.

LANCASHIRE

A crumbly, white cheese, slightly salty, with a full-bodied flavour. The richer farmhouse version usually uses unpasteurised milk. The cheese is the softest of English pressed cheeses and melts well, so is ideal for toasting and cooking.

WENSLEYDALE

Usually eaten young, Wensleydale is a white cheese with a close, smooth texture and a mild, refreshing flavour. Blue Wensleydale is hard to come by, and has an extremely delicate and delicious flavour.

LANCASHIRE

WENSLEYDALE

BOTTON

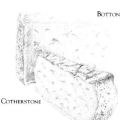

COTHERSTONE

COTHERSTONE

Made in a white or blue-veined version, from unpasteurised milk, Cotherstone is open-textured with a sharp, slightly acidic flavour. It develops a natural crust, similar to Camembert, which changes from gold to pink as it ages. Not easily found.

BOTTON

A newly developed cheese made to a traditional recipe in Danby, Yorkshire. Semi-hard and made from unpasteurised cows' milk, it is similar to Cheddar. Not widely available.

A thirst-quenching drink from the clear waters of Grasmere. Enough cattle are kept in the Lake District to produce over 500 million litres of milk a year.

local farmhouses and dairies, that cows' milk was introduced into the recipe. The North Country way to eat Wensleydale is with a slice of apple pie, gingerbread or fruit cake.

Cotherstone is another cheese, originally made by monks, which is enjoying a revival today. It is not widely available, since it is made only by a small number of producers in Yorkshire. There are several other locally produced cheeses, all of which are made on a small scale.

An area that gives so much milk inevitably produces butter as well. Cumberland rum butter is a delicious local speciality, of butter flavoured with rum, Barbados sugar and spices. It was traditionally served to celebrate the birth of a baby, and coins were placed in the empty butter bowl, where they stuck to the remains, to ensure a happy and prosperous life for the newborn.

Not surprisingly, for a region which has so much rugged land, goats and sheep are widely farmed, and their milk increasingly used for yogurts and cheeses.

LOTS OF LAMB AND INTERESTING OFFAL

Huge numbers of sheep are reared on the hill farms and moorlands of the North Country. Cumbria has a sheep population of three million, and there are two million in Yorkshire. Hardy breeds are favoured, which can withstand the cold winds and bitter winters. The North Country Mule is a cross breed common in Cumbria, and Cheviot sheep are found on the moors in Yorkshire. One advantage of these tough creatures is that they can survive all but the worst weather on what little they can crop from the ground, and need no extra food from the farmer.

Sheep produce their lambs in spring and the youngest, tenderest meat is available from June to August. Lambs born later do not reach the shops until further on in the year and have a more mature flavour. Mutton, the meat of a fully grown sheep, once staple

A North-country cross-bred ewe, with two black-faced Suffolk-cross lambs, pictured in the Yorkshire Dales. These animals are farmed intensively for meat.

fare throughout the country but no longer produced in any quantity, can still occasionally be bought in the Lakes, where it comes from Herdwick sheep. Many regional dishes use lamb. Shepherd's Pie (see recipe, page 120) is one national favourite that originated in the North, and Lancashire Hot Pot is a popular and flavoursome way to cook lamb chops.

The hard life of the North, both in the industrial cities and among the farming communities, meant that Northerners developed a thrifty approach to food that still exists today. No part of the animal was wasted, and butchers' stalls are arrayed not just with the more usual liver, kidneys and hearts, but with other types of offal that are seldom, if ever, found further south. Tripe is very popular – there is a recipe for tripe and onions on page 182 – and brains, chitterlings (pig's intestines), lamb's fry (testicles), elder (pressed cow's udder), cow heel for enriching pies and stews, and sweetbreads are all on sale.

Black pudding is a great delicacy and the best ones are said to come from Bury. They are made from fresh blood and oatmeal, and there are as many different variations to the texture and seasoning as there are makers. Every year the butchers compete with their French counterparts to see who can produce the best black pudding. Besides these delicacies are pressed and potted meats, jellied veal, faggots, cooked chicken, tongue and brisket, and much more. And all over Lancashire, stalls sell hot meat pies, to eat there and then or take home.

Bacon is prepared in the same way as it is in Scotland, with the joint rolled, so that the 'middle cut' has both streaky and back meat. York hams are cured in oak smoke and come from the meat of the Large White pig, a sizeable, sturdy breed. Tradition has it that the hams were first smoked over fires of the sawdust that came from building York Minster. Over on the other side of the country, Cumberland hams, although hard to come by, are worth looking out for. They are dry-cured, salted and rubbed with brown sugar, and are usually sold

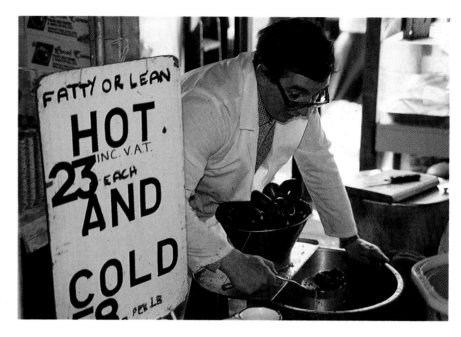

unsmoked. Cumberland sausages are a delicacy which has found its way south. They contain nothing but meat, flavoured with herbs and spices, and can be up to four feet long. These sausages are easily recognised because each one is sold wound into a plump coil.

The beef of northern England has a reputation for being juicier and tastier than that of the south. Whether or not this is true, there is no dish that spells the best of British cooking more than roast beef, accompanied of course by Yorkshire pudding. Steak and Kidney Pie (see recipe, page 130) is another much-loved dish that originates from the North.

The wild moors, mountains and dales are home to all sorts of game. There is some venison, as well as grouse, pheasant and partridge, and both venison and quail are farmed. Jugged hare is regarded as a local speciality. Derwentwater duck (see recipe, page 165) is delicious served with piquant Cumberland sauce.

The notice spells out the choice at Chadwicks' black pudding stall, in Bury's famous open market, Lancashire. These are real North Country favourites, rich, savoury and full of goodness and flavour.

Delicious black puddings and fresh tripe front the impressive display in Walmsley's butcher's shop in Ramsbottom, Lancashire. Beautifully presented cuts of lamb and beef, joints of lean pink ham, and fat sausages surround these northern delicacies.

FISH FROM SEA, RIVER AND LAKE

With sea to both east and west, the tradition of fishing is naturally well established. Fleets from Humberside trawl the North Sea for huge quantities of white fish, including cod, haddock, whiting and plaice. Many foreign vessels also use these ports. More cod comes through Grimsby than any other English port, some of it destined for the processing plants of a major freezing company based in the town. To underline the importance of the fishing industry here, the National Federation of Fish Friers runs courses to teach people the art of running a fish and chip shop.

In some places along the Yorkshire coast, a boat based on the design of the Viking long boat, called a coble, can still be seen. These days they are mostly motorised, although in the past they relied on sail power.

Shellfish, including crabs, lobsters and scallops, are caught in all northern waters, and tiny scallops are found off the Isle of Man. From Morecambe Bay, on the west coast, come small brown shrimps, sadly rarer now than they used to be, but still delicious eaten in the traditional way, potted with butter. There are good fish markets throughout Lancashire, where you might find hake, shrimp or herring. A tasty herring recipe for fish stuffed and served with mustard sauce comes from Cumbria (page 197).

Fine kippers are made in Northumbria, where the smokehouses at Craster have their own special light cure, based on a technique originally used for salmon, which hasn't changed for more than 100 years. The kippers have an appetising flavour and good, rich colour that owes nothing to artificial dyes or additives but comes instead from lengthy smoking over a slow oak

Boats venture far out into the North Sea, to bring home the best catches. The trawl net is towed between two vessels and, when the tow is completed, the full net, seen here, is winched alongside and hoisted on board.

fire. Few of the herrings used are caught locally, however. The Isle of Man also produces memorable kippers, and from other smokeries in the North come delicious haddock, trout, salmon and prawns, among other delicacies.

Freshwater fish, such as trout and salmon, inhabit the Lakes and many of the rivers which flow down to the sea from the Pennines and Cheviots. A strange method of river fishing still survives in parts of the north-west, where an enormous net called a 'heave' or 'haaf' is used. The nets can be as much as 18 feet wide and the fishermen have to stand in the water rather than on the bank to handle them effectively. Fish farming is a growing business in the North, with trout being the most commonly produced variety.

An unusual freshwater fish which is found in the deep waters of the Lake District is the char. A relative of the salmon, char was left behind in the inland lakes after the glacial waters of the Ice Age receded. The fish has a delicate flavour and pink-tinged flesh, and was generally served in pies or potted. Char are caught with long lines, which plunge deep into the waters, weighted by bright metal spinners made of bronze, copper or even silver. It is sometimes possible to buy these fish locally.

PLENTIFUL PRODUCE

Lancashire boasts nearly 30,000 acres of fertile agricultural land. Hardly any fruit is grown but instead a profusion of vegetables, especially potatoes, is produced. Other roots are important and salad vegetables, such as cucumbers, tomatoes and lettuce, are grown under glass. A high percentage of this abundance of fresh vegetables is consumed locally, some sold in farm shops and the rest taken to shops and markets in the surrounding towns and cities. Golden Vegetable Soup (see recipe, page 84) is a North Country recipe which puts a wide variety of vegetables to good use.

Gooseberries and forced rhubarb are the two big fruit crops to come from the North. Yorkshire produces nearly 70 per cent of early rhubarb, but because the

Craster kippers hanging from the smokehouse rafters look rather like so many copper-coloured bats! Northumbria claims to have invented this particular method of preserving fish.

harvesting needs a lot of labour, the future of this crop is endangered by increasing costs. Intense rivalry surrounds domestic gooseberry growing, and an annual Gooseberry Show at Egton Bridge sees a fiercely fought contest, where one year a champion berry tipped the scales at over 2 lb (1 kg). Commerical growing centres are found in Lancashire, however, rather than Yorkshire.

The climate of the North is generally unsuitable for fruit growing, although damsons, known locally as witherslacks, are grown around Lake Windermere. These fruits have a tart flavour, but can be used very successfully for cooking (Damson and Apple Tansy, see recipe, page 244).

CAKES, BAKES AND SWEET THINGS

Comforting cakes to cheer up chilly afternoons are a speciality of the North and a multitude of recipes come from the area, some of them with intriguing names. Singing hinnies, from the north-east, are made from a scone-like mixture and are so named because they sizzle on the griddle as they cook. Many recipes from the north-east feature oats, which were one of the staple crops grown here.

Kendal Mint Cake from the Lake District isn't a cake

at all but a peppermint-flavoured sweet, which is said to be very sustaining and ideal for climbers and walkers trekking across the hills. Eccles Cakes (see recipe, page 272) are filled with a mincemeat-style mixture of dried fruits, sugar and spices, in a crisp flaky pastry crust. They come from the town of Eccles in Lancashire. Their origins are not known for sure, but they may originally have had a religious significance.

Gingerbread is popular all over the North and perhaps the most famous comes from the Lake District village of Grasmere. The Grasmere Gingerbread Shop still exists, and the cake is baked on the premises; it has been made to Sarah Nelson's secret recipe since 1855.

Rum features as a flavouring in many Lake District dishes, because the liquor was brought over in ships from the West Indies during the 18th century. Cumberland Rum Nicky (see recipe, page 240) is a traditional dessert from the area, which is rather like a mince pie flavoured with rum. Curd tarts are found here as in other parts of the country, and deserve to be made more often. Try Yorkshire Curd Tarts (see recipe, page 274) to see how light and delicious they are.

Perhaps the most famous 'bake' from the North Country is Yorkshire pudding. This was originally flatter than the puffy version we know today, because the batter was cooked on an open fire, beneath the spit where the joint was roasting, to catch all the delicious juices as they dripped down. Although it is often thought of purely as an accompaniment to roast beef, Yorkshire pudding in the North is served as a pub snack with onion gravy or a meat-based filling, such as steak and kidney. In the past it was often eaten as a course on its own, before the meat, to take the edge off ravenous

TART TOPPINGS FROM THE NORTH OF ENGLAND

Open-plate tarts filled with jam are a familiar feature of North Country cooking, and offer the cook a chance to be imaginative in the decoration and use of different colours and flavours in the filling, as shown here.

Above:
Redcurrant jelly was used to make a 'red cross' in the centre.

Each section of the star pattern could have a different filling.

Four separate portions, each one a different flavour (left).

A traditional lattice design, often used for treacle tarts (left).

The pastry edging was cut at intervals, and alternate sections folded into the centre (right).

The decorative coil design, made from a long strip of pastry, could be varied in thickness and number of loops (right).

FOOD FAIRS AND FESTIVALS

EASTERTIDE	JULY	AUGUST	SEPTEMBER
Egg Decorating and Rolling Competitions, Cusworth Hall Museum, Cusworth, Doncaster, South Yorkshire; Avenham Park, Preston, Lancashire; and other venues: display of painted eggs made by children; hard-boiled eggs are rolled downhill in a race, then eaten.	Blessing the Boats, Whitby, Yorkshire: a quayside procession to bless the fishing fleet. The Great Yorkshire show, Hookstone Oval, Harrogate, Yorkshire: major agricultural show, livestock, sheep-shearing, poultry, bee-keeping, etc. Cumberland Show, Bitts Park, Carlisle: livestock and agricultural show.	Carnival Day, Denby Dale, nr Barnsley, South Yorkshire: held intermittently, this features a 2-ton pie made of mixed meat and potatoes. Old Gooseberry Show, Egton Bridge, North Yorkshire: numerous examples of gooseberry species.	First Fruits Harvest Ceremony, Market Place, Richmond, North Yorkshire: greeting the first farmer to bring his year's corn to the Market Square.

appetites and make the meat stretch further. And it can also be enjoyed with jam or fruit – a truly versatile dish.

NORTHERN BREWS

The North may not have the climate to grow its own hops, which it imports from other parts of the country as well as from overseas, but nonetheless it is great beer country and nowhere will the drinker find a wider range of brews to choose from. Many independent brewers thrive in the North, producing some of the best real ales in Britain. Northerners like their beer strong – the strongest draught beer in the world was brewed by a pub called the Frog and Parrot in Sheffield in 1985. Strength depends on how long the malted barley is allowed to ferment: the longer the fermentation, the higher the alcohol content. The trick is to get the balance between strength and body just right, since a long fermentation reduces the body of the beer. In Yorkshire, brewing is done by the two-tier method, which separates out excess yeast and draws it off without disturbing the fermenting beer. This produces rich ales, which are particularly full-bodied. It is a fine art, and each brewery has their own closely guarded recipe for success. Whether the ale is dark or light, the way to drink it is from a straight-sided glass, with a high creamy head of foam that lasts right down to the bottom.

Lindisfarne Mead, from Holy Island off Northumberland, is a drink with an ancient history. It is made from honey and, since it is known that bees have been kept in this area for many centuries, the drink was probably made by the monks who settled here 1,300 years ago. The modern winery stands opposite the ruins of the monastery. Mead is a sweet, alcoholic drink and can be bought by visitors to the island. It is also sold throughout the country to lend an authentic taste to medieval banquets. Another delicious honey-based drink from the North is Brontë Yorkshire liqueur, which is subtly flavoured with herbs and spices and gets a kick from brandy.

BEERS FROM THE NORTH

A proliferation of breweries is found in the North, with many that are still family-owned independent ones, each producing beers that differ greatly in flavour and style. Some can only be found locally, others are more widely distributed. These are a few of the many companies that brew in the North:

J. W. CAMERON & CO, Hartlepool. An independent brewery producing a full range of mild and strong bitters, but famous for their 'Strong Arm' premium bitter.

HARTLEY, Ulverston, part of Frederic Robinson (see below). Brewers since 1755 making mild, bitter and best bitter. This, their best-known bitter, is a premium bitter, with a sweet heavy flavour. It is called 'XB', the X being the old method of denoting strength.

JOSEPH HOLT, Manchester. A traditional family company with about 90 pubs in the Manchester area, they produce what some consider the most bitter bitter in the country – Holt's bitter. An acquired taste, but worth the effort!

HYDES, Manchester. A small family-owned independent brewery making bitter under the Anvil label. They produce two draught milds, one dark and sweetish, the other a lighter, hoppy mild, and an ale known as Anvil Strong Ale. This heavy brew is also available on draught in winter.

JOSHUA TETLEY, Leeds. Part of the National Allied Breweries group, but has been brewing since 1746. Produces a light creamy bitter, a stronger, premium bitter and a dark mild, widely available in Lancashire.

MITCHELLS, Lancaster. A small family company brewing a mild, a bitter, and a strong bitter – 'ESB' – which is fairly heavy and full-bodied.

OLD MILL, Snaithe. A small, new brewery producing two beers, Old Mill Traditional, a standard hoppy bitter, and Bullion, their premium, award-winning bitter.

FREDERIC ROBINSON, Stockport. Large company with about 350 pubs in the north-west of England. They brew a very distinctive best bitter, well-hopped, full-bodied and strong, called Old Tom. They have a unicorn as their logo.

SAMUEL SMITH'S, Tadcaster. Yorkshire's oldest brewery, serving a wide area. Their best known is Old Brewery Bitter, malty, smooth, full-bodied and very distinctive. Their beer is still available in wooden casks – from the wood – rare in these days.

TIMOTHY TAYLOR, Keighley. A small traditional family company with one of the largest ranges of cask-conditioned ales in the country. They are famous for their 'Landlord' beer, a premium bitter, distinctive and full-bodied. Going for highest quality in all ingredients, Taylor's are producers of 'Championship beers' and have won more medals than any other company.

T & R THEAKSTON, Masham and Carlisle. Makes four traditional ales, the best known of which is 'Old Peculier', a very strong, heavy, dark, rich, sweet beer. A winter warmer that leaves knees wobbling.

DANIEL THWAITES, Blackburn. An independent brewer famous for their award-winning mild, reputed to be the best in the country. They produce two – one is a dark, nutty brew, the other, their best mild, is a slightly maltier, heavier brew.

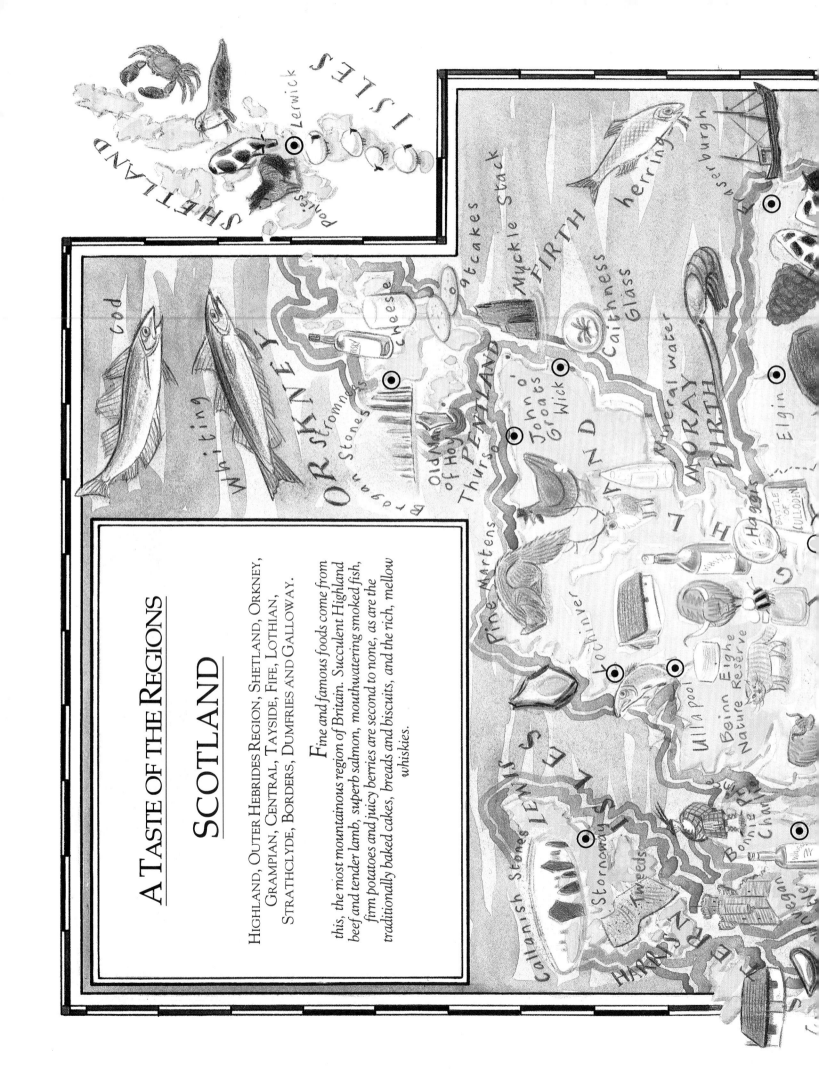

A TASTE OF THE REGIONS

SCOTLAND

HIGHLAND, OUTER HEBRIDES REGION, SHETLAND, ORKNEY, GRAMPIAN, CENTRAL, TAYSIDE, FIFE, LOTHIAN, STRATHCLYDE, BORDERS, DUMFRIES AND GALLOWAY.

Fine and famous foods come from this, the most mountainous region of Britain. Succulent Highland beef and tender lamb, superb salmon, mouthwatering smoked fish, firm potatoes and juicy berries are second to none, as are the traditionally baked cakes, breads and biscuits, and the rich, mellow whiskies.

Scotland conjures up images of hills and mountains. Most parts, however, are low-lying and fertile, producing soft fruits and good harvests of wheat and barley. About one-third of the countryside is hostile to all but the hardiest of animals and crops. Mountain sheep and tough Highland cattle do thrive in these areas, however. And there are plenty of fish and shellfish to be had from the seas and inland waters. Add to that the delectable products of Scottish baking and the age-old skills of distilling, and you have the picture of a country with a wealth of good food to offer.

CHEESE-MAKING REVIVAL

Dairy farming is practised in most parts of Scotland, although it is largely concentrated in the lower lands of the south, particularly in the fertile pastures of Dumfries & Galloway and Strathclyde. The most southerly islands of the Hebrides also have a climate well suited to dairying, and all these areas produce milk, butter and yogurt as well as cheese.

Recent years have seen a cheese-making revival and many manufacturers have begun making interesting cheeses, although often on a small scale. However, Scottish Cheddar still accounts for 90 per cent of cheese production, and comes in all shapes and sizes: mild or mature, white or coloured. Dunlop, an exclusively Scottish cheese, is similar in style to Cheddar but lighter in colour and texture. It is named after the Ayrshire village where it was first made but is now produced on the islands of Arran and Islay. Both Dunlop and Cheddar are available with many unusual flavourings, including herbs, mustard and Drambuie.

Among the newer hard cheeses, Pentland and Lothian, from the Lowlands, are similar in style to Brie and Camembert. A soft, peat-smoked cheese comes from the same area. Midlothian produces Langskaill, a Gouda-type, and Howgate, a cream cheese with an oatmeal coating.

The Highlands specialise in soft cheeses, of which Crowdie, said to have been introduced by the Vikings, is probably the best known. In the days when every cottage had a cow, Crowdie was made regularly from the excess milk. It is low in fat, similar to cottage cheese in style, and was sometimes eaten mixed with cream.

ABOVE

Part of the cheese making process in which the vat temperature is raised almost to blood heat for about an hour to firm the curd. Any changes in acidity are also checked – too much acid causes toughening of the curd.

RIGHT

Wild red deer stags in winter. Scotland is the only place where these animals live in the open, taking refuge in high, remote areas. Usually, they prefer to shelter in forests.

SMOKED FISH

Fish has been dried and smoked for hundreds of years, probably since prehistoric times. Not only does the process preserve the fish, it also adds distinctive and delicious flavours. Many varieties, including trout, mackerel and eel, are suitable for smoking, but those illustrated here are the best-known, traditional Scottish smoked fish.

SMOKED SALMON

Soaked in salt for 24 hours to bring out the flavour, then cold-smoked over oak sawdust. Succulent, with mild flavour. No need to cook before eating. Delicious as a starter, thinly sliced, with lemon and brown bread and butter, or can be used in recipes.

ARBROATH SMOKIES

Made first in Auchmithie, and now in Arbroath, both fishing towns of the north-east. Small haddock, heads removed, are salted for two hours, then hot-smoked in pairs over oak or beech for less than an hour. No colour is added. Can be eaten cold or grilled.

KIPPERS

Those from the area around Loch Fyne, on the west coast, are the best known. Herrings are split, gutted and brined, then smoked over oak for up to 12 hours. They are silvery-gold in colour. Buy whole fish, with head on. Cook by grilling or poaching in water.

FINNAN HADDOCK

From Findon, north of Arbroath. The fish are split and cleaned, lightly brined, then cold-smoked for up to six hours over oak sawdust. No dye is added and the fish are a pale lemon colour. Must be cooked before eating; can be grilled or poached. Eyemouth Pales, from the Borders, are prepared in a similar way.

Serve it with fruit or spread on oatcakes. Caboc, a rich double-cream cheese rolled in crunchy oatmeal, was first made in the Western Highlands in the 15th century by a chieftain's daughter. The recipe was revived in the 1960s.

The upsurge of interest in a wider range of products has meant an increase in the production of sheep and goat cheeses. Lanark Blue, made in Strathclyde, is a delicious blue-veined sheep's cheese, said to taste like French Roquefort.

FISH FARMING – A BOOM INDUSTRY

Fishing in Scotland has provided many communities with a livelihood over the centuries. Peterhead is the largest port, and Aberdeen is also very important. Huge catches of haddock, cod, whiting, halibut, sole, mackerel and many other varieties of seafish are landed. Herring is often thought of as the typical Scottish fish and still makes up the main catch of the Highlands, where over half of Scottish fish are caught, but the number fished off the east coast has dwindled now because of EEC regulations. Herring are a very nutritious, oily fish, which are best cooked simply. The Scottish way is to coat them with oatmeal and fry them until they are crisp and golden.

It was during the 14th century that fishing first began to grow as an industry in the Border country. Lobster and shrimp, as well as white fish, feature in the catch here. Crabs and lobsters are caught in creels off the coast of Fife, while the Western Isles add more white fish to the picture, as well as excellent shellfish, including lobsters, crabs, scallops and winkles.

Scotland also has a fine reputation for freshwater fish, from the pure waters of the deep lochs and fast-flowing rivers. Trout and salmon from the Tay and

Tweed are caught by traditional methods, and are considered a great delicacy. But the biggest news to hit the Scottish fish industry recently is the huge expansion in fish farming.

Salmon hatcheries started to take off in the Seventies and production is soaring, so that ten times more farmed salmon than wild salmon now come on to the market. The fish are hatched in rivers and then transferred to fresh or seawater lochs to grow in the

That triumphant smile says it all! The wild Atlantic salmon which has just met its match on the other end of the fishing line probably weighs around 4.5 kg (10 lb). This king of fish can be recognised by its small head, plump body and forked tail, and by its shining skin, that merges from steely grey on the back to white on the belly.

Haddock hangs on racks in the kiln, to be smoked to a full and succulent flavour. These fish are found in abundance around the British Isles and belong to the same family as cod.

Small by modern standards, the Arbroath fishing fleet lands its catch of white fish from the North Sea – mainly haddock, cod and whiting – every day. Most are sold in the town's daily market to small local fish processors, and it is here that the famous 'Arbroath Smokies' are made, that are exported all over the world.

safety of special cages, where they cannot be harmed by predators. The farms are found mainly in the Highlands and islands, although there is a good scattering across the rest of Scotland. Rainbow trout are also reared in the same way, and the farming of oysters, mussels and scallops, although still in its infancy, is on the increase and shows huge potential for growth. Experiments into halibut farming have also been reported, although they are still at an early stage.

Some farmed salmon and trout are turned into another of Scotland's finest foods – smoked fish. Smoking is also used to treat herrings and haddock. The traditions of smoking go back hundreds of years, when it was an important method of storing fish for long periods.

MEAT FROM MOOR AND MOUNTAIN

Scottish beef and lamb are renowned throughout the world for their excellence. The Aberdeen Angus breed of beef cattle was first developed in the north-east of Scotland in the early 19th century. These animals have a good proportion of lean to fat and, although they are relatively small, yield a good weight for their size. The meat is lightly veined with fat, which makes it tender, juicy and full of flavour. Other breeds include the Galloway and the Highland Shorthorn. Cattle are usually bred on hill and upland farms, then brought to maturity on the lush lowlands. The Highlands and islands have some of the best grazing in Europe, with the rich summer pastures of Orkney, Islay and Kintyre. Orkney beef, from milk-fed calves, is marketed as such, and can sometimes be found in other parts of the country. You will find ideas for using Scottish beef in Chapter 3, in the section on beef beginning on page 124.

Sheep are particularly well suited to life on the rough Scottish slopes. The Black-faced breed grazes on heather, which gives the meat a specially sweet and delicious flavour. These sheep do not lamb until June and the young are allowed to mature until the following year. Cheviots, bred in the Border hills and the lower lands of the north, are known for their wool as well as their meat. The Shetland breed, which inhabits the islands of the same name, is hardy, lean and small. It feeds on grass, heather and seaweed, which gives the

flesh a gamey flavour. The meat is very tender and needs only light cooking.

Haggis is probably the best-known Scottish meat dish although it is not widely consumed by the Scots themselves. It is made of minced offal parcelled in a sheep's gut, like a big spicy sausage, and is traditionally served with great ceremony on Burns Night – 25 January.

Hens, turkeys and pigs are all produced in quantity in Lothian, and some of the best pork and bacon comes from Aberdeenshire and the north-east, though Ayrshire bacon, too, is renowned.

Scotland is also renowned for the abundance of game that inhabits the moors and forests of the country. Over 90 per cent is exported to the Continent but some still finds its way into the shops as fresh or smoked joints, or in sausages and pâtés. Roe and fallow deer, and the more common red deer are found wild throughout the Highlands, as well as being farmed. Red grouse is the finest game bird, and hare, pheasant and many other types of game bird are also bagged in large numbers.

LATE AND EARLY RIPENERS

Scotland produces two-thirds of British raspberries, and fine fruits they are, with an intensity of flavour that is unsurpassable. Fruit farming is centred on Tayside, around Blairgowrie, and stretches south to Lothian and north to the shores of the Moray Firth. The bulk of the crop is canned or made into jam.

Other soft fruits, such as tayberries, gooseberries, strawberries and black- and redcurrants, do well in the Scottish climate. They take longer to ripen than in the south and so come into season later. The raspberry-growing regions also produce peas, beans, potatoes and other roots, which are sold at pick-your-own farms and farm shops as well as being sent to market.

Potatoes are a common crop in Scotland, which produces some of the earliest earlies in the country. The Borders grow oil-seed rape, used for cooking oils and cattle fodder, as well as turnips, peas and potatoes. Lothian produces excellent leeks, while in the Clyde valley they specialise in plums and salad greens. The Scottish climate is very suitable for hardier herbs, such as coriander, dill, fennel and marjoram, and research is being done with a view to large-scale farming of these varieties in the future.

ABOVE
Highland cattle are well equipped to withstand the tough climate, and have thick, shaggy coats to keep out the bitter winter winds.

BELOW LEFT
The Scottish raspberry industry started to develop commercially about 70 years ago.

SCOTTISH GAME

The term 'game' describes wild birds and animals that are shot for sport during a specified season. The meat has a strong flavour, and needs to be properly hung. See page 172 for roasting methods and times.

VENISON

The meat of the deer. Marinade, then roast, casserole or use in pies and pâtés. Wild deer are in season from July to end February; venison from deer farms is available all year.

RED GROUSE

Shooting starts on the 'glorious 12th' of August and goes on until 10 December. Found only in Scotland. Feeds on berries and young heather, has a fine, subtle flavour. Serve roasted or in pies or stews.

PHEASANT

The season is from 1 October to 1 February. Pheasants have rich, tender flesh and can be roasted or casseroled.

HARE

The season runs from 1 August to the last day of February. Can be roasted, jugged or casseroled.

BERRIES

England is catching up with Scotland on the quantity of soft fruit production, but the Scots would say that their berries have the finest concentration of flavour, due to slow ripening.

RASPBERRIES

Grown on canes. Eat raw, or use in jams, tarts and desserts. Store in fridge and use as soon as possible after purchase. Can be frozen successfully. (End June to October.)

LOGANBERRIES

A cross between a raspberry and an American dewberry, mainly used for canning. First raised in late 19th century. Larger, darker and softer than raspberries, with a sharp flavour. (Early July to late August.)

TAYBERRIES

A cross between a blackberry and a raspberry. Easy to pick, although the canes are thorny. Large, conical and bright deep purple, with a rich flavour. (Early July to mid-August.)

STRAWBERRIES

Can be grown under glass or plastic, or outdoors. Eat raw or use in desserts or jams. Store in a cool place and use quickly: they do not keep well. Can be frozen but become mushy when thawed. (Late May to October.)

RIGHT
Scotch whisky has a distinctive flavour depending on where it was made. The water, the exact process used and, of course, the magical balance achieved in blending, all have an effect on the finished product.

WHAT ELSE BUT WHISKY?

The national drink of Scotland, whisky, is also a best-selling spirit worldwide. The name comes from the ancient Gaelic *uisge beatha,* meaning 'water of life'. Whisky has been distilled in Scotland for many hundreds of years, although it has only existed as a commercial concern since the mid-19th century.

Two kinds of whisky are made, malt and grain. Most malt whisky is made in the Highlands and islands, and uses malted barley only, in the pot still process. The barley is malted by germination, which is halted by drying in a peat-fired kiln. The aromatic smoke helps to flavour the whisky. The barley is then mashed and fermented before being distilled in the swan-necked copper pot stills. Most malt whiskies are distilled twice before being transferred to oak barrels to mature, a process which takes a minimum of three years and can often take considerably longer.

Grain whisky is made all over Scotland, from a mixture of unmalted and malted grains, distilled by a continuous process, and does not have the subtleties of flavour found in malts. Once mature, the whiskies are blended before packaging. Some are sold as single, unblended varieties but by far the majority are blends, consisting of anything from 15 to 50 different single whiskies, carefully chosen to complement and enhance each other.

Malt whiskies are particularly sought after for their pronounced bouquet and flavour, attributed to the soft water, the peat used in malting and the soft, Scottish air that infiltrates the casks during maturing. Whisky can only be described as Scotch if it has been wholly distilled and matured in Scotland. Eighty per cent is exported, but of the Scotch whisky sold in Britain 80 to 85 per cent is consumed outside Scotland.

The country also produces Drambuie, a whisky-based liqueur said to be made to Bonnie Prince Charlie's secret recipe, left behind when he fled from Skye. Fruit and flowers are used for country wines on a small commercial scale in the Highlands. And Scottish ales and lagers, introduced by the monks of the Border abbeys, are produced in quantity, especially around Edinburgh, a traditional brewing centre.

Some of Scotland's pure water is bottled and sold, including Caithness Spring Water and Sutherland Spring, which is golden in colour and has a peaty flavour.

TEA-TIME FEASTS

The delights of Scottish baking are renowned. Oats are the most important cereal, because they can withstand poor soils and harsh weather, and oatmeal features widely in baking as well as in the traditional Scottish breakfast dish, porridge. Nothing is more warming than a bowl of well-made porridge on a cold morning, seasoned with salt, or perhaps topped with a spoonful of heather honey, another Scottish speciality. Fruity Dundee marmalade also deserves a place on the breakfast table, spread perhaps on morning rolls. Served warm, these soft, oval, floury baps are baked fresh each day by local bakeries.

FOOD FAIRS AND FESTIVALS

JANUARY

Burns Suppers: various venues throughout Scotland. The numerous Burns Clubs celebrate the birth on 25 January 1759 of Scotland's national poet, Robert Burns, with the ceremony of piping in the haggis.

MARCH

Highland Cattle Show and Sale, Oban: pedigree Highland cattle.
International Festival of Food and Wine, St Andrews, Fife: hotels and restaurants offer culinary theme nights.

APRIL

Scottish Connection, Aberdeen: festival of all things Scottish, including food and drink; various city centre locations.
Agricultural Show, Ayr.

MAY

Catrine Agricultural Show, Kingencleugh, nr Mauchline: cattle, sheep, goats, baking, handicrafts, Highland dancing and show-jumping.
Lesmahgow Farmers' Society Annual Show, Langside Farm, Kirkfield Bank, Lanark: annual cattle show with sheep and pony sections.

JUNE

Baking Days, Highland Folk Museum, Duke Street, Kingussie.
Royal Highland Show, Edinburgh and Exhibition Trade Centre, Ingliston, Edinburgh: Scotland's premier agricultural show.

JULY

Caithness County Show, Riverside, Wick, Caithness.
Deeside Agricultural Show, King George V Park, Banchory, Kincardineshire.
New Deer Show, Craigieford Park, Aberdeenshire: agricultural show.
Palnackie Flounder Tramping World Championship, Palnackie Village, by Dalbeattie, Kirkcudbrightshire: competition, in aid of the RNLI, to catch the biggest flounder by tramping on it in the shallows.
Sutherland Agricultural Show. The Links, Dornoch, Sutherland.

AUGUST

Aberdeen Fish Festival, Aberdeen Harbour: all about how fish are caught and cooked.
Argyll County Show, Selma, Benderloch, by Oban, Argyll: agricultural show with livestock, produce, Highland dancing, terrier racing and sheep-shearing demonstration.
East Mainland Agricultural Show, Show Park, St Andrews, Orkney.
Islay Agricultural Show, Showfield, Islay, Argyll: agricultural show with trade stands, country dancing, bands and tossing the sheaf.
Orkney Agricultural Show, Bignold Park, Bignold Park Road, Kirkwall, Orkney: agricultural show with sports and side-shows.
Perthshire Agricultural Show, South Inch, Perth: large agricultural show.

SEPTEMBER

Eskdale Agricultural Society Open Show, The Castleholm, Langholm, Dumfriesshire: livestock with show-jumping, pony games, tug-o'-war and terrier racing.
Keith Horticultural Society Summer Show, Longmore Halls, Banff Road, Keith, Banffshire: flower and produce show with classes for flowers, vegetables, wines and baking.

OCTOBER

Aberdeen Angus Show and Perth Bull Sales, The Market, Caledonian Road, Perth: judging for champion on first day; sale of bulls by auction on second.

Oatcakes are thin, crisp biscuits, good with cheese (see recipe, page 280). Bannocks are made from enriched oatmeal bread dough, while Selkirk Bannock, a famous variation which was much admired by Queen Victoria, is like a fruit teabread, with fruit and spices.

High tea is the time to savour a slice of rich, almond-topped Dundee cake (see recipe, page 262). Black Bun, or Yule Cake, is traditionally baked at the year's end for Hogmanay and is rather like a giant mince-pie, with a pastry case enclosing a dried fruit filling. Shortbread is widely made, and the best contains pure butter and melts in the mouth (see recipe, page 281). Much flour is milled in Lothian, from Scottish wheat.

The Scots are very fond of their 'sweeties'. Edinburgh Rock is nothing like seaside rock, but is a soft, pale confection. Peppermint is a favourite flavouring, used in Jethart Snails – dark toffees introduced by a French prisoner from the Napoleonic wars – and in Hawick Balls, which also contain cinnamon. Galashiels Soor Plooms, round, green sweets with an acid tang, are said to commemorate the day when a gang of English marauders were overcome, having been caught unawares as they feasted on unripe plums.

FAR LEFT
Preparing for an old-fashioned tea in the Orkney Islands. The griddle plate suspended over an open fire is economical and simple to use.

LEFT
Scottish hospitality is famous and this table spread with all manner of cakes, breads and biscuits displays the best of home baking.

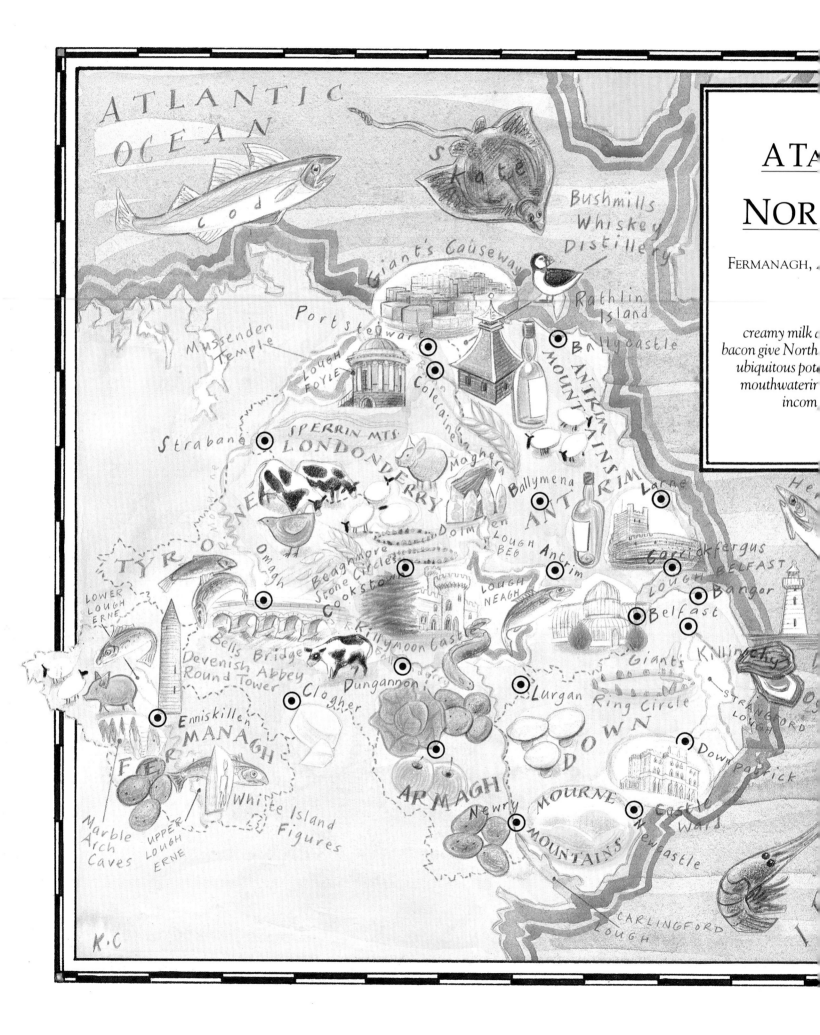

ATLANTIC OCEAN

Giant's Causeway

Bushmills
Whiskey
Distillery

Rathlin
Island

Ballycastle

Skate

Cod

Mussenden
Temple

Portstewart

Lough
FOYLE

Coleraine

ANTRIM MOUNTAINS

Strabane

SPERRIN MTS
LONDONDERRY

Maghera

Ballymena

Larne

TYRONE

Omagh

Beaghmore
Stone Circles
Cookstown

Dolmen

LOUGH
BEG

Antrim

LOUGH
NEAGH

Carrickfergus

LOUGH BELFAST

Bangor

Belfast

LOWER
LOUGH
ERNE

Bells Bridge

R.Killymoon Castle

Giant's

Killinchy

Devenish Abbey
Round Tower

Clogher

Dungannon

Lurgan

Ring Circle

STRANGFORD
LOUGH

DOWN

Enniskillen

FERMANAGH

White Island
Figures

ARMAGH

Newry

MOURNE

MOUNTAINS

Downpatrick

Castle
Newcastle

Marble
Arch
Caves

UPPER
LOUGH
ERNE

CARLINGFORD
LOUGH

A TA
NOR

FERMANAGH,

creamy milk
bacon give Nort
ubiquitous pot
mouthwaterin
incom

K.C

TE OF THE REGIONS

HERN IRELAND

AGH, DOWN, ANTRIM, LONDONDERRY, TYRONE.

*Rivers and seas teeming with fish,
utter, top-quality meat, and excellent ham and
eland its reputation for fine, simple food. The
ooked in all manner of ways, is always
ood. And to savour afterwards, there's the
le smoothness of Irish whiskey.*

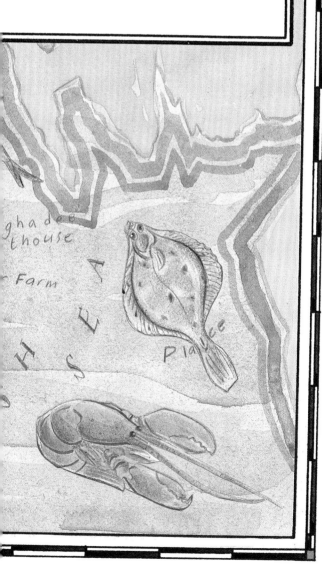

A diet based on simple things has sustained the people here for centuries. Milk, butter and cream, fish and meat, home-baked breads and cakes, and above all potatoes, dug straight from the crumbly, black soil and cooked in their skins to keep all the goodness in – these have been the culinary mainstays. It has been said that no one in Northern Ireland is more than three generations from the land and with such close links with farming it is not surprising that home cooking and baking remain important aspects of domestic life in Northern Ireland. Simple, unfussy cooking using natural, wholesome products of Northern Ireland's most important industry, agriculture, is the basis of the cuisine in this part of the United Kingdom.

The region's best-known dish, Irish stew, was originally made with young kid, but now uses lamb or mutton. There's a recipe on page 116. More and more lamb is being produced here and high-quality beef cattle are also reared on an increasingly important scale. And of course the countryside provides perfect cover for all types of game, feathered and furred.

POTATO COUNTRY

Think of Ireland and you think of potatoes, a staple crop and an important part of the economy since the 17th century. The main eating varieties grown here are the Dunbar Standard, Pentland Dell and Kerr's Pinks, and enough of these are now produced to allow a considerable export to Great Britain. Traditionally they were – and still are – cooked in every possible way. There's potato soup (see recipe, page 86), cake, bread,

Emerald green pastures provide perfect fodder for Ireland's many cattle. In the background is Strangford Lough, a magnificent, 18-mile-long inland sea which is a sanctuary for countless geese, ducks and swans. And the waters are rich in fish, including haddock, whiting and mackerel.

pie and pancakes. And of course, as an accompaniment to fish and meat, the floury boiled potatoes or crispy jackets of Northern Ireland are superb.

If Kent is the Garden of England, Armagh is the Orchard of Ireland, and there are dozens of fruit orchards, mostly growing apples, especially Bramley's. Other produce includes cabbage and, surprisingly, cultivated mushrooms, 70 per cent of which find their way across the water.

BEST FOR BACON

Nearly a quarter of all UK bacon comes from Ulster's Landrace and Large White pigs. Most is processed by a method known as the Wiltshire cure, but more traditional methods still survive, such as the Ulster Roll, which uses dry salt. Belfast hams, smoked over peat, are delicious and have been produced for over a hundred years.

A LAND OF MILK AND CREAM

The famous 'soft' climate of Northern Ireland encourages rich grass to grow, so the cattle are never short of good grazing. The people enjoy the natural goodness of dairy products and consume more milk and butter per head every year than their counterparts across the water. There is no great tradition of cheese-making. Although Cheddar is the most popular kind, an increasing range of cheese is being made to meet the demand by consumers for greater variety.

FRUITFUL WATERS

The rivers and lakes of Northern Ireland are alive with fish – the whole area is an angler's delight. Brown trout, sea trout, salmon, perch, pike, are all caught in abundance. From Lough Neagh, the biggest lake in the British Isles, come eels, which are often smoked. The River Mourne is one of the best salmon rivers, but it's almost impossible to choose between so many superb fishing waters.

FAR RIGHT
The Mourne Mountains form a dramatic backdrop to the farmlands of County Down. Barley, oats and potatoes are the most important crops to Irish farmers.

BELOW
The River Mourne eventually joins with the rivers Derg and Finn, to form the Foyle. The whole system of waters is a maze of wild salmon and trout grounds, and rainbow trout are also farmed in the area.

BEEF

Ireland's lush green pastures are ideal for extensive beef production. Beef from Northern Ireland, from animals fed on grass all year round, is more succulent and flavoursome, it is claimed, than intensively produced beef.

The traditional indigenous breeds, the Hereford and Aberdeen Angus, are rapidly being supplanted by continental breeds such as Charolais and Limousin, which produce more, leaner, meat.

Out to sea there's more fish – mackerel, plaice, cod, skate and lobster are brought ashore all round the coast. Prawns are landed from the colourful fishing fleet at Portavogie. Pubs often sell reasonably priced shellfish dishes at lunchtime and there are many different types of locally smoked fish to sample. Oysters are commercially grown in Strangford's unpolluted waters and are available all year round.

HOME FOR HIGH TEA

Every little town has its home bakery and the shelves are laden with farls – the word means a 'fourth part' of a round cake, and the loaves are shaped like triangles, with one rounded side. Soda bread (see recipe, page 288) is popular, with its crisp crust and moist crumb. It

ABOVE
Portavogie, in County Down, is a traditional little fishing village. The prawns that come ashore here are a speciality of a region renowned for seafood.

RIGHT
The main crop of potatoes is harvested during September and October, and the machinery is designed to ensure that the tubers are not damaged. It is also important to keep the potatoes dry during lifting, so that they will keep well.

FOOD FAIRS AND FESTIVALS

JANUARY

Royal Ulster Agricultural Show and Sale, The Showground, Balmoral, Belfast: show for pedigree dairy and beef cattle.

MARCH

Horse Ploughing Match and Heavy Horse Show, Fair Head, Ballycastle: ploughmen's competition.

APRIL

Greenmount Garden Fair, Greenmount College, Antrim: demonstrations and talks, including greenhouse cropping, fruit growing and wine-making.

MAY

Sealink Classic Fishing Festival, Fermanagh Lakeland: coarse fishing competition. Royal Ulster Agricultural Society Show, Balmoral, Belfast: competitions, side-shows and much more, going on late into evening.

JUNE

Irish Festival of Good Beer, Hilden Brewery, Lisburn.

AUGUST

Oul' Lammas Fair, Ballycastle: big traditional fair, with sheep and pony sales, side-stalls; 'Yellow man' toffee (similar to honeycomb but made to a secret recipe) and dulse (a seaweed which can be eaten raw in salads or cooked) on sale.

SEPTEMBER

Harvest Fair, Newtownards, Co. Down: held since 1613.

OCTOBER

Mounthill Fair, Larne: horse fair dating from 17th century; livestock, competitions, side-stalls. Royal Ulster Agricultural Society Autumn Show, Balmoral, Belfast: show and sale of pedigree pigs and cattle.

NOVEMBER

International Ploughing Championships, Moygannon, Donacloney, Co. Down: 50 ploughmen and 50 tractors plough 100 acres in unison.

was originally cooked on a griddle over a peat fire. Potato bread is widely made and, although good cold, is even better fried in bacon fat for breakfast.

High tea is a favourite meal, the table groaning with home-baked cakes and breads. Barm brack, a yeasted fruit bread (see recipe, page 287), is delicious sliced and buttered.

A TOAST TO FINE WHISKEY

You're never far from a pub or bar in Ireland, and whiskey was being made here long before it arrived across the water. Old Bushmills Distillery, situated on the Antrim coast, was granted the very first licence to distil whiskey in 1608. Local barley and water from St Columb's Rill are still used in production. But a strong, smooth liquor called poitín, or poteen, was being discreetly made in these parts for hundreds of years before that and who's to say that the ancient tradition of illicit distilling has died out even today?

Some independent brewing goes on in Northern Ireland. Hilden Brewery in County Antrim makes strong, hoppy, distinctive bitter as well as other beers, which are available in local pubs.

BELOW LEFT

Irish whiskey is triple-distilled to give it a subtle, pure taste. The malt is roasted in closed kilns, rather than over peat as in Scotland, and this also contributes to the mellowness of the flavour.

BELOW RIGHT

Traditional stooks of corn in a field near Ballintoy, County Antrim. Here, local shops are well stocked with different loaves and cakes.

RECIPES

BEST OF BRITISH . . .

All the recipes in this book have been chosen for the interesting use they make of all types of British produce, whether recently introduced to the country or grown here for centuries. The recipes represent the wide variety of British produce and many are also traditional favourites. Although many of the recipes have been chosen for use on special occasions, the emphasis is on inexpensive yet delicious dishes for family meals. For ease of use, the recipes have been arranged according to types of meal, with additional chapters on cakes, breads and preserves. There is a comprehensive index at the back of the book which lists recipes and produce.

. . . FROM EVERY REGION

Below the title of every recipe you will see the name of a region. These correspond to those used in the first part of the book, 'A Taste of the Regions', and have been categorised in this way either because they originally came from that area or because the main ingredient or ingredients originate there. Recipes said to be countrywide are those whose earliest origins are unclear or which are common to the whole country. Each recipe has a brief introduction explaining its origin, giving information about ingredients or giving serving suggestions. Details are always given about how many people a dish will serve.

MAKING THE MOST OF YOUR MICROWAVE   *The symbols* indicate whether a dish can be successfully frozen ✳ or cooked in a microwave ⊿. Where a recipe is suitable for microwaving, the ⊿ symbol is repeated at the bottom of the recipe with the microwaving instructions. Sometimes you will first need to complete certain steps in the standard recipe before beginning the special microwave technique. In these cases the microwave instructions will say, for instance, 'Complete steps 1, 2 and 3' before leading into the microwave steps.

Further recipe notes can be found on pages 310–11.

SOUPS & STARTERS

Here you will find the best of British soups – from Scottish cock-a-leekie, Irish potato and parsley soup to Welsh leek soup or London Particular. There are both hot and cold soups and those suitable for a starter or light meal. A rich selection of starters such as pâtés, mousses and dips, made from vegetables, fruit, fish, shellfish and dairy produce provides a great variety of choice.

2. Pour in the stock, add the sage and cloves. Bring to the boil, cover then simmer for 30 minutes, until the parsnip is softened.

3. Remove the sage leaves and cloves, leave to cool slightly, then purée in a blender or food processor.

4. Return to the saucepan and reheat gently with the cream. Season to taste. Serve hot, garnished with the sage or parsley and croûtons.

TO MICROWAVE

 Cut the butter into small pieces and melt in a large bowl on HIGH for 45 seconds. Add the parsnips, apple, stock, sage leaves and cloves, cover and cook on HIGH for 20 minutes, until the parsnip is tender. Complete step 3. Return the soup to the bowl, add the cream and reheat on HIGH for 2–3 minutes without boiling. Complete the remainder of step 4.

TURKEY AND HAZELNUT SOUP

THE EASTERN COUNTIES

Cooked leftovers work well in this recipe if you're using up the remains of the Christmas bird. Just add them to the stock and simmer for 2 to 3 minutes, until hot. Make the soup at other times of year using a Norfolk turkey breast fillet. Chopped hazelnuts add a hint of nuttiness and a hearty texture.

SERVES 4–6 (AS A MEAL)

✳

75 g (3 oz) hazelnuts
15 g (½ oz) butter
1 medium onion, skinned and roughly chopped
2.5 ml (½ tsp) paprika
225 g (8 oz) turkey breast fillet, skinned and chopped
900 ml (1½ pints) chicken stock
1 egg yolk
150 ml (5 fl oz) fresh single cream
15 ml (1 tbsp) chopped fresh chervil or 5 ml (1 tsp) dried chervil
salt and pepper
fresh chervil sprigs, to garnish

1. Toast the hazelnuts on a sheet of foil under the grill, turning frequently. Put in a blender or food processor and very finely chop.

2. Melt the butter in a saucepan, add the onion and paprika, cover and cook for 5 minutes, until soft.

3. Add the turkey breast and stock and simmer for 5 minutes, until tender. Do not over-cook or the turkey will become rubbery.

4. Allow to cool slightly, then purée in a blender or food processor.

5. Blend the egg yolk with the cream and add to the soup. Return the soup to the pan and reheat without boiling, stirring all the time.

PARSNIP AND APPLE SOUP. A smooth soup with an interesting garnish of diamond-shaped croûtons and fresh sage leaves.

PARSNIP AND APPLE SOUP

THE EASTERN COUNTIES

The velvety texture of a creamy soup is always welcoming, and the unmistakable flavour of parsnips, blended with a hint of tart cooking apple, is very warming. Root crops of all types thrive in fertile East Anglian soil, but parsnips don't reach their peak until after one or two hard frosts.

SERVES 6–8 (AS A STARTER)

✳

25 g (1 oz) butter
700 g (1½ lb) parsnips, peeled and roughly chopped
1 Bramley cooking apple, cored, peeled and roughly chopped
1.1 litres (2 pints) chicken stock
4 fresh sage leaves or 2.5 ml (½ tsp) dried sage
2 cloves
150 ml (5 fl oz) fresh single cream
salt and pepper
fresh sage leaves or parsley and croûtons, to garnish

1. Melt the butter in a large saucepan, add the parsnips and apple, cover and cook gently for 10 minutes, stirring occasionally.

6. Add the hazelnuts, chopped chervil and season to taste. Serve hot, garnished with sprigs of fresh chervil.

TO MICROWAVE

 Complete step 1. Cut the butter into small pieces and melt in a large bowl on HIGH for 30 seconds. Add the onion and paprika, cover and cook on HIGH for 3–4 minutes, until softened. Add the turkey and the stock, re-cover and cook on HIGH for 5–6 minutes, until tender. Complete step 4. Blend the egg yolk with the cream and add to the soup. Return the soup to the bowl and cook on HIGH for 1–2 minutes without boiling, stirring once. Complete step 6.

COCK·A·LEEKIE SOUP

SCOTLAND

This is a very substantial soup which could also be a main course. It originally contained beef as well as chicken so if you have a small quantity of leftover joint or uncooked beef around add it to the dish. Cooked beef should be added towards the end of cooking time to prevent it becoming tough.

SERVES 4 (AS A MEAL)

❋

15 g (½ oz) butter
275–350 g (10–12 oz) chicken (1 large or 2 small chicken portions)
350 g (12 oz) leeks, trimmed
1.1 litres (2 pints) chicken stock
1 bouquet garni
salt and pepper
6 prunes, stoned and halved
fresh parsley sprigs, to garnish

1. Melt the butter in a large saucepan and fry the chicken quickly until golden on all sides.
2. Cut the white part of the leeks into four lengthways and chop into 2.5 cm (1 inch) pieces, reserving the green parts. Wash well. Add the white parts to the pan and fry for 5 minutes, until soft.
3. Add the stock and bouquet garni and season to taste. Bring to the boil and simmer for 30 minutes or until the chicken is tender.
4. Shred the reserved green parts of the leeks, then add to the pan with the prunes. Simmer for a further 30 minutes.
5. To serve, remove the chicken, then cut the meat into large pieces, discarding the skin and bones. Put the meat in a warmed soup tureen and pour over the soup. Serve hot, garnished with parsley sprigs.

SCOTCH BROTH

SCOTLAND

This has been described as the national soup of Scotland and is both hearty and filling. Either cook it slowly for a long time on the hob to tenderise the ingredients or put the meat and water in a pressure cooker, bring to the boil and skim the surface. Add the remaining ingredients, put on the lid, bring to HIGH (15 lb) pressure and cook under pressure for 25 minutes. If made the day before needed, the soup can be allowed to cool so the layer of fat can be removed from the top.

SERVES 4 (AS A MEAL)

❋

700 g (1½ lb) shin of beef, cut into pieces
salt and pepper
1 medium carrot, peeled and chopped
1 medium turnip, peeled and chopped
1 medium onion, skinned and chopped
2 medium leeks, trimmed, chopped and washed
45 ml (3 tbsp) pearl barley
chopped fresh parsley, to garnish

1. Put the meat into a saucepan, cover with 2.3 litres (4 pints) water, season to taste and bring slowly to the boil. Cover and simmer for 1½ hours.
2. Add the vegetables and barley. Continue to simmer, covered, for a further hour or until the vegetables and barley are soft. Skim off any fat and serve the soup hot, garnished with chopped parsley.

COCK·A·LEEKIE SOUP. The clear golden liquid reveals all the good things that go to make this soup – prunes, leeks and juicy mouthfuls of chicken.

CULLEN SKINK. Served as a main course, this traditional, creamily thick soup is hearty enough to satisfy appetites that have been sharpened by the cold.

flesh, then set aside. Return the bones and strained stock to the pan with the milk. Cover and simmer gently for a further hour.

3. Meanwhile, peel and roughly chop the potatoes, then cook in boiling salted water until tender. Drain well, then mash.

4. Strain the liquid from the bones and return it to the pan with the flaked fish. Add the mashed potato and butter and stir well to give a thick creamy consistency. Adjust the seasoning and garnish with parsley. Serve with crusty bread.

TO MICROWAVE

 Put the haddock, onion and 600 ml (1 pint) boiling water in a large bowl. Cover and cook on HIGH for 10 minutes, until the haddock is cooked. Drain off the liquid and reserve. Remove the bones from the haddock and flake the flesh, then set aside. Return the bones and strained stock to the bowl with the milk, cover and cook on HIGH for 20 minutes. Meanwhile complete step 3. Strain the liquid from the bones and return it to the bowl with the flaked fish. Add the mashed potato and butter and stir well to give a thick creamy consistency. Adjust the seasoning, garnish with parsley and serve with crusty bread.

CULLEN SKINK

SCOTLAND

This classic fish and potato soup is good and filling. The word 'skink' means stock or broth but the strong flavour of the fish means that water and milk can be used for the liquor; there is no need to go to the trouble of making fish stock. For a smoother but less traditional texture you can whizz the soup in a food processor or blender.

SERVES 4 (AS A MEAL)

1 Finnan haddock, weighing about 350 g (12 oz), skinned

900 ml (1½ pints) boiling water

1 medium onion, skinned and chopped

568 ml (1 pint) fresh milk

700 g (1½ lb) potatoes

knob of butter

salt and pepper

chopped fresh parsley, to garnish

1. Put the haddock into a medium saucepan, just cover it with the boiling water and bring to the boil again. Add the onion, cover and simmer for 10–15 minutes, until the haddock is tender. Drain off the liquid and reserve.

2. Remove the bones from the haddock and flake the

GOLDEN VEGETABLE SOUP

THE NORTH

Served in larger quantities this hearty soup can make a meal in itself. You can use any other orange or light coloured vegetables (such as potatoes, sweetcorn, yellow courgettes, pumpkins, turnips) that have a firm enough texture not to disintegrate during cooking. Be sparing with the turmeric; it is for colour only and too much will spoil the taste.

SERVES 4 (AS A STARTER)

25 g (1 oz) butter

1 large carrot, peeled and cut into 4 cm (1½ inch) match sticks

2 celery sticks, cut into 4 cm (1½ inch) match sticks

100 g (4 oz) swede, peeled and cut into 4 cm (1½ inch) match sticks

225 g (8 oz) cauliflower, broken into florets

1 medium onion, skinned and sliced

2.5 ml (½ tsp) ground turmeric

1 litre (1¾ pints) vegetable stock

salt and pepper

fresh snipped chives, to garnish

1. Melt the butter in a saucepan, add all the vegetables and cook for 2 minutes, stirring occasionally.

2. Add the turmeric and cook for 1 minute. Pour over the stock and adjust seasoning. Bring to the boil and simmer for 20 minutes. Garnish with snipped chives and serve with crusty brown bread.

TO MICROWAVE

 Melt the butter in a large bowl on HIGH for 45 seconds, then cook the vegetables, covered, on HIGH for 2 minutes. Add the turmeric and cook on HIGH for 1 minute. Blend in the stock and cook on HIGH for 10 minutes. Garnish and serve.

LONDON PARTICULAR

THE SOUTH-EAST

It's a long time since London was blanketed regularly in thick fogs known as 'pea-soupers'. But that's how this gloriously green soup got its delightful name! And it's still a dish that's perfectly designed to keep out the chill on a misty autumn evening.

SERVES 8 (AS A STARTER)

※

good.

15 g (½ oz) butter
50 g (2 oz) streaky bacon rashers, rinded and chopped
1 medium onion, skinned and roughly chopped
1 medium carrot, diced
1 celery stick, chopped
450 g (1 lb) split dried peas
2.3 litres (4 pints) chicken or ham stock
salt and pepper
60 ml (4 tbsp) natural yogurt
chopped grilled bacon and croûtons, to garnish

1. Melt the butter in a large saucepan. Add the bacon, onion, carrot and celery and cook for 5–10 minutes, until beginning to soften.
2. Add the peas and stock and bring to the boil, then cover and simmer for 1 hour, until the peas are soft.
3. Allow to cool slightly, then purée in a blender or food processor until smooth.
4. Return the soup to the pan. Season to taste, add the yogurt and reheat gently. Serve hot, garnished with chopped grilled bacon and croûtons.

TO MICROWAVE

 Halve the ingredients. Melt the butter in a large bowl on HIGH for 30 seconds. Add the bacon, onion, carrot and celery, cover and cook on HIGH for 5–7 minutes, until softened. Add the peas and the stock, cover and cook on HIGH for 25–30 minutes, until the peas are soft. Complete step 3. Return the soup to the bowl, season to taste with salt and pepper, stir in the yogurt and reheat on HIGH for 2–3 minutes, without boiling. Garnish with the bacon and croûtons. Serves 4.

LEFT
LONDON PARTICULAR.
The underlying flavour of bacon in this recipe is brought out by the garnish of chopped, grilled rashers.

RIGHT
GOLDEN VEGETABLE SOUP. A good choice for making the most of a glut. The small pieces of neatly cut vegetables are easy to spoon up.

BROAD BEAN AND BACON SOUP. A thick soup to whet the appetite. Some of the vegetables are puréed and the rest left whole, for an interesting texture.

2. Purée one-third of the soup in a blender or food processor and add to the remaining soup, then season to taste. Reheat gently. Serve hot, garnished with chopped bacon.

TO MICROWAVE

 Cook the vegetables, milk and stock in a large bowl on HIGH for 20–25 minutes, stirring occasionally. Complete step 2, reheating on HIGH for 2–3 minutes.

IRISH POTATO AND PARSLEY SOUP

NORTHERN IRELAND

Potatoes have been a staple part of the Irish diet for hundreds of years, and find their way into all sorts of dishes. Use a variety such as Pentland Dell or King Edward to make this thick and sustaining soup, with green flecks of parsley added for extra flavour.

SERVES 6–8 (AS A STARTER)

☒ ☒

2 streaky bacon rashers, rinded and chopped

25 g (1 oz) butter

450 g (1 lb) potatoes, chopped

450 g (1 lb) onions, skinned and roughly chopped

900 ml (1½ pints) chicken stock

300 ml (½ pint) fresh milk

salt and pepper

25 g (1 oz) chopped fresh parsley

150 ml (5 fl oz) fresh single cream

croûtons, to garnish

1. Fry the bacon in a large saucepan for 2–3 minutes, until the fat just starts to run.
2. Add the butter, potatoes and onions and cook for 10 minutes, until beginning to soften, stirring occasionally.
3. Add the stock and milk. Season to taste, bring to the boil, then cover and simmer for 30 minutes, until the vegetables are tender.
4. Allow to cool slightly, then purée the soup in a blender or food processor.
5. Return the soup to the pan and stir in the parsley and cream. Reheat gently, then serve hot, garnished with croûtons.

TO MICROWAVE

 Cut the butter into small pieces and melt in a large bowl on HIGH for 45 seconds. Add the bacon, potatoes and onions and cook on HIGH for 5 minutes, stirring once. Add the stock and milk. Season to taste, cover and cook on HIGH for 15–20 minutes or until the vegetables are tender. Complete step 4. Return the soup to the bowl, stir in the parsley and cream. Reheat on HIGH for 2–3 minutes without boiling.

BROAD BEAN AND BACON SOUP

COUNTRYWIDE

An unusual way to use broad beans, which are often under-rated. Their flavour is delicate, and the beans are especially good when very young and tender. They are only in season from June to August, but you can substitute frozen beans or peas when the fresh vegetables are not available.

SERVES 4 (AS A STARTER)

☒ ☒

225 g (8 oz) shelled broad beans

225 g (8 oz) shelled peas

1 large onion, skinned and chopped

450 ml (¾ pint) fresh milk

300 ml (½ pint) vegetable stock

salt and pepper

2 rashers back bacon, rinded, grilled and chopped, to garnish

1. In a large saucepan, simmer the broad beans, peas and onion in the milk and stock for 20 minutes, until the beans are tender.

WELSH LEEK SOUP

WALES

This delicious vegetable soup features the national emblem of Wales, the leek, and is also known as Cawl Cennin, the word 'cawl' meaning broth. Because the leek season is short (January to March) it's a good idea to freeze some since all the other ingredients for the soup are available all year round.

SERVES 6–8 (AS A STARTER)

25 g (1 oz) butter

700 g (1½ lb) leeks, trimmed, sliced and washed

2 medium onions, skinned and roughly chopped

2 celery sticks, chopped

1.1 litres (2 pints) chicken stock

salt and pepper

150 g (5 oz) natural yogurt

snipped fresh chives, to garnish

1. Melt the butter in a large saucepan, add the leeks, onions and celery and cook gently for 10 minutes, until softened but not browned.
2. Add the stock. Season to taste and bring to the boil, then cover and simmer for 30 minutes, until the vegetables are tender.
3. Allow to cool slightly, then purée in a blender or food processor until smooth.
4. Return to the saucepan, stir in the yogurt. Adjust the seasoning and reheat gently without boiling. Serve hot, garnished with snipped chives.

TO MICROWAVE

Cut the butter into small pieces and melt in a large bowl on HIGH for 45 seconds. Add the leeks, onions and celery, then cover and cook on HIGH for 7–10 minutes, until softened. Add the stock and salt and pepper, re-cover and cook on HIGH for 15–20 minutes, until the vegetables are tender. Complete step 3. Return the soup to the bowl, stir in the yogurt, adjust the seasoning and reheat on HIGH for 2–3 minutes, without boiling. Garnish with chives.

CHILLED ASPARAGUS SOUP

THE EASTERN COUNTIES

Thick-stemmed, succulent asparagus from the eastern counties is always a treat, and here the superb flavour shines out. Go for tight heads, fresh-looking stalks and a good colour when shopping. Chilled soup makes an excellent start to a dinner party on a warm evening and this one, with its pretty green colour and luxurious consistency, is a particularly good choice.

SERVES 6 (AS A STARTER)

700 g (1½ lb) asparagus

salt and pepper

25 g (1 oz) butter

2 medium onions, skinned and roughly chopped

1.4 litres (2½ pints) chicken stock

150 ml (5 fl oz) fresh single cream

grated lemon rind, to garnish

1. Cut the heads off the asparagus and simmer them very gently in salted water for 3–5 minutes, until just tender. Drain well and refresh with cold water.
2. Scrape the asparagus stalks with a potato peeler or knife to remove any scales and cut off the woody ends. Thinly slice the stalks.
3. Melt the butter in a large saucepan. Add the asparagus stalks and onions, cover and cook for 5–10 minutes, until beginning to soften.
4. Add the stock and season to taste. Bring to the boil, cover and simmer for 30–40 minutes, until the asparagus and onion are tender.
5. Allow to cool slightly, then purée in a blender or food processor until smooth. Sieve to remove any stringy particles, then stir in the cream.
6. Cover and chill in the refrigerator for 2–3 hours. Serve, garnished with the reserved asparagus tips and grated lemon rind.

TO MICROWAVE

Cut the heads off the asparagus and arrange the heads around the edge of a large shallow dish. Pour over 30 ml (2 tbsp) water, cover and cook on HIGH for 2–3 minutes, until just tender. Drain and refresh with cold water. Complete step 2. Cut the butter into small pieces and melt in a large bowl on HIGH for 45 seconds. Add the asparagus stalks and onions, cover and cook on HIGH for 7–10 minutes, until softened. Add the stock, re-cover and cook on HIGH for 20–25 minutes, until tender. Complete steps 5 and 6.

CHILLED ASPARAGUS SOUP. A few fine strands of lemon rind are all that's needed to finish this summery recipe.

87

ICED TOMATO AND
BASIL SOUP. Glass bowls
show this pretty soup off in all
its rich, red glory. A generous
measure of basil gives it
marvellous, fresh flavour.

ICED TOMATO AND BASIL SOUP

COUNTRYWIDE

*A refreshing chilled soup, best made when tomatoes are at
their cheapest and most flavoursome. The pungency of fresh
basil adds a delicious herbiness.*

SERVES 4 (AS A STARTER)

450 g (1 lb) tomatoes, chopped

1 small onion, skinned and chopped

15 ml (1 tbsp) tomato purée

15 ml (1 tbsp) chopped fresh basil

568 ml (1 pint) chicken stock

salt and pepper

30 ml (2 tbsp) fresh soured cream, to garnish (optional)

1. Purée the tomatoes, onion, tomato purée and basil
in a blender or food processor. Pass through a sieve into
a medium saucepan, then stir in the stock and heat
gently to remove froth. Season to taste.
2. Chill before serving, garnished with swirls of soured
cream, if liked.

STARTERS

PRAWN AND CUCUMBER SALAD

COUNTRYWIDE

*A light and attractive starter for a summer dinner party. Dill
adds a pleasant flavour to all types of fish, and the feathery
fronds of the fresh herb make a pretty garnish.*

SERVES 4

1 cucumber, thinly sliced

salt and pepper

45 ml (3 tbsp) white wine vinegar

15 g (½ oz) sugar

225 g (8 oz) peeled cooked prawns, thawed if frozen

30 ml (2 tbsp) chopped fresh dill or 5 ml (1 tsp) dried

15 ml (1 tbsp) snipped fresh chives (optional)

150 ml (5 fl oz) fresh soured cream

chopped fresh dill or chives, to garnish

1. Put the cucumber slices in a colander, sprinkling
each layer with salt. Cover with a plate and weigh
down. Leave to drain for 30 minutes.
2. Meanwhile, put the vinegar, 45 ml (3 tbsp) water
and sugar in a small saucepan and heat gently until the

sugar dissolves. Boil for 1 minute, then remove from the heat and leave to cool.

3. Rinse the cucumber under cold running water and pat dry. Place in a bowl with the prawns and half of the dill. Pour over the cold vinegar mixture. Cover and chill for at least 30 minutes or overnight.

4. Just before serving, mix the remaining dill and the chives with the soured cream and season with salt and pepper. Spoon the prawns and cucumber on to four plates and top each with a spoonful of the flavoured soured cream. Garnish with dill or chives and serve with crusty granary bread.

WARM WATERCRESS, POTATO AND BACON SALAD

THE SOUTH-EAST

Tender little new potatoes are bathed in a vinaigrette dressing while still warm to sop up the maximum flavour. Peppery watercress from the Hampshire beds and crispy bits of bacon add more colour and texture to this interesting and attractive salad.

SERVES 4

450 g (1 lb) very small new potatoes
salt and pepper
8 rashers streaky bacon, rinded and chopped
45 ml (3 tbsp) vegetable oil
15 ml (1 tbsp) white wine vinegar
1 bunch watercress, trimmed and roughly chopped

1. Cook the potatoes in boiling salted water for 10–15 minutes, until tender.
2. Meanwhile, fry the bacon in its own fat for 5 minutes, until crisp. Add the oil and vinegar to the bacon fat and bring to the boil, stirring in any sediment from the bottom of the pan. Season with pepper.
3. Drain the cooked potatoes and put in a serving dish. Pour over the bacon and dressing while they are still warm and toss together. Toss in the watercress and serve warm.

TO MICROWAVE

Put the potatoes in a large bowl with 45 ml (3 tbsp) water. Cover and cook on HIGH for 6–8 minutes, until tender.

MARINATED MACKEREL

THE WEST

Mackerel are good value in the shops and even more delicious if you've taken a fishing trip anywhere round the south-west coast and caught your own. Clean, wash and wipe them well. They are filling so serve small ones for a starter, larger ones for a main course.

SERVES 4

4 mackerel, each weighing about 225 g (8 oz), cleaned
4 bay leaves
30 ml (2 tbsp) demerara sugar
salt
6 black peppercorns
150 ml (¼ pint) cider vinegar
150 ml (¼ pint) cold black tea

1. Arrange the mackerel in a shallow ovenproof dish, placing a bay leaf inside each one. Sprinkle with the sugar and a little salt, then add the peppercorns.
2. Mix the vinegar and tea together and pour over the mackerel.
3. Cover the dish and bake at 180°C (350°F) mark 4 for 45 minutes or until tender. Allow to cool. Serve cold with a little of the juice which sets to a light jelly, and triangles of buttered brown bread.

BACK
WARM WATERCRESS, POTATO AND BACON SALAD. The flavours blend perfectly in this colourful salad.

FRONT
PRAWN AND CUCUMBER SALAD. Good-looking and very simply made, this salad gets lots of flavour from its dressing.

SMOKED TROUT PATE

THE EASTERN COUNTIES

The brilliantly simple idea of making smoked fish into a paste to spread on toast originated in Great Yarmouth, home of the bloater. The method is suitable for many other types of smoked fish and here trout is blended with lemon juice, butter and cream to make a rich pâté.

SERVES 4

2 smoked trout, each weighing about 275 g (10 oz), skinned and boned

50 g (2 oz) butter, softened

30 ml (2 tbsp) lemon juice

60 ml (4 tbsp) fresh single cream

pepper

pinch of ground mace

cucumber and lemon slices, to garnish

1. Put the trout flesh in a blender or food processor.
2. Add the butter, lemon juice, cream, pepper and mace and blend together until smooth.
3. Divide the pâté equally between 4 ramekin dishes. Chill for 1 hour before serving. Garnish with cucumber and lemon slices. Serve accompanied with fingers of wholemeal toast.

COD'S ROE RAMEKINS

COUNTRYWIDE

Smoked cod's roe has a delicious flavour and a little of it goes a long way. These light, airy soufflés are very quickly cooked, so do be ready to serve them immediately.

SERVES 6

225 g (8 oz) smoked cod's roe, skinned

50 g (2 oz) fresh breadcrumbs

15 ml (1 tbsp) chopped fresh parsley

30 ml (2 tbsp) lemon juice

1 egg, separated

150 g (5 oz) natural yogurt

pinch of ground mace

salt and pepper

1. Put the roe in a blender or food processor. Add the breadcrumbs, parsley, lemon juice, egg yolk, yogurt and mace. Season to taste and work together until smooth. Turn into a bowl.
2. Whisk the egg white until stiff, then fold into the mixture.
3. Spoon into 6 greased ramekin dishes. Bake at 200°C (400°F) mark 6 for 15–20 minutes, until well risen and golden brown. Serve at once, accompanied with fingers of toast.

COUNTRY MUSHROOMS

COUNTRYWIDE

Choose button mushrooms for their delicate flavour. There's no need to wash or peel them – a wipe with a damp cloth is all that's needed. Tarragon is very distinctive and marries well with mushrooms. Soured cream gives a hint of piquancy.

SERVES 4

25 g (1 oz) butter

450 g (1 lb) button mushrooms

15 ml (1 tbsp) plain flour

150 ml (¼ pint) fresh milk

10 ml (2 tsp) wholegrain mustard

10 ml (2 tsp) chopped fresh tarragon or 2.5 ml (½ tsp) dried tarragon

45 ml (3 tbsp) fresh soured cream

chicory and lettuce, to serve

fresh tarragon leaves, to garnish

1. Melt the butter in a medium saucepan, then fry the mushrooms for 2 minutes.

LEFT
COUNTRY MUSHROOMS. A refreshing starter for summer, that's extremely easy to make.

RIGHT
LYMESWOLD WITH REDCURRANT JELLY. Simplicity itself: slices of creamy cheese, coated in egg and breadcrumbs and swiftly fried until piping hot and ready to ooze deliciously when cut open.

RINDED SOFT CHEESES

Soft, ripened cheeses are no longer an exclusively French speciality. Britain too can offer a range of tasty creamy home-produced cheeses, particularly from the lush pasture lands of the West. They are often excellent for cooking as well as for eating with crusty bread and crisp biscuits.

WHITE LYMESWOLD

BLUE LYMESWOLD

LYMESWOLD

Full-fat, blue-veined, mild cheese made by Dairy Crest near Bridgwater in Somerset. Launched to great acclaim in 1982, it's now obtainable nationwide. White Lymeswold is also now available. Lymeswold's creamy texture makes it a good cooking cheese, as in the flan on page 210 or as here, lightly fried as a starter.

CAPRICORN

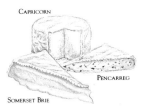

PENCARREG

SOMERSET BRIE

2. Stir in the flour and milk. Heat, stirring continuously until the sauce thickens, boils and is smooth. Simmer for 1–2 minutes.
3. Stir in the mustard, tarragon and soured cream.
4. Serve hot on a nest of chicory and lettuce leaves, garnished with fresh tarragon.

TO MICROWAVE

☑ Melt the butter in a medium bowl on HIGH for 45 seconds. Add the mushrooms and cook on HIGH for 2 minutes, then add the flour and cook on HIGH for 1 minute. Stir in the milk and cook on HIGH for 3 minutes, until boiling and thickened, stirring frequently. Complete steps 3 and 4.

LYMESWOLD WITH REDCURRANT JELLY

THE MIDLANDS

The relatively newly developed cheese Lymeswold can be substituted by Somerset Brie.

SERVES 4

| 150 g (5 oz) white Lymeswold cheese |
| 1 egg, beaten |
| 50 g (2 oz) fresh wholemeal breadcrumbs |
| vegetable oil for frying |
| 30 ml (2 tbsp) redcurrant jelly |
| shredded lettuce, to serve |
| redcurrants, to garnish |

1. Cut the cheese into 4 slices. Brush with beaten egg and coat in the breadcrumbs.
2. Heat some oil in a large frying pan and fry the cheese slices for 10 seconds on each side, until golden. Drain on absorbent kitchen paper. Fry in batches if necessary.
3. Put the redcurrant jelly and 15 ml (1 tbsp) water in a saucepan and heat gently until the jelly melts.
4. Place each slice of cheese on a bed of shredded lettuce and pour over the redcurrant sauce. Garnish with the redcurrants and serve at once.

PENCARREG

Made in Lampeter, Dyfed, with pasteurized cows' milk from organic farms, this resembles Brie in appearance but has a softer texture and a much stronger flavour. It's available from specialist cheese shops and is gradually reaching supermarkets. Chive and garlic flavoured versions have recently been developed.

SOMERSET BRIE

Made at Crewkerne in Somerset exactly according to traditional French methods. It's considered by many to be as fine as any French Brie, with its straw colour and creamy, tangy flavour.

CAPRICORN

Also from Crewkerne, this is one of Britain's few commercially available goats' cheeses, made from pasteurized milk. Relatively mild compared with continental goats' cheese, with an appetizing piquancy. Try it in the salad on page 212.

 Put the butter, flour and milk in a medium bowl and cook on HIGH for 4–5 minutes, until boiling and thickened, whisking frequently. Complete steps 2, 3 and 4.

VEGETABLE TERRINE

COUNTRYWIDE

Stunningly striped in cream and orange layers of puréed cauliflower and carrot, this is an eye-catching dish that is perfect for a dinner party. The name comes from a covered French cooking dish called a terrine but you can always use a loaf-tin as we have here.

SERVES 8

700 g (1½ lb) cauliflower florets
salt and pepper
700 g (1½ lb) carrots, peeled and sliced
300 ml (10 fl oz) fresh double cream
2 eggs
1.25 ml (¼ tsp) freshly grated nutmeg
1.25 ml (¼ tsp) ground coriander
90 ml (6 tbsp) vegetable oil
30 ml (2 tbsp) white wine vinegar
5 ml (1 tsp) tomato purée
pinch of mustard powder
pinch of sugar

1. Cook the cauliflower in boiling salted water for 10 minutes, until just tender.
2. Meanwhile, put the carrots in a separate saucepan, cover with cold water and season. Bring to the boil and cook for 10 minutes or until completely tender. Drain both the cauliflower and carrots.
3. Purée the cauliflower in a blender or food processor until smooth. Transfer to a bowl. Purée the carrots in the same way, then transfer to a separate bowl.
4. Add 1 egg and 150 ml (5 fl oz) cream to each purée and mix well. Season each with salt and pepper. Stir the grated nutmeg into the cauliflower purée and the coriander into the carrot purée.
5. Grease a 1.4 litre (2½ pint) loaf tin. Put half of the cauliflower purée in the bottom, making sure it is quite level. Cover with a layer of half of the carrot purée, followed by the remaining cauliflower purée and finally remaining carrot purée.
6. Cover the tin tightly with foil. Bake at 180°C (350°F) mark 4 for about 1¼–1½ hours or until firm.
7. When the terrine is cooked, allow to cool slightly, then turn out carefully on to a serving plate.
8. Just before serving, whisk together the oil, vinegar, tomato purée, mustard, sugar and salt and pepper until blended. Do not let the dressing stand before serving or it will separate.
9. Serve the terrine hot or cold, cut into slices, with the dressing handed separately.

VEGETABLE TERRINE. Pretty as a picture, served in a pool of mustardy vinaigrette, this recipe is easier than it looks to prepare.

SAGE DERBY SOUFFLES

THE MIDLANDS

Soufflés are an airy French dish lightened with whisked egg whites, which take their name from the specific flavouring used. Here the popular British cheese marbled with chopped sage adds flavour and colour.

SERVES 6

40 g (1½ oz) butter
40 g (1½ oz) plain flour
200 ml (7 fl oz) fresh milk
75 g (3 oz) Sage Derby cheese, grated
salt and pepper
2 eggs, separated

1. Put the butter, flour and milk in a saucepan. Heat, whisking continuously, until the sauce thickens, boils and is smooth. Simmer for 1–2 minutes.
2. Remove pan from the heat, add the cheese and stir until melted. Season to taste. Beat in the egg yolks.
3. Whisk the egg whites until stiff and fold into the sauce with a large metal spoon.
4. Pour the mixture into 6 greased ramekin dishes and bake at 190°C (375°F) mark 5 for 30 minutes, until risen and golden brown. Serve immediately with brown bread and butter.

VARIATIONS

Cheese Other cheese can be used. Use a hard cheese such as Cheddar or Stilton.
Ham Omit the cheese and add 75 g (3 oz) cooked ham.
Fish Omit the cheese and add 75 g (3 oz) cooked smoked haddock, finely flaked.

TO MICROWAVE

📷 Put the cauliflower in a roasting bag with 30 ml (2 tbsp) water. Put the carrots in a roasting bag with 30 ml (2 tbsp) water. Loosely seal the bags and cook both at once on HIGH for 20 minutes, or until very tender. Drain. Complete steps 3, 4 and 5 (using a 1.7 litre (3 pint) microwave loaf dish). Stand on a roasting rack, cover with kitchen paper and cook on MEDIUM for about 20 minutes, until just firm to the touch. Complete steps 7, 8 and 9.

STILTON PEARS

THE MIDLANDS

Cheese and pears are a delightful combination, and dessert pears make a refreshing change from avocados in this starter. Comice are a good choice, as they are mouthwateringly juicy when fully ripe. Make sure they are still firm, though, because, as with all pears, they have to be eaten at just the right moment.

SERVES 4

| 2 large dessert pears, ripe but firm |
| 30 ml (2 tbsp) lemon juice |
| 50 g (2 oz) curd cheese |
| 75 g (3 oz) Stilton cheese, crumbled |
| 30 ml (2 tbsp) vegetable oil |
| 15 ml (1 tbsp) mayonnaise |
| pinch of mustard powder |
| pinch of sugar |
| 5 ml (1 tsp) poppy seeds |
| salt and pepper |

1. Using an apple corer, remove the cores from the pears. Sprinkle the cavities with 15 ml (1 tbsp) of the lemon juice.
2. Cream together the two cheeses. Press as much mixture as possible into the cavities, then cover and chill until ready to serve.
3. Just before serving, whisk the oil, mayonnaise, remaining lemon juice, mustard, sugar, poppy seeds, salt and pepper together. Spoon on to 4 individual plates. Cut each pear in half lengthways then slice, fan out and arrange, cut side down, in the dressing. Serve at once.

STILTON PEARS. No cooking needed for an appealing starter of stuffed pears, fanned out and served in a creamy, poppy-seed dressing.

SMOKED SALMON MOUSSES

SCOTLAND

Scottish salmon is thought by many to have the best flavour of all and Scotland has always been justly famous for its traditional smokehouses which put flavour into fish with just wooden chips and no additives. This mousse tastes just as good if made from cheap end cuts or flakes which can be bought in the required quantity.

SERVES 6

300 ml (10 fl oz) fresh single cream
2 bay leaves
100 g (4 oz) smoked salmon
15 ml (1 tbsp) lemon juice
large pinch of paprika
about 150 ml (¼ pint) fresh milk
15 ml (3 tsp) gelatine
cucumber slices, to garnish

1. Gently heat the cream and bay leaves together in a small saucepan. When warm, remove from the heat and leave to infuse for 2–3 hours.
2. Discard the bay leaves. Pour the cream into a blender or food processor, add the salmon, reserving one small slice to garnish, the lemon juice and paprika and blend together.
3. Transfer to a measuring jug and add enough milk to make up the quantity to 568 ml (1 pint) and stir well together.
4. Sprinkle the gelatine over 45 ml (3 tbsp) water in a small bowl and leave to soak for a few minutes. Place the bowl over a saucepan of simmering water and stir until dissolved. Leave to cool slightly, then whisk into the salmon mixture.
5. Pour the mixture into 6 ramekin dishes and leave to chill for at least 2 hours. Serve garnished with a small piece of the reserved salmon and cucumber slices.

SMOKED SALMON MOUSSES. These individual mousses are just the right size to whet the appetite without being too filling.

TOMATO AND CAERPHILLY SALAD

WALES

Caerphilly, originally a Welsh cheese, is now mostly made in Devon, Dorset, Somerset and Wiltshire. It is soft and white with a mild, salty flavour. With sun-ripened tomatoes and a sprinkling of fresh herbs, it makes a tasty and pretty salad.

SERVES 4

175 g (6 oz) Caerphilly cheese
4 medium tomatoes
15 ml (1 tbsp) vegetable oil
150 g (5 oz) natural yogurt
pinch of mustard powder
30 ml (2 tbsp) chopped fresh mixed herbs such as chives, marjoram, parsley
salt and pepper
chopped fresh herbs, to garnish

1. Slice the cheese (do not worry if it crumbles) and the tomatoes. Arrange on individual serving plates.
2. Whisk together the oil, yogurt, mustard, herbs and salt and pepper until well blended.
3. Spoon the dressing over the cheese and tomatoes, then serve garnished with chopped fresh herbs.

CARROT AND GARLIC DIP

COUNTRYWIDE

Everyone loves to scoop up mouthfuls of a smooth dip on pieces of crunchy raw vegetable. Here, a purée of cooked carrot is blended with creamy natural yogurt and lightly spiced to make a very more-ish mixture.

SERVES 6

350 g (12 oz) carrots, sliced
1–2 garlic cloves, skinned and crushed
300 g (10 oz) natural yogurt
2.5 ml (½ tsp) ground coriander
cayenne pepper
salt
selection of raw fresh vegetables such as celery, red and green peppers, courgettes, radishes and cauliflower, cut into neat pieces or strips

1. Cook the carrots in boiling salted water until just tender. Drain thoroughly, refresh with cold water and drain again.
2. Put into a blender or food processor with the garlic and yogurt and coriander and purée until smooth. Season generously with cayenne pepper and a little salt. Turn into a serving dish and leave for about 1 hour to let the flavours develop. Serve with the vegetables.

SPINACH TIMBALES.
Cream, eggs and cheese are all
used in these
mouthwateringly savoury
starters. A light seasoning of
nutmeg is good with spinach.

TO MICROWAVE

 Put the carrots and 30 ml (2 tbsp) water in a large bowl. Cover and cook on HIGH for 10–12 minutes, or until tender, stirring once. Complete the remainder of step 1 and step 2.

SPINACH TIMBALES

COUNTRYWIDE

These light spinach, cheese and egg starters take their name from the round moulds with straight or slightly sloping sides in which they were originally baked, called timbales. This version is cooked in more readily available ramekin dishes.

SERVES 6

15 g (½ oz) butter

1 small onion, skinned and finely chopped

450 g (1 lb) fresh spinach, trimmed and finely chopped, or 225 g (8 oz) frozen chopped spinach, thawed

150 ml (5 fl oz) fresh single cream

2 eggs, beaten

50 g (2 oz) Cheddar cheese, grated

25 g (1 oz) fresh wholemeal breadcrumbs

pinch of freshly grated nutmeg

salt and pepper

lemon slices, to garnish

1. Melt the butter in a large saucepan, stir in the onion and cook gently for about 5 minutes, until soft.
2. Stir in the spinach and cook for a further 5 minutes if using fresh spinach, 2–3 minutes if using frozen, stirring occasionally, until soft. Stir in the cream.
3. Beat the eggs in a bowl and stir in the spinach mixture, cheese, breadcrumbs and nutmeg. Season to taste. Spoon the mixture into 6 ramekin dishes, level the surfaces, cover each one with foil and place in a roasting tin, half filled with hot water.
4. Bake at 180°C (350°F) mark 4 for 1 hour, until firm to the touch and a knife inserted in the centre comes out clean. Remove the dishes and leave for 5 minutes. Turn out on to individual plates and garnish with lemon slices.

TO MICROWAVE

 Melt the butter in a medium bowl on HIGH for 30 seconds. Add the onion, cover and cook on HIGH for 4–5 minutes, until softened. Add the spinach, re-cover and cook on HIGH for 2–3 minutes, until softened. Stir in the cream, eggs, cheese, breadcrumbs, nutmeg and salt and pepper. Spoon into 6 ramekin dishes. Arrange in a circle in the cooker and cook on MEDIUM for about 12 minutes or until firm to the touch. Leave to stand for 5 minutes, then complete step 6.

LIGHT MEALS
& SNACKS

The wide variety of British cheeses are ideal for both eating and cooking. When combined with eggs or other ingredients they can be turned into quick, nourishing meals. In this chapter you will find a variety of regional specialities – from Scotch woodcock and pan haggerty to Glamorgan sausages and herrings in oatmeal – as well as new recipes suitable for today's fast living. There's something here for everyone.

EGGS

One of nature's most complete, inexpensive, versatile and nutritious foods, rich in protein, valuable A, D and B Group vitamins and iron. Eggs have many uses in baking, batters and sauces, to bind sweet and savoury mixtures, coat fried food and glaze pastry. There's also a vast range of low-budget main egg dishes.

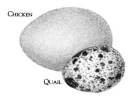

CHICKEN

QUAIL

CHICKEN EGGS

White or brown shell, the most widely available type of egg. Chicken eggs are carefully graded for quality and size:
Grade A: perfectly clean, fresh, intact eggs.
Grade B: eggs with slight imperfections, which have been cleaned or preserved in some way.
Free range chicken eggs are from non-battery reared hens.
Size 1: 70 g or over
Size 2: 65–70 g
Size 3: 60–65 g
Size 4: 55–60 g
Size 5: 50–55 g
Size 6: 45–50 g
Size 7: under 45 g
Eggs used in the recipes in this book are size 2 unless otherwise stated.

QUAIL EGGS

A recognised delicacy, these increasingly popular, tiny mottled eggs are available from specialist food shops and good supermarkets. Serve hard-boiled in salad or set in aspic, or poached in a crisp pastry shell for an elegant starter.

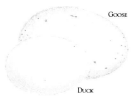

GOOSE

DUCK

GOOSE EGGS

White shell, can weigh up to 300 g (11 oz), slightly oily flavour. Use like duck eggs.

DUCK EGGS

Ivory shell, average weight 75 g (3 oz), rich flavour, available from farm and health food shops. Duck eggs are thin-shelled and often contain more bacteria than other types, so they should be used very fresh and never served soft-boiled. Excellent for baking.

SCOTCH WOODCOCK
SCOTLAND

This savoury dish was popular in Victorian and Edwardian days, when it was served at the end of a meal. With today's trend towards lighter eating habits, savouries have gone out of fashion but this dish is sufficiently tasty to be served as a snack at any time. It's very salty so make sure you have a long cool drink with it.

SERVES 2

---

2 large slices wholemeal bread

butter for spreading

Gentleman's Relish or anchovy paste for spreading

60–90 ml (4–6 tbsp) fresh milk

2 eggs

pinch cayenne pepper

50 g (1¾ oz) can anchovies, drained

---

1. Toast the bread, remove the crusts and spread with butter. Cut in half and spread with Gentleman's Relish or anchovy paste.
2. Melt a knob of butter in a saucepan. Whisk together the milk, eggs and cayenne pepper, then pour into the pan and stir slowly over a gentle heat until the mixture begins to thicken. Remove from the heat and stir until creamy.
3. Divide the mixture between the anchovy toasts and top with thin strips of anchovy fillet, arranged in a criss-cross pattern.

TO MICROWAVE

Complete step 1. Melt a knob of butter in a medium bowl on HIGH for 30 seconds. Add the milk, eggs and cayenne pepper and whisk together. Cook on MEDIUM for 2–3 minutes or until the eggs are lightly scrambled, stirring frequently. Complete step 3.

BUBBLE AND SQUEAK
THE SOUTH-EAST

A classic dish of leftover cooked potatoes, cabbage and beef. The name imitates the sounds of cooking, the vegetables and meat first bubbling away as they boiled and later squeaking in the frying pan. Simple and old-fashioned it may be, but it's still an appetising way to deal with the remains of a joint.

SERVES 2

---

25 g (1 oz) butter

1 medium onion, skinned and finely chopped

450 g (1 lb) potatoes, cooked and mashed

225 g (8 oz) cooked cabbage, finely chopped

4–8 slices cooked beef, chopped

salt and pepper

---

1. Melt the butter in a large frying pan. Add the onion and cook for 4–5 minutes, stirring frequently, until softened.
2. Add the potatoes, cabbage and beef. Season to taste. Fry over medium heat for about 15 minutes, stirring frequently, until browned. Serve hot.

CHEESE RAMEKINS
THE WEST

More substantial than a soufflé, these flavoursome ramekins are also a good way of using up odd leftovers of different cheeses. The name comes from the small, round ovenproof container it is baked in, a ramekin dish.

SERVES 4

---

50 g (2 oz) Double Gloucester cheese, grated

50 g (2 oz) Cheshire cheese, grated

60 ml (4 tbsp) fresh single cream or milk

50 g (2 oz) cooked ham, finely chopped

50 g (2 oz) fresh wholemeal breadcrumbs

few drops of Worcestershire sauce

pinch of ground mixed spice

salt and pepper

2 eggs, separated

---

1. Put the cheeses into a bowl, then beat in the cream, ham, breadcrumbs, Worcestershire sauce and mixed spice. Season to taste. Grease 4 ramekin dishes and stand on a baking sheet.
2. Beat the egg yolks into the mixture. Whisk the egg whites until stiff, then fold into the mixture.
3. Spoon into the ramekin dishes and bake at 200°C (400°F) mark 6 for 10–15 minutes, until golden and risen. Serve at once.

GLOUCESTER CHEESE AND ALE
THE WEST

Food and drink are combined for a filling snack that was originally served – with more ale to wash it down – after the meat or poultry course of the evening meal at posting houses and inns. Double Gloucester cheese has a stronger flavour than Single Gloucester which is also very difficult to track down in the shops.

MAKES 4

---

175 g (6 oz) Double Gloucester cheese, thinly sliced

5 ml (1 tsp) prepared English mustard

about 120 ml (4½ fl oz) brown ale

4 thick slices of wholemeal bread

---

1. Arrange the cheese slices in the bottom of a large shallow ovenproof dish and spread the mustard over the top of them.

2. Pour in enough brown ale to just cover the cheese. Cover with foil, then bake at 190°C (375°F) mark 5 for about 10 minutes, until the cheese has softened.
3. Meanwhile, toast the bread. Pour the warm ale and cheese over the toast and serve immediately.

MOCK CRAB

COUNTRYWIDE

A simple Victorian luncheon dish, cleverly invented to deceive the eye, and even the palate. The 'crab' is in fact finely shredded chicken and grated Red Leicester cheese, and the fishy disguise is made all the more convincing with anchovy flavouring.

SERVES 2

1 hard-boiled egg, the yolk sieved, white chopped

15 g (½ oz) butter

7.5 ml (1½ tsp) prepared English mustard

few drops of anchovy essence

pepper

100 g (4 oz) Red Leicester cheese, grated

2 cooked chicken breast fillets, skinned and finely chopped

lettuce leaves, sliced tomato and cucumber, to garnish

1. Reserve a little of the egg yolk and mix the remainder with the butter, mustard, anchovy essence and pepper to taste.
2. Mix in the cheese with a fork so that it is evenly blended but as many shreds as possible of the cheese remain separate.
3. Mix in the chicken lightly, then taste and adjust the seasoning if necessary. Cover and leave in a cool place for at least 2 hours for the flavours to develop.
4. Serve on a small bed of lettuce, in crab shells if available, garnished with the reserved egg yolk, chopped egg white and a little sliced tomato and cucumber. Accompany with thinly sliced wholemeal bread and butter.

MOCK CRAB. Cheaper than the real thing, but just as tasty, serve this savoury concoction in crab shells to complete the deception.

LEFT
GLAMORGAN
SAUSAGES. Crisp and
cheesy 'sausages', which make
a good, economical dish to
serve at any time of day.

RIGHT
BREAKFAST PANCAKES.
Give yourself a weekend treat
with freshly made, well-filled
pancakes.

BREAKFAST PANCAKES

COUNTRYWIDE

There's no need to save pancakes for Shrove Tuesday. They're quick and easy to prepare, and good at any time of day. This breakfast recipe uses a mix of wholemeal flour and oatmeal and makes a welcome change from toast topped with grilled bacon, scrambled eggs and tomato slices.

MAKES 4

25 g (1 oz) plain wholemeal flour

25 g (1 oz) medium oatmeal

salt and pepper

4 eggs, beaten

250 ml (9 fl oz) fresh milk

butter for frying

100 g (4 oz) back bacon, grilled and chopped

2 tomatoes, sliced and grilled

1. Put the flour, oatmeal, salt and 15 ml (1 tbsp) egg into a bowl. Gradually add 150 ml (¼ pint) milk to form a smooth batter.
2. Heat a little butter in a 20.5 cm (8 inch) frying pan. When hot, pour in 45 ml (3 tbsp) of the batter, tilting pan to cover base. Cook until pancake moves freely, turn over and cook until golden. Make 4 pancakes.
3. Beat together the remaining eggs, milk and salt and pepper. Scramble in a small saucepan over gentle heat, stirring until the egg starts to set.
4. Place spoonfuls of the egg into the pancakes, add the bacon and tomato slices. Fold the pancakes over. Serve warm as a snack or for breakfast.

TO MICROWAVE

Complete steps 1 and 2. To scramble the eggs, cook in a medium bowl on HIGH for 3–4 minutes, stirring frequently. Complete step 4.

GLAMORGAN SAUSAGES

WALES

These were the poor man's meatless substitute for the real thing, and are today an interesting dish for vegetarians.

MAKES 8

175 g (6 oz) fresh breadcrumbs

100 g (4 oz) Caerphilly cheese, grated

1 small leek, washed and very finely chopped
15 ml (1 tbsp) chopped fresh parsley
large pinch of mustard powder
salt and pepper
2 eggs, separated
about 60 ml (4 tbsp) fresh milk to mix
plain flour for coating
15 ml (1 tbsp) vegetable oil
15 g (½ oz) butter

1. In a large bowl, mix together the breadcrumbs, cheese, leek, parsley and mustard. Season to taste. Add 1 whole egg and 1 egg yolk and mix thoroughly. Add enough milk to bind the mixture together.
2. Divide the mixture into 8 and shape into sausages.
3. Beat the remaining egg white on a plate with a fork until frothy. Dip the sausages into the egg white, then roll in the flour to coat.
4. Heat the oil and the butter in a frying pan and fry the sausages for 5–10 minutes until golden brown. Serve hot or cold.

TO MICROWAVE

☑ Complete steps 1, 2 and 3. Heat a large browning dish on HIGH for 5–8 minutes or according to the manufacturer's instructions. When the browning dish is hot, add 15 ml (1 tbsp) oil and quickly put the sausages into the dish and cook on HIGH for 1½ minutes. Turn the sausages over and cook on HIGH for a further 1 minute.

HAM AND PINEAPPLE TOP KNOT
COUNTRYWIDE

Ham and pineapple are always a favourite combination, and here they make a satisfying snack. The base is a toasted crumpet which soaks up the deliciously gooey topping of Cheddar, hot English mustard and cream.

SERVES 1

1 round ham steak
1 canned pineapple ring, drained
1 crumpet
25 g (1 oz) Cheddar cheese, grated
2.5 ml (½ tsp) mustard powder
15 ml (1 tbsp) fresh single cream
watercress, to garnish

1. Grill the ham steak and pineapple, and toast the crumpet.
2. Mix together the cheese, mustard and cream. Spread on top of the crumpet and grill until golden.
3. Top with the ham steak and pineapple. Garnish with watercress and serve at once.

PAN HAGGERTY
THE NORTH

A warming filling dish at a bargain price. It's a good choice if you're planning an evening at the pub or for satisfying hungry teenage appetites. Use firm fleshed potatoes such as Desirée, Romano or Maris Piper as they will keep their shape and not crumble into mash at the end of the cooking time.

SERVES 4

25 g (1 oz) butter
15 ml (1 tbsp) vegetable oil
450 g (1 lb) potatoes, peeled and thinly sliced
2 medium onions, skinned and thinly sliced
100 g (4 oz) Cheddar or Lancashire cheese, grated
salt and pepper

1. Heat the butter and oil in a large heavy-based frying pan. Remove the pan from the heat and put in layers of potatoes, onions and grated cheese, seasoning well with salt and pepper between each layer, and ending with a top layer of cheese.
2. Cover and cook the vegetables gently for about 30 minutes or until the potatoes and onions are almost cooked.
3. Uncover and brown the top of the dish under a hot grill. Serve straight from the pan.

PAN HAGGERTY.
Succulent layers of potatoes, onions and cheese, given a bubbling brown finish under the grill.

MIXED BEAN SALAD

COUNTRYWIDE

Charnwood, or Applewood, cheese is a mature Cheddar variation, smoked and coated with paprika. Cubed, it adds colour and bite to this summertime salad, which mixes fresh French and broad beans with canned kidney beans.

SERVES 4

450 g (1 lb) broad beans
salt and pepper
225 g (8 oz) French beans, trimmed
15 ml (1 tbsp) vegetable oil
150 g (5 oz) natural yogurt
15 ml (1 tbsp) mild wholegrain mustard
15 ml (1 tbsp) lemon juice
397 g (14 oz) can red kidney beans, drained and rinsed
225 g (8 oz) Charnwood or Applewood cheese, cubed
chopped fresh parsley, to garnish

1. Shell the broad beans and cook in boiling salted water for 10 minutes. Add the French beans and continue to cook for 5–10 minutes, until both are tender.
2. Meanwhile, mix together the oil, yogurt, mustard, lemon juice and salt and pepper until well blended.
3. Drain the cooked beans and while still hot, combine with the kidney beans and dressing. Leave to cool.
4. Toss in the cubes of cheese and garnish with chopped fresh parsley just before serving.

TO MICROWAVE

Put the broad beans in a small bowl with 30 ml (2 tbsp) water. Cover and cook on HIGH for 10–12 minutes or until tender. Put the French beans and 15 ml (1 tbsp) water in a small bowl, cover and cook on HIGH for 4–5 minutes, until tender, stirring once. Complete steps 2, 3 and 4.

BACON FROISE

COUNTRYWIDE

An old English dish dating back to the 15th century, froise (or fraize) is a batter-like mixture, which was probably originally cooked in the hot fat that dripped from a spit-roasted joint. It's a tasty economical recipe, delicious served with mushrooms, lightly cooked in a little lemon juice flavoured with black pepper and grilled tomatoes.

SERVES 2

50 g (2 oz) plain flour
1 egg
150 ml (¼ pint) fresh milk
black pepper
4 rashers streaky bacon, rinded and cut into strips
1 egg white
butter for frying
grilled mushrooms and tomatoes, to serve

1. Sift the flour into a bowl. Break in the egg. Gradually add the milk, beating to form a smooth batter. Season with pepper.
2. Gently cook the bacon in a non-stick frying pan until the fat runs and the bacon is crisp. Drain on absorbent kitchen paper.
3. Whisk the egg white until stiff, but not dry, and lightly fold into the batter.
4. Melt a little butter in the frying pan, then, when sizzling, add half the batter and spread out to cover the base of the pan. Cook over a moderate heat until the bottom is a light golden brown and the top is just set.
5. Scatter the bacon over the surface of the batter and cover with the remaining batter. Cook until the top is set, then turn the 'cake' over and brown the other side.
6. Transfer to a warmed plate and cut into wedges. Serve accompanied by mushrooms and tomatoes.

MIXED BEAN SALAD. An attractive mixture of shapes, colours and textures make this an interesting salad. The natural yogurt dressing adds a pleasing sharpness.

MACARONI AND BROCCOLI CHEESE

COUNTRYWIDE

Macaroni Cheese has been popular family fare since Victorian times, when it was fashionable to give a British slant to traditional Italian dishes. This modern version uses British Red Leicester cheese, wholewheat pasta, and broccoli. If you have never used wholewheat pasta before you will find the flavour stronger and nuttier than the plain kind.

SERVES 2

75 g (3 oz) wholewheat macaroni
salt and pepper
25 g (1 oz) butter
25 g (1 oz) plain flour
300 ml (½ pint) fresh milk
75 g (3 oz) Red Leicester cheese, grated
100 g (4 oz) broccoli florets
15 ml (1 tbsp) fresh wholemeal breadcrumbs

1. Cook the macaroni in 1.1 litres (2 pints) boiling salted water for 15 minutes. Drain.

2. Put the butter, flour and milk in a saucepan. Heat, whisking continuously, until the sauce boils, thickens and is smooth. Simmer for 1–2 minutes.
3. Remove pan from the heat, add most of the cheese and stir until melted. Season to taste.
4. Blanch the broccoli in boiling water for 7 minutes or until tender. Drain well.
5. Put the broccoli in the base of a 900 ml (1½ pint) flameproof serving dish. Cover with the macaroni and cheese sauce. Sprinkle with remaining cheese and breadcrumbs. Brown under a hot grill.

TO MICROWAVE

Put the macaroni in a large bowl. Pour over boiling water to cover the pasta by about 2.5 cm (1 inch). Cover and cook on HIGH for 4 minutes. Stand for 3 minutes. Put the butter, flour and milk in a medium bowl and cook on HIGH for about 4 minutes, until boiling and thickened, whisking frequently. Complete step 3. Cook the broccoli in a large bowl in 45 ml (3 tbsp) water on HIGH for 3½ minutes. Drain well. Complete step 5.

MACARONI AND BROCCOLI CHEESE. Substantial and very nourishing, this crisply topped supper dish is sure to become a firm favourite.

RIBBON NOODLES IN CURD CHEESE AND HERBS. Pasta variations are always popular. Use a mix of green and white noodles to give the dish extra colour.

RIBBON NOODLES IN CURD CHEESE AND HERBS

COUNTRYWIDE

Renaissance cooks brought pasta to England from Italy and it has remained a firm favourite ever since. Ribbon noodles, tagliatelle in Italian, make a filling dish served like this.

SERVES 2

| 15 g (½ oz) butter |
| 1 garlic clove, skinned and crushed |
| 50 g (2 oz) mushrooms, sliced |
| 5 ml (1 tsp) chopped fresh sage or 2.5 ml (½ tsp) dried |
| 50 g (2 oz) cooked ham, diced |
| salt |
| 100 g (4 oz) ribbon noodles |
| 50 g (2 oz) medium fat curd cheese |

1. Melt the butter in a frying pan and fry the garlic, mushrooms and sage for 2 minutes, then stir in the ham.
2. Bring 900 ml (1½ pints) salted water to the boil and cook the noodles for 10 minutes or according to packet instructions. Drain well and keep warm.
3. Heat the cheese with the mushroom mixture until melted, then stir in the noodles. Serve immediately.

TO MICROWAVE

Melt the butter in a medium bowl on HIGH for 30 seconds. Cook the mushrooms, garlic and sage on HIGH for 1 minute, then stir in the ham. Put the noodles in a large bowl. Pour over *boiling* water to cover the pasta by about 2.5 cm (1 inch). Cover and cook on HIGH for 5 minutes. Stand for 3 minutes. Drain. Heat the cheese with the mushroom mixture on HIGH for 1 minute. Stir in noodles and serve.

POACHED EGGS WITH CREAM AND PARSLEY SAUCE

COUNTRYWIDE

An attractive pale green sauce, well speckled with parsley, tops carefully poached fresh eggs. A little mature Cheddar gives a lovely taste. Also good served on noodles.

SERVES 1–2

| 15 g (½ oz) butter |
| 15 g (½ oz) plain flour |
| 150 ml (¼ pint) fresh milk |
| 5 ml (1 tsp) chopped fresh parsley |
| salt and pepper |
| 25 g (1 oz) mature Cheddar cheese, grated |
| 15 ml (1 tbsp) fresh soured cream |
| 2 eggs |
| 2 slices wholemeal bread, toasted |

1. Put the butter, flour, milk and parsley in a saucepan. Heat, whisking continuously, until the sauce thickens, boils and is smooth. Simmer for 1–2 minutes. Season.

2. Remove the pan from the heat, add the cheese and stir until melted. Fold in the cream.
3. Poach the eggs by breaking them into a pan of barely simmering water and cook for 3 minutes. Lift out with a draining spoon and drain on absorbent kitchen paper.
4. Place 1 egg on each slice of toast and cover with parsley sauce.

TO MICROWAVE

 Put the butter, flour, milk and parsley in a medium bowl and cook on HIGH for about 4 minutes, until boiling and thickened, whisking frequently. Add salt and pepper. Complete steps 2, 3 and 4.

CHESHIRE
POTTED CHEESE
THE MIDLANDS

This is an excellent way to use up odd pieces of cheese. They can be grated up together. As long as the butter seal is unbroken, this mixture keeps in the refrigerator for several weeks.

MAKES ABOUT 350 g (12 oz)

225 g (8 oz) Cheshire cheese, grated
about 50 g (2 oz) butter, softened
1.25 ml (¼ tsp) ground mace or allspice
30 ml (2 tbsp) sweet sherry or Madeira
melted butter for sealing

1. Mix the cheese with the softened butter and spice. The exact amount of butter will depend to a certain extent on how dry or moist the cheese is. Beat thoroughly. Add the sherry and mix again.
2. When the cheese is well amalgamated with the other ingredients, put it into small pots or ramekin dishes, pressing it well down and smoothing the tops. Cover each with melted butter and store in a refrigerator. Remove from the refrigerator about 1 hour before serving. Serve spread on toast or bread with fruit and celery.

CAULIFLOWER CHEESE
AND TOMATOES
COUNTRYWIDE

The smoothness of the cheese sauce contrasts well with the slight crispness of the cauliflower. Double Gloucester is a pale, mild cheese with a gentle, salty tang. Worcestershire sauce and chutney give a lively depth of flavour to this dish.

SERVES 2

✳ ⊞

225 g (8 oz) cauliflower florets
salt

25 g (1 oz) plain wholemeal flour
25 g (1 oz) butter
300 ml (½ pint) fresh milk
75 g (3 oz) Double Gloucester cheese, grated
10 ml (2 tsp) Worcestershire sauce
2 tomatoes, skinned and chopped
15 ml (1 tbsp) tomato chutney

1. Blanch the cauliflower in boiling salted water for 10 minutes or until tender. Drain well.
2. Put the flour, butter and milk in a saucepan. Heat, whisking continuously, until the sauce thickens, boils and is smooth. Simmer for 2–3 minutes.
3. Remove the pan from the heat, add most of the cheese and stir until melted. Mix in the Worcestershire sauce.
4. Place the tomatoes and chutney in the base of a 750 ml (1¼ pint) flameproof dish. Cover with the cauliflower and cheese sauce.
5. Sprinkle with the remaining cheese and grill until bubbling and golden brown. Serve with brown bread.

TO MICROWAVE

 Blanch the cauliflower in a large bowl in 45 ml (3 tbsp) water on HIGH for 5 minutes. Drain. Put the butter, flour and milk in a medium bowl and cook on HIGH for about 4 minutes, until boiling and thickened, whisking frequently. Complete steps 3, 4 and 5.

CHESHIRE POTTED CHEESE. Round off a meal with a change from the cheeseboard. The creamy mixture, flavoured with sherry and spice, spreads smoothly and tastes delicious.

HERRINGS IN OATMEAL
To remove backbone, press
lightly down middle of back.

Turn fish over and ease up
backbone.

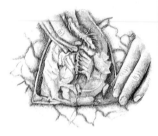

HERRINGS IN
OATMEAL. Nothing could
be simpler, or more delicious,
than piping hot fish in a crispy
coating, served fresh from the
pan with lemon wedges.

HERRINGS
IN OATMEAL
SCOTLAND

*The oatmeal in this dish adds to its bulk and fibre as well as
absorbing the rich oiliness of the herrings. Herrings are
economical fare, in season all year and at their best from
June to September. Ask your fishmonger to prepare them.*

SERVES 2

2 medium herrings, cleaned, heads and tails removed
salt and pepper
50 g (2 oz) medium oatmeal
15 ml (1 tbsp) vegetable oil
15 g (½ oz) butter
lemon wedges, to serve

1. To remove the backbone of the fish, put on a board,
cut side down, and press lightly with the fingers down
the middle of the back. Turn the fish over and ease the
backbone up with the fingers. Fold the fish in half.
Season well and coat with the oatmeal.
2. Heat the oil and butter in a large frying pan, and fry
the herrings for about 5 minutes on each side. Drain
well before serving hot with lemon wedges.

TO MICROWAVE

Complete step 1. Heat a large browning dish on
HIGH for 5–8 minutes according to manufacturer's
instructions. Put the oil and butter into the browning
dish, then quickly add the herrings. Microwave on
HIGH for 1 minute, then turn over and microwave on
HIGH for 1–2 minutes or until tender. Serve hot with
lemon wedges.

SPRING VEGETABLE
OMELETTE
COUNTRYWIDE

*Spring greens, or unhearted young cabbages, can usually be
found in the shops all year round, despite their name. They
need only light cooking and should keep a bit of crunch.*

SERVES 2

225 g (8 oz) spring greens, prepared and finely shredded
1 medium onion, skinned and thinly sliced
salt and pepper
15 g (½ oz) butter
3 tomatoes, cut into eighths
100 g (4 oz) frozen sweetcorn kernels
3 eggs

1. Blanch the spring greens and onion in boiling salted
water for 3 minutes. Drain well.
2. Put in a 20.5 cm (8 inch) dry omelette pan and
cook, stirring, over a medium heat for 3–5 minutes, to
evaporate excess moisture.
3. Add the butter and fry for about 8 minutes, until the
greens are just tender.
4. Add the tomatoes to the pan with the sweetcorn and
cook, stirring, for a further 3 minutes. Season.
5. Lightly whisk the eggs with seasoning, then pour
over the vegetables. Cook for about 5 minutes or until
just set, stirring once or twice to allow the egg mixture
to run through the vegetables.
6. Flash under the grill until the surface begins to
brown. Cut in half and serve at once.

QUICK PAN PIZZA
COUNTRYWIDE

*The scone base gives a very English feel to this much loved
Italian dish. Mozzarella is a mellow cheese with a subtle
flavour and is produced by several manufacturers in Britain.*

SERVES 4

75 g (3 oz) plain flour
salt and pepper
50 g (2 oz) butter
75 ml (3 fl oz) fresh milk
100 g (4 oz) streaky bacon rashers, rinded and chopped
1 medium onion, skinned and sliced
4 tomatoes, skinned and chopped
30 ml (2 tbsp) tomato chutney
15 ml (1 tbsp) chopped fresh oregano
100 g (4 oz) mozzarella cheese, grated
fresh parsley and sliced tomato, to garnish

1. Put the flour and a pinch of salt into a bowl. Rub in
40 g (1½ oz) of the butter until the mixture resembles
fine breadcrumbs. Add enough milk to form a soft

SPINACH PANCAKES.
Inside is a lemony sauce,
packed with choice chunks of
smoked and fresh fish.

dough. Roll out on a floured work surface to the size of
20.5 cm (8 inch) frying pan.
2. Melt the remaining butter in a frying pan and fry the
dough on one side until golden brown for 8 minutes.
Turn over.
3. Meanwhile, fry the bacon in its own fat with the
onion until soft. Add the tomatoes, chutney and
oregano. Season and simmer gently for a few minutes.
4. Spread the tomato mixture over the pizza, then
sprinkle with the mozzarella.
5. Cook gently for about 10 minutes. Brown under a
hot grill if desired. Garnish with parsley and tomato.

TO MICROWAVE

Complete steps 1 and 2. Cook the bacon and onion
in a medium bowl, covered, on HIGH for 2 minutes,
then add the tomatoes, chutney and oregano. Season
and cook, uncovered, for 2 minutes. Complete steps
4 and 5.

SPINACH PANCAKES

COUNTRYWIDE

*In this mouth-watering variation on the pancake theme,
chopped spinach is added to the batter, to make pretty green
pancakes with a delicious flavour.*

SERVES 4

✳ 〰

75 g (3 oz) plain flour

pinch of salt

1 egg, size 6

450 ml (¾ pint) fresh milk

50 g (2 oz) spinach, trimmed and finely chopped

25 g (1 oz) butter, plus extra for frying

grated rind of lemon

1 bay leaf

100 g (4 oz) smoked haddock, skinned and cubed

100 g (4 oz) cod, skinned and cubed

1. Sift 50 g (2 oz) of the flour and salt into a bowl.
Break in the egg. Gradually add 150 ml (¼ pint) milk,
beating to form a smooth batter. Stir in the spinach.
2. Heat a little butter in a 20.5 cm (8 inch) frying pan.
When hot pour in 45 ml (3 tbsp) batter, tilting pan to
cover base. Cook until the pancake moves freely, turn,
cook until golden. Make 4 pancakes.
3. Put the remaining butter, flour and milk in a
saucepan. Heat, whisking continuously, until the sauce
thickens, boils and is smooth. Stir in the lemon rind,
bay leaf and fish. Cook for 6 minutes.
4. Divide the mixture equally between the pancakes,
then roll up. Serve hot with a green salad.

TO MICROWAVE

Complete steps 1 and 2. Put the butter, remaining
flour and milk in a medium bowl and cook on HIGH for
about 4 minutes, until boiling and thickened, whisking
frequently. Stir in the lemon rind, bay leaf and fish.
Cook, covered, on HIGH for 3 minutes. Complete
step 4.

JACKET POTATOES

COUNTRYWIDE

Choose large, unblemished potatoes of roughly the same size. Maris Piper, Pentland Squire and a relatively new variety called Cara are particularly good baking potatoes. When cooked, make a crosswise slit on top and squeeze gently at the bottom to open. Then pile high with one of these simple but very tasty fillings, or serve simply with butter, grated cheese, or soured cream.

SERVES 2

2 large potatoes, scrubbed and pricked

Bake in their jackets at 200°C (400°F) mark 6 for 1½ hours, until tender. Slit the top of the potatoes.

TO MICROWAVE

Prick the potatoes with a fork, then put on absorbent kitchen paper and cook on HIGH for 10 minutes or until soft when squeezed gently.

FILLINGS

COTTAGE CHEESE AND CUCUMBER

225 g (8 oz) cottage cheese

50 g (2 oz) cucumber, diced

5 ml (1 tsp) snipped fresh chives

salt and pepper

2 cooked jacket potatoes (see above)

JACKET POTATOES. An old favourite that always goes down well. Ring the changes with unusual fillings.

LEFT TO RIGHT

Smoked haddock and chives, cheese and bacon, cottage cheese and cucumber, prawn special.

1. Combine the cottage cheese, cucumber, chives and salt and pepper to taste. Pile the filling into the potatoes and serve at once.

CHEESE AND RED PEPPER

100 g (4 oz) low-fat curd cheese

30 ml (2 tbsp) natural yogurt

50 g (2 oz) red pepper, cored, seeded and diced

1 egg, hard-boiled and chopped

salt and pepper

2 cooked jacket potatoes (see above)

Beat together the cheese and yogurt until soft. Stir in the red pepper, egg and salt and pepper to taste. Pile the filling into the potatoes and serve at once.

CHEESE AND BACON

100 g (4 oz) lean bacon, roughly chopped and fried

50 g (2 oz) Cheddar cheese, grated

salt and pepper

2 cooked jacket potatoes (see above)

Combine the bacon, cheese and salt and pepper to taste. Pile the filling into the potatoes and serve at once.

SMOKED HADDOCK AND CHIVES

100 g (4 oz) smoked haddock, cooked and mashed

15 ml (1 tbsp) snipped chives

10 ml (2 tsp) lemon juice

pepper

2 cooked jacket potatoes (see above)

Combine the haddock, chives, lemon juice and pepper to taste. Pile the filling into the potatoes and serve at once.

PRAWN SPECIAL

25 g (1 oz) butter

25 g (1 oz) plain flour

225 ml (8 fl oz) fresh milk

salt and pepper

50 g (2 oz) peeled cooked prawns

30 ml (2 tbsp) white wine

2 cooked jacket potatoes (see above)

1. Put the butter, flour and milk into a saucepan. Heat, whisking continuously, until the sauce thickens, boils

and is smooth. Simmer for 1–2 minutes. Season to taste.
2. Stir in the prawns and white wine. Cook for 1 minute. Pile the filling into the potatoes and serve at once.

TO MICROWAVE

⬚ Put the butter, flour and milk in a medium bowl. Cook on HIGH for 2–3 minutes, until boiling and thickened, whisking frequently. Add the salt and pepper, prawns and wine, cook on HIGH for 30 seconds. Complete step 2.

SAUSAGE AND SPINACH FLAN

COUNTRYWIDE

This flan, with its wholemeal pastry case, is good served warm with vegetables or cold with a salad. It makes hearty picnic food and can be baked the day before it's needed. Use firm, meaty sausages.

SERVES 4

✳ ⬚

15 g (½ oz) butter
225 g (8 oz) chipolata sausages, halved
1 large onion, skinned and chopped
25 g (1 oz) plain wholemeal flour
300 ml (½ pint) fresh milk
salt and pepper
50 g (2 oz) spinach, trimmed, blanched and chopped
1 egg, beaten
18 cm (7 inch) uncooked wholemeal pastry case

1. Melt the butter in a large frying pan and lightly fry the sausages and onion for 8 minutes, stirring occasionally. Stir in the flour and cook for 1 minute. Gradually add the milk, stirring continuously, until the sauce thickens, boils and is smooth. Simmer for 1–2 minutes. Season to taste.
2. Stir in the spinach and cook for 1 minute. Beat in the egg.
3. Pour the mixture into the pastry case and bake at 190°C (375°F) mark 5 for 45 minutes. Serve hot or cold with salad.

TO MICROWAVE

⬚ Melt the butter in a large bowl on HIGH for 30 seconds, then add the sausages and onion and cook, covered, on HIGH for 7 minutes. Stir in the flour and cook on HIGH for 1 minute, then add the milk, cook on HIGH for 4–5 minutes, until boiling and thickened, whisking frequently. Add the spinach and egg and cook on HIGH for 1 minute. Complete step 3.

EGGY BREAD

COUNTRYWIDE

A childhood favourite that's as popular now as it has ever been. If time allows, let the bread stand in the eggy mixture until it is all absorbed, before frying until beautifully brown and crisp. This version has a cheese and pickle topping and is popped under the grill to finish off.

SERVES 1–2

65 ml (2½ fl oz) fresh milk
1 egg, size 6
2 slices wholemeal bread
25 g (1 oz) butter
100 g (4 oz) Caerphilly cheese, grated
30 ml (2 tbsp) pickle
3 pickled onions, chopped

1. Beat together the milk and egg. Dip both slices of bread into the egg mixture, coating well on both sides.
2. Melt the butter in a large frying pan and fry the bread until golden brown on both sides. Keep warm.
3. Mix together the Caerphilly cheese, pickle and pickled onions. Spread the cheese mixture over the bread, then grill until golden and bubbling. Serve immediately.

SAUSAGE AND SPINACH FLAN. This is a really satisfying dish that bakes to an appetising golden brown on top.

MAIN COURSES

In this chapter is a superb collection of main course recipes – including lamb, beef, veal, pork, poultry and game, fish and shellfish. There are main course meals for everyday, dishes to serve when entertaining and substantial vegetarian recipes to enjoy at any time.

LAMB

CROWN ROAST
THE SOUTH-EAST

A spectacular dinner party dish. Some supermarkets now stock prepared crown roasts, or ask your butcher in advance to prepare one for you. If you're doing it, make sure that only the best ends of neck are chined, that is, the backbone sawn through so that the joint can be carved more easily. The cutlet bones must be left in one piece. Use a well-flavoured variety of apple for the filling such as Discovery or Jonagold.

SERVES 6

2 best end necks of lamb, each with 6 cutlets, chined
15 g (½ oz) butter
1 medium onion, skinned and chopped
3 celery sticks, chopped
2 eating apples, cored and chopped
100 g (4 oz) fresh breadcrumbs
30 ml (2 tbsp) chopped fresh mint
grated rind and juice of ½ lemon
1 egg
salt and pepper
30 ml (2 tbsp) plain flour
450 ml (¾ pint) lamb or beef stock
mint sprigs, to garnish

1. Trim each cutlet bone to a depth of 2.5 cm (1 inch).
2. Bend the joints around, fat side inwards, and sew together using strong cotton or fine string to form a crown. Cover the exposed bones with foil.
3. Melt the butter in a saucepan and cook the onion, celery and apples until brown. Stir in the breadcrumbs, mint, lemon rind and juice and egg. Season to taste and cool, then fill the centre of the joint with the stuffing and weigh.
4. Place the joint in a small roasting tin. Roast at 180°C (350°F) mark 4 for 25 minutes per 450 g (1 lb) plus 25 minutes. Baste occasionally and cover with foil if necessary.

PARSON'S VENISON.
Cooked to a turn, to leave just
a hint of juicy pinkness in the
centre. The stuffing helps to
keep the meat moist.

5. Transfer the roast to a warmed serving dish and keep warm. Drain off all but 30 ml (2 tbsp) of the fat in the roasting tin, then add the flour and blend well. Cook for 2–3 minutes, stirring continuously. Add the stock and boil for 2–3 minutes. Adjust the seasoning and serve hot with the joint. Garnish with sprigs of mint.

TO MICROWAVE

Complete steps 1 and 2. To prepare stuffing, put the butter, onion, celery and apples in a large bowl. Cover and cook on HIGH for 7-8 minutes, until softened. Complete step 3. Cook, uncovered, on HIGH for 10 minutes per 450 g (1 lb). Turn round halfway through cooking. Wrap crown in foil and stand for 10 minutes before serving.

GUARD OF HONOUR

Like Crown Roast, this is prepared from two best ends of neck. Trim as above but interlace the bones, fat side outwards, to form an arch. Fill the cavity with the stuffing, as above, and fasten with strong cotton or fine string.

PARSON'S VENISON

COUNTRYWIDE

Not venison at all but a leg of lamb, given a richer, fuller flavour reminiscent of game. The boned joint is stuffed with a savoury mushroom mixture, then marinated and cooked in a heady concoction of wine and port, seasoned with spices.

SERVES 4–6

25 g (1 oz) butter
1 small onion, skinned and finely chopped
100 g (4 oz) mushrooms, chopped
100 g (4 oz) cooked ham, chopped
30 ml (2 tbsp) snipped fresh chives
salt and pepper
1.8–2 kg (4–4½ lb) leg of lamb, skinned and boned
200 ml (7 fl oz) dry red wine
75 ml (3 fl oz) port
6 juniper berries, crushed
1.25 ml (¼ tsp) ground allspice
45 ml (3 tbsp) red wine vinegar
1 bay leaf
1.25 ml (¼ tsp) freshly grated nutmeg

1. Melt half the butter in a saucepan, add the onion and mushrooms and cook, stirring frequently, until the onion is soft but not browned. Stir in the ham and chives and season to taste. Leave to cool.
2. Season the lamb inside and out with pepper, then spread onion mixture over inside. Roll up tightly and tie securely. Place in a large glass bowl or casserole.
3. To make the marinade, mix remaining ingredients, except butter, pour over lamb, cover and leave in a cool place for 24 hours, turning occasionally.
4. Remove the meat from the marinade, drain and dry. Reserve the marinade. Melt the remaining butter in a flameproof casserole. Add the meat and brown on all sides over medium to high heat.
5. Pour in the marinade, bring almost to the boil, cover and roast at 180°C (350°F) mark 4 for 1¾–2 hours, until the meat is tender, basting occasionally with marinade.
6. Transfer meat to a warmed plate. Skim fat from surface of liquid, then boil rapidly until reduced. Remove bay leaf, adjust seasoning and serve with meat.

LEFT
CROWN ROAST OF
LAMB. A joint to carry
triumphantly to the table,
standing up proudly from a
bed of buttery baby
vegetables. Little paper ruffs
add to the finishing
decorative touch.

Bend the joints around, fat
side inwards, and sew together
using strong cotton or fine
string to form a crown.

NEW LAMB CUTS

The traditional roasting joints, leg (sold on the bone whole or as the fillet half and the knuckle or shank end) and shoulder (sold on the bone whole or as the blade or knuckle half) are now especially popular boned and rolled for easy carving – they may also be sold ready-stuffed.

Boning large cuts means that the butcher is able to remove some of the fat during the process and produce joints of uniform size, which also makes calculating servings easier.

Smaller boneless lamb cuts include best end neck fillets (see Gloucestershire Squab Pie, page 119) and prime steak cut from the leg (see recipe, page 121) or chump end of the loin.

Ready-cubed boneless lamb is ideal for kebabs and lean lamb mince makes delicious rissoles and lamb burgers (see page 122).

LAMB CUTLETS REFORM
THE SOUTH-EAST

Reform sauce is mouth-wateringly piquant and deliciously seasoned with herbs and spices. It was invented in the 1830s by the great French chef Alexis Soyer. At the time he was Chef de Cuisine of the Reform Club in London's Pall Mall, a favourite meeting place for politicians after Parliament. The club still exists, with Lamb Cutlets Reform a popular item on the menu.

This recipe is a simplified version of the traditional one, and omits ingredients such as hard-boiled egg white and cooked tongue which would make the sauce too elaborate for modern tastes.

SERVES 4

15 g (½ oz) butter

1 small onion, skinned and finely chopped

1 medium carrot, finely sliced

50 g (2 oz) lean ham, cut into thin strips

60 ml (4 tbsp) red wine vinegar

45 ml (3 tbsp) port

568 ml (1 pint) lamb or chicken stock

2 cloves

2 blades of mace

1 bay leaf

4 juniper berries, crushed

pinch of dried thyme

8 lamb cutlets, each weighing about 75 g (3 oz)

50 g (2 oz) cooked ham, finely minced

50 g (2 oz) fresh breadcrumbs

1 egg, beaten

15 ml (1 tbsp) cornflour

1. To make the Reform sauce, melt the butter in a medium saucepan, then add the onion, carrot and ham strips and cook gently until just turning brown. Add the vinegar and port and boil rapidly until almost all the liquid evaporates.
2. Remove the pan from the heat and add the stock, cloves, mace, bay leaf, juniper berries and thyme. Stir well, return to the heat and bring to the boil. Lower the heat and simmer gently for about 30 minutes.
3. Meanwhile, trim the cutlets to remove most of the surrounding fat. Scrape the bone absolutely clean to within 2.5 cm (1 inch) of the 'eye' of the meat.
4. Mix the minced ham and breadcrumbs together. Brush each cutlet with beaten egg and coat with the ham and breadcrumb mixture. Cover and chill until required.
5. Blend the cornflour with about 30 ml (2 tbsp) water and add to the sauce. Stir well and bring the sauce to the boil, stirring continuously. Simmer until thickened.
6. Grill the cutlets for about 4 minutes on each side, until golden brown. Arrange the cutlets on a warmed serving dish and garnish each one with a cutlet frill. Reheat the sauce gently and serve separately.

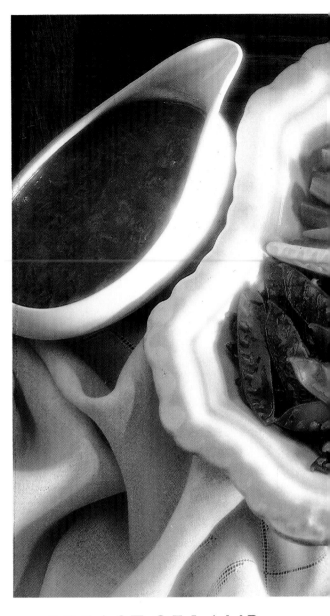

BREAST OF LAMB WITH MINT STUFFING
THE SOUTH-EAST

An inexpensive cut with a good flavour, breast of lamb can be rather fatty, so be sure to trim it well.

SERVES 6

2 lamb breasts, each weighing about 900 g (2 lb), boned

15 g (½ oz) butter

1 medium onion, skinned and finely chopped

1 egg, beaten

30 ml (2 tbsp) milk

100 g (4 oz) fresh wholemeal breadcrumbs

60 ml (4 tbsp) chopped mixed fresh mint and parsley

salt and pepper

pinch of sugar

1. Flatten the meat and remove excess fat.

2. Melt the butter in a medium frying pan and fry the onion until soft but not brown. In a separate bowl, beat the egg with the milk and mash in the breadcrumbs. Mix together the onion, herbs and eggy-bread mixture and season to taste with the salt and pepper and sugar.
3. Divide the mixture between the two breasts of lamb and spread it out evenly, then roll up the meat as tightly as possible and secure well with strong cotton or fine string. Cover with foil and roast at 230°C (450°F) mark 8 for 40 minutes. Remove the foil so that the meat can brown and roast for a further 15 minutes.

A WELSH WAY WITH LAMB

WALES

Although Welsh lamb is delicious served plain, adding sweet and spicy ingredients makes it a truly flavoursome dish.

SERVES 6

1 leg or shoulder of lamb, weighing about 1.4 kg (3 lb)

salt and pepper
5 ml (1 tsp) ground ginger
45–60 ml (3–4 tbsp) honey
fresh rosemary sprigs
300 ml (½ pint) dry cider

1. Weigh the lamb joint, then put it into a roasting tin and sprinkle with salt and pepper and the ground ginger. Pour over the honey (heated if it is very stiff), put the rosemary on top and pour round the cider.
2. Roast at 220°C (425°F) mark 7 for 30 minutes, then reduce the heat to 200°C (400°F) mark 6 and continue to roast until the lamb is tender, allowing 20 minutes per 450 g (1 lb). Baste several times during the cooking, and if the top looks as if it is getting too dark – the honey is inclined to scorch – protect it with foil. If necessary, add a little more cider. The cider and honey form the gravy and nothing more is needed. Skim off any excess fat.

LAMB CUTLETS REFORM. It's the savoury sauce which really makes this dish. The cutlets are coated in a tasty mixture of minced ham and breadcrumbs, which forms a crispy coating when grilled.

LAMB WITH CHERRIES
THE SOUTH-EAST

Juicy red cherries from the orchards of Kent add a slight sharpness to this unusual casserole. Flavours and textures blend deliciously as the ingredients cook together in red wine.

SERVES 6

225 g (8 oz) streaky bacon rashers, rinded and chopped

15 g (½ oz) butter

1.4 kg (3 lb) boneless leg or shoulder of lamb, cut into 4 cm (1½ inch) cubes

1 medium onion, skinned and sliced

1 medium carrot, sliced

1 celery stick, sliced

1 garlic clove, skinned and sliced

568 ml (1 pint) dry red wine

bouquet garni

freshly grated nutmeg

salt and pepper

450 g (1 lb) fresh red cherries, stoned

1. In a large frying pan, fry the bacon in its own fat until browned. Add the butter to the pan and fry the lamb, a little at a time, until browned. Remove from the pan with the bacon and put in the casserole.
2. Fry the onion, carrot, celery and garlic in the fat remaining in the pan for about 5 minutes, until lightly browned. Add the vegetables to the casserole.
3. Pour over the wine and add the bouquet garni, pinch of nutmeg and salt and pepper. Cover and bake at 150°C (300°F) mark 3 for about 2½ hours, until tender.
4. Thirty minutes before the end of the cooking time, stir the cherries into the casserole and continue to cook until the meat is tender and the cherries soft. Serve hot with courgettes and new potatoes.

IRISH STEW
NORTHERN IRELAND

A simple dish of lamb, potatoes and onions, well flavoured with herbs. If any other ingredients are added, the result is not an authentic Irish stew. Use a deep casserole to hold the layers of meat and vegetables, and allow for long slow cooking so that the liquid is thickened and enriched. Use a firm potato such as the Romano or Maris Piper varieties.

SERVES 4

※

700 g (1½ lb) middle neck of lamb, cut into cutlets and trimmed

2 medium onions, skinned and sliced

450 g (1 lb) old potatoes, thinly sliced

15 ml (1 tbsp) chopped fresh parsley

5 ml (1 tsp) dried thyme

salt and pepper

chopped fresh parsley, to garnish

1. Make layers of meat, vegetables, herbs and salt and pepper in a deep casserole, ending with a top layer of potato to make a neat 'lid'.

LAMB WITH CHERRIES. Plump fruits are a pleasing addition to this comforting casserole, which gets its mellow flavour from bacon, herbs and spices.

2. Pour in 300 ml (½ pint) water and cover with greaseproof paper or foil and then the casserole lid. Bake at 170°C (325°F) mark 3 for about 2 hours or until the meat and vegetables are tender. Serve hot, garnished with parsley.

PORTMANTEAU LAMB CHOPS
THE SOUTH-EAST

This dish is so called because it resembles the travelling bag known as a portmanteau when stuffed with chicken livers and mushrooms, which complement the flavour of the lamb. Use chops which are thick enough to hold the stuffing.

SERVES 4

4 thick lamb loin chops
40 g (1½ oz) butter
100 g (4 oz) chicken livers, thawed if frozen and finely chopped
100 g (4 oz) mushrooms, finely chopped
salt and pepper
1 egg, beaten
50 g (2 oz) fresh wholemeal breadcrumbs
fresh parsley sprigs, to garnish

1. Using a sharp, pointed knife, make a horizontal cut in each chop, working from the outside fat edge to the bone, to form a pocket.
2. To make the stuffing, melt 15 g (½ oz) of the butter in a frying pan, add the chicken livers and mushrooms and fry for 4–5 minutes, until soft but not brown. Season to taste.
3. Leave the stuffing to cool slightly, then spoon into the cavity in the chops and secure the open edges with wooden cocktail sticks.
4. Dip the chops in the beaten egg, then in the breadcrumbs to coat thoroughly.
5. Put the chops in a roasting tin. Melt the remaining butter and pour over the chops. Bake at 200°C (400°F) mark 6 for 15 minutes, then turn and bake for a further 15 minutes, until golden brown. Serve hot, garnished with parsley sprigs.

LAMB AND BARLEY STEW
THE SOUTH-EAST

Lamb from the Weald of Kent is particularly tasty and pearl barley is a good bulking ingredient to use in stews and casseroles. It will keep for up to 18 months in an air-tight container.

SERVES 4–6

✳

1.4 kg (3 lb) boned leg or shoulder of lamb, trimmed of fat and cubed

30 ml (2 tbsp) plain wholemeal flour
salt and pepper
3 streaky bacon rashers, rinded and chopped
25 g (1 oz) butter
2 medium onions, skinned and chopped
2 medium carrots, sliced
100 g (4 oz) turnip or swede, peeled and diced
2 celery sticks, diced
30 ml (2 tbsp) pearl barley
10 ml (2 tsp) mixed chopped fresh herbs, such as thyme, rosemary, parsley, basil
300 ml (½ pint) lamb or beef stock
chopped fresh parsley, to garnish

1. Toss the lamb in the flour, seasoned with salt and pepper.
2. Dry fry the bacon in a large flameproof casserole. Add the butter and the lamb and fry until browned all over, stirring. Remove the lamb and the bacon from the casserole with a slotted spoon and set aside.
3. Add the onions, carrots, turnip or swede and celery to the casserole and fry for 5–10 minutes, until beginning to brown.
4. Return the lamb to the casserole, add the pearl barley and herbs and pour in the stock.
5. Bring to the boil, then cover and simmer for 2 hours, stirring occasionally to prevent sticking, until the lamb is tender.
6. Serve hot, sprinkled with chopped parsley.

PORTMANTEAU LAMB CHOPS. Inviting parcels, filled with a rich, savoury stuffing, and oven-baked until golden brown.

and keep warm.
3. Add the wine to the roasting tin, stirring in any sediment from the bottom of the tin. Stir in the redcurrant jelly. Bring to the boil, then stir in the remaining soured cream and boil for 2–3 minutes, until thickened slightly.
4. Thickly slice the lamb and serve with the sauce spooned over. Accompany with new boiled potatoes and courgettes.

TO MICROWAVE

 Complete step 1. Put the lamb in a shallow dish and spoon over the garlic mixture. Cook, uncovered, on HIGH for 3 minutes. Cover and cook on MEDIUM for 10–15 minutes, rearranging twice, until cooked to your liking. Transfer the lamb to a warmed serving dish. Stir the remaining soured cream, the wine and redcurrant jelly into the dish. Cook on HIGH for 1–2 minutes, stirring occasionally, until hot. Complete step 4.

BROWN RAGOO OF LAMB

COUNTRYWIDE

The strange name of this dish comes from the French word ragoût, *meaning a thick meat or poultry stew, enriched with a well-flavoured stock and also containing plenty of mixed vegetables. It is an example of France's influence on British cooking. Carrots, onions and mushrooms are always easy to find, and you can substitute peas for the broad beans if necessary.*

SERVES 6

❄

25 g (1 oz) butter
900 g (2 lb) leg of lamb, cut into 2.5 cm (1 inch) cubes
12 small onions, skinned
3 carrots, cut into quarters
4 cloves
1 medium onion, skinned
3 fresh parsley sprigs
2 fresh thyme sprigs
2 bay leaves
small fresh rosemary sprig
750 ml (1¼ pints) lamb or beef stock
salt and pepper
100 g (4 oz) button mushrooms
175 g (6 oz) broad beans, cooked
squeeze of lemon juice
chopped fresh parsley, to garnish

1. Melt the butter in a large, heavy-based frying pan, add the lamb in batches and cook until an even golden brown. Transfer to a casserole dish using a slotted spoon. Add the small onions and the carrots to the frying pan and fry until lightly browned. Transfer to the casserole dish.

LAMB FILLET WITH REDCURRANT SAUCE. The sharpness of redcurrants is the perfect foil for thick, succulent slices of lamb, which need only simple vegetables to accompany.

LAMB FILLET WITH REDCURRANT SAUCE

COUNTRYWIDE

Try this idea next time you're cooking for a special occasion. Tender lamb fillet is coated with a garlic and mustard mixture before roasting. The savoury pan juices are used as the basis of a scrumptious red wine and soured cream sauce, which is poured over the thickly sliced meat to serve.

SERVES 3

90 ml (6 tbsp) fresh soured cream
1 garlic clove, skinned and crushed
5 ml (1 tsp) wholegrain mustard
salt and pepper
450 g (1 lb) lamb fillet
30 ml (2 tbsp) dry red wine
15 ml (1 tbsp) redcurrant jelly

1. Mix 30 ml (2 tbsp) of the soured cream with the garlic and mustard. Season to taste.
2. Put the lamb fillet in a roasting tin and spoon the garlic mixture all over. Roast at 180°C (350°F) mark 4 for 30 minutes, until tender and cooked to your liking. Transfer the lamb to a warmed serving dish

OPPOSITE
GLOUCESTERSHIRE SQUAB PIE. A golden pastry crust sliced open to reveal a delectable filling of juicy lamb and apple slices.

2. Stick the cloves in the onion and add to the casserole with the herbs and stock. Season to taste and bring to the boil.

3. Cover tightly and bake at 180°C (350°F) mark 4 for about 2½ hours, stirring occasionally.

4. Remove the onion stuck with cloves from the casserole, then stir in the mushrooms, broad beans and lemon juice and continue to cook for 10 minutes.

5. Using a slotted spoon, lift the meat and vegetables from the casserole, arrange on a large serving plate and keep warm. Boil the liquid until it is reduced to about 400 ml (14 fl oz). Pour some of the sauce over the meat and vegetables. Garnish with chopped parsley and serve with the rest of the sauce handed separately. Accompany with boiled or mashed potatoes.

GLOUCESTERSHIRE SQUAB PIE

THE WEST

You'd be forgiven for thinking this dish might contain young pigeons, otherwise known as squabs, but this pie has always been made with lamb. If you can buy it locally in the Cotswolds the flavour will be delicious set off by the sharp apple and spices.

SERVES 4

225 g (8 oz) plain flour
salt and pepper
50 g (2 oz) butter
50 g (2 oz) lard
700 g (1½ lb) lamb neck fillets, sliced into 12 pieces
1 large cooking apple, peeled, cored and sliced
450 g (1 lb) onions, skinned and thinly sliced
1.25 ml (¼ tsp) ground allspice
1.25 ml (¼ tsp) grated nutmeg
150 ml (¼ pint) lamb or beef stock
fresh milk, to glaze

1. Put the flour and a pinch of salt in a bowl. Rub in the butter and lard until the mixture resembles fine breadcrumbs. Add enough cold water and mix in to form a firm dough. Knead lightly until smooth, then chill until required.

2. Place half the lamb in the base of a 900 ml (1½ pint) pie dish. Arrange half the apple slices and half the onion slices over the top. Sprinkle over the allspice and nutmeg and season to taste. Repeat the layers, then pour over the stock.

3. Roll out the pastry to fit the dish and use to cover the pie, moistening the edges so the pastry is well sealed. Use any pastry trimming to decorate.

4. Brush the pastry with milk and bake at 200°C (400°F) mark 6 for 20 minutes. Reduce the temperature to 180°C (350°F) mark 4 and cook for a further 1 hour 15 minutes. Cover the pastry if it shows signs of becoming too brown. Serve hot.

Onions, garlic and leeks, members of the same family, all have their own individual flavouring qualities. Most onions can be obtained through the year, garlic is most commonly available dried, and leeks enjoy a long season.

SPANISH ONION

British grown despite the name, these are large, sweet and mild. Use cooked when less pronounced flavour is required; delicious stuffed (see recipe, page 217) in a tart or as sauce for lamb.

RED ONION

Of Italian origin. Particularly attractive sliced raw into rings and added to salads for colour as well as flavour.

GARLIC

Very pungent, use sparingly. Cut into slivers to flavour roast lamb, chop finely or crush in garlic press or with knife blade for soups, casseroles and stuffings. Also available as powder and salt.

SHALLOT

Smaller and less pungent than most onions, delicious in subtle sauces for fish and steak, or glazed as an accompanying vegetable (see recipe, page 228).

SPRING ONION

Cropped before bulb forms fully. Excellent in salads, for garnish, or finely chopped to give mild flavour.

LEEK

Available August to May. National vegetable of Wales. Less strong-flavoured than onions, delicious braised or puréed as an accompanying vegetable; baby leeks can be shredded raw in salads. Leeks are excellent in soups (see recipes, pages 83, 87) and casseroles, or to make a creamy flan (page 211).

SHEPHERD'S PIE

THE NORTH

Few seemingly simple and traditional dishes have so much controversy about their names. There are those who hold that it is shepherd's pie when made with lamb and cottage pie when made with beef – and vice versa. Some people say it should be made with raw meat, others with cooked. This version has more flavoursome ingredients than some recipes and tastes excellent.

SERVES 4

| 450 g (1 lb) minced lamb |
| 1 large onion, skinned and chopped |
| 1 bay leaf |
| 50 g (2 oz) mushrooms, sliced |
| 2 carrots, sliced |
| 25 g (1 oz) plain wholemeal flour |
| 300 ml (½ pint) lamb or beef stock |
| 15 ml (1 tbsp) tomato purée |
| salt and pepper |
| 700 g (1½ lb) potatoes, peeled and chopped |
| 25 g (1 oz) butter |
| 60 ml (4 tbsp) fresh milk |
| 50 g (2 oz) Lancashire cheese, crumbled |

1. Dry fry the lamb with the onion, bay leaf, mushrooms and carrots for 8–10 minutes.
2. Add the flour and cook, stirring, for 1 minute. Gradually blend in the stock and tomato purée. Cook, stirring, until the mixture thickens and boils.
3. Cover and simmer gently for 25 minutes. Remove the bay leaf and season to taste. Spoon into a 1.7 litre (3 pint) ovenproof serving dish.
4. Meanwhile, cook the potatoes in boiling salted water for 20 minutes, until tender. Drain well. Mash with the butter and milk and mix well. Pile on to the mince mixture and sprinkle over the cheese.
5. Bake at 200°C (400°F) mark 6 for 15–20 minutes. Serve hot with a green vegetable.

TO MICROWAVE

Dry fry the lamb, onion, bay leaf, mushrooms and carrots in a 1.7 litre (3 pint) shallow heatproof dish, covered, on HIGH for 8 minutes. Add the flour and cook on HIGH for 1 minute. Gradually blend in the stock and tomato purée, then cook on HIGH for 5 minutes, stirring occasionally. Cook the potatoes in a large bowl in 150 ml (¼ pint) water for 15 minutes. Complete steps 4 and 5.

OXFORD JOHN STEAKS WITH CAPER SAUCE. Generous, tender steaks need only the simplest cooking. The mouthwateringly sharp capers add a refreshing bite to the sauce.

OXFORD JOHN STEAKS WITH CAPER SAUCE

THE SOUTH-EAST

At Oxford's indoor market there are butchers who have for years supplied the colleges with high quality meat. A speciality is Oxford John, the local name for a lamb leg steak. It's a tender cut that just needs gentle frying before serving with a piquant sauce.

SERVES 4

| 4 lamb leg steaks, each weighing about 175 g (6 oz) |
| salt and pepper |
| 25 g (1 oz) butter |
| 5 ml (1 tsp) plain flour |
| 300 ml (½ pint) lamb or beef stock |
| 30 ml (2 tbsp) drained capers |
| 15 ml (1 tbsp) vinegar from the capers |

1. Season the lamb steaks to taste. Heat the butter in a frying pan and fry the steaks gently for 10–15 minutes, turning occasionally, until browned on both sides. Remove from the pan with a slotted spoon and transfer to a warmed dish.
2. Stir to loosen any sediment at the bottom of the pan, then stir in the flour and cook for 1–2 minutes. Gradually add the stock, stirring all the time, then cook until the sauce thickens, boils and is smooth. Add the capers and vinegar and simmer for 1–2 minutes.
3. Return the lamb steaks to the pan and simmer for 5 minutes or until the lamb is cooked to your liking. Serve hot.

LAMB AND WATERCRESS BAKE
COUNTRYWIDE

Methods of watercress cultivation have improved so that it is now available all year round. Bought vacuum-packed, it keeps unopened for up to five days, but wilts quickly when exposed to the air. If you buy watercress in bunches, store them upside down, with the leaves plunged into cold water.

SERVES 4–6

450 g (1 lb) minced lamb
2 large onions, skinned and finely chopped
2 bunches watercress, trimmed and finely chopped
10 ml (2 tsp) dried oregano
105 ml (7 tbsp) plain flour
300 ml (½ pint) lamb or chicken stock
50 ml (2 fl oz) dry white wine
25 g (1 oz) butter
salt and pepper
568 ml (1 pint) fresh milk
175 g (6 oz) Lancashire cheese, crumbled
225 g (8 oz) oven-ready lasagne verdi

1. Brown the lamb well in its own fat in a large saucepan. Pour off excess fat. Add the onion and cook for 5 minutes, stirring occasionally. Add the watercress, oregano and 30 ml (2 tbsp) of the flour. Cook for 1–2 minutes, then gradually stir in the stock and wine and season with salt and pepper. Bring to the boil, then simmer gently, uncovered, for 45 minutes, stirring occasionally.
2. Put the butter, remaining flour and milk in a saucepan. Heat, whisking continuously, until the sauce thickens, boils and is smooth. Simmer for 1–2 minutes. Remove the pan from the heat and stir in 100 g (4 oz) of the cheese, stir until melted and season with salt and pepper.
3. Layer the mince mixture with the uncooked lasagne in a fairly deep ovenproof serving dish. Spoon over the cheese sauce. Sprinkle over remaining cheese.
4. Bake at 190°C (375°F) mark 5 for about 40 minutes, until browned. Serve hot straight from the dish.

TO MICROWAVE

The cheese sauce can be prepared in the microwave. Put the butter, remaining flour and milk in a medium bowl and stir together. Cook on HIGH for 5–6 minutes, until the sauce has boiled and thickened, whisking frequently. Complete the sauce as in step 2.

CHUMP CHOPS WITH BLACKCURRANT SAUCE
COUNTRYWIDE

Make the most of the superb sharpness of blackcurrants during their summer season. They are particularly good with lamb, because their natural acidity acts as a foil to the lamb's fattiness. The easiest way to remove fresh blackcurrants from their stalks is to run a fork down the stem.

SERVES 4

4 lamb chump chops, each weighing about 225 g (8 oz)
1 medium onion, skinned and chopped
15 ml (1 tbsp) chopped fresh rosemary
15 ml (1 tbsp) chopped fresh parsley
grated rind of 1 lemon
300 ml (½ pint) apple and blackcurrant juice
15 ml (1 tbsp) blackcurrant jelly
50 g (2 oz) blackcurrants, stripped
30 ml (2 tbsp) fresh soured cream

1. Dry fry the chops in a large non-stick frying pan until brown and sealed on both sides.
2. Add the onion, rosemary, parsley and lemon rind, lightly fry for 2 minutes, then pour in the apple and blackcurrant juice. Simmer gently, covered, for 20–25 minutes until the chops are tender.
3. Remove the chops from the pan, put on to a warmed serving plate and keep hot.
4. Add the blackcurrant jelly and most of the blackcurrants to the pan, then boil the juices to reduce by half. Add the soured cream and reheat gently, then pour over the chops. Serve garnished with the remaining blackcurrants. Accompany with creamed potatoes and sliced carrots.

LAMB AND WATERCRESS BAKE. A sustaining variation of lasagne. The smooth, cheesy topping conceals the mouthwatering layers of meat sauce and pasta.

LEFT
MINTED LAMB BURGERS
WITH CUCUMBER. Neat
little burgers in a sherry sauce
are an out-of-the-ordinary
way to use minced lamb.

RIGHT
LAMB KEBABS IN SPICY
YOGURT DRESSING. Bite-
size cubes of lamb, skewered
with still-crisp vegetables and
topped off with a well-
flavoured dressing.

LAMB KEBABS IN SPICY YOGURT DRESSING

COUNTRYWIDE

A good dish for the end of summer, when corn-on-the-cob comes into the shops. The kebabs can be grilled, or cooked outdoors on a barbecue. A few hours in the marinade helps tenderise them, as well as adding flavour and moisture.

SERVES 4

1 large corn-on-the-cob
salt and pepper
8 shallots
150 g (5 oz) natural yogurt
1 garlic clove, skinned and crushed
2 bay leaves, crumbled
15 ml (1 tbsp) lemon juice
5 ml (1 tsp) ground allspice
15 ml (1 tbsp) coriander seeds
700 g (1½ lb) boned leg of lamb, trimmed and cut into 2.5 cm (1 inch) cubes
225 g (8 oz) courgettes, topped and tailed and cut into 0.5 cm (¼ inch) slices
4 tomatoes, halved
lemon wedges, to garnish

1. Blanch the corn in boiling salted water for 1 minute, drain well, cut into 8 pieces and set aside. Blanch the shallots in boiling salted water for 1 minute, skin and set aside.
2. To make the marinade, pour the yogurt into a shallow dish and stir in the garlic, bay leaves, lemon juice, allspice, coriander seeds and salt and pepper.
3. Thread the lamb cubes on to eight skewers with the courgettes, tomatoes, corn and shallots. Place in the dish, spoon over the marinade, cover and leave for 2–3 hours, turning occasionally to ensure even coating.
4. Grill the kebabs for about 15–20 minutes, turning and brushing with the marinade occasionally. To serve, spoon remaining marinade over the kebabs and garnish with lemon wedges. Accompany with boiled rice.

MINTED LAMB BURGERS WITH CUCUMBER

COUNTRYWIDE

Lamb and mint were made for each other, and the flavours marry perfectly in these quick burgers. When buying cucumbers, feel the stalk end and only buy if it is firm. Don't peel the cucumber, as both appearance and flavour are improved if the skin is left on.

SERVES 4

450 g (1 lb) minced lamb
1 small onion, skinned and finely chopped
100 g (4 oz) fresh breadcrumbs
finely grated rind of ½ lemon
45 ml (3 tbsp) chopped fresh mint
1 egg, beaten
salt and pepper
30 ml (2 tbsp) plain flour
½ cucumber, cut into 5 cm (2 inch) long wedges
6 spring onions, trimmed and cut into 1 cm (½ inch) pieces
200 ml (7 fl oz) lamb or chicken stock
15 ml (1 tbsp) dry sherry

1. Mix the lamb, onion, breadcrumbs and lemon rind with 15 ml (1 tbsp) of the chopped mint and egg. Season.
2. Shape into 8 burgers with floured hands, then completely coat in the flour.
3. Dry fry the burgers in a large heavy-based non-stick frying pan for about 6 minutes, until lightly browned, turning once. Add the cucumber and spring onions.
4. Pour in the stock and sherry, then add the remaining mint and salt and pepper to taste. Bring to the boil, cover and simmer gently for about 20 minutes or until the meat is tender. Skim off any excess fat before serving, and taste and adjust seasoning. Serve with boiled new potatoes.

TO MICROWAVE

⊠ Heat a large browning dish on HIGH for 5–8 minutes or according to the manufacturer's instructions. Meanwhile, complete steps 1 and 2. Add 10 ml (2 tsp) oil to the browning dish, then quickly add the burgers and cook on HIGH for 2 minutes. Turn over and cook on HIGH for 2–3 minutes or until browned. Add the cucumbers, spring onions, 150 ml (¼ pint) stock, the sherry and the remaining mint. Cook on HIGH for 4–5 minutes or until the liquid is boiling and slightly reduced. Skim off any excess fat and season. Serve with boiled new potatoes.

MARINATED LAMB WITH ONION PUREE

COUNTRYWIDE

Even a short soak in a piquant marinade improves the flavour of everyday chops. Go easy on the sage – just a hint is all that's needed, as the flavour can be overpowering.

SERVES 4

⊠

45 ml (3 tbsp) vegetable oil
15 ml (1 tbsp) white wine vinegar
1.25 ml (¼ tsp) dried sage
1 garlic clove, skinned and crushed
4 lamb chump chops, each about 225 g (8 oz), trimmed
2 medium onions, skinned and finely chopped
30 ml (2 tbsp) plain flour
300 ml (½ pint) fresh milk
1 clove
30 ml (2 tbsp) fresh single cream
salt and pepper
fresh sage sprigs, to garnish

1. To make the marinade, whisk together the oil, vinegar, sage and crushed garlic.
2. Place the chops flat in a shallow dish. Pour over the marinade, cover and leave to marinate in a cool place for 1 hour.
3. Remove the chops from the marinade and place under a hot grill. Cook for 7–10 minutes on each side.
4. Meanwhile, put the marinade and chopped onions

in a small saucepan. Cover and cook over low heat for about 10–15 minutes, until onions are soft.
5. Stir in the flour, then gradually stir in the milk. Add the clove. Bring to the boil, stirring occasionally, and simmer for 2 minutes. Discard the clove, transfer to a blender or food processor and purée until smooth. Return the sauce to the rinsed-out pan. Add the cream and salt and pepper to taste and reheat gently. Arrange the chops on a warmed serving dish and garnish with sprigs of sage. Serve the onion purée separately.

TO MICROWAVE

⊠ Complete steps 1, 2 and 3. Meanwhile, put the marinade and chopped onions in a medium bowl. Cover and cook on HIGH for 7–10 minutes, until softened. Stir in the flour, milk and the clove. Cook on HIGH for 2–3 minutes until boiling and thickened, whisking frequently. Discard the clove. Transfer the sauce to a blender or food processor and purée until smooth. Transfer the purée to a heatproof serving bowl and cook on HIGH for 2 minutes or until hot. Stir in the cream and salt and pepper to taste. Complete the remainder of step 5.

LOIN OF LAMB WITH APRICOT AND HERB STUFFING

COUNTRYWIDE

A fruity stuffing goes well with lamb and here no-soak dried apricots save time. Ask the butcher to bone the loin for you, then it's simple to roll and tie it into a neat joint.

SERVES 6

15 g (½ oz) butter
1 medium onion, skinned and finely chopped
30 ml (2 tbsp) chopped fresh thyme or mint
75 g (3 oz) fresh wholemeal breadcrumbs
salt and pepper
100 g (4 oz) no-soak dried apricots, finely chopped
1 egg, beaten
1.6 kg (3½ lb) loin of lamb, boned
fresh thyme or mint sprigs, to garnish

1. Melt the butter in a large frying pan. Add the onion and fry for 5 minutes, until softened. Stir in thyme or mint, breadcrumbs and seasoning. Set aside to cool.
2. Add the apricots to the mixture with the egg and mix well together.
3. Lay the meat out flat, fat side down, and spread the stuffing over the lamb.
4. Roll up the meat to enclose the stuffing and tie with strong cotton or fine string at regular intervals. Put the joint in a roasting tin and bake at 180°C (350°F) mark 4 for about 12 hour or until cooked to your liking.
5. To serve, remove the string and carve into thick slices. Garnish with sprigs of fresh thyme or mint.

BEEF

ROAST BEEF AND YORKSHIRE PUDDING

THE NORTH

The North may claim it for its own but all over Britain this is recognised as a traditional dish, especially for Sunday lunch time. Using semi-skimmed instead of whole milk will produce the same effect as using half milk and half water in the Yorkshire pudding. Keep the meat warm, resting under a tent of foil, until you are ready to carve it.

* ALLOW 175 g (6 oz) OFF THE BONE PER PERSON; 225–350 g (8–12 oz) ON THE BONE PER PERSON

SERVES 4–8

sirloin, rib, rump or topside*
25 g (1 oz) beef drippings (optional)
salt and pepper
5 ml (1 tsp) mustard powder (optional)
Prepared English mustard or horseradish sauce, to serve
For the Yorkshire pudding
100 g (4 oz) plain flour
pinch of salt
1 egg
200 ml (7 fl oz) fresh milk
For the gravy
10 ml (2 tsp) plain flour
300 ml (½ pint) beef stock

1. Weigh the meat and calculate the cooking time: for rare beef allow 15 minutes per 450 g (1 lb) plus 15 minutes; for medium beef allow 20 minutes per 450 g (1 lb) plus 20 minutes; and for well-done beef allow 25 minutes per 450 g (1 lb) plus 25 minutes. Put the meat into a shallow roasting tin, preferably on a roasting rack, with the thickest layer of fat uppermost and the cut sides exposed to the heat. Add drippings if the meat is lean. Season the meat with pepper and mustard powder, if wished.

2. Roast at 180°C (350°F) mark 4 for the calculated time, basting occasionally with the juices from the tin. Forty-five minutes before the end of the cooking time, cover the joint with foil and place on the bottom shelf of the oven. Increase the oven temperature to 220°C (425°F) mark 7.

3. To make the Yorkshire pudding, mix the flour and a pinch of salt in a bowl, then make a well in the centre and break in the egg.

4. Add half the milk and, using a wooden spoon, gradually work in the flour. Beat the mixture until it is smooth, then add the remaining milk and 100 ml (3 fl oz) water. Beat until well mixed and the surface is covered with tiny bubbles.

5. Put 30 ml (2 tbsp) fat from the beef into a baking tin and place in the oven at 220°C (425°F) mark 7 until the fat is very hot.

6. Pour in the batter and return to the oven to cook for 40–45 minutes, until risen and golden brown. Do not open the oven door for 30 minutes.

7. After 30 minutes, transfer the cooked meat to a warmed serving plate and leave to rest for 20 minutes, covered, before carving.

8. To make the gravy, the meat juices alone may be used. For a thicker gravy, skim some of the fat from the surface and place the tin over moderate heat. Sprinkle the flour into the tin and stir it into the pan juices, scraping up the brown sediment. Cook over high heat, stirring constantly, until the flour has browned slightly. (When the meat is carved, any juices from the meat can be added to the gravy.) Add up to 300 ml (½ pint) of beef stock to the tin and stir well. Bring it to the boil, simmer for 2–3 minutes and season to taste. Pour into a sauce boat or jug.

9. Serve the carved beef with the Yorkshire pudding, cut into portions. Accompany with the gravy and mustard or horseradish sauce.

VARIATION

For individual Yorkshire Puddings or Popovers, use 50 g (2 oz) plain flour, a pinch of salt, 1 egg and 150 ml (¼ pint) milk and water mixed. Cook for 15–20 minutes. This quantity will fill 12 patty tins.

BEEF WELLINGTON. An impressive dish, using a fine cut of meat. The pastry casing is crisply browned, while the meat within stays moist and juicy.

BEEF WELLINGTON

THE SOUTH-EAST

The Duke of Wellington was a highly prominent statesman and soldier of the nineteenth century. This dish, however, bears his name not because he was a great gourmet but because the finished joint was thought to resemble one of the brown shiny military boots which were called after him.

SERVES 8

1.4 kg (3 lb) fillet of beef
pepper
15 ml (1 tbsp) vegetable oil
40 g (1½ oz) butter
225 g (8 oz) button mushrooms, sliced
175 g (6 oz) smooth liver pâté
368 g (13 oz) packet frozen puff pastry, thawed
1 egg, beaten, to glaze

1. Trim and tie up the fillet at intervals so it retains its shape. Season to taste with pepper. Heat the oil and 15 g (½ oz) of the butter in a large frying pan, add the meat and fry briskly on all sides. Press down with a wooden spoon while frying to seal well.
2. Roast at 220°C (425°F) mark 7 for 20 minutes, then set the beef aside to allow it to cool and remove the string.
3. Meanwhile, cook the mushrooms in the remaining butter until soft; leave until cold, then blend with the pâté.
4. On a lightly floured surface, roll out the pastry to a large rectangle about 33×28 cm (13×11 inches) and 0.5 cm (¼ inch) thick.
5. Spread the pâté mixture down the centre of the pastry. Place the meat on top in the centre. Brush the edges of the pastry with the egg.
6. Fold the pastry edges over lengthways and turn the parcel over so that the join is underneath. Fold the ends under the meat on a baking sheet.
7. Decorate with leaves cut from the pastry trimmings. Brush with the remaining egg and bake at 220°C (425°F) mark 7 for 50–60 minutes, depending how well done you like your beef, covering with foil after 25 minutes. Allow the Beef Wellington to rest for 10 minutes before serving.

BEEF WELLINGTON
Tie the beef fillet at regular intervals.

Fold the pastry edges over to cover the meat.

BEEF CUTS

*We all
enjoy traditional British beef
dishes using cuts like sirloin, rib
or topside for Roast Beef and
Yorkshire (see recipe, page 124)
or silverside for boiled beef (see
recipes, opposite). However,
today's demand is increasingly
for quick-cooking cuts which are
ready-trimmed for convenience
and economy, and lean for
health, often labelled according
to fat content (e.g. less than 5%,
10% or 15%).*

*For a roasting joint, boneless rib,
or a combination of rolled and
boned back and top rib, and
rolled top rump are good choices.*

*New small beef cuts include
specially tenderised quick-grill as
well as flash-fry steak, and thin
slices of beef such as topside for
making beef olives (see recipe,
page 129).*

*Trimmed steak for braising and
stewing is sold cubed or sliced.
Extra lean mince is available
fine-textured for hamburgers
and coarse-cut for dishes like
shepherd's pie.*

*Beef cuts often have different
names in different parts of the
country but are becoming
increasingly standardised.*

SPICED BEEF

NORTHERN IRELAND AND THE MIDLANDS

*If the meat has not had a prolonged salting it may not need
soaking, so check with your butcher when buying. Leisurely
simmering ensures that the silverside is meltingly tender and
a spicy mixture spread over it before roasting keeps the joint
moist as it takes on a delicious flavour.*

SERVES 6

1.8 kg (4 lb) salted rolled silverside
1 medium onion, skinned and sliced
4 medium carrots, sliced
1 small turnip, peeled and sliced
8 cloves
100 g (4 oz) dark soft brown sugar
2.5 ml (½ tsp) mustard powder
5 ml (1 tsp) ground cinnamon
juice of 1 lemon

1. If necessary, soak the meat in cold water for several
hours or overnight, then rinse. Tie up the meat to form
a neat joint and put in a large saucepan or flameproof
casserole with the vegetables.
2. Cover with water and bring slowly to the boil. Skim
the surface, cover and simmer for 3–4 hours, until
tender. Leave to cool completely in the liquid for
3–4 hours.
3. Drain the meat well, then put into a roasting tin and
stick the cloves into the fat. Mix together the

remaining ingredients and spread over the meat.
4. Bake at 180°C (350°F) mark 4 for 45 minutes to
1 hour, until tender, basting from time to time. Serve
hot or cold.

BOILED BEEF
AND CARROTS

THE SOUTH-EAST

*Immortalised by the old music hall song, this is a truly
traditional Cockney dish. The length of time the meat is
soaked depends on how salty it is; check with the butcher.
The greyish colour turns an appetising pink when cooked.*

SERVES 6

✳

1.6 kg (3½ lb) lean salted silverside or brisket of beef
bouquet garni
6 black peppercorns, lightly crushed
2 small onions, skinned and quartered
8 cloves
2 small turnips, peeled and quartered
2 celery sticks, chopped
1 leek, trimmed, chopped and washed
18 small carrots

1. If necessary, soak the meat in cold water for several
hours or overnight, then rinse. Tie up into a neat joint.
2. Place the beef in a large saucepan, add just enough

SPICED BEEF. A handsome
joint makes a pleasant change
from the Christmas turkey.
The meat has a tangy,
mustard-flavoured crust,
which darkens to a
mouthwatering brown during
cooking.

BOILED BEEF AND
CARROTS. Look for carrots
which still have some of their
feathery foliage, and leave the
stems on while they cook for a
pretty effect. Long, slow
cooking ensures that the meat
is beautifully tender.

water to cover and bring slowly to the boil. Skim the
surface, add the bouquet garni, peppercorns, onions,
each quarter stuck with a clove, turnip, celery and leek.
Lower the heat and simmer very gently for about
2 hours.

3. Add the small carrots and simmer gently for a further
30–40 minutes or until the carrots are tender.

4. Carefully transfer the beef and small carrots to a
warmed serving plate and keep warm.

5. Skim the fat from the surface of the cooking liquor,
then strain. Boil the liquid to reduce slightly, then pour
into a warmed sauceboat or jug.

6. Serve the beef surrounded by the carrots, with the
sauce handed separately. Accompany with peas and
mashed potatoes or dumplings.

BRAISED BEEF WITH CHESTNUTS AND CELERY

COUNTRYWIDE

*An unusual casserole, which dates from the eighteenth
century. Make it in the late autumn and winter when both
celery and fresh chestnuts are available. It's well worth
spending the extra time needed to shell the chestnuts, as they
do add a very special flavour to the finished dish.*

SERVES 6

✳

18 fresh chestnuts, skins split

15 g (½ oz) butter

15 ml (1 tbsp) vegetable oil

2 bacon rashers, rinded and chopped

900 g (2 lb) stewing steak, cubed

1 medium onion, skinned and chopped

15 ml (1 tbsp) plain flour

300 ml (½ pint) brown ale

300 ml (½ pint) beef stock

pinch of freshly grated nutmeg

finely grated rind and juice of 1 orange

salt and pepper

3 celery sticks, chopped

chopped fresh parsley, to garnish

1. Cook the chestnuts in simmering water for about
7 minutes. Peel off the thick outer skin and thin inner
skin while still warm, removing from the water one at a
time.

2. Heat the butter and oil in a flameproof casserole,
add the bacon and beef in batches and cook, stirring
occasionally, until browned. Remove the meat with a
slotted spoon.

3. Add the onion to the casserole and fry, stirring,
until softened. Drain off most of the fat. Return the
meat to the casserole, sprinkle in the flour and cook,
stirring, for 1–2 minutes.

4. Stir in the brown ale, stock, nutmeg, orange juice
and half the rind. Season to taste. Bring to the boil, stir
well to loosen the sediment, then add the chestnuts.
Cover tightly with foil and a lid and bake at 170°C
(325°F) mark 3 for about 45 minutes.

5. After 45 minutes baking time, add the celery to the
casserole and continue baking for about 1 hour until the
meat is tender. Serve with the remaining orange rind
and the parsley sprinkled over the top.

BEEF IN STOUT. Leave this stew to simmer gently until the meat is meltingly tender. The stout lends a good depth of flavour.

BEEF POCKETS STUFFED WITH MUSHROOMS To form pocket, make horizontal cut in steak without cutting all the way through.

BEEF IN STOUT

NORTHERN IRELAND

This is a simple dish but one that's packed with goodness. Stout gets its dark colour and bitterness from the roasted malt or barley used in its brewing. It makes a delicious gravy when used in a casserole, and a touch of sugar brings out the flavour even more.

SERVES 4–6

15 g (½ oz) butter
about 15 ml (1 tbsp) vegetable oil
900 g (2 lb) stewing steak, cut into 5 cm (2 inch) cubes
4 medium onions, skinned and sliced
225 g (8 oz) button mushrooms, halved
salt and pepper
30 ml (2 tbsp) plain flour
300 ml (½ pint) stout
1 bay leaf
5 ml (1 tsp) soft dark brown sugar

1. Heat the butter and oil in a large flameproof casserole and cook the meat for 10 minutes, until browned all over. Remove the meat from the pan with a slotted spoon.

2. Add the onions and mushrooms to the pan, adding more oil if necessary, and fry until softened. Season to taste, add the flour and stir well so that the flour absorbs the fat.

3. Return the meat to the pan, pour in the stout and add the bay leaf and brown sugar. Stir well to mix.

4. Cover and cook gently, either on top of the stove or in the oven at 180°C (350°F) mark 4 for about 2½ hours or until the meat is tender.

BEEF POCKETS STUFFED WITH MUSHROOMS

SCOTLAND

Mushrooms make marvellous stuffings and as a year-round crop are always available. Ginger wine is an English speciality which appeals to the British palate's desire for strong positive flavours. Even this small quantity makes a significant difference to the recipe.

SERVES 4

4 thick-cut steaks, each weighing 175 g (6 oz)
salt and pepper
15 g (½ oz) butter
175 g (6 oz) mushrooms, finely chopped
1 garlic clove, skinned and crushed
1 large onion, skinned and finely chopped
15 ml (1 tbsp) chopped fresh parsley
15 ml (1 tbsp) ginger wine
15 ml (1 tbsp) fresh wholemeal breadcrumbs
15 ml (1 tbsp) fresh double cream

1. Using a sharp, pointed knife, make a horizontal cut in each steak without cutting all the way through. Season to taste.

2. Melt the butter in a medium saucepan and lightly cook the mushrooms, garlic and onion for 5 minutes, until softened. Remove from the heat.

3. Add the parsley, ginger wine, breadcrumbs and cream. Mix together well.

4. Generously fill each pocket of the steaks with the stuffing.

5. Grill the steaks for 5–15 minutes, until the meat is cooked to taste (see page 131 for times). Serve at once with new potatoes and broccoli.

TO MICROWAVE

Complete step 1. Melt the butter in a shallow dish on HIGH for 30 seconds. Add the mushrooms, garlic and onion and cook on HIGH for 7 minutes. Complete steps 3 and 4. Preheat a large browning dish on HIGH for 5–8 minutes or according to manufacturer's instructions. Quickly put the steaks in the browning dish and cook on HIGH for 2 minutes. Turn and cook on HIGH for 3–5 minutes, until cooked to taste. Serve with new potatoes and broccoli.

HEREFORD BEEF OLIVES

Hereford cattle produce some of the best beef in Britain, very tender with excellent flavour. Choose a snug-fitting dish for this recipe so the sauce does not evaporate.

SERVES 4

75 g (3 oz) streaky bacon rashers, rinded and finely chopped
1 small onion, skinned and chopped
10 ml (2 tsp) chopped fresh parsley
100 g (4 oz) fresh breadcrumbs
50 g (2 oz) shredded beef suet
1.25 ml (¼ tsp) dried mixed herbs
1 egg, size 6
1 lemon
salt and pepper
8 thin slices topside beef, weighing about 700 g (1½ lb)
15 ml (1 tbsp) prepared English mustard
45 ml (3 tbsp) seasoned flour
25 g (1 oz) butter
30 ml (2 tbsp) vegetable oil
450 ml (¾ pint) beef stock
2 medium onions, skinned and sliced

1. Mix the bacon with the onion, parsley, breadcrumbs, suet, herbs and egg. Add the grated rind of ½ of the lemon and 5 ml (1 tsp) juice and season.
2. Put the meat between greaseproof paper and beat out with a meat mallet or rolling pin.
3. Spread mustard thinly over the meat, then divide stuffing equally between the pieces. Roll up and secure with strong cotton or fine string. Toss in seasoned flour.
4. Heat the butter and oil in a shallow flameproof casserole into which all the beef olives will just fit. Brown them well, then remove from the pan.
5. Stir the remaining seasoned flour into the pan residue and brown lightly. Gradually stir in stock and bring to boil. Season to taste, then return meat to pan.
6. Scatter the onions over the meat. Cover and bake at 170°C (325°F) mark 3 for 1½ hours or until tender.

BEEF HARE

Although chuck steak is a tougher cut, it should be lean and not too fatty. When cooked slowly and cleverly spiced it comes up meltingly tender and, in this recipe, has a gamey flavour rather like hare.

SERVES 4

plain flour, to coat
salt and pepper

freshly grated nutmeg
900 g (2 lb) chuck steak, cut into 7.5 × 2.5 cm (3 × 1 inch) strips
5 ml (1 tbsp) celery seeds
8 cloves
1 medium onion, skinned and quartered
1 small young parsnip, peeled and grated
150 ml (¼ pint) dry red wine

1. Season the flour with salt and pepper and plenty of nutmeg, then toss the meat in it to coat, shaking off any excess.
2. Pack the meat into a deep 900 ml (1½ pint) ovenproof earthenware dish, scattering celery seeds in between the layers.
3. Stick 2 cloves into each onion quarter, then arrange the onion and parsnip on top of the meat. Pour in the wine, cover tightly and leave for about 2 hours.
4. Place in an oven at 220°C (425°F) mark 7 and immediately reduce the temperature to 170°C (325°F) mark 3. Bake for 2¼ hours or until the beef is tender.

HEREFORD BEEF OLIVES. Juicy rolls of succulent beef, wrapped round a herby filling and braised slowly in a well-seasoned stock.

STEAK AND KIDNEY PIE

THE NORTH

When originally developed, this dish used oysters rather than mushrooms for additional flavour, mushrooms being considerably the more expensive ingredient. Times have changed but the popularity of this filling dish has not. Be sure to cook the filling slowly and thoroughly to allow the different flavours to intermingle.

SERVES 4

❋ ⬗

200 g (7 oz) plain flour

salt and pepper

700 g (1½ lb) braising steak, trimmed and cubed

175 g (6 oz) ox kidney, cored and chopped

100 g (4 oz) butter

1–2 garlic cloves, skinned and crushed

1 large onion, skinned and chopped

100 g (4 oz) mushrooms

150 ml (¼ pint) beef stock

150 ml (¼ pint) brown ale

1 bay leaf

sprig of fresh thyme or 2.5 ml (½ tsp) dried thyme

15 ml (1 tbsp) Worcestershire sauce

15 ml (1 tbsp) tomato purée

fresh milk, to glaze

1. Season 25 g (1 oz) of the flour, then toss the steak and kidney in the flour, shaking off any excess.
2. Melt 25 g (1 oz) of the butter in a large saucepan and lightly fry the garlic, onion and mushrooms for 3 minutes. Add the steak, kidney and remaining coating flour and cook for 5 minutes, until lightly browned.
3. Gradually stir in the stock, ale, bay leaf, thyme, Worcestershire sauce and tomato purée. Cover and simmer gently for about 1¼ hours. Spoon the mixture into a 1.7 litre (3 pint) pie dish.
4. Put the remaining flour and a pinch of salt into a bowl. Rub in the remaining butter until the mixture resembles fine breadcrumbs. Add 60 ml (4 tbsp) cold water and mix to form a dough.
5. Roll out on a lightly floured work surface to 5 cm (2 inch) wider than the pie dish. Cut a 2.5 cm (1 inch) wide strip from the outer edge and place on the dampened rim of the dish. Brush the strip with water. Cover with the pastry lid, press lightly to seal the edges. Trim off excess pastry, knot the edges back to seal and crimp. Garnish with pastry leaves, brush with milk and bake at 200°C (400°F) mark 6 for 30–45 minutes.

For Steak and Kidney Pudding

Make a suet crust pastry by mixing 225 g (8 oz) self-raising flour, 75 g (3 oz) beef suet and a pinch of salt. Add about 120–150 ml (8–10 tbsp) cold water to mix into a soft dough. Roll out two-thirds of the dough on a lightly floured work surface and use to line a 1.7 litre (3 pint) pudding basin. Leave any extra pastry hanging over the sides. Complete steps 1, 2 and 3, then fill the pudding with the steak and kidney mixture. Brush the

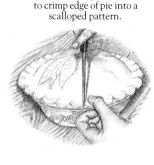

STEAK AND KIDNEY PIE. Use thumb and point of knife to crimp edge of pie into a scalloped pattern.

STEAK AND KIDNEY PIE. Crisp and light shortcrust pastry tops a mixture of richly flavoured meats in this all-time classic winter dish.

top edge of the pastry with water, roll out remaining pastry and lay over the pudding. Press the edges together and trim off extra pastry. Cover the top with loosely fitting greaseproof paper. Tie in place with string, put into a large pan with boiling water halfway up the sides of the basin. Simmer gently for 2 hours.

TO MICROWAVE

 Complete step 1. Dice the butter in a large bowl on HIGH for 45 seconds. Add the garlic, onion and mushrooms and cook on HIGH for 5–7 minutes. Add the meats and flour, cook on HIGH for 4 minutes. Gradually add the stock, 50 ml (2 fl oz) of the ale, bay leaf, thyme, Worcestershire sauce and tomato purée. Cook on HIGH for 10 minutes, stirring occasionally. Stand for 5 minutes, complete steps 4 and 5. *For a steak and kidney pudding,* cook on HIGH for 8 minutes and stand for 8 minutes.

GRILLED STEAKS WITH HORSERADISH SAUCE

COUNTRYWIDE

Horseradish is the traditional fiery accompaniment to roast beef but it's equally good served with a sizzling hot steak. Use fresh horseradish root if you can find it – but prepare to shed tears during the preparation. If you're lucky enough to come across it in jars, ready grated, you'll get the right results if you use half the quantity given below.

SERVES 4

30 ml (2 tbsp) creamed horseradish
5 ml (1 tsp) lemon juice
pinch of mustard powder
salt and pepper
75 ml (3 fl oz) fresh double cream
4 rump or sirloin steaks, each weighing about 225 g (8 oz)

1. To make the sauce, mix together the horseradish, lemon juice and mustard. Season to taste.
2. Whip the cream until stiff, then fold in the horseradish mixture. Turn into a serving bowl and chill until ready to serve. Eat the same day.
3. To cook the steaks, preheat the grill. Then cook, turning frequently, for the times below, depending how you like your steak. Season to taste.

COOKING TIMES FOR STEAKS
(total in minutes)

Thickness	Rare	Medium Rare	Well-done
2 cm (¾ inch)	5	9–10	12–15
2.5 cm (1 inch)	6–7	10	15
4 cm (1½ inches)	10	12–14	18–20

4. Serve hot with the horseradish sauce. Accompany with boiled new potatoes and a salad.

SIRLOIN STEAKS WITH TEWKESBURY MUSTARD

THE WEST

Beef and mustard are a traditional pair; Tewkesbury mustard gives an unusual flavour, being made from a mixture of crushed mustard seeds and grated horseradish. If you can't buy it, use a wholegrain mustard and, in any case, wash the dish down with a draught of good British beer.

SERVES 4

50 g (2 oz) Tewkesbury mustard
15 g (½ oz) plain flour
4 sirloin steaks, each weighing about 175 g (6 oz)
30 ml (2 tbsp) chopped fresh parsley
30 ml (2 tbsp) chopped fresh thyme

1. Mix together the mustard and flour, then spread on top of each steak.
2. Line a grill pan with foil, sprinkle with herbs and put the steaks on top. Grill for 5–15 minutes, turning them frequently until the steaks are cooked to taste (see previous recipe for times). Serve at once.

TO MICROWAVE

 Complete step 1. Preheat a large browning dish on HIGH for 8–10 minutes or according to manufacturer's instructions. Quickly put the herbs and steaks in the browning dish and cook on HIGH for 5–7 minutes, according to taste.

SIRLOIN STEAKS WITH TEWKESBURY MUSTARD. A simple but very effective way to liven up grilled steaks. The herb and mustard topping takes only a minute to make before spreading over the meat.

DORSET JUGGED STEAK

THE WEST

This traditional Dorset dish was often prepared to be eaten on days when the fair came to town since it is good tempered enough to wait until the revellers come home, although the forcemeat balls should not be cooked for too long. Jugging is a method of slow cooking which retains all the flavours of the meat while mingling them with those of the other ingredients.

SERVES 4

✳

700 g (1½ lb) stewing steak, cut into 2.5 cm (1 inch) cubes

25 g (1 oz) plain wholemeal flour

1 medium onion, skinned and sliced

4 cloves

salt and pepper

150 ml (¼ pint) port

about 450 ml (¾ pint) beef stock, to cover

225 g (8 oz) sausagemeat

50 g (2 oz) fresh wholemeal breadcrumbs

30 ml (2 tbsp) chopped fresh parsley

15 ml (1 tbsp) redcurrant jelly

1. Toss the meat in the flour, shaking off excess, and put into an ovenproof casserole.
2. Add the onion and cloves and season to taste. Pour in the port and just enough stock to cover the meat.
3. Cover the casserole and bake at 170°C (325°F) mark 3 for about 3 hours, until the meat is tender.
4. Meanwhile, mix together the sausagemeat, breadcrumbs and parsley and season to taste. With floured hands, form the mixture into 8 balls.
5. Forty minutes before the end of the cooking time, stir the redcurrant jelly into the casserole. Add the forcemeat balls and cook, uncovered, until the forcemeat balls are cooked and slightly brown. Skim off any excess fat and serve hot.

DORSET JUGGED STEAK. Chunks of steak and succulent forcemeat balls are cooked together in a port-enriched gravy, flavoured with just a hint of cloves.

CELERIAC AND MUSTARD BEEF
COUNTRYWIDE

It's easier to ask your butcher to cut the slices of silverside, rather than attempting to do it yourself. That way you need only buy as much as you need to make this juicy variation on beef olives. Bat the slices out until paper-thin so that they will be perfectly tender when cooked.

SERVES 4

✳

8 thin slices silverside, about 700 g (1½ lb) total weight
3 medium carrots, grated
1 medium onion, skinned and thinly sliced
175 g (6 oz) celeriac, grated and sprinkled with lemon juice
75 ml (5 tbsp) wholegrain mustard
75 ml (5 tbsp) chopped fresh parsley
salt and pepper
15 g (½ oz) butter
30 ml (2 tbsp) vegetable oil
30 ml (2 tbsp) plain flour
300 ml (½ pint) beef stock
60 ml (4 tbsp) Madeira or medium sherry
extra chopped fresh parsley, to garnish

1. Put the meat between 2 sheets of dampened greaseproof paper and bat out with a meat mallet or rolling pin.
2. Place all the vegetables in a saucepan. Cover with cold water and bring to the boil. Drain immediately.
3. Stir half the mustard and half the parsley into the vegetable mixture and season to taste.
4. Spoon a little of the vegetable mixture on to each slice of beef. Fold in the edges and roll up to enclose the filling. Secure with wooden cocktail sticks or tie neatly with strong cotton or fine string.
5. Heat the butter and oil in a large frying pan, add the beef rolls and brown quickly. Transfer to a 2 litre (3½ pint) ovenproof casserole with a slotted spoon.
6. Stir the flour into the frying pan. Cook, stirring, for 1–2 minutes, then gradually add the stock, Madeira, remaining mustard and parsley. Bring to the boil.
7. Pour the sauce over the beef, cover the casserole and bake at 180°C (350°F) mark 4 for about 1½ hours or until the beef is tender. Garnish with chopped parsley and serve hot. Accompany with boiled rice and seasonal vegetables.

STILTON STEAKS
THE MIDLANDS

Stilton is the only British cheese to have its name protected by copyright, which means that it can only be produced in the three counties of Derbyshire, Nottinghamshire and Leicestershire. It's a rich, creamy cheese, immediately recognisable with its pattern of blue veins, and has a distinctive mellow flavour.

SERVES 4

100 g (4 oz) Stilton cheese, crumbled
25 g (1 oz) butter, softened
50–75 g (2–3 oz) shelled walnut pieces, finely chopped
pepper
4 sirloin or fillet steaks, each weighing about 100–175 g (4–6 oz), trimmed

1. Put the cheese in a bowl and mash with a fork. Add the butter and walnuts and mix in. Season to taste.
2. Put the steaks on the grill rack and season with plenty of pepper. Put under a preheated hot grill and cook for 2–10 minutes on each side, according to the thickness of the steaks and how well done you like them (see page 131 for times).
3. Remove the steaks from under the grill, sprinkle the cheese and nut mixture evenly over them and press down with a palette knife. Grill for 1 further minute or until the topping is melted and bubbling. Serve hot, accompanied with boiled new potatoes and a mixed salad.

STILTON STEAKS. The mouthwateringly savoury cheese topping gets an unexpected crunchiness from finely chopped walnuts. Simple accompaniments are all that's needed to complete the meal.

STRIPS OF BEEF IN WHISKY SAUCE. The creamy sauce has a deliciously boozy flavour, and the dish is very quick to cook.

2. Stir in the liqueur and cream. Heat gently to reduce slightly. Serve at once with vegetables and brown rice.

TO MICROWAVE

 Preheat a large browning dish on HIGH for 8–10 minutes or according to manufacturer's instructions. Quickly put the butter, beef and onions in the browning dish. Cook on HIGH for 5–7 minutes, until meat is cooked to taste, stirring frequently. Stir in the liqueur and season to taste. Cook on HIGH for 1 minute, then stir in the cream and serve.

MEAT BALLS IN TOMATO SAUCE

COUNTRYWIDE

There's an Italian influence here. Serve these meat balls with spaghetti as a change from Bolognese sauce.

SERVES 4

| 150 g (5 oz) crustless wholemeal bread |
| 150 ml (¼ pint) fresh milk |
| 25 g (1 oz) butter |
| 20 ml (4 tsp) plain wholemeal flour |
| 200 ml (7 fl oz) beef stock |
| 397 g (14 oz) can tomatoes, sieved with their juice |
| pinch of sugar |
| 2.5 ml (½ tsp) dried thyme |
| salt and pepper |
| 1 large onion, skinned and finely chopped |
| 450 g (1 lb) lean minced beef |
| 5 ml (1 tsp) paprika |
| 15 ml (1 tbsp) vegetable oil |

1. Crumble the bread into a bowl, pour over the milk and leave to soak for about 30 minutes.
2. Meanwhile, put 15 g (½ oz) of the butter, flour and stock in a saucepan. Heat, whisking continuously, until the sauce thickens, boils and is smooth.
3. Add the tomatoes, sugar and thyme. Season to taste and simmer, covered, for 30 minutes.
4. Put the onion and the mince in a bowl and add the soaked bread together with any remaining milk and paprika. Season to taste. Using floured hands, shape the mixture into 16 balls.
5. Heat the oil and remaining butter in a frying pan, add the meat balls, a few at a time, and fry until browned all over.
6. Place the meat balls in a single layer in a shallow ovenproof serving dish and pour over the sauce. Cover and bake at 180°C (350°F) mark 4 for about 30 minutes. Serve hot, over spaghetti.

TO MICROWAVE

 Complete step 1. Meanwhile, put half the butter, flour and stock in a large bowl and cook on HIGH for

STRIPS OF BEEF IN WHISKY SAUCE

SCOTLAND

This quick-cooking dish requires prime meat. Whisky liqueur will reduce to a sweet glistening glaze.

SERVES 4

| 15 g (½ oz) butter |
| 700 g (1½ lb) sirloin steak, cut into strips |
| 1 large onion, skinned and chopped |
| 75 ml (3 tbsp) whisky liqueur such as Drambuie |
| 75 ml (3 fl oz) fresh double cream |
| salt and pepper |

1. Melt the butter in a medium frying pan. Add the beef strips and onion and cook for 5–10 minutes, until the beef is brown and cooked to taste.

3–4 minutes, whisking frequently until boiling and thickened. Add the tomatoes, sugar and thyme. Season to taste, cover and cook on HIGH for 15 minutes, stirring occasionally. Meanwhile, complete steps 4 and 5. Place the meatballs in a shallow dish, pour over the sauce, cover and cook on HIGH for 14 minutes or until cooked. Serve with freshly cooked spaghetti.

TEVIOTDALE PIE

SCOTLAND

Originating in the Borders where good meat is taken for granted, this dish is a kind of suet pie which makes a small amount of meat go a long way. Vegetables can be incorporated with the meat under the suet crust, making it a true one-pot meal if liked.

SERVES 4

---

450 g (1 lb) lean minced beef

1 medium onion, skinned and chopped

300 ml (½ pint) beef stock

5 ml (1 tsp) Worcestershire sauce

salt and pepper

225 g (8 oz) self-raising flour

25 g (1 oz) cornflour

75 g (3 oz) shredded beef suet

about 300 ml (½ pint) fresh milk

1.   Put the meat in a large saucepan, preferably non-stick, over medium heat and cook in its own fat until beginning to brown. Add the onion and cook for a further 5 minutes until softened.
2.   Add the stock and Worcestershire sauce. Season to taste and simmer for 15–20 minutes.
3.   Put the self-raising flour, cornflour and suet in a bowl, then gradually stir in the milk to form a thick batter. Season well.
4.   Put the meat in a 1.1 litre (2 pint) pie dish. Cover with the batter mixture. Bake at 180°C (350°F) mark 4 for about 30–35 minutes, until risen and browned.

BEEF IN WINE WITH WALNUTS

COUNTRYWIDE

Ground walnuts add an interesting texture to this tasty casserole. Buy walnut pieces, which are cheaper than halves. Shin of beef is a good value cut which can be left cooking in a low oven for hours without spoiling.

SERVES 6

✳

---

900 g (2 lb) shin of beef, trimmed and cut into 2.5 cm (1 inch) cubes

150 ml (¼ pint) dry red wine

3 medium parsnips, peeled

15 ml (1 tbsp) vegetable oil

15 g (½ oz) butter

1 small onion, skinned and finely chopped

1 garlic clove, skinned and crushed

5 ml (1 tsp) ground allspice

30 ml (2 tbsp) plain flour

150 ml (¼ pint) beef stock

50 g (2 oz) shelled walnut pieces, ground

salt and pepper

chopped walnuts, to garnish

1.   Put the beef in a bowl with the wine and mix well. Cover and leave to marinate overnight, stirring occasionally.
2.   Cut the parsnips into 5 cm (2 inch) lengths, about 1 cm (½ inch) wide. Drain the meat from the marinade, reserving the marinade. Heat the oil and butter in a large frying pan, add the beef, a few pieces at a time, and brown quickly. Transfer to an ovenproof casserole with a slotted spoon.
3.   Add the onion and garlic to the frying pan and fry until beginning to brown. Stir in the allspice, flour, reserved marinade, stock and walnuts. Bring to the boil, stirring constantly.
4.   Pour into the casserole and add the parsnips. Season lightly to taste. Cover and bake at 170°C (325°F) mark 3 for 2½–3 hours or until the meat is really tender.
5.   Serve hot, straight from the casserole, sprinkled with the chopped walnuts. Accompany with boiled rice and a green salad.

BEEF IN WINE WITH WALNUTS. Soaking the meat overnight in red wine guarantees a fine flavour and tender result in this casserole, which also uses chunks of parsnip.

MEAT LOAF WITH ONION SAUCE. An economical recipe, to serve hot one day, cold the next. The loaf has a good, firm texture and plenty of flavour.

MEAT LOAF WITH ONION SAUCE

COUNTRYWIDE

A tasty and economical dish that's good served hot with the onion sauce, or cold with pickles and chutney. Do choose good quality mince, as if the meat is too cheap it will tend to be fatty and lacking in flavour.

SERVES 4

25 g (1 oz) butter
2 medium onions, skinned and finely chopped
5 ml (1 tsp) paprika
450 g (1 lb) lean minced beef
75 g (3 oz) fresh breadcrumbs
1 garlic clove, skinned and crushed
60 ml (4 tbsp) tomato purée
15 ml (1 tbsp) chopped fresh mixed herbs or 5 ml (1 tsp) dried
salt and pepper
1 egg, beaten
15 g (½ oz) plain wholemeal flour
300 ml (½ pint) fresh milk

1. Grease a 900 ml (1½ pint) loaf tin, then line the base with greased greaseproof paper. Set aside.
2. Melt 15 g (½ oz) of the butter in a frying pan. Add half of the onions and cook until softened. Add the paprika and cook for 1 minute, stirring. Remove from the heat.

3. Add the beef, breadcrumbs, garlic, tomato purée and herbs. Season to taste. Stir thoroughly until evenly mixed, then bind with the beaten egg.
4. Spoon the mixture into the loaf tin, level the surface and cover tightly with foil. Stand the tin in a roasting tin and pour in water to a depth of 2.5 cm (1 inch). Bake the meat loaf at 180°C (350°F) mark 4 for 1½ hours.
5. Meanwhile, melt the remaining butter in a saucepan. Add the rest of the onion and cook over low heat, stirring occasionally, for 10 minutes until soft but not coloured. Add the flour and cook over low heat, stirring, for 1–2 minutes.
6. Remove the pan from the heat and gradually stir in the milk, stirring after each addition to prevent lumps forming. Bring to the boil slowly and continue to cook, stirring continuously, then simmer for 2–3 minutes until thick and smooth. Simmer very gently for a further 2–3 minutes. Add salt and pepper to taste. To serve, turn out the meat loaf on to a warmed serving plate and peel off the lining paper. Serve with the hot onion sauce. Accompany with creamed potatoes and courgettes.

TO MICROWAVE

Complete step 1 using a 900 ml (2 pint) loaf dish. Melt 15 g (½ oz) of the butter on HIGH in a large bowl for 30 seconds. Add half of the onions and the paprika, cover and cook on HIGH for 5–7 minutes, until the onions are softened. Complete step 3. Spoon into the loaf dish, stand on a roasting rack, cover with kitchen paper and cook on MEDIUM for 25 minutes or until cooked. Leave to stand for 5 minutes. Meanwhile, complete the recipe.

VEAL

SCOTCH COLLOPS
SCOTLAND

Collop is another word for escalope, the thick slice of meat off the bone which is cut across the grain. Collops may be beef, lamb or venison, as well as veal, and should always be flattened before use. A rolling pin will do less damage to the meat fibres than a meat mallet.

SERVES 4

4 veal escalopes, each weighing 175 g (6 oz), halved
40 g (1½ oz) butter
1 small onion, skinned and chopped
175 ml (6 fl oz) dry white wine
400 ml (14 fl oz) veal or chicken stock
5–10 ml (1–2 tsp) mushroom ketchup
about 15 ml (1 tbsp) lemon juice
10 ml (2 tsp) plain flour
salt and pepper
pinch of ground mace
crisp bacon rolls, fried button mushrooms, lemon twists and parsley sprigs, to garnish

1. Flatten each veal escalope between two sheets of greaseproof paper with a rolling pin or meat mallet.
2. Melt 25 g (1 oz) of the butter in a large frying pan, add the veal and cook for about 2 minutes on each side. Transfer to a warmed serving plate and keep warm.
3. Add the onion to the pan and cook for about 3 minutes, stirring frequently, until softened but not browned. Stir in the wine and boil until almost evaporated. Stir in the stock, mushroom ketchup and lemon juice. Bring to the boil and simmer until reduced to 225 ml (8 fl oz).
4. Work the flour into the remaining butter, then gradually whisk into the stock to thicken slightly. Season with salt, pepper and mace, taste and add more mushroom ketchup and lemon juice, if necessary.
5. Arrange the collops, overlapping each other, on the serving dish and spoon some sauce down the centre. Garnish with bacon rolls, mushrooms, lemon twists and parsley. Serve remaining sauce separately.

VEAL WITH COURGETTES
COUNTRYWIDE

Courgettes are grown in Britain, from seed, sown under glass early in the year. Strips of veal, combined with the crispness of the courgettes and the sharpness of grapefruit, makes this a special dish.

SERVES 4

2 grapefruits
30 ml (2 tbsp) vegetable oil
450 g (1 lb) veal fillet in one piece, very thinly sliced
15 g (½ oz) butter
450 g (1 lb) courgettes, thinly sliced
salt and pepper

1. Using a potato peeler, pare rind off one grapefruit. Cut into julienne strips. Squeeze juice and reserve.
2. Using a serrated knife, peel the remaining grapefruit, removing all skin and pith. Thinly slice the flesh and reserve.
3. Heat the oil in a large frying pan. Add the veal slices, a few at a time, and fry for 2–3 minutes until well browned on both sides. Transfer to a warmed serving dish. Cover and keep warm in a low oven.
4. Add the butter to the pan then fry the courgettes for 2–3 minutes until beginning to brown. Add the julienne strips and 90 ml (6 tbsp) of the reserved juice.
5. Bring to the boil then simmer for 4–5 minutes or until the liquid is well reduced. Stir in the reserved flesh and season with salt and pepper to taste.
6. Spoon the contents of the pan over the veal and serve immediately.

VEAL CUTS

Veal is a naturally very lean, tender meat, with virtually no fat or gristle, and many veal cuts contain less than 5% fat.

Veal escalope, cut across the grain of the meat, is one of the most popular cuts (see recipes, pages 137, 139).

Cutlets and rump steaks, good with a creamy mushroom sauce, or with apples, are new additions to the veal range.

Veal braising steak, or pie veal as it is traditionally called, makes a delicious blanquette (see recipe, right) and veal mince is perfect for Veal and Ham Pie and light-textured meatballs.

VEAL AND HAM PIE. A lovely firm, meaty filling, with its surprise centrepiece of hard-boiled egg, is baked in a rich, golden crust.

VEAL AND HAM PIE

COUNTRYWIDE

This raised meat pie with a row of hard-boiled eggs at its centre is traditional British picnic food. The hot-water crust should not be allowed to cool completely before lining the tin. This type of pastry is particularly good for pies as it absorbs the delicious juices inside while keeping its crisp crust outside.

SERVES 8–10

450 g (1 lb) minced veal
100 g (4 oz) boiled ham, minced
30 ml (2 tbsp) chopped fresh parsley
2.5 ml (½ tsp) ground mace
1.25 ml (¼ tsp) ground bay leaves
finely grated rind of 1 lemon
2 medium onions, skinned and finely chopped
salt and pepper
100 g (4 oz) lard, plus extra for greasing tin
350 g (12 oz) plain wholemeal flour
1 egg yolk
3 eggs, hard-boiled and shelled
10 ml (2 tsp) powdered aspic jelly

1. Grease a 1.4 litre (2½ pint) loaf tin and line the base with greased greaseproof paper.
2. Put the first 7 ingredients in a bowl, 5 ml (1 tsp) salt and 1.25 ml (¼ tsp) pepper. Mix well to combine.
3. Put the lard and 200 ml (7 fl oz) water in a saucepan and gently heat until the lard has melted. Bring to the boil, remove from the heat and tip in the flour with 2.5 ml (½ tsp) salt. Beat well to form a soft dough.
4. Beat the egg yolk into the dough. Cover with a damp tea towel and rest in a warm place for 20 minutes, until the dough is elastic and easy to work. Do not allow the dough to cool.
5. Pat two-thirds of the pastry into the base and sides of the prepared tin, making sure it is evenly distributed. Press in half of the meat mixture and place the eggs down the centre. Fill with the remaining meat mixture.
6. Roll out the remaining pastry for the lid. Cover the pie with the pastry and seal the edges. Use the pastry trimmings to decorate the top, then make 1 large hole in the centre of the pie.
7. Bake at 180°C (350°F) mark 4 for 1½ hours. If necessary, cover the pastry with foil towards the end of cooking to prevent overbrowning. Leave to cool for 3–4 hours.
8. Make up the aspic jelly to 300 ml (½ pint) with water. Cool for about 10 minutes.
9. Pour the liquid aspic through the hole in the top of the pie. Chill the pie for about 1 hour. Leave to stand at room temperature for about 1 hour before removing from the tin.

VEAL BLANQUETTE

THE SOUTH-EAST

Veal is a delicate, tender meat which is not fatty. It should look moist and be a good deep pink colour. This simple recipe provides a creamy sauce which enhances the flavour of the meat without masking it.

SERVES 4–6

✳ at the end of step 3

700 g (1½ lb) pie veal, trimmed and cubed
2 medium onions, skinned and chopped
2 medium carrots, chopped
squeeze of lemon juice
bouquet garni
salt and pepper
25 g (1 oz) butter
45 ml (3 tbsp) plain flour
1 egg yolk
30–45 ml (2–3 tbsp) fresh single cream
4–6 streaky bacon rashers, rinded, rolled and grilled
chopped fresh parsley, to garnish

1. Put the meat, onions, carrots, lemon juice and bouquet garni and seasonings into a large saucepan with enough water to cover. Cover and gently simmer for about 1 hour, until the meat is tender.
2. Strain off the cooking liquid, reserving 568 ml (1 pint) and keep the meat and vegetables warm.
3. Melt the butter in a pan, stir in the flour and cook gently for 1 minute. Remove from the heat and gradually stir in the reserved liquid. Return to the heat, slowly bring to the boil and continue cooking, stirring, until the sauce thickens.
4. Adjust the seasoning, remove from the heat and when slightly cooled stir in the egg yolk and cream. Add the meat and vegetables and reheat without boiling for 5 minutes. Serve garnished with the bacon rolls and parsley.

VEAL ESCALOPES IN
MUSHROOM SAUCE. The
wafer-thin slices of meat are
rolled round a chunky apple
and celery stuffing and served
with a delicately flavoured
sauce.

VEAL ESCALOPES IN MUSHROOM SAUCE

COUNTRYWIDE

Veal is the best choice for this dish, as it has a tenderness and subtle flavour that's hard to beat. If you can't find veal, however, slices of turkey or pork fillet or tenderloin can be used instead. Fromage frais adds smoothness to the sauce.

SERVES 4

4 veal escalopes, each weighing 175 g (6 oz)
2 slices cooked ham, halved
50 g (2 oz) butter
1 stick celery, chopped
1 eating apple, peeled and chopped
25 g (1 oz) Cheddar cheese, grated
1 small onion, skinned and chopped
100 g (4 oz) button mushrooms, sliced
25 g (1 oz) plain flour
300 ml (½ pint) fresh milk
salt and pepper
30 ml (2 tbsp) fromage frais
celery leaves, to garnish

1. Put each escalope between a sheet of greaseproof paper and beat till thin with a meat mallet or rolling pin.

2. Place a ham slice on each escalope.

3. Melt 15 g (½ oz) of the butter in a large frying pan and lightly fry the celery and apple for 3–4 minutes. Stir in the cheese.

4. Place some of the stuffing on each escalope and roll up, securing with wooden cocktail sticks or fine string or strong cotton.

5. Melt the remaining butter in the pan. Add the veal rolls, brown on all sides and cook for 10 minutes. Remove from the pan, place on a warmed serving plate and keep hot.

6. Add the onion and mushrooms to the pan and cook about 5 minutes, until softened. Stir in the flour and cook for 2 minutes, then gradually add the milk, stirring continuously, until the sauce thickens, boils and is smooth. Simmer for 1–2 minutes. Season to taste.

7. Stir in the fromage frais. Pour the sauce over the escalopes and garnish with celery leaves. Serve at once.

TO MICROWAVE

Complete steps 1 and 2. Melt half the butter in a shallow dish on HIGH for 30 seconds. Add the celery and apple and cook on HIGH for 3 minutes. Stir in the cheese. Complete step 4. Melt remaining butter in the same dish on HIGH for 1 minute, add the veal and cook on HIGH for 3½–4 minutes. Complete the remainder of step 5. Add the onion and mushrooms to the dish, cook on HIGH for 5–7 minutes, then stir in the flour and milk. Cook on HIGH for 4–5 minutes, until boiling and thickened, stirring frequently. Season to taste. Complete step 7.

PORK

ROAST PORK WITH APPLES
COUNTRYWIDE

Crisp crackling is one of the best things about roast pork. To make sure that yours is good and crunchy, score deeply through the skin with a sharp knife, following the natural grain of the meat, then rub in butter and coarse salt before roasting. Baked apples make a delicious accompaniment.

SERVES 6–8

1.6 kg (3½ lb) loin of pork
40 g (1½ oz) butter
coarse salt
fresh rosemary sprig
6 large Cox's Orange Pippin apples, cored
salt and pepper
150 ml (¼ pint) dry white wine (optional)
150 ml (¼ pint) chicken stock
fresh watercress sprigs, to garnish

1. Score the pork rind all over with a sharp knife. Rub with the butter, then sprinkle with coarse salt.
2. Place the rosemary on a rack in a roasting tin, put the pork on top and roast at 180°C (350°F) mark 4 for 2 hours.
3. Season the apples to taste inside and make a shallow cut through the skin around the apples about one third of the way down. Place in a tin or dish and baste with some of the fat from the pork. Cook on a lower shelf for the last 30 minutes of the cooking time.
4. Keep the pork warm on a rack. Drain off most of the fat from the roasting tin, leaving the meat juices. Stir in the wine, if using, loosening the sediment at the bottom of the pan. Boil until almost completely evaporated. Stir in the stock and boil for 2–3 minutes. Strain into a sauceboat.
5. Arrange the apples around the pork, garnish with watercress and serve accompanied by the gravy.

OPPOSITE
ROAST PORK WITH
APPLES. A sprig of rosemary,
placed under the joint during
cooking, imparts a subtle
flavour. Whole baked apples
are an attractive and unusual
alternative to apple sauce.

LEFT
LIKKY PIE. A flavoursome
sauce, enriched with cream
and eggs, is used in the filling
of this pie, which also
contains leeks and tender
cubes of pork.

PORK FILLET IN MUSTARD CREAM SAUCE

THE WEST

A rich dish combining the best of the West – pork, mustard and cream. Take care when flattening the pork not to use the indented side of a meat mallet or it will look battered.

SERVES 4

700 g (1½ lb) pork fillet or tenderloin, cut into 1.25 cm (½ inch) slices

15 g (½ oz) butter

15 ml (1 tbsp) vegetable oil

1 garlic clove, skinned and crushed

150 ml (¼ pint) medium-dry white wine

150 ml (5 fl oz) fresh soured cream

50 ml (2 tbsp) mild wholegrain mustard

salt and pepper

1. Slightly flatten each piece of pork with a rolling pin or meat mallet.
2. Heat the butter and oil in a large frying pan and fry the garlic for 1 minute without browning it. Add the meat and brown on both sides.
3. Push the meat to one side of the pan and pour in the wine. Stir to loosen any sediment at the bottom of the pan, then add the soured cream and mustard. Mix the meat into the sauce and cook for 2–3 minutes, stirring. Season with salt and pepper. Serve hot.

LIKKY PIE

THE WEST

This feast-day dish, more grammatically known as Leek Pie, has a delicate subtle flavour.

SERVES 4

✳ before step 5

225 g (8 oz) leeks, trimmed, sliced and washed

salt and pepper

450 g (1 lb) lean boneless pork, cut into 2.5 cm (1 inch) cubes

150 ml (¼ pint) fresh milk

75 ml (3 fl oz) fresh single cream

2 eggs, lightly beaten

212 g (7½ oz) packet frozen puff pastry, thawed

1. Parboil the leeks in salted water for about 5 minutes. Drain well. Fill a 1.1 litre (2 pint) pie dish with the leeks and pork. Season to taste and pour in the milk.
2. Cover with foil and bake at 200°C (400°F) mark 6 for about 1 hour. (Don't worry if it looks curdled.)
3. Stir the cream into the eggs, then pour into the dish. Allow the pie to cool.
4. Roll out the pastry on a lightly floured surface to 5 cm (2 inches) wider than the dish. Cut a 2.5 cm (1 inch) strip from the outer edge and use to line the dampened rim of the pie dish. Dampen the pastry rim with water, cover with the pastry lid and seal the edges well, then knock up and flute. Make a hole in the centre of the pie and use pastry trimmings to decorate.
5. Bake at 220°C (425°F) mark 7 for about 25–30 minutes, until risen and golden brown.

POT ROAST OF PORK AND RED CABBAGE

THE EASTERN COUNTIES

Pork shoulder is an economical cut that is good for pot roasting. Cabbage and apple are traditional accompaniments to pork. Here they are cooked with the meat and take on a delicious flavour from the juices.

SERVES 4

45 ml (3 tbsp) red wine vinegar

450 g (1 lb) red cabbage, shredded

225 g (8 oz) cooking apple, peeled, cored and sliced

15 ml (1 tbsp) demerara sugar

15 ml (1 tbsp) plain flour

salt and pepper

700 g (1½ lb) boneless pork shoulder, rinded

chopped fresh parsley, to garnish

1. Bring a large saucepan of water with 15 ml (1 tbsp) of the vinegar to the boil. When boiling, add the cabbage and bring back to the boil, then drain well.
2. Place the apple slices and the cabbage in an ovenproof casserole just wide enough to hold the pork joint.
3. Add the sugar, the remaining vinegar and the flour. Season to taste and stir together well.
4. Slash the fat side of the joint several times and sprinkle with salt and pepper. Place on top of the cabbage and cover the casserole.
5. Bake at 190°C (375°F) mark 5 for about 1¾ hours or until the pork is tender. Serve the pork sliced on a warmed serving platter, surrounded by cabbage. Garnish with chopped parsley and serve the remaining cabbage in a serving dish. Accompany with mashed potatoes.

SOMERSET HONEYED PORK STEW

THE WEST

Pork lends itself to sweet sauces with a touch of tartness which counteract the rich flavour of the meat. Pork and honey go particularly well together. Try to buy Somerset or other regional honey which has a strong flavour and scent which recalls the flowers on which the bees have feasted.

SERVES 4–6

450 g (1 lb) lean belly pork, rinded, boned and cut into chunky cubes

225 g (8 oz) dried black-eye or haricot beans, soaked overnight in cold water

15 ml (1 tbsp) clear honey

568 ml (1 pint) chicken stock

300 ml (½ pint) apple juice

1 medium onion, skinned and stuck with a few whole cloves

bouquet garni

3 medium carrots, peeled and sliced

2 leeks, trimmed, sliced and washed

2 celery sticks, sliced

30 ml (2 tbsp) Worcestershire sauce

15 ml (1 tbsp) tomato purée

salt and pepper

1. Cook the pork in a flameproof casserole over a brisk heat until the fat runs.
2. Drain the beans and add to the pork with the honey, stock, apple juice, onion and bouquet garni. Slowly bring to the boil, then cover and simmer for 1 hour or until the beans are just becoming tender.
3. Add the carrots, leeks and celery to the casserole with the Worcestershire sauce and tomato purée, season to taste. Continue simmering for a further 15–30 minutes or until the beans are really tender. Discard the bouquet garni before serving. Accompany with crusty bread.

PORK CHOPS WITH CHEESE AND BEER

THE WEST

This substantial savoury dish combines good home-produced ingredients. Rutland cheese is an unusual mixture made from Cheddar, beer, garlic and parsley. If you can't find it, use plain Cheddar and add garlic and parsley to the mixture.

SERVES 4

✳ ▱

4 loin chops, each weighing 175 g (6 oz)

100 g (4 oz) Rutland cheese, grated

5 ml (1 tsp) prepared English mustard

45 ml (3 tbsp) brown ale

tomato halves and watercress sprigs, to garnish

1. Grill the chops under a moderate grill for 7–10 minutes depending on the thickness. Turn over and grill for 7–10 minutes, until cooked through.
2. Mix together the cheese, mustard and brown ale. Spread over the chops and grill until the cheese has melted. Transfer to a warm serving plate and garnish with tomato halves and watercress sprigs.

TO MICROWAVE

▱ Remove the fat from the chops. Preheat a large browning dish on HIGH for 5–8 minutes or according to manufacturer's instructions. Quickly put the chops in the browning dish. Cook on HIGH for 5 minutes, turn over and cook on HIGH for 5 minutes. Stand, covered, for 5 minutes. Mix together the cheese, mustard and brown ale, then spread over the chops. Cook on HIGH for 2 minutes. Complete the remainder of step 2.

PORK STEAKS WITH
PEPPERS
COUNTRYWIDE

A quick and easy dish with a piquant sauce that makes itself. Sweet peppers are grown under glass on a small scale in Britain and these are available from May to October. Choose fresh, bright peppers with firm, unwrinkled skin. Store for a few days if necessary in the salad drawer of the fridge.

SERVES 4

15 ml (1 tbsp) vegetable oil
15 g (½ oz) butter
1 medium onion, skinned and chopped
2.5 cm (1 inch) piece fresh root ginger, peeled and finely grated
1 garlic clove, skinned and crushed
4 boneless pork loin steaks, each weighing 150 g (5 oz)
1 red pepper, seeded and thinly sliced
1 green pepper, seeded and thinly sliced
45 ml (3 tbsp) dry sherry
30 ml (2 tbsp) soy sauce
150 ml (¼ pint) unsweetened pineapple juice
salt and pepper

1. Heat the oil and butter in a large frying pan, add the onion, ginger and garlic and gently fry for 5 minutes, until soft. Push to one side of the pan.
2. Add the steaks and brown on both sides, then add the remaining ingredients and mix thoroughly together.
3. Cover tightly and simmer gently for 8–10 minutes, until the steaks are tender and the peppers are soft. Transfer the steaks and peppers to warmed serving plates. Bring the remaining liquid in the pan to the boil and boil for 2–3 minutes until reduced slightly. Spoon over the steaks and serve with boiled rice.

PORK IN PLUM SAUCE. Fruit works well in offsetting the fattiness of pork, and here the juice from plums, simmered in rosé wine, is used to make an interesting sauce.

the garlic, juniper berries and sage. The milky cooking juices will look curdled, so rub the sauce through a sieve or liquidise in a blender or food processor until smooth. Taste and adjust the seasoning.

4. Carve the pork into thick slices. Pour a little of the sauce over the slices and serve the remaining sauce separately. Garnish with sprigs of sage. Accompany with boiled new potatoes and a green salad.

PORK IN PLUM SAUCE
COUNTRYWIDE

There are many varieties of plum and one type or another should be available from late July through to October. Monarch, a large, black cooking plum, in season from mid-September, would be a good choice, or the widely grown Victoria, which comes into the shops a little earlier, could be used instead. And damsons, if you happen to find them, can also be substituted.

SERVES 4

| 450 g (1 lb) plums |
| 300 ml (½ pint) rosé wine |
| salt and pepper |
| 25 g (1 oz) plain wholemeal flour |
| 700 g (1½ lb) pork fillet or tenderloin, trimmed and cubed |
| 25 g (1 oz) butter |
| 1 large onion, skinned and chopped |
| 175 g (6 oz) white cabbage, shredded |
| 30 ml (2 tbsp) natural yogurt |

1. Simmer the plums in the wine for 5 minutes, until tender. Strain, reserving the juice. Remove the stones from the plums and purée half in a blender or food processor.
2. Season the flour, then coat the pork cubes.
3. Melt the butter in a large saucepan or flameproof casserole and lightly fry the onion and cabbage for 3–4 minutes. Add the meat and fry until brown on all sides.
4. Pour in the reserved plum juice and puréed plums, then simmer, uncovered, for 10–15 minutes, until tender. Just before serving add the remaining plums and yogurt and reheat gently.

TO MICROWAVE

Put the plums and wine in a large bowl and cook on HIGH for 3–4 minutes. Complete the remainder of step 1 and step 2. Melt the butter in a large bowl on HIGH for 45 seconds. Add the onion and cabbage and cook on HIGH for 7 minutes, stirring occasionally. Add the pork and cook on HIGH for 3 minutes. Pour in 200 ml (7 fl oz) plum juice and the puréed plums and cook on HIGH for 3–4 minutes, until boiling, stirring occasionally. Cook on LOW for 7–8 minutes, until the pork is tender. Stir in the remaining plums and yogurt. Stand, covered, for 5 minutes.

BRAISED PORK
COUNTRYWIDE

It may seem odd to cook pork in milk but in fact the richness of the milk, coupled with long, slow cooking, produces mouth-wateringly tender results. Loin is a particularly lean cut and can be rather dry if roasted, but this recipe keeps it moist and succulent. And the use of garlic, juniper and sage makes the dish delightfully aromatic.

SERVES 6

| 15 ml (1 tbsp) vegetable oil |
| 25 g (1 oz) butter |
| 1 kg (2¼ lb) loin of pork, rinded |
| 2 garlic cloves, skinned |
| 1 large onion, skinned and chopped |
| 568 ml (1 pint) fresh milk |
| 5 juniper berries |
| 4 fresh sage sprigs, plus extra for garnish |
| salt and pepper |

1. Heat the oil and the butter in a large saucepan or flameproof casserole into which the meat will just fit. Fry the pork, garlic and onion for about 15 minutes, until the pork is browned on all sides. Add the milk, juniper berries and sage. Season to taste.
2. Bring to the boil, cover and simmer for 1½–2 hours, until the pork is tender and cooked through, turning and basting from time to time.
3. Transfer the pork to a warmed serving dish. Discard

PORK FILLET IN WINE AND CORIANDER

COUNTRYWIDE

Coriander seeds quickly lose their mild, orangy flavour when ground, so try to buy whole seeds to crush yourself.

SERVES 4

700 g (1½ lb) pork fillet or tenderloin, trimmed and cut into 1.25 cm (½ inch) slices

15 g (½ oz) butter

15 ml (1 tbsp) vegetable oil

1 small green pepper, seeded and sliced into rings

1 medium onion, skinned and chopped

15 g (½ oz) plain flour

15 ml (1 tbsp) coriander seeds, ground

150 ml (¼ pint) chicken stock

150 ml (¼ pint) dry white wine

salt and pepper

1. Place the pork between 2 sheets of greaseproof paper and flatten with a mallet or rolling pin until thin.
2. Melt the butter and oil in a large saucepan, add the pork and brown on both sides. Add the pepper and onion and lightly cook for 8–10 minutes, until softened.
3. Stir in the flour and coriander and cook for 1 minute. Gradually add the stock and wine, stirring until the sauce thickens, boils and is smooth. Season to taste. Simmer gently for 5–10 minutes, until the pork is tender and cooked through.

TO MICROWAVE

Complete step 1. Put the butter in a shallow dish and cook on HIGH for 30 seconds. Stir in the pepper and onion and cook on HIGH for 5 minutes. Stir in the flour and coriander and cook on HIGH for 1 minute. Gradually add the stock and wine. Cook on HIGH for 4–5 minutes, stirring frequently, until boiling and thickened. Add the pork and cook on HIGH for 5 minutes, until boiling, stirring occasionally. Cook on LOW for 4 minutes, until the pork is tender and cooked through. Stand, covered, for 5 minutes before serving.

PORK FILLET IN WINE AND CORIANDER. Gently spiced, and given a full-bodied flavour with white wine, this dish needs only plain boiled rice as an accompaniment.

BARBECUED SPARERIBS

COUNTRYWIDE

There's nothing nicer to chew on than a succulent sparerib coated in deliciously sticky sauce. You only get one or two mouthfuls per rib, so buy plenty. It's worth asking for them specially if the butcher doesn't have them on display, as they are one of the most economical cuts you can buy, but don't confuse them with sparerib chops, which are thicker and meatier. Chinese-style spareribs should be eaten with the fingers. Provide finger bowls and plenty of napkins, for easy eating.

SERVES 4

about 1.8 kg (4 lb) Chinese-style pork spareribs, cut into individual chops

salt and pepper

100 g (4 oz) clear honey

60 ml (4 tbsp) dark soft brown sugar

60 ml (4 tbsp) tomato ketchup

30 ml (2 tbsp) Worcestershire sauce

30 ml (2 tbsp) prepared English mustard

30 ml (2 tbsp) red wine vinegar

1. Place the ribs in a single layer in 2 roasting tins and sprinkle with salt and pepper. Roast at 190°C (375°F) mark 5 for 30 minutes.

2. Meanwhile, put the remaining ingredients in a jug and stir well until mixed together.
3. Pour the sauce into the tins and turn the ribs until well coated. Return to the oven and roast for a further 1–1¼ hours, until the meat is tender and the sauce syrupy. Turn the ribs in the sauce several times during cooking and swap over the shelf positions of the 2 roasting tins, if necessary, to ensure that the ribs cook through evenly.
4. Serve hot, with the sauce poured over the ribs. Accompany with plain boiled rice and a dish of mixed stir-fried vegetables such as thinly sliced carrots, shredded leeks and baby sweetcorn.

OXFORD SAUSAGES

THE MIDLANDS

An Oxford butcher probably created this recipe in the days when every shop sold its own special home-made sausages. These are succulent and meaty, well flavoured with herbs and lemon. They are shaped in the hands before frying, and do not have skins.

MAKES ABOUT 18

✳ before step 3

450 g (1 lb) lean boneless pork

450 g (1 lb) lean boneless veal

350 g (12 oz) shredded suet

225 g (8 oz) fresh breadcrumbs

BARBECUED SPARERIBS. Easy to prepare, this tasty dish is ideal for summer al fresco meals. The sweet sauce has a slight tang that perfectly complements the crisply roasted ribs.

grated rind of ½ lemon

5 ml (1 tsp) freshly grated nutmeg

15 ml (1 tbsp) chopped fresh mixed herbs or 5 ml (1 tsp) dried mixed herbs

5 ml (1 tsp) chopped fresh sage or a pinch of dried

salt and pepper

1 egg, lightly beaten

plain flour for coating

1. Mince or very finely chop the pork and veal. Put the minced meat in a large mixing bowl and add the suet, breadcrumbs, lemon rind, nutmeg and herbs. Mix together and season to taste. Add the egg yolks to the mixture and mix well with a fork until all the ingredients are thoroughly combined and bound together.

2. With floured hands, form the mixture into sausage shapes. Coat each sausage in flour, shaking off any excess.

3. Cook the sausages under a hot grill, turning frequently, until evenly browned and cooked through. Serve the sausages with mashed potatoes and a green vegetable as a main meal, or with grilled bacon and tomatoes for breakfast.

STUFFED CABBAGE PARCELS

COUNTRYWIDE

Savoy cabbages stand up well to frost and are in the shops right through winter. Their leaves are very curly and they have a less dense heart than other types. Look for bright, healthy leaves, with no sign of wilting or insect damage. Savoy cabbages will keep well for up to a week if stored in a cool place.

SERVES 4

✳ before step 8

350 g (12 oz) lean minced pork

1 medium onion, skinned and finely chopped

227 g (8 oz) can tomatoes

salt and pepper

283 g (10 oz) can red kidney beans, drained and rinsed

16 large Savoy cabbage leaves

40 g (1½ oz) butter

40 g (1½ oz) plain flour

450 ml (¾ pint) fresh milk

50 g (2 oz) mature Cheddar cheese, grated

pinch of cayenne or paprika, to finish

1. Put the minced pork in a large saucepan, preferably non-stick, over medium heat and cook in its own fat until beginning to brown, stirring from time to time to ensure that it does not stick.

2. Add the onion and fry until softened and lightly coloured. Add the tomatoes with their juice and bring to the boil, stirring. Season to taste, then simmer over moderate heat for 20 minutes, stirring occasionally, until the pork is cooked and the sauce thick and well

reduced. Stir in the kidney beans and remove the pan from the heat. Set aside, covered, while preparing the cabbage leaves for stuffing.

3. Blanch the cabbage for 3 minutes, in batches of 4 leaves at a time, in a large pan of boiling salted water. Drain the cabbage leaves, rinse them under cold running water and pat them dry with absorbent kitchen paper.

4. Lay the cabbage leaves flat on a chopping board. Using a sharp knife, cut out and discard the thick central stalks.

5. Put 15–25 ml (1–1½ tbsp) filling mixture at the stalk end of each cabbage leaf. Fold the 2 sides inwards to cover the filling mixture, then roll up to make a neat, compact parcel.

6. Arrange the cabbage parcels, seam side down, close together in a single layer in a well-buttered flameproof serving dish.

7. Put the butter, flour and milk in a saucepan. Heat, whisking continuously, until the sauce thickens, boils and is smooth. Simmer for 1–2 minutes. Season to taste. Pour the sauce evenly over the cabbage parcels in the dish.

8. Sprinkle with the cheese and cayenne or paprika, and place under a preheated grill for about 5 minutes, until golden brown and bubbling. Serve the cabbage parcels hot, straight from the dish. Accompany them with boiled rice.

TO MICROWAVE

▨ The sauce can be prepared in the microwave. Put the butter, flour and milk in a medium bowl and stir together. Cook on HIGH for 5 minutes, until boiling and thickened, whisking frequently.

STUFFED CABBAGE PARCELS. Tempting food for cold weather eating, shown here as an individual portion. Kidney beans and lean minced pork are used in the stuffing, and a sprinkling of tangy Cheddar adds last-minute flavour.

PORK AND MUSHROOM
SALAD. The ingredients are
marinaded in a mustard and
sour cream dressing for several
hours before serving, to let the
flavours develop. A scattering
of fresh herbs and a dash of
lemon add the finishing
touches.

PORK AND MUSHROOM SALAD

COUNTRYWIDE

An unusual cold dish for summer, when pork prices are usually at their lowest. Cutting the meat and vegetables up into neat strips will improve the appearance of the finished dish, which should be served well chilled.

SERVES 6

2 pork fillets or tenderloins, each weighing about 350 g (12 oz), well trimmed
vegetable oil
knob of butter
225 g (8 oz) small button mushrooms
juice of ½ a lemon
1 small onion, skinned and finely sliced
1 small green pepper, seeded and finely shredded
10 green olives, stoned and chopped
150 ml (5 fl oz) fresh soured cream
1.25 ml (¼ tsp) mustard powder
salt and pepper
5 ml (1 tsp) chopped fresh marjoram or mint
lemon wedges, to garnish

1. Cut the pork into 1 cm (½ inch) slices on the diagonal, then cut each slice into neat strips, about 5 cm × 0.5 cm (2 × ¼ inch).
2. Heat a little oil and the butter in a large frying pan, add half the pork and fry quickly to seal the meat. Repeat with remaining meat, then return all to the pan. Lower the heat and slowly cook for about 10–15 minutes, until very tender. Using a slotted spoon lift the meat out of the pan and leave to cool.
3. Add the mushrooms to the pan with 50 ml (2 fl oz) water and the lemon juice. Cook, stirring, for 1–2 minutes. Using a slotted spoon remove from the pan and leave to cool.
4. Put the onion and green pepper in a pan of cold water, bring to the boil and simmer for 1–2 minutes. Drain and cool under running cold water. Stir into the pork with the cooled mushrooms and olives.
5. Mix the soured cream with the mustard, season to taste and stir into the pork mixture. Cover and chill for at least 3 hours.
6. Stir the salad well before serving sprinkled with marjoram or mint and garnished with lemon wedges.

MELTON MOWBRAY PORK PIE

THE MIDLANDS

A robust pie from the Shires, justly famous for its juicy, jellied filling. A little anchovy essence gives the meat an extra savoury tang that is very appetising. The pies were originally served at high tea after a long day's hunt.

SERVES ABOUT 8

450 g (1 lb) plain flour
salt and pepper
1 egg yolk
175 g (6 oz) lard, diced
100 ml (4 fl oz) fresh milk and water mixed
900 g (2 lb) lean pork, cut into 0.5 cm (¼ inch) dice
3 bacon rashers, rinded and finely diced
5 ml (1 tsp) finely chopped fresh sage or 1.25 ml (¼ tsp) dried
5 ml (1 tsp) finely chopped fresh thyme or 1.25 ml (¼ tsp) dried
5 ml (1 tsp) anchovy essence
2.5 ml (½ tsp) ground mace
2.5 ml (½ tsp) ground allspice
568 ml (1 pint) chicken stock
1 egg, beaten, to glaze
15 g (½ oz) gelatine

1. To make the pastry, warm a mixing bowl and sieve the flour and a pinch of salt into it. Make a well in the centre and add the egg yolk.
2. Gently heat the lard in the milk and water until it has melted, then bring rapidly to the boil. Pour immediately into the well in the flour and draw the ingredients together with a wooden spoon to form a

PAINSWICK BACON CHOPS IN CIDER. Bacon chops are a good choice for mid-week meals, particularly with such a tasty sauce.

soft, pliable but not sticky ball of dough.

3. Transfer to a lightly floured surface and knead until it is smooth and elastic and easy to work. Cover the dough and leave to rest in a warm place for 20–30 minutes.

4. Mix together the pork, bacon, sage, thyme, anchovy essence and spices. Lightly season. Moisten with 45 ml (3 tbsp) of the stock.

5. Roll out two thirds of the pastry on a lightly floured surface and mould round a 1.1 kg (2½ lb) floured straight-sided jam jar, or line a raised pie mould or drop-sided terrine. If using a jar, leave the pastry to set on a baking sheet, then gently ease out the jar.

6. Pack the meat mixture into the pastry. Roll out the remaining pastry to make a lid for the pie. Press the edges together tightly to seal. Scallop the edges and decorate with pastry leaves. Cut a hole in the centre of the pastry lid. Tie a double thickness of buttered greaseproof paper around the outside of the pie if formed using a jam jar. Brush the top with beaten egg. Place on a baking sheet if using a mould or terrine.

7. Bake at 200°C (400°F) mark 6 for 20 minutes, then reduce the temperature to 180°C (350°F) mark 4 and bake for a further 2¼ hours. Remove the mould or greaseproof paper, brush the sides and top with egg and return to oven for 10–15 minutes, until well browned. Remove from oven, leave until almost cold.

8. Heat the stock in a saucepan and sprinkle in the gelatine. Stir briskly until dissolved. Leave to cool slightly. Pour liquid through hole in pastry lid. Leave in a cool place overnight. Serve cut in thick slices.

PAINSWICK BACON CHOPS IN CIDER

THE WEST

Cider is a popular ingredient of West Country dishes. For a stronger cider flavour, use one-third to one-half more than the recipe states and reduce it by boiling to concentrate.

SERVES 4

4 bacon chops, each weighing about 175 g (6 oz)
15 ml (1 tbsp) prepared English mustard
25 g (1 oz) demerara sugar
300 ml (½ pint) dry cider
15 g (½ oz) butter
25 ml (1½ tbsp) plain flour
chopped fresh parsley, to garnish

1. Put chops side by side in a large ovenproof dish. Mix mustard and sugar with cider to make a smooth paste. Spread over chops. Leave for 30 minutes.

2. Bake at 200°C (400°F) mark 6 for 15 minutes.

3. Meanwhile, put the butter, flour and remaining cider in a saucepan. Heat, whisking continuously, until the sauce thickens, boils and is smooth. Simmer for 1–2 minutes. Season to taste.

4. Pour over chops. Bake for a further 15 minutes, until cooked through. Serve garnished with parsley.

BACON CHOPS WITH
GOOSEBERRY SAUCE.
A purée of gooseberries and
onions makes a refreshing
sauce. This is a very quick and
easy dish, which you can
rustle up in half an hour.

BACON CHOPS WITH GOOSEBERRY SAUCE

THE MIDLANDS

At the start of the season gooseberries are too acid and hard to be eaten raw, but are perfect for cooking. Look for thick prime back bacon chops, good for gentle braising.

SERVES 4

✳

15 ml (1 tbsp) soft brown sugar

5 ml (1 tsp) mustard powder

pepper

4 bacon chops, each weighing 175 g (6 oz)

15 g (½ oz) butter

1 large onion, skinned and chopped

150 ml (¼ pint) vegetable stock

100 g (4 oz) gooseberries, topped and tailed

1. Mix together the brown sugar, mustard and pepper and rub into both sides of the bacon chops.
2. Melt the butter in a large frying pan or flameproof casserole. Cook the onion for 2 minutes, then add the bacon chops, half the stock and the gooseberries. Simmer gently for 15 minutes.
3. Remove chops. Purée onions and gooseberries in blender or food processor until smooth.
4. Return the chops and purée to the pan with the remaining stock. Simmer gently for 10 minutes, until the chops are tender and cooked through. Serve at once with boiled sliced red cabbage.

HUNTINGDON FIDGET PIE

THE EASTERN COUNTIES

A lovely old-fashioned recipe – no one knows how it got its peculiar name. Bacon, onions and apples are the traditional filling and the pie was originally made round harvest time to feed the hungry workers. Potatoes can be added to make the dish even more sustaining.

SERVES 4

250 g (9 oz) plain flour

100 g (4 oz) butter, diced

salt and pepper

225 g (8 oz) back bacon, rinded and roughly chopped

1 medium onion, skinned and roughly chopped

225 g (8 oz) cooking apples, peeled, cored and roughly chopped

15 ml (1 tbsp) chopped fresh parsley

150 ml (¼ pint) medium-dry cider

1 egg, beaten, to glaze

1. To make the pastry, sift 225 g (8 oz) of the flour and a pinch of salt into a bowl. Rub in the butter until the mixture resembles breadcrumbs. Add just enough water to mix to a firm dough.
2. Gather the dough into a ball and knead lightly. Wrap the dough in foil and chill in the refrigerator for 30 minutes.

3. Meanwhile, combine the bacon, onion and apples in a 568 ml (1 pint) pie dish. Add the parsley and season to taste.

4. Blend the remaining flour with the cider, a little at a time, then pour into the pie dish.

5. Roll out the pastry. Cut out a thin strip long enough to go around the rim of the pie dish. Moisten the rim with water and place the pastry strip on the rim. Press down lightly all the way round.

6. Moisten the strip of pastry, then place the lid on top and press to seal. Knock up and flute the edge.

7. Make a diagonal cross in the centre almost to the edges of the dish, then fold the pastry back to reveal the filling.

8. Brush the pastry with the egg. Bake at 190°C (375°F) mark 5 for about 45 minutes or until the pastry is golden and the filling is cooked. Serve the pie hot with a green vegetable or cold with salad.

BOILED BACON AND PARSLEY SAUCE

WALES

The choice of bacon joints today is wide and suits all pockets. Gammon is leanest but costs more, while collar and forehock are more economical. All cuts taste equally good cold so it can be worth buying a bigger joint than is required for one meal, and serving the leftover meat with jacket baked potatoes and a mixed salad.

SERVES 6–8

| 1.4 kg (3 lb) piece of gammon, collar or forehock bacon |
| 2 medium onions, skinned |
| 2 medium carrots, thickly sliced |
| 2 celery sticks, chopped |
| 1 bay leaf |
| 4 black peppercorns |
| *For the Parsley Sauce* |
| 15 g (½ oz) butter |
| 15 g (½ oz) plain flour |
| 300 ml (½ pint) fresh milk |
| salt and pepper |
| 30 ml (2 tbsp) chopped fresh parsley |

1. Weigh the joint and calculate the cooking time, allowing 20 minutes per 450 g (1 lb) plus 20 minutes. To remove the salt, place the joint in a large saucepan with enough cold water to cover. Slowly bring to the boil, then discard the water.

2. Place the joint in a large saucepan or preserving pan, add the vegetables, bay leaf and peppercorns, cover with cold water and bring slowly to the boil. Skim the surface with a slotted spoon. Cover and calculate the cooking time from this point.

3. To make the Parsley Sauce, put the butter, flour and milk in a saucepan. Heat, whisking continuously, until the sauce thickens, boils and is smooth. Simmer for 1–2 minutes. Season to taste and add the parsley.

4. When the bacon is cooked, ease off the rind and remove any excess fat. Serve the bacon hot, sliced, with the Parsley Sauce.

BRITISH CHARTER
QUALITY BACON MARK

*Look for
this mark when buying bacon. It
appears on most supermarket
packs and guarantees tasty
rashers, pre-cut and pre-
packaged, with just the right
blend of fat and lean.*

HUNTINGDON FIDGET
PIE. Hearty appetites will be
more than satisfied by this
warming and nourishing pie.
The filling is temptingly
revealed in the centre.

RIGHT
BAKED HAM. Succulent, tender ham is excellent served hot after roasting, and is also extremely good eaten cold. Not a scrap will be wasted.

OPPOSITE
STOVED CHICKEN. Chicken and bacon are baked gently between layers of potato and onion, until everything is done to a turn.

BAKED HAM
Score the gammon surface fat in a diamond pattern, then stud each diamond with a clove.

BAKED HAM
COUNTRYWIDE

A ham is the leg of a pig that is cured separately and sold cooked. However, this recipe uses a gammon joint, which is cured as part of the whole side of the pig and sold uncooked.

SERVES 8–10

1.8 kg (4 lb) middle gammon joint
2 medium onions, skinned and quartered
2 medium carrots, thickly sliced
1 bay leaf
5 black peppercorns
cloves, to garnish
demerara sugar, to glaze

1. Weigh the gammon and calculate the cooking time, allowing 20 minutes per 450 g (1 lb) plus 20 minutes. Place the gammon in a large pan and cover with cold water. Bring slowly to the boil, then drain.
2. Return the gammon to the saucepan. Add the vegetables, bay leaf and peppercorns, cover with cold water and bring slowly to the boil. Skim the surface with a slotted spoon. Cover and boil for half the calculated cooking time.
3. Drain and wrap the gammon in foil. Place in a roasting tin and bake at 180°C (350°F) mark 4 until 30 minutes before the cooking time is completed.
4. Remove the foil and rind from the gammon. Score the fat in diamonds and stud with cloves. Sprinkle the surface with demerara sugar and pat in.
5. Bake at 220°C (425°F) mark 7 for 30 minutes, until crisp and golden. Serve hot or cold.

SAUSAGE AND BEAN STEW
COUNTRYWIDE

A favourite with children, and a warming dish for a winter day. Cider is used for extra flavour, and for a hint of spiciness, add 15 ml (1 tbsp) chilli seasoning. Substitute with dried kidney beans, if liked, using 225 g (8 oz) dried beans, cooked before adding to the stew.

SERVES 4

✳

15 ml (1 tbsp) vegetable oil
15 g (½ oz) butter
450 g (1 lb) pork sausages
1 large onion, skinned and sliced
two 397 g (14 oz) cans red kidney beans, drained
227 g (8 oz) can tomatoes
30 ml (2 tbsp) tomato purée
350 ml (12 fl oz) dry cider
salt and pepper

1. Heat the oil and butter in a large flameproof casserole and fry the sausages for about 5 minutes, until browned. Cut each sausage in half crossways.
2. Add the onions to the casserole and fry for 5 minutes, until golden brown. Drain off any excess fat. Return the sausages to the casserole together with the beans, tomatoes and their juice, tomato purée, cider and salt and pepper to taste.
3. Cover and cook gently for about 15 minutes or until the sausages are tender. Accompany with crusty bread, boiled rice or mashed potatoes.

POULTRY & GAME

STOVED CHICKEN

SCOTLAND

Sometimes also called 'stovies' this Scottish recipe derives from the French etouffer, to cook in a closed pot, and dates from the strong Scottish/French links of the seventeenth century. It makes a filling family dish which can safely be left to its own devices; a little extra cooking time will not spoil the flavour.

SERVES 4

25 g (1 oz) butter
15 ml (1 tbsp) vegetable oil
4 chicken quarters, halved
100 g (4 oz) lean back bacon, rinded and chopped
1.1 kg (2½ lb) floury potatoes, such as King Edwards, peeled and cut into 0.5 cm (¼ inch) slices
2 large onions, skinned and sliced
salt and pepper
10 ml (2 tsp) chopped fresh thyme or 2.5 ml (½ tsp) dried thyme
568 ml (1 pint) chicken stock
fresh chives, to garnish

1. Heat half of the butter and the oil in a large frying pan and fry the chicken and bacon for 5 minutes, until lightly browned.
2. Place a thick layer of potato slices, then onion slices, in the base of a large ovenproof casserole. Season well, add the thyme and dot with half the remaining butter.
3. Add the chicken and bacon, season to taste and dot with the remaining butter. Cover with the remaining onions and finally a layer of potatoes. Season and dot with butter. Pour over the stock.
4. Cover and bake at 150°C (300°F) mark 2 for about 2 hours, until the chicken is tender and the potatoes are cooked, adding a little more hot stock if necessary.
5. Just before serving sprinkle with snipped chives.

CHICKEN AND BROCCOLI PIE. There are carrots, onions and mushrooms as well as broccoli in this generous pie, with its creamy sauce and golden crust.

CHICKEN AND BROCCOLI PIE

THE SOUTH-EAST

The sauce in this recipe uses plain wholemeal flour and is delicately flavoured with just a hint of lemon. For variation, you could top the pie with wholemeal shortcrust pastry.

SERVES 4–6

25 g (1 oz) butter
2 carrots, diced
8 button onions, skinned
100 g (4 oz) button mushrooms
25 g (1 oz) plain wholemeal flour
450 ml (¾ pint) fresh milk, plus extra to glaze
450 g (1 lb) boneless cooked chicken, cut into strips
175 g (6 oz) broccoli, blanched
grated rind of ½ lemon
30 ml (2 tbsp) fresh single cream
salt and pepper
225 g (8 oz) frozen puff pastry, thawed

1. Melt the butter in a large saucepan and lightly fry the carrots, onions and mushrooms for 8 minutes, stirring occasionally.
2. Stir in the flour and cook for 1–2 minutes. Gradually add the milk, stirring continuously until the sauce thickens, boils and is smooth. Simmer for 3–4 minutes.
3. Add the chicken, broccoli, lemon rind and cream to the sauce. Season to taste and pour into a 1.1 litre (2 pint) pie dish.
4. Roll out the pastry on a lightly floured surface large enough to fit the dish. Cover the pie with the pastry and moisten the edges so the pastry is well sealed. Use any pastry trimmings to decorate. Brush with milk to glaze.
5. Bake at 200°C (400°F) mark 6 for 25 minutes, until the pastry is golden brown. Serve at once.

TO MICROWAVE

Melt the butter in a large bowl on HIGH for 45 seconds. Add the carrots, onions and mushrooms and cook on HIGH for 5 minutes, stirring occasionally. Add the flour and cook on HIGH for 1 minute, then gradually add the milk and cook on HIGH for 8 minutes, until boiling and thickened, whisking frequently. Complete steps 3, 4 and 5.

GREEN FRICASSEE OF CHICKEN
COUNTRYWIDE

Fricassee is the French name for a stew which has been used in British cooking for centuries. It contains chicken, rabbit or veal and vegetables, and is finished with cream and egg yolks. This version gets its appetising green colour from spinach, which also adds its own subtle flavour.

SERVES 4

30 ml (2 tbsp) plain wholemeal flour
salt and pepper
4 chicken quarters, halved
15 g (½ oz) butter
15 ml (1 tbsp) vegetable oil
300 ml (½ pint) dry white wine
900 g (2 lb) spinach, trimmed
2 egg yolks
150 ml (5 fl oz) fresh single cream
45 ml (3 tbsp) chopped fresh parsley
freshly grated nutmeg

1. Season the flour with salt and pepper, then use to coat the chicken. Heat the butter and oil in a large frying pan and fry the chicken until browned on all sides. Pour in the wine, cover and simmer gently for 20–30 minutes or until the chicken is tender.
2. Meanwhile, thoroughly wash the spinach, then put into a large saucepan with just the water clinging to the leaves. Cover with a tightly fitting lid and cook for about 5 minutes or until the spinach is just tender. Drain very thoroughly, then transfer to a large casserole.
3. Arrange the chicken pieces on top of the spinach. Cover and bake at 170°C (325°F) mark 3 for 20 minutes.
4. When ready to serve, beat the egg yolks and cream together. Reheat the wine juices in the pan, then remove from the heat and stir in the cream and egg yolk mixture. Stir in the parsley and season to taste with salt, pepper and nutmeg.
5. Pour the sauce evenly over the chicken and serve immediately with rice, noodles or baked potatoes.

TO MICROWAVE

Complete step 1. Wash the spinach thoroughly, then put into a large bowl with just the water clinging to the leaves. Cover and cook on HIGH for 5 minutes or until just tender. Arrange the chicken on top of the spinach. Cover and cook on HIGH for 5 minutes. Complete steps 4 and 5.

CHICKEN IN WHITE WINE
COUNTRYWIDE

Chicken is always a good choice for entertaining because it is so versatile and most people like it. Slowly cooked in white wine and given lots of flavour with garlic, herbs and bacon, it makes an ideal dinner party dish that is also quick and easy to prepare.

SERVES 6

100 g (4 oz) lean bacon, rinded and diced
450 g (1 lb) button onions, skinned
225 g (8 oz) button mushrooms
6 chicken quarters, halved
50 g (2 oz) plain flour
salt and pepper
25 g (1 oz) butter
30 ml (2 tbsp) vegetable oil
300 ml (½ pint) dry white wine
300 ml (½ pint) chicken stock
1 garlic clove, skinned and crushed
sprigs of fresh thyme or 2.5 ml (½ tsp) dried
2 bay leaves
chopped fresh parsley, to garnish

1. Fry the bacon in its own fat in a large frying pan until beginning to brown. Add the onions and fry until browned, then add the mushrooms and fry for 2 minutes. Transfer the bacon and vegetables to a flameproof casserole with a slotted spoon.
2. Coat the chicken joints with the flour, seasoned with salt and pepper. Heat the butter and the oil in the frying pan, add the chicken and fry until browned all over. Transfer the chicken to the casserole.
3. Gradually stir the white wine into the frying pan. Bring to the boil, scraping any sediment from the bottom of the pan, then pour over the chicken joints in the casserole.
4. Add the chicken stock, garlic herbs and seasoning to taste to the frying pan. Bring to the boil, then pour over the chicken.
5. Cover and cook in the oven at 170°C (325°F) mark 3 for 1 hour or until the chicken is tender. Skim any fat from the cooking liquid. Garnish with chopped parsley.

TO MICROWAVE

Complete steps 1 and 2, transferring the bacon, vegetables and chicken to a large bowl. Complete steps 3 and 4. Cover and cook on HIGH for 25–30 minutes, stirring occasionally. Complete the recipe.

CHICKEN

Chicken is produced extensively countrywide to meet increasing demand for its high-protein, low-fat meat. Broiler chickens' intensively reared for the table under closely supervised conditions (look for the Quality British Chicken Mark) are sold whole or divided into portions. Chicken is very versatile, lending itself to many different cooking methods and dishes. Producers have matched this with a corresponding variety of types of chicken, free range as well as intensively farmed, fresh or frozen, with or without giblets.

ROASTING

Usually up to 2.7 kg (6 lb) though can be larger. Delicious cooked in own juices in chicken brick. Leftover carcase can be used for stock.

BOILING

Larger, older birds ideal for soup like Cock-a-Leekie (see recipe, page 83).

POUSSIN

Baby chicken, single serving size, ideal spatch-cocked (ie split open and flattened), grilled, roasted or sautéed.

PORTIONS

Breasts on the bone or in fillets are good for special dishes like Chicken with Grapes, Lemon and Cream (page 160) deep- and stir-frying (see recipes, pages 157, 161). Legs (thigh and drumstick) are suitable for casseroles like Chicken in White Wine (see recipe, left). Drumsticks are very good for buffets and picnics, as finger food. Thighs are excellent cheap, multi-purpose meat.

FLAVOURED

Corn-fed chicken has a distinctive yellow colour and the flavour is also distinctive. Smoked chicken is good in special salads. Pre-basted, herbed, ready-stuffed birds are also increasingly available.

CHICKEN THIGHS WITH SPICY TOMATO SAUCE

COUNTRYWIDE

Meaty little chicken thighs make a good, inexpensive mid-week meal. The tasty tomato sauce is well spiced with cumin and coriander, and a pinch of chilli powder adds a pleasant heat without being fiery.

SERVES 4

| 15 g (½ oz) butter |
| 15 ml (1 tbsp) vegetable oil |
| 1 medium onion, skinned and chopped |
| 1 garlic clove, skinned and crushed |
| 5 ml (1 tsp) ground cumin |
| 5 ml (1 tsp) ground coriander |
| large pinch of chilli powder |
| 8 chicken thighs |
| 397 g (14 oz) can tomatoes |
| 15 ml (1 tbsp) tomato purée |
| salt and pepper |
| 30 ml (2 tbsp) chopped fresh parsley |

1. Heat the butter and oil in a large frying pan, add the onion and garlic, cover and cook for 4–5 minutes, until the onion is softened. Add the cumin, coriander and chilli powder and cook for 1 minute, stirring continuously.
2. Push the onions to one side of the pan, then add the chicken and brown on both sides. Stir in the tomatoes and the tomato purée and season to taste.
3. Bring to the boil, stirring continuously. Cover and simmer gently for about 30 minutes or until the chicken is tender. Stir in the parsley and serve immediately with boiled rice.

TO MICROWAVE

Put everything, except the butter, oil, chicken and parsley, in a large bowl. Cover and cook on HIGH for 10 minutes. Meanwhile, melt the butter and oil in a frying pan and brown the chicken on both sides. Add the chicken to the sauce, re-cover and cook on HIGH for 15 minutes or until the chicken is tender, stirring occasionally. Stir in the parsley and serve immediately.

CORNISH CAUDLE CHICKEN PIE

THE WEST

The caudle in this rich and tasty pie is the mixture of egg and cream that is poured into the filling towards the end of cooking time.

SERVES 4

| 15 g (½ oz) butter |
| 15 ml (1 tbsp) vegetable oil |
| 1 medium onion, skinned and finely chopped |
| 4 chicken drumsticks or thighs, skinned and boned |
| 30 ml (2 tbsp) chopped fresh parsley |
| 4 spring onions, trimmed and chopped |
| salt and pepper |
| 150 ml (¼ pint) fresh milk |
| 212 g (7½ oz) packet frozen puff pastry, thawed |
| 150 ml (5 fl oz) fresh soured cream |
| 2 eggs, beaten |

1. Heat the butter and oil in a small frying pan, add the onion, cover and cook over a low heat, until softened but not browned. Transfer to a 1.1 litre (2 pint) pie dish using a slotted spoon.
2. Add the chicken and cook until evenly browned. Arrange on top of the onion in a single layer. Stir the parsley, spring onions, seasonings and milk into the pan and bring gently to the boil. Simmer for 2–3 minutes, then pour over the chicken.
3. Cover with foil and bake at 180°C (350°F) mark 4 for 30 minutes, until the chicken is tender. Remove from the oven and leave to cool.
4. Meanwhile, roll out the pastry on a lightly floured surface until about 2.5 cm (1 inch) larger all round than pie dish. Leave pastry to relax while filling is cooling.

CHICKEN THIGHS WITH SPICY TOMATO SAUCE. Bursting with flavour, this is an easy-cook dish which just uses one big frying pan from start to finish.

SHREDDED CHICKEN
WITH MUSHROOMS
AND WALNUTS. Cook
Chinese for a change, with
this aromatic stir-fry. For the
fullest flavour, let the meat
marinate for at least an hour
before you get to work with
the wok.

*good – J doesn't like
ginger!*

*? less. soy sauce
easy on ginger.*

5. Cut off a strip from all round the edge of the pastry. Place the strip on the rim of the pie dish, moisten with a little water, then place the pastry lid on top. Crimp the edges, make a small hole in the top.

6. Beat the soured cream and the eggs together, then brush the top of the pie with a little of the mixture. Bake at 220°C (425°F) mark 7 for 15–20 minutes, until a light golden brown. Reduce the temperature to 180°C (350°F) mark 4.

7. Pour the soured cream and egg mixture into the pie through the hole. Shake the dish to distribute the cream mixture and return the pie to the oven for 15 minutes. Remove from the oven and leave to stand in a warm place for 5–10 minutes before serving or leave to cool completely and serve cold.

SHREDDED CHICKEN
WITH MUSHROOMS
AND WALNUTS

COUNTRYWIDE

This stir-fried dish ends up a delicious mixture of juicy chicken strips, firm mushrooms, crisp cucumber chunks and crunchy nuts, all coated in a piquant, spicy sauce.

SERVES 4

4 chicken breast fillets, each weighing about 100 g (4 oz), skinned and cut into thin strips

5 cm (2 inch) piece of fresh root ginger, peeled and thinly sliced

45 ml (3 tbsp) soy sauce

60 ml (4 tbsp) dry sherry

5 ml (1 tsp) five spice powder

45 ml (3 tbsp) vegetable oil

100 g (4 oz) mushrooms, halved

¼ cucumber, cut into chunks

75 g (3 oz) walnut pieces, roughly chopped

pepper

1. Put the chicken in a bowl with the ginger, soy sauce, sherry and five spice powder. Stir well to mix, then cover and leave to marinate for at least 1 hour.

2. Remove the chicken from the marinade with a slotted spoon, reserving the marinade.

3. Heat the oil in a large frying pan or wok. Add the chicken and cook for 3–4 minutes, stirring continuously.

4. Add the mushrooms, cucumber and walnuts and continue to cook for 1–2 minutes, until the chicken is cooked and the vegetables are tender but still crisp.

5. Stir in the reserved marinade and cook for 1 minute, until hot. Season to taste with pepper. Serve immediately with rice or noodles.

TO MICROWAVE

 Complete steps 1 and 2. Put the chicken, reserving the marinade, the oil, mushrooms, cucumber and walnuts in a large bowl. Cook on HIGH for 5–6 minutes, stirring frequently. Stir in the reserved marinade and cook on HIGH for 1 minute, until hot. Season to taste with pepper. Serve immediately with rice or noodles.

SPICED CHICKEN. Chunks of chicken in a temptingly fragrant curry sauce. Fresh soured cream drizzled over the finished dish adds a cooling note.

2. Melt the butter in a large saucepan and lightly fry the chicken and onion for 5–6 minutes, until the chicken is brown and the onion lightly coloured.
3. Stir in the remaining flour. Gradually blend in the milk, stirring continuously, until the sauce thickens, boils and is smooth.
4. Add the chutney and sultanas and simmer gently for 30–35 minutes, until the chicken is tender.
5. Remove the pan from the heat and drizzle with the cream. Sprinkle with the paprika and serve at once with boiled rice.

TO MICROWAVE

☑ Complete step 1. Cube the butter and melt in a large bowl on HIGH for 1 minute. Cook the onion on HIGH for 5 minutes. Add the chicken and cook on HIGH for 3–4 minutes, stirring occasionally. Stir in the flour. Gradually blend in the milk and cook on HIGH for 7–8 minutes, whisking frequently, until boiling and thickened. Add the chutney and sultanas and cook on MEDIUM for 12–15 minutes, until the chicken is tender. Drizzle with the cream. Serve at once with boiled rice.

CHICKEN IN CREAM

COUNTRYWIDE

Simplicity is the key to this very easy recipe. Soured cream gives a hint of sharpness, but fresh double cream is also good. Add a few tablespoons of chopped fresh mixed herbs and some thinly sliced mushrooms to make an equally delicious variation.

SERVES 4

15 g (½ oz) butter
15 ml (1 tbsp) vegetable oil
4 chicken quarters, halved
salt and pepper
150 ml (5 fl oz) fresh double cream
chopped fresh parsley, to garnish

1. Heat the butter and oil in a large flameproof casserole and fry the chicken pieces quickly until lightly browned on all sides.
2. Season the chicken to taste, then pour over the cream. Cover and bake at 200°C (400°F) mark 6 for 45 minutes–1 hour, until tender, turning the chicken pieces over twice during cooking. Serve garnished with chopped parsley.

TO MICROWAVE

☑ Complete step 1. Transfer the chicken to a dish. Season the chicken to taste, then pour over the cream. Cover and cook on HIGH for 20–25 minutes or until the chicken is tender, stirring occasionally. Serve garnished with chopped parsley.

SPICED CHICKEN

COUNTRYWIDE

Curry powder is increasingly used in British cuisine these days and most supermarkets stock a selection of them in varying strengths. Cayenne pepper used sparingly adds heat. Add mango or peach chutney instead of apple if you prefer.

SERVES 4

350 g (12 oz) boneless chicken, skinned and diced
40 g (1½ oz) plain wholemeal flour
5 ml (1 tsp) curry powder
2.5 ml (½ tsp) cayenne pepper
40 g (1½ oz) butter
1 medium onion, skinned and chopped
450 ml (¾ pint) fresh milk
60 ml (4 tbsp) apple chutney
100 g (4 oz) sultanas
150 ml (5 fl oz) fresh soured cream
2.5 ml (½ tsp) paprika

1. Toss the chicken in the flour, curry powder and cayenne pepper, shaking off any excess.

CHICKEN IN RED WINE WITH RAISINS

THE SOUTH-EAST

This is a medieval recipe, originally intended for rabbit, but equally good with chicken. The sauce is spicy and sweetish, and is used to marinate the meat and fruits before cooking. In this way the chicken takes on a marvellous flavour and the raisins and apricots become juicy and plump.

SERVES 4

✱

300 ml (½ pint) red wine
45 ml (3 tbsp) red wine vinegar
100 g (4 oz) seedless raisins
175 g (6 oz) no-soak dried apricots, halved
5 ml (1 tsp) ground ginger
5 ml (1 tsp) ground cinnamon
1 cm (½ inch) piece of fresh root ginger, peeled and grated
4 cloves
4 juniper berries, lightly crushed
4 chicken breast fillets, with skin on, each weighing about 175 g (6 oz)
30 ml (2 tbsp) plain wholemeal flour
salt and pepper
15 g (½ oz) butter
15 ml (1 tbsp) vegetable oil
300 ml (½ pint) chicken stock
orange segments, to garnish

1. Put the wine, vinegar, raisins, apricots, ground ginger, cinnamon, fresh ginger, cloves and juniper berries in a dish. Add the chicken breasts and spoon the liquid over them. Cover and leave to marinate in a cool place for 3–4 hours or overnight.
2. Remove the chicken from the marinade and dry with kitchen paper. Coat in the flour, seasoned with salt and pepper. Heat the butter and oil in a large flameproof casserole, add the chicken, skin side down, and fry until lightly browned, turn over and fry the other side. Drain on kitchen paper.
3. Pour off any excess fat from the casserole, then stir in the chicken stock, reserved marinade and fruit and bring to the boil. Return the chicken to the casserole, cover tightly and cook for about 30 minutes, until the chicken is tender.
4. Transfer the chicken to a warmed serving plate and keep warm. Boil the liquid until reduced and thickened, then pour over the chicken. Serve garnished with orange segments. Accompany with boiled rice.

CHICKEN AND BEAN LAYER

COUNTRYWIDE

Green beans are in the shops from June to September. Buy them young and fresh – snap one in half and make sure that it is crisp and juicy. Red Leicester cheese adds an appetising golden glow to the sauce.

SERVES 4

✱ ⚡

40 g (1½ oz) butter
40 g (1½ oz) plain wholemeal flour
568 ml (1 pint) fresh milk
75 g (3 oz) Red Leicester cheese, grated
2.5 ml (½ tsp) mustard powder
2.5 ml (½ tsp) cayenne pepper
freshly ground pepper
450 g (1 lb) green beans, cooked
450 g (1 lb) boned cooked chicken, skinned and chopped
50 g (2 oz) no-soak dried apricots, chopped
25 g (1 oz) flaked almonds

1. Put the butter, flour and milk in a saucepan. Heat, whisking continuously, until the sauce thickens, boils and is smooth. Simmer for 2–3 minutes. Remove the pan from the heat, add the cheese, mustard and peppers, then stir until the cheese has melted.
2. Layer the beans, chicken, apricots and sauce in a 1.7 litre (3 pint) ovenproof serving dish. Sprinkle with almonds.
3. Bake, uncovered, at 180°C (350°F) mark 4 for 25 minutes. Serve with baked potatoes.

TO MICROWAVE

⚡ Put the beans in a medium bowl with 30 ml (2 tbsp) water and cook on HIGH for 8 minutes. To make the sauce, put the butter, flour and milk in a medium bowl and cook on HIGH for 9–10 minutes, whisking frequently, until boiling and thickened. Add the cheese, mustard and peppers and stir until the cheese has melted. Complete step 2 but do not sprinkle with almonds. Instead, toast them under a grill. Meanwhile, cook the dish on HIGH for 10–12 minutes. Sprinkle with almonds.

onion is transparent. Stir in the flour and curry powder and cook, stirring, for 1 minute. Remove from the heat and gradually stir in the stock. Bring to the boil, stirring continuously, then simmer for 2–3 minutes, until thickened.

2. Reduce the heat, add the lemon juice and chicken and season to taste. Leave to cool.

3. When the chicken mixture is cool, roll out the pastry on a lightly floured surface to a 35.5 cm (14 inch) square. Using a sharp knife, cut into 4 squares.

4. Place the pastry on dampened baking sheets, then spoon the chicken mixture on to the pastry, leaving a border round the edges. Brush the edges of each square lightly with water. Fold each square in half and seal and crimp the edges to make a parcel.

5. Make 2 small slashes on the top of each parcel. Brush with beaten egg to glaze.

6. Bake at 220°C (425°F) mark 7 for 15–20 minutes or until the pastry is golden brown. Serve with a mixed salad or Brussels sprouts.

CHICKEN PARCELS. The tasty filling is a simple yet delicious way to use up cooked chicken leftovers.

CHICKEN PARCELS
COUNTRYWIDE

These neat puff pastry pasties are filled with a lovely, spicy mixture of chicken chunks, carrots and onion. They are perfect picnic food as they can be made in advance and eaten cold in the fingers, but are also good served hot with accompanying vegetables.

SERVES 4

✳

15 g (½ oz) butter
1 small onion, skinned and chopped
2 medium carrots, diced
15 ml (1 tbsp) plain wholemeal flour
5 ml (1 tsp) mild curry powder
300 ml (½ pint) chicken stock
5 ml (1 tsp) lemon juice
225 g (8 oz) boneless cooked chicken, chopped
salt and pepper
368 g (13 oz) packet frozen puff pastry, thawed
beaten egg, to glaze

1. Melt the butter in a large saucepan, add the onion and carrots, cover and cook for 4–5 minutes, until the

CHICKEN WITH GRAPES, LEMON AND CREAM
COUNTRYWIDE

Everyday chicken takes on a note of luxury, in this pretty dish with its garnish of seedless green grapes. The creamy sauce is well flavoured with lemon and herbs, and the recipe is ready in little more than 30 minutes from start to finish.

SERVES 4

15 g (½ oz) butter
15 ml (1 tbsp) vegetable oil
4 chicken breast fillets, skinned, each weighing about 100 g (4 oz)
150 ml (¼ pint) chicken stock
finely grated rind and juice of 1 lemon
5 ml (1 tsp) fresh chopped rosemary or 2.5 ml (½ level tsp) dried
salt and pepper
150 ml (5 fl oz) fresh single cream
225 g (8 oz) seedless green grapes, halved

1. Heat the butter and oil in a large frying pan, add the chicken and cook quickly until lightly browned on both sides.

2. Reduce the heat and add the stock, lemon rind and juice and rosemary. Season to taste, cover and simmer gently for about 10 minutes, until the chicken is tender.

3. Remove the chicken from the pan, cover and keep warm. Boil the cooking juices to reduce a little. Add the chicken, cream and grapes and heat through gently, then adjust seasoning. Serve with noodles or boiled rice.

TO MICROWAVE

 Put the butter and oil in a large shallow dish and cook on HIGH for 45 seconds, until melted. Add the chicken, stock, lemon rind and juice, rosemary and seasoning. Cover and cook on HIGH for 6–8 minutes or until the chicken is tender. Remove the chicken from the dish and keep warm. Cook the sauce, uncovered, on HIGH for 3 minutes to reduce slightly, then add the chicken, cream and grapes. Cook on HIGH for 2 minutes. Season to taste and serve.

STIR-FRIED CHICKEN WITH COURGETTES

COUNTRYWIDE

The ancient Chinese art of stir-frying has been a welcome addition to British cooking techniques. It's a speedy, healthy way to cook, as the food is only over the heat for a few minutes and so keeps much of its bite, colour and vitamins.

SERVES 4

30 ml (2 tbsp) vegetable oil

1 garlic clove, skinned and crushed

450 g (1 lb) chicken breast fillets, skinned and cut into thin strips

450 g (1 lb) courgettes, cut into thin strips

1 red pepper, seeded and cut into thin strips

45 ml (3 tbsp) dry sherry

15 ml (1 tbsp) soy sauce

60 ml (4 tbsp) natural yogurt

pepper

1. Heat the oil in a large frying pan or a wok and fry the garlic for 1 minute. Add the chicken and cook for 3–4 minutes, stirring continuously.
2. Add the courgettes and pepper and continue to cook for 1–2 minutes, until the chicken is cooked and the vegetables are tender but still crisp.
3. Stir in the sherry and soy sauce and cook for 1 minute, until hot. Stir in the yogurt and season to taste with pepper. Serve immediately with boiled rice or noodles.

TO MICROWAVE

 Put all of the ingredients, except the yogurt, in a large bowl or browning dish. Cook on HIGH for 6–8 minutes, stirring frequently. Stir in the yogurt and serve immediately with boiled rice or noodles.

STIR-FRIED CHICKEN WITH COURGETTES. Beautifully bright, the vegetables keep all their crispness as well as their colour. Succulent strips of chicken are mingled with a soy and sherry sauce.

CHICKEN AND BLUE CHEESE SALAD

COUNTRYWIDE

Blue Cheshire is rich and creamy with an excellent flavour. Other blue cheeses, such as Shropshire Blue or Stilton, could also be used in this recipe. Radishes bought fresh, with the leaves still attached, should be eaten as soon as possible. If pre-packed, however, they will keep for a day or two in the fridge.

SERVES 4

250 g (9 oz) boneless cooked chicken, diced

75 g (3 oz) brown rice, cooked

100 g (4 oz) Blue Cheshire cheese, cubed

50 g (2 oz) radishes, sliced

25 g (1 oz) sultanas

2 celery sticks, sliced

1 Cox's eating apple, cored and diced

15 ml (1 tbsp) lemon juice

150 g (5 oz) natural yogurt

30 ml (2 tbsp) mayonnaise

fresh watercress sprigs and red apple slices, to garnish

1. Mix the chicken, rice, cheese, radishes, sultanas and celery together in a large bowl.
2. Coat the apple in lemon juice, then add to the salad.
3. Mix together the yogurt and mayonnaise and fold into the salad mixture. Cover and chill until ready to serve. Serve in a large salad bowl, garnished with watercress and apple slices.

CHICKEN WITH TARRAGON MAYONNAISE

COUNTRYWIDE

It is important to use fresh tarragon in this dish: dried tarragon is a poor substitute.

SERVES 6

6 chicken breast fillets, skinned

2 celery sticks, trimmed and sliced

200 ml (7 fl oz) dry white wine

30 ml (2 tbsp) chopped fresh tarragon

salt and pepper

300 ml (½ pint) lemon mayonnaise

fresh tarragon sprigs, to garnish

1. Put the chicken breasts in a large frying pan. Add the celery, wine, tarragon, salt and pepper. Cover and simmer for 20–30 minutes until tender. Leave to cool.
2. When cool, strain the juices into a pan and boil rapidly until reduced to 90 ml (6 tbsp). Leave to cool.
3. Arrange the chicken on a serving plate. Stir the reduced marinade into the mayonnaise and spoon over the chicken. Serve, garnished with tarragon.

SALMAGUNDI

THE NORTH

Salmagundi has been a popular cold dish for centuries, often incorporating other cold meats, fish and a variety of vegetables. This recipe can be made using chicken only and leaving out the duck. Select firm-textured vegetables and arrange the ingredients in ever-widening circles to create an attractive effect.

SERVES 8

1 oven-ready duckling, weighing about 2.3 kg (5 lb), thawed if frozen

salt and pepper

1 oven-ready chicken, weighing about 2 kg (4½ lb), thawed if frozen

450 g (1 lb) carrots, cut into 0.5 cm (¼ inch) wide strips

450 g (1 lb) potatoes, peeled

150 ml (¼ pint) vegetable oil

75 ml (5 tbsp) lemon juice

pinch of mustard powder

pinch of sugar

450 g (1 lb) shelled peas, cooked

1 cucumber, sliced

225 g (8 oz) tomatoes, thinly sliced

4 celery sticks, thinly sliced

4 eggs, hard-boiled (optional)

mayonnaise (optional)

slices of stuffed olives and radishes, to garnish

1. Weigh the duckling, prick the skin all over with a skewer or sharp fork and sprinkle with salt. Place breast-side down on a rack or trivet in a roasting tin. Roast in the top of the oven at 200°C (400°F) mark 6, basting occasionally, for 20 minutes per 450 g (1 lb).
2. Weigh the chicken and sprinkle with salt and pepper. Place in a shallow roasting tin and roast below the duck on the lowest shelf of the oven for 20 minutes per 450 g (1 lb) plus 20 minutes. Cool both for 1–2 hours or until cool enough to handle.
3. Using a sharp knife, make a slit along each side of the breastbone of both the chicken and duck. Remove and discard the skin.
4. Carefully remove all the flesh from the carcasses of both birds. Discard the carcasses and cut the flesh of the birds into thin strips, about 5 cm (2 inches) long.
5. Cook the carrots in boiling salted water for 8 minutes or until just tender. Drain and rinse in cold water. Cook the potatoes in boiling salted water for 15 minutes until tender. Drain and leave to cool, then dice finely.
6. Make the dressing by whisking the oil, lemon juice, mustard and sugar together with salt and pepper to taste.
7. Choose a large oval platter for making up the salmagundi. Place the potato and peas in the bottom of the dish to give a flat base. Arrange the carrot strips or a layer of cucumber on top, following the oval shape of the platter.

8. Pour over a little dressing. Next, arrange a layer of cucumber or carrot, slightly inside the first layer so that it may be easily seen.

9. Top with more layers of chicken meat, peas, tomato slices, celery and duck meat. Make each layer smaller than the previous one so that the lower layers can all be seen. Sprinkle each one with dressing. Continue layering until all the ingredients are used.

10. If using the eggs, shell and halve them, then top each half with a little mayonnaise, if used. Garnish with a few radish slices and stuffed olives, arranged round the edge of the dish.

TO MICROWAVE

Weigh the duckling. Prick the skin all over with a skewer or sharp fork. Place breast-side down on a microwave roasting rack, standing in a dish. Cover with a split roasting bag to prevent spitting. Cook on HIGH for 8 minutes per 450 g (1 lb), turning over halfway through cooking. Leave to cool. Drain the fat from the dish. Weigh the chicken and stand on the roasting rack. Cover with a split roasting bag and cook on HIGH for 8 minutes per 450 g (1 lb). Leave to cool. Complete steps 5 and 6, then complete the recipe from step 3.

SALMAGUNDI. A stunning salad, that uses cold cooked chicken, duck and vegetables. Definitely a dish to make when you're feeding a crowd.

DUCKLING WITH GREEN PEAS. Roast duck is a deliciously succulent meat, and, in this recipe, comes with its own colourful vegetable accompaniment.

DUCKLING WITH GREEN PEAS

THE EASTERN COUNTIES

In this mouthwatering recipe the vegetables are cooked round the duck and take on plenty of flavour, yet without being too fatty. If fresh peas are not in season – they are only available from June to August – you can use frozen instead.

SERVES 4

1 oven-ready duckling, weighing about 2 kg (4½ lb), thawed if frozen

salt and pepper

16 pickling or small onions, skinned

50 g (2 oz) smoked streaky bacon rashers, rinded and diced

450 g (1 lb) shelled fresh or frozen peas

60 ml (4 tbsp) chicken stock

few sprigs of fresh herbs, such as savory, thyme, mint

1. Weigh the duckling, prick the skin all over with a sharp skewer or fork and rub with salt. Place duckling on a wire rack or trivet in a roasting tin. Roast at 180°C (350°F) mark 4 for 30–35 minutes per 450 g (1 lb).

2. Thirty minutes before the end of cooking time, drain off the fat from the roasting tin, transferring 30 ml (2 tbsp) of it to a saucepan, and discarding the remainder. Add the onions to the pan and cook, turning frequently, until lightly browned. Add the bacon and cook for 2 minutes, until the fat starts to run.

3. If using fresh peas, blanch them for 3 minutes, refresh and drain well. Do not blanch frozen peas. Mix the peas with the onions, bacon and herbs and season to taste with pepper.

4. Stir the stock into the sediment in the roasting tin, then stir in the pea mixture. Return the duckling to the roasting tin, still on the rack, and continue cooking for the remaining 30 minutes. Serve the duckling on a large platter surrounded by the vegetables and the cooking juices.

TO MICROWAVE

Complete step 1, placing the duckling, breast-side down, on a microwave roasting rack, standing in a dish. Do not rub with salt. Cover with a split roasting bag to prevent spitting. Cook on HIGH for 8 minutes per 450 g (1 lb), turning over halfway through cooking. Fifteen minutes before the end of the cooking time, complete steps 2, 3 and 4, cooking the duckling for the remaining 15 minutes. Serve the duckling on a large platter surrounded by the vegetables and cooking juices.

ROAST DUCKLING

THE EASTERN COUNTIES

Make sure you buy a bird large enough for the number of people you are feeding, as there is much less flesh on a duck than on a chicken of the same weight. Aylesbury ducks take their name from the Vale in Buckinghamshire where they used to be reared. However, nowadays most ducklings are produced in Lincolnshire and Norfolk, and the Aylesbury is no longer a speciality of its home region.

* ALLOW AT LEAST 450 g (1 lb) DRESSED WEIGHT PER PERSON

1 oven-ready duckling*
25 g (1 oz) butter
1 medium onion, skinned and finely chopped
100 g (4 oz) fresh wholemeal breadcrumbs
15 ml (1 tbsp) chopped fresh sage or 5 ml (1 tsp) dried
1 small eating apple, peeled, cored and grated
1 egg
salt and pepper
450 g (1 lb) cooking apples, peeled, cored and sliced
sugar (optional)

1. If frozen, thaw the duckling completely. Leave it in its bag and thaw at room temperature. Remove the giblets as soon as possible. Wash and pat the carcass dry both inside and out. A duckling that is not thoroughly dried will not crisp as easily.
2. To make the stuffing, melt half the butter in a medium saucepan and cook the onion gently until softened, but not browned. Stir in the breadcrumbs, sage, eating apple and egg and season to taste. Shape the stuffing into small balls and place in a roasting tin.
3. Weigh the duckling, prick the skin all over with a skewer or sharp fork and sprinkle with salt. (This helps to draw out the fat and crisp the skin.)
4. Place the duckling on a wire rack or trivet in a roasting tin. Roast at 180°C (350°F) mark 4 for 30–35 minutes per 450 g (1 lb). Cook the stuffing balls for the last 30 minutes of the calculated time.
5. Meanwhile, make the apple sauce. Put the sliced apples in a heavy-based saucepan together with 15 ml (1 tbsp) water. Cover tightly and cook for about 10 minutes, until the apples are tender, shaking the pan occasionally. Stir in the remaining butter and beat with a wooden spoon until smooth. Stir in a little sugar, if liked. Serve the duckling with the apple sauce and thin gravy.

TO MICROWAVE

Complete steps 1, 2 and 3 but do not rub with salt. Place the duckling, breast-side down, on a microwave roasting rack, standing in a dish. Cover with a split roasting bag to prevent spitting. Cook on HIGH for 8 minutes per 450 g (1 lb), turning over halfway through cooking. Meanwhile, cook the stuffing balls in a conventional oven for 30 minutes. When the duckling is cooked, put under a grill to brown. Complete step 5.

DERWENTWATER DUCK WITH CUMBERLAND SAUCE

THE NORTH

Game flourishes on the moors and lakes of the North and the wild duck of Derwentwater are especially valued for their tenderness and flavour. You can, of course, use any other duck for this recipe; the rich flesh is admirably partnered by the sweet sharp flavour of Cumberland sauce. Croquette potatoes would go well with this dish.

SERVES 4

4 duckling portions
salt and pepper
finely shredded rind and juice of 1 large orange
finely shredded rind and juice of 1 lemon
60 ml (4 tbsp) redcurrant jelly
10 ml (2 tsp) cornflour
60 ml (4 tbsp) port
30 ml (2 tbsp) brandy
fresh watercress sprigs and orange slices, to garnish

1. Prick the duckling portions all over with a sharp skewer or fork, then sprinkle with salt and pepper.
2. Place the duckling portions on a wire rack over a roasting tin. Roast at 190°C (375°F) mark 5 for 45–60 minutes, until the skin is crisp and the juices run clear when the thickest part of the duckling is pricked with a skewer.
3. Meanwhile, make the sauce. Put the orange and lemon juices into a small saucepan, add the shreds of orange and lemon rind, cover and simmer gently for 5 minutes.
4. Add the redcurrant jelly and let it melt slowly over a gentle heat. Mix the cornflour with the port, then stir into the sauce and bring to the boil, stirring until the sauce thickens.
5. When the duckling portions are cooked put them on to a warmed serving dish and keep hot while the sauce is finished. Pour off the fat from the roasting tin, leaving the cooking juices behind, then add the brandy and stir over a gentle heat to stir in the sediment in the bottom of the tin.
6. Add the orange sauce, stir well and serve with the duckling. Garnish with sprigs of watercress and orange slices.

TO MICROWAVE

Complete step 1 but do not rub with salt. Weigh the duckling portions, then place, breast-side down, on a microwave roasting rack, standing in a dish. Cover with a split roasting bag to prevent spitting. Cook on HIGH for 8 minutes per 450 g (1 lb), turning over halfway through cooking. When the duckling portions are cooked, put under a grill to brown. Complete the recipe.

ROAST TURKEY WITH PARSLEY AND LEMON STUFFING

COUNTRYWIDE

The trick when roasting a turkey is to keep the breast meat moist while the darker meat on the legs, which takes longer to cook, is finishing off. To do this, cover the breast with streaky bacon rashers, baste well from time to time and protect it with foil if it shows signs of becoming too brown.

* 3.6–5 kg (8–11¼ lb) SERVES 10–15; 5–6.8 kg (11¼–15 lb) SERVES 15–20; 6.8–9 kg (15–20¼ lb) SERVES 20–30

25 g (1 oz) butter
2 medium onions, skinned and finely chopped
2 celery sticks, finely chopped
225 g (8 oz) fresh wholemeal breadcrumbs
60 ml (4 tbsp) chopped fresh parsley
finely grated rind of 2 lemons
salt and pepper
1 egg, beaten
1 oven-ready turkey, thawed if frozen*
streaky bacon rashers

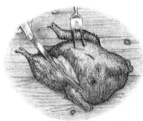

Use a carving fork to hold the bird firmly in place.

Carve down between thigh and breast.

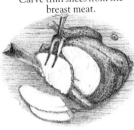

Carve thin slices from the breast meat.

1. To make the stuffing, melt the butter in a large saucepan, add the onions and celery, cover and cook gently for about 10 minutes, until really soft, stirring occasionally.
2. Remove from the heat and add the breadcrumbs, parsley and lemon rind. Season and stir in the egg.
3. Wash the inside of the bird and stuff at the neck end before folding the neck skin over. Make the turkey plump and as even in shape as possible, then truss it with the wings folded under the body and the legs tied together.
4. Weigh the turkey and calculate the cooking time, allowing 20 minutes per 450 g (1 lb) plus 20 minutes.
5. Place the turkey in a roasting tin, then sprinkle with salt and pepper.
6. Place the streaky bacon rashers over the breast to prevent it from becoming dry. Roast at 180°C (350°F) mark 4, basting occasionally. Put a piece of foil over the bird if it shows signs of becoming too brown.
7. Leave the turkey to rest for 10 minutes, then carve as illustrated. Serve the roast turkey with the traditional accompaniments of thin gravy, bread sauce, small sausages and bacon rolls.

NORFOLK TURKEY BREAST WITH ASPARAGUS

THE EASTERN COUNTIES

This recipe combines two of East Anglia's most celebrated products. Norfolk has long been an important turkey farming centre and the small joints and breasts that are readily available mean that the meat can be served at any time of year. Choose thin sprue asparagus for this dish.

SERVES 4

225 g (8 oz) thin asparagus stalks

2 turkey breast fillets, each weighing about 225 g (8 oz), skinned and halved

30 ml (2 tbsp) plain flour

salt and pepper

15 g (½ oz) butter

15 ml (1 tbsp) vegetable oil

300 ml (½ pint) chicken stock

5 ml (1 tsp) chopped fresh sage or 2.5 ml (½ tsp) dried

60 ml (4 tbsp) dry white wine

150 ml (5 fl oz) fresh soured cream

1. Cut off the ends of the asparagus if they are tough and woody. Trim them all to the same length, cut off the tips and cut the stalks into 3 pieces.

2. Bat out each turkey breast slightly with a rolling pin or meat mallet. Coat in the flour seasoned with salt and pepper, shaking off any excess. Heat the butter and oil in a large frying pan and fry the turkey until lightly browned on both sides. Add the chicken stock, asparagus stalks, reserving the tips, the sage and wine, cover and cook gently for 15–20 minutes, until tender.

3. Five minutes before the end of the cooking time, add the reserved asparagus tips and the cream. Season to taste. Serve with new potatoes.

TO MICROWAVE

Complete step 1. Heat a large browning dish on HIGH for 5–8 minutes or according to the manufacturer's instructions. Meanwhile, bat out the turkey breasts slightly with a rolling pin or meat mallet. Coat in the seasoned flour, shaking off any excess. Add 15 ml (1 tbsp) vegetable oil to the browning dish (omit butter), then quickly add the turkey breasts and cook on HIGH for 1 minute, turn over and cook on HIGH for 1 minute. Add 150 ml (¼ pint) chicken stock, the asparagus stalks and asparagus tips, the sage and wine, cover and cook on HIGH for 5–6 minutes or until tender. Add the cream, re-cover and cook for 1–2 minutes, until heated through. Season to taste.

OPPOSITE
ROAST TURKEY WITH PARSLEY AND LEMON STUFFING. Proudly plump and golden, there's nothing to beat a turkey with all the trimmings, at any time of year.

BELOW
NORFOLK TURKEY BREAST WITH ASPARAGUS. The unmistakable flavour of asparagus is delicious in this creamy sauce. Remember to save a few tips for the pretty garnish.

TURKEY ESCALOPES WITH DAMSONS. Dark, shiny damsons or plums look attractive in an unusual sauce that is flavoured with apple juice, sherry and garlic.

TURKEY ESCALOPES
WITH DAMSONS
COUNTRYWIDE

This is a lovely way to perk up plain turkey breasts, with a fruity, piquant marinade. It's a very quick dish to cook, but you do need to plan ahead and let the meat marinate overnight, or at least for a few hours, for maximum flavour.

SERVES 4

2 turkey breast fillets, each weighing about 225 g (8 oz), skinned and cut widthways into 5 cm (2 inch) slices

75 ml (3 fl oz) unsweetened apple juice

45 ml (3 tbsp) soy sauce

45 ml (3 tbsp) dry sherry

1 small garlic clove, skinned and crushed

5 ml (1 tsp) chopped fresh thyme or 1.25 ml (¼ tsp) dried thyme

15 g (½ oz) butter

15 ml (1 tbsp) vegetable oil

225 g (8 oz) damsons or plums, halved and stoned

pepper

1. Bat out the turkey slices with a rolling pin or meat mallet until about 2.5 cm (1 inch) thick.
2. Place in a large shallow dish and pour over the apple juice, soy sauce, sherry, garlic and thyme. Cover and leave in the refrigerator to marinate for 3–4 hours or overnight.
3. Remove the turkey from the marinade, reserving the marinade. Heat the butter and oil in a large frying pan and quickly fry the turkey until browned on both sides. Add the damsons or plums, reserved marinade and pepper to taste.
4. Cover and simmer gently for 10–15 minutes, until tender, stirring occasionally. Serve with green beans and boiled or mashed potatoes.

TO MICROWAVE

Complete steps 1 and 2. Remove the turkey from the marinade, reserving the marinade. Heat a large browning dish on HIGH for 5–8 minutes or according to the manufacturer's instructions. Add 15 ml (1 tbsp) vegetable oil (omit butter), then quickly add the turkey and cook on HIGH for 2 minutes, stirring once. Add the damsons and pepper to taste. Cover and cook on HIGH for 5 minutes or until tender, stirring once. Serve hot.

TURKEY WITH CELERY SAUCE

COUNTRYWIDE

This magnificent stuffed turkey would once have formed the centrepiece on a Victorian sideboard, flanked by a boiled ham, tongue or pickled pork. The celery sauce is a traditional accompaniment, although an oyster stuffing and sauce were sometimes served in the days when oysters were cheaper and less of a luxury than today.

SERVES 6

175 g (6 oz) back bacon rashers, rinded and minced

2 medium onions, skinned and finely chopped

100 g (4 oz) lean veal, minced

175 g (6 oz) fresh wholemeal breadcrumbs

100 g (4 oz) mushrooms, chopped

30 ml (2 tbsp) chopped fresh parsley

salt and pepper

1 egg

a little milk, if necessary

1 oven-ready turkey, weighing about 2.7 kg (6 lb), thawed if frozen

1 head of celery, sliced

568 ml (1 pint) chicken stock

1 bouquet garni

30 ml (2 tbsp) cornflour

45 ml (3 tbsp) fresh single cream

1. To make the stuffing, dry fry the bacon in a large heavy-based frying pan until the fat starts to run. Add half of the chopped onion and cook gently for about 5 minutes, until softened, stirring. Add the veal, breadcrumbs, mushrooms and parsley and mix together thoroughly. Season to taste and bind together with the egg, adding a little milk if the mixture is too stiff.
2. Stuff the neck end of the turkey with the stuffing. Cover the stuffing with the neck skin. Truss the turkey with the wings folded under the body and the legs tied together.
3. Weigh the turkey and calculate the cooking time, allowing 20 minutes per 450 g (1 lb) plus 20 minutes. Place in a roasting tin, then sprinkle with salt and pepper.
4. Roast at 180°C (350°F) mark 4, basting occasionally. Put a piece of foil over the bird if it shows signs of becoming too brown.
5. Meanwhile, make the sauce. Put the celery, remaining onion, stock and bouquet garni in a large saucepan. Bring to the boil, then cover and simmer gently for 45 minutes, until really tender. Cool slightly, remove the bouquet garni, and purée in a blender or food processor. Return to the pan.
6. Blend the cornflour to a paste with a little water and stir into the purée. Bring to the boil, stirring continuously. Stir in the cream and season to taste.
7. When the turkey is cooked, gently reheat the celery sauce but do not boil or it will curdle. Serve the carved turkey with the sauce handed separately.

TURKEY AND LEEK CRUMBLE

COUNTRYWIDE

A hint of mustard gives a good tang to the crumble topping, which gets an extra crunchy texture from porridge oats. Leeks are available for most of the year, except for three months or so in high summer.

SERVES 4

75 g (3 oz) butter

450 g (1 lb) boneless turkey, skinned and cubed

150 g (5 oz) plain wholemeal flour

450 ml (¾ pint) fresh milk

salt and pepper

10 ml (2 tsp) chopped fresh sage

450 g (1 lb) leeks, trimmed, sliced and washed

100 g (4 oz) small button mushrooms

5 ml (1 tsp) mustard powder

5 ml (1 tsp) paprika

50 g (2 oz) Cheddar cheese, grated

25 g (1 oz) porridge oats

1. Melt 25 g (1 oz) butter in a large saucepan, then add the turkey and fry for 5–6 minutes, until lightly browned.
2. Stir in 25 g (1 oz) of the flour and cook for 2–3 minutes, then gradually blend in the milk. Heat, whisking continuously, until the sauce thickens, boils and is smooth. Simmer gently for 15 minutes. Season to taste.
3. Add the sage, leeks and mushrooms to the sauce and simmer for 10 minutes.
4. Rub the remaining butter into the remaining flour, mustard and paprika, then stir in the cheese and oats.
5. Pour the turkey and leek sauce into a 1.7 litre (3 pint) ovenproof serving dish. Sprinkle with the crumble mixture and bake at 200°C (400°F) mark 6 for 25 minutes.

TO MICROWAVE

Melt 25 g (1 oz) of the butter in a large bowl on HIGH for 45 seconds. Add the turkey and cook on HIGH for 4 minutes. Stir in 25 g (1 oz) of the flour and cook on HIGH for 1 minute. Gradually blend in the milk and cook on HIGH for 7–8 minutes, until sauce thickens, boils and is smooth, whisking frequently. Add the sage, leeks and mushrooms to the sauce and cook on HIGH for 7–8 minutes. Complete steps 4 and 5.

ROAST MICHAELMAS GOOSE WITH APPLES AND PRUNES

NORTHERN IRELAND AND THE NORTH

'Green' geese, which had fed on pasture, made a traditional feast for Michaelmas, in late September, and were less fatty than Christmas geese. In Ireland and northern England, it was thought that if you ate goose at Michaelmas you would have good luck for the rest of the year. The roast bird was always accompanied by apples, as windfalls were plentiful. Geese are in season from September to December but are not widely stocked, so you will probably have to order in advance, especially for Christmas.

SERVES 8

4–5 kg (9–11 lb) oven-ready goose, with giblets, thawed if frozen
salt and pepper
15 g (½ oz) butter
1 large onion, skinned and chopped
450 g (1 lb) no-soak prunes
60 ml (4 tbsp) port
15 ml (1 tbsp) chopped fresh sage or 5 ml (1 tsp) dried
100 g (4 oz) fresh wholemeal breadcrumbs
6 Cox's Orange Pippin apples
300 ml (½ pint) dry white wine

1. Prick the skin of the goose all over with a sharp skewer or fork and pull the inside fat out of the bird and reserve. Rub salt over the skin.
2. To make the stuffing, melt the butter in a large frying pan, add the onion and cook for 5–6 minutes, until softened. Separate the goose liver from the giblets and chop finely, then add to the onion and cook gently for 2–3 minutes.
3. Remove the stones from half of the prunes and discard. Chop the prunes roughly and stir into the onion with the port. Cover and simmer gently for 5 minutes. Add the sage and breadcrumbs and mix thoroughly together. Season the stuffing mixture to taste.
4. Spoon the stuffing into the neck end of the goose, then truss with strong cotton or fine string. Weigh the bird.
5. Put on a wire rack placed in a roasting tin. Cover the breast with the reserved fat and then with foil. Roast at 200°C (400°F) mark 6 for 15 minutes per 450 g (1 lb) plus 15 minutes, basting frequently.
6. Thirty minutes before the end of the cooking time, drain off the fat and discard. Core the apples and cut into eighths, then add to the tin with the remaining prunes and wine. Place the bird on top, standing on the roasting rack. Remove the foil and the fat and cook, uncovered, for the last 30 minutes.
7. Serve the roast goose with the cooking juices and the apples and the prunes. Plain boiled or mashed potatoes go well with the richness of goose. Braised red cabbage is also a traditional accompaniment.

KENTISH PIGEONS IN A POT WITH PLUMS

THE SOUTH-EAST

Fruit is widely used in savoury recipes in Kent and the delicate, slightly sharp flavour of plums goes well with game. Pigeons are widely available in early autumn, when plums are at their best.

SERVES 4

25 g (1 oz) butter
15 ml (1 tbsp) vegetable oil

4 young pigeons, prepared

10 ml (2 tsp) plain wholemeal flour

1 medium onion, skinned and chopped

2 cloves

15 ml (1 tbsp) chopped fresh mixed herbs, such as rosemary, sage, thyme, or 5 ml (1 tsp) dried

100 ml (4 fl oz) port

450 g (1 lb) purple plums, stoned and halved

salt and pepper

freshly grated nutmeg

1. Heat the butter and oil in a large frying pan. Coat the pigeons lightly in the flour, shaking off any excess, then add to the pan and fry, turning occasionally, until lightly browned on all sides. Transfer to an ovenproof casserole.

2. Stir the onion into the frying pan and fry gently until beginning to soften. Spoon over the pigeons, then sprinkle the cloves and herbs over the top.

3. Stir the port into the frying pan, bring to the boil, then pour over the pigeons. Arrange the plums over the top. Cover tightly and bake at 170°C (325°F) mark 3 for 1½ hours, until the pigeons are tender.

4. Transfer the pigeons and plums to a warmed serving platter. Boil the juices for 2–3 minutes to thicken them and concentrate the flavour. Season to taste with salt, pepper and nutmeg, then pour over the pigeons. Serve at once.

ROAST MICHAELMAS GOOSE WITH APPLES. Goose makes a real treat, and this fruity recipe adds a refreshing tang to offset the richness of the bird.

171

OPPOSITE
ROAST PHEASANT. The rich, gamey flavour and superb tenderness of the meat make pheasant a must to enjoy through the autumn and winter. See the Roast Game chart on this page for cooking instructions. Don't forget the traditional accompaniments for a truly memorable meal.

ROAST GAME
COUNTRYWIDE

The rules for roasting are much the same for all game birds – keep the breast moist with streaky bacon rashers and cook at a fairly high temperature. Large birds are carved in the same way as chicken; smaller ones, such as partridge, can be cut in half; and the smallest of all, for instance quail, can be served whole, with two birds per person.

Bird	Number of Servings	Oven Temperature	Cooking Time
Grouse	1 per person	200°C (400°F) mark 6	35–40 minutes
Guinea fowl	3–4 servings	200°C (400°F) mark 6	45–60 minutes
Partridge	1 per person	200°C (400°F) mark 6	40 minutes
Pheasant	Female birds give 2 servings, male birds give 3 servings	230°C (450°F) mark 8 Then reduce to 200°C (400°F) mark 6	10 minutes Then 30–50 minutes
Quail	2 per person	190°C (375°F) mark 5	15–20 minutes

1. If the bird is frozen, thaw it completely before cooking.
2. Wash the bird inside and out and dry on kitchen paper. If it is to be stuffed, put the stuffing in the neck end only. If placed in the body cavity, stuffing can prevent the bird cooking through thoroughly. Pull the skin over the stuffing and truss the bird neatly to keep it in good shape. If you are not using stuffing, you can add extra flavour by putting half an onion or an apple inside the body cavity and seasoning the inside well. Lean birds benefit from a little butter flavoured with lemon rind or herbs inside the cavity.
3. Add extra fat to the breast such as softened butter and streaky bacon rashers.
4. Preheat the oven and have the bird at room temperature before it goes in. Time the cooking according to the chart. Baste frequently with butter and cover towards the end of the cooking time if the breast is browning too quickly.
5. Serve garnished with fresh watercress sprigs and accompany with thin gravy, bread sauce, game chips and a green vegetable.

PHEASANT WITH CHESTNUTS
COUNTRYWIDE

Many supermarkets now sell oven-ready fresh or frozen pheasant during the season, which runs from 1 October to 1 February (10 December in Scotland). You may also be able to buy fresh game from your butcher, in which case ask for the bird to be plucked and drawn. The tender flesh is deliciously contrasted with crunchy chestnuts in this richly flavoured dish.

SERVES 4
✳

25 g (1 oz) butter
15 ml (1 tbsp) vegetable oil
2 oven-ready pheasants, jointed
2 medium onions, skinned and sliced
225 g (8 oz) peeled chestnuts
45 ml (3 tbsp) plain wholemeal flour
450 ml (¾ pint) chicken stock
150 ml (¼ pint) dry red wine
salt and pepper
grated rind and juice of ½ orange
10 ml (2 tsp) redcurrant jelly
bouquet garni
chopped fresh parsley, to garnish

1. Heat the butter and oil in a large frying pan and fry the pheasant joints for about 5 minutes, until browned. Remove from the pan and put into an ovenproof casserole.
2. Fry the onions and chestnuts in the remaining oil and butter for a few minutes until brown, then add to the pheasant.
3. Stir the flour into the fat in the pan and cook, stirring, for 2–3 minutes. Remove from the heat and gradually stir in the stock and wine. Bring to the boil, stirring continuously, until thickened and smooth. Season to taste and pour over the pheasant in the casserole. Add the orange rind and juice, redcurrant jelly and bouquet garni.
4. Cover the casserole and bake at 180°C (350°F) mark 4 for about 1 hour or until the pheasant is tender. Remove the bouquet garni before serving, garnished with parsley. Accompany with jacket potatoes.

Accompaniments

The traditional accompaniments to serve with Roast Game are:

Thin Gravy   Add 150 ml (¼ pint) water or meat stock to the roasting tin and, with a spoon, rub down any cooking juices left in the tin. Bring to the boil and boil for 2–3 minutes. Remove all fat from the surface with a metal spoon, season to taste and strain before serving.

Fried Crumbs   Fry 50–100 g (2–4 oz) fresh breadcrumbs in 25–50 g (1–2 oz) butter until golden brown. Stir from time to time to ensure even browning.

Game Chips   Peel and cut potatoes into very thin slices. Then deep fry until golden.

Bread Sauce   Stick **2 cloves** into a skinned **onion** and put in a saucepan with a **bay leaf** and **450 ml (¾ pint) fresh milk**. Bring slowly to the boil, remove from the heat, cover and leave to infuse for 10 minutes, then remove the bay leaf and onion. Add **75 g (3 oz) fresh breadcrumbs** and **salt and pepper**, return to the heat, cover and simmer for 10–15 minutes, stirring occasionally. Stir in **15 g (½ oz) butter** and **30 ml (2 tbsp) fresh single cream**.

Toast   Small birds such as grouse are roasted and served on a slice of toast or bread.

VENISON ESCALOPES WITH RED WINE.
Redcurrant jelly adds a touch of sweetness to the savoury sauce poured over the tender meat.

VENISON ESCALOPES WITH RED WINE

SCOTLAND

You can buy venison from any butcher with a game licence. Young venison is usually tender enough not to need hanging but older, tougher animals benefit from it. Your butcher can advise on this.

SERVES 6

| 6 escalopes of venison cut from the haunch (leg), each weighing about 175 g (6 oz) |
| 1 small onion, skinned and finely chopped |
| 1 bay leaf |
| 2 fresh parsley sprigs |
| 8 juniper berries |
| 300 ml (½ pint) dry red wine |
| 15 g (½ oz) butter |

| 15 ml (1 tbsp) vegetable oil |
| 30 ml (2 tbsp) redcurrant jelly |
| salt and pepper |

1. Put the escalopes in a large shallow dish and sprinkle with the onion, bay leaf, parsley and juniper berries. Pour on the wine, cover and marinate in the refrigerator for 3–4 hours or overnight, turning the escalopes occasionally.

2. Remove the escalopes from the marinade, reserving the marinade. Heat the butter and oil in a large frying pan and fry the escalopes for 3–4 minutes on each side. Transfer to a warmed serving dish and keep warm while making the sauce.

3. Strain the reserved marinade into the frying pan and stir to loosen any sediment. Increase the heat and boil rapidly for 3–4 minutes, until reduced. Stir in the redcurrant jelly and season the mixture to taste. Cook for 1–2 minutes, stirring, then pour over the escalopes. Serve immediately with game chips and carrots.

VENISON STEW
SCOTLAND

Venison is becoming more widely available with the development of deer farming and can be bought all year round because of freezing techniques. The rich gamey flavour of venison comes out well in this slow-cooked dish.

SERVES 4

✳

700 g (1½ lb) shoulder of venison, cut into 1 cm (½ inch) cubes	
50 g (2 oz) plain flour	
salt and pepper	
25 g (1 oz) butter	
15 ml (1 tbsp) vegetable oil	
2 medium onions, skinned and chopped	
2 carrots, sliced	
300 ml (½ pint) beef stock	
150 ml (¼ pint) dry red wine	
bouquet garni	
10 ml (2 tsp) red wine vinegar	

1. Toss the venison in the flour seasoned with salt and pepper, shaking off any excess. Heat the butter and the oil in a large frying pan and fry the meat for about 10 minutes, until well browned on all sides. Using a slotted spoon, transfer to an ovenproof casserole.
2. Fry the vegetables in the fat remaining in the frying pan until golden. Drain well and add to the meat in the casserole. Stir the rest of the flour into the fat in the pan and cook gently, stirring, until brown. Remove the pan from the heat and gradually stir in the stock and wine. Bring to the boil, stirring, until thickened.
3. Pour the sauce over the venison and season to taste, then add the bouquet garni and the vinegar.
4. Cover the casserole and bake at 170°C (325°F) mark 3 for about 2 hours or until the meat is tender. Remove the bouquet garni before serving.

POACHER'S PIE
THE EASTERN COUNTIES

Rabbit recipes feature widely in the traditional cooking of the Eastern Counties because there used to be a big surplus of wild rabbits and hares, which were partially controlled by shooting for game. If wild rabbit is not available, use commercially produced meat, on sale in many supermarkets.

SERVES 4

✳

225 g (8 oz) plain flour	
salt and pepper	
50 g (2 oz) butter	
50 g (2 oz) lard	
450 g (1 lb) boneless rabbit, skinned and cubed	
100 g (4 oz) streaky bacon rashers, rinded and chopped	
2 medium potatoes, sliced	
1 medium leek, trimmed, sliced and washed	

15 ml (1 tbsp) chopped fresh parsley	
1.25 ml (¼ tsp) mixed dried herbs	
chicken stock	
1 egg, beaten, to glaze	

1. Put the flour and a pinch of salt into a bowl and rub in the butter and lard until the mixture resembles fine breadcrumbs. Add 45–60 ml (3–4 tbsp) cold water and mix to form a firm dough.
2. Fill a 1.7 litre (3 pint) pie dish with alternate layers of rabbit, bacon and vegetables, sprinkling with seasoning and herbs. Half-fill with stock.
3. Roll out the pastry on a lightly floured surface to 5 cm (2 inches) wider than the top of the dish. Cut a 2.5 cm (1 inch) strip from the outer edge and line the dampened rim of the dish. Dampen the pastry rim and cover with the pastry lid. Trim and seal the edges. Make a hole in the centre to let the steam escape.
4. Decorate with pastry leaves and brush with egg. Bake in the oven at 190°C (375°F) mark 5 for 30 minutes. Cover loosely with foil, then reduce to 180°C (350°F) mark 4 for a further hour. Serve hot.

RABBIT CIDER HOT POT
THE WEST

One medium-sized rabbit, jointed, should weigh about 1.1 kg (2½ lb). If you are using smaller joints to make up this total weight, cut down the cooking time accordingly.

SERVES 4

6 rabbit joints, total weight about 1.1 kg (2½ lb)	
12 prunes	
450 ml (15 fl oz) can dry cider	
2 medium onions, skinned and sliced	
30 ml (2 tbsp) wholegrain mustard	
4 bay leaves	
salt and pepper	
60 ml (4 tbsp) plain flour	
30 ml (2 tbsp) vegetable oil	
15 g (½ oz) butter	
450 g (1 lb) parsnips, peeled and cut into chunks	
397 g (14 oz) can red kidney beans, drained	

1. Rinse and dry the rabbit joints. Put in a large bowl with the prunes, cider, onions, mustard, bay leaves and 450 ml (15 fl oz) water. Season, then stir gently to mix. Cover tightly and refrigerate overnight.
2. The next day, lift rabbit joints out of marinade and dry. Toss in flour. Heat oil and butter in a large flameproof casserole, add joints and fry until brown.
3. Sprinkle any remaining flour into the casserole. Pour in the marinade, reserving the prunes. Add the parsnips. Bring to the boil and cover tightly.
4. Bake at 180°C (350°F) mark 4 for about 40 minutes. Add the prunes and beans, cover again and bake for a further 20–30 minutes or until everything is tender.

175

RABBIT CASSEROLE WITH DUMPLINGS.
Celery, leek, carrot and bacon add flavour, while herby dumplings give substance to this heart-warming dish.

1. Fry the bacon in a flameproof casserole until the fat runs. Add the rabbit and fry gently until browned. Add the celery, leeks, bay leaf and carrots and mix well. Sprinkle in the wholemeal flour and stir well. Cook for 1 minute, then remove from the heat and gradually add the stock. Bring to the boil, stirring continuously. Season to taste.
2. Cover and bake at 170°C (325°F) mark 3 for about 1½ hours or until the rabbit is tender.
3. To make the dumplings, mix the self-raising flour, suet, chives and salt and pepper together. Add enough cold water to make a soft dough.
4. Twenty to twenty-five minutes before the end of the cooking time, shape the dough into 12 balls and place on top of the casserole. Cover again and bake until the dumplings are well risen and cooked through. Serve immediately with runner beans.

RABBIT IN THE DAIRY

COUNTRYWIDE

Young rabbit is a tender, white meat, which tastes rather like chicken and should not be swamped with strong herbs. This recipe uses milk to enhance the delicacy of flavour, and is deliberately left pale.

SERVES 4

| 1 small celery stick, finely chopped |
| 1 small onion, skinned and finely chopped |
| 25 g (1 oz) cooked ham, finely chopped |
| 8 rabbit joints |
| salt and pepper |
| 2 bay leaves |
| 300 ml (½ pint) fresh milk |

1. Put the celery, onion and ham in an ovenproof casserole. Place the pieces of rabbit on top, season to taste and add the bay leaves.
2. Bring the milk to the boil, then pour over the rabbit. Cover tightly and bake at 170°C (325°F) mark 3 for about 2 hours, until the rabbit is tender. Accompany with broad beans or carrots and boiled new potatoes.

TO MICROWAVE

Complete step 1. Bring the milk to the boil and pour over the rabbit. Cover and cook on HIGH for 10 minutes, then on MEDIUM for 45 minutes or until the rabbit is tender.

RABBIT CASSEROLE WITH DUMPLINGS

THE EASTERN COUNTIES

Country families were always glad to get their hands on a fresh rabbit to help stretch the week's food. And rabbit still makes a cheap meal, served in a well-flavoured casserole with plenty of vegetables. Dumplings are an East Anglian favourite – to be called a 'Norfolk dumpling' just means you are delightfully plump!

SERVES 4

| 100 g (4 oz) streaky bacon rashers, rinded and chopped |
| 4 rabbit portions |
| 4 celery sticks, chopped |
| 2 leeks, trimmed, sliced and washed |
| 1 bay leaf |
| 225 g (8 oz) carrots, sliced |
| 30 ml (2 tbsp) plain wholemeal flour |
| 568 ml (1 pint) chicken stock |
| salt and pepper |
| 75 g (3 oz) self-raising flour |
| 40 g (1½ oz) shredded beef suet |
| 15 ml (1 tbsp) snipped fresh chives |

OFFAL

LAMBS' LIVER AND MUSHROOMS
COUNTRYWIDE

A dish that's quick to put together but good enough to serve to guests. Simply fry the lambs' liver and mushrooms for a few minutes before adding tomatoes and an all-important dash of Worcestershire sauce. A flourish of soured cream stirred in at the end of cooking makes the result into something a bit special.

SERVES 3

15 g (½ oz) butter
1 medium onion, skinned and sliced
450 g (1 lb) lambs' liver, cut into strips
15 ml (1 tbsp) plain flour
100 g (4 oz) button mushrooms
150 ml (¼ pint) beef stock
4 tomatoes, skinned and roughly chopped
30 ml (2 tbsp) Worcestershire sauce
salt and pepper
150 ml (5 fl oz) fresh soured cream

1. Melt the butter in a large frying pan and gently fry the onion for 5 minutes, until softened.
2. Coat the liver strips with the flour and add to the pan with the mushrooms. Fry for 5 minutes, stirring well, then add the stock and bring to the boil.
3. Stir in the tomatoes and Worcestershire sauce. Season to taste, then simmer for 3–4 minutes. Stir in the soured cream, and reheat without boiling. Serve hot with ribbon noodles.

TO MICROWAVE

Cut the butter into small pieces and melt in a large bowl on HIGH for 30 seconds. Add the onion, cover and cook on HIGH for 5–7 minutes, until softened. Coat the liver in the flour and add to the bowl with the mushrooms. Cover and cook on HIGH for 2–3 minutes or until the liver just changes colour, stirring once. Add the stock, tomatoes, Worcestershire sauce and salt and pepper, re-cover and cook on HIGH for 2–3 minutes or until boiling, stirring once. Stir in the soured cream and serve immediately.

LAMBS' LIVER AND MUSHROOMS. Meltingly tender liver and juicy mushrooms make a mouthwatering combination. Serve with a bed of ribbon noodles.

WELSH FAGGOTS
WALES

These are also known as 'poor man's goose' or 'savoury duck' and are a traditional, filling and economical dish. The word faggots is a corruption of fegato, the Italian for liver.

SERVES 4

❄ ⚡

450 g (1 lb) pigs' liver

2 medium onions, skinned

75 g (3 oz) shredded beef suet

100 g (4 oz) fresh breadcrumbs

5 ml (1 tsp) finely chopped fresh sage or 2.5 ml (½ tsp) dried sage

salt and pepper

300 ml (½ pint) boiling beef stock

1. In a food processor or blender, finely chop the liver with the onions. Stir in the suet, breadcrumbs and sage. Season to taste.
2. Roll the mixture into 12 balls and place them in a well-greased, shallow ovenproof dish.
3. Pour the stock into the dish, cover and bake at 180°C (350°F) mark 4 for about 30 minutes, until the juices run clear. Uncover and continue cooking for 10 minutes. Traditionally faggots are served with a purée of dried peas.

TO MICROWAVE

⚡ Complete steps 1 and 2. Pour 150 ml (¼ pint) boiling stock into the dish, cover and cook on HIGH for 12–14 minutes or until cooked through. Uncover and brown under a hot grill.

LIVER WITH SAGE
COUNTRYWIDE

Calves' liver, with its meltingly tender texture, would be ideal in this dish, but it's not always easy to find and tends to be pricey. Lambs' liver also gives excellent results. If you can, use fresh sage; the flavour is not as subtle with dried.

SERVES 4

⚡

25 g (1 oz) butter

1 medium onion, skinned and chopped

30 ml (2 tbsp) chopped fresh sage or 5 ml (1 tsp) dried

450 g (1 lb) liver, sliced

25 g (1 oz) plain wholemeal flour

300 ml (½ pint) fresh milk

salt and pepper

1. Melt the butter in a medium saucepan and fry the onion and sage for 3 minutes. Coat the liver in the flour, then add to the pan and cook for 3 minutes on one side. Turn over and cook for a further 3 minutes.
2. Gradually stir in the milk and bring to the boil, stirring, until the sauce thickens, boils and is smooth. Season to taste. Cook for 1–2 minutes. Serve with jacket potatoes or rice and a green vegetable.

TO MICROWAVE

⚡ Melt the butter in a shallow dish on HIGH for 45 seconds. Add the onions and sage and cook, covered, on HIGH for 5 minutes. Add the liver coated in flour and cook, covered, on HIGH for 2 minutes, then turn and cook on HIGH for a further 2 minutes. Gradually add the milk and cook on HIGH for 4–5 minutes, until boiling and thickened, stirring frequently. Serve with jacket potatoes or rice and a green vegetable.

STIR-FRIED LIVER WITH CABBAGE AND CARAWAY
COUNTRYWIDE

Take a tip from the Chinese and try stir-frying to keep vegetables crisp and meat moist. It takes just a few minutes from start to finish to cook this inexpensive dish, in which apple and caraway seeds add to the flavour.

SERVES 4

⚡

450 g (1 lb) lambs' liver, thinly sliced

15 g (½ oz) butter

15 ml (1 tbsp) vegetable oil

350 g (12 oz) green cabbage, finely shredded

1 large onion, skinned and chopped

1 Discovery or Crispin apple, quartered, cored and thinly sliced

15 ml (1 tbsp) caraway seeds

30 ml (2 tbsp) cider vinegar

15 ml (1 tbsp) demerara sugar

1. Cut the liver into narrow 5 cm (2 inch) strips.
2. Heat the butter and oil in a large deep frying pan or wok. Brown the liver a few pieces at a time, stirring all the time – don't overcook them, the centres should be juicy. Remove with a slotted spoon.
3. Stir the cabbage and onions into the pan. Stir over a high heat for 4–5 minutes, until the vegetables begin to soften.
4. Add the apple, caraway seeds, vinegar and sugar. Continue to cook, stirring, over a moderate heat for 1–2 minutes. Return the liver to the pan, season and reheat very quickly. Serve immediately.

TO MICROWAVE

⚡ Complete step 1. Put the butter and oil in a large bowl and cook on HIGH for 2 minutes or until melted and hot. Add the liver and cook on HIGH for 2 minutes or until it just changes colour, stirring once. Remove

with a slotted spoon. Add the onion, cover and cook on HIGH for 2 minutes, then add the cabbage, apple, caraway seeds, vinegar and sugar. Cover and continue to cook on HIGH for 2 minutes or until the cabbage is softened. Add the liver, re-cover and cook on HIGH for 2 minutes or until hot. Season and serve immediately.

CHICKEN LIVERS IN SHERRY CREAM SAUCE

COUNTRYWIDE

Rich chicken livers have a very moist, crumbly texture. This dish can be served in small quantities as a starter, or as a main course. If grapes are not available, substitute with 25 g (1 oz) sultanas.

SERVES 2

225 g (8 oz) chicken livers, thawed if frozen

25 g (1 oz) plain flour

salt and pepper

25 g (1 oz) butter

75 ml (3 fl oz) sherry

50 ml (2 fl oz) chicken stock

50 g (2 oz) black or green seedless grapes, halved

150 ml (5 fl oz) fresh soured cream

1. Coat the livers in well-seasoned flour.
2. Melt the butter in a medium frying pan and fry the livers with any remaining flour for about 4 minutes, stirring once or twice. Gradually stir in the sherry and stock and simmer for 1–2 minutes.
3. Add the grapes and soured cream. Heat through gently and serve hot with brown rice.

TO MICROWAVE

Complete step 1. Melt the butter in a large shallow dish on HIGH for 45 seconds. Add the livers with any remaining flour and cook on HIGH for 2 minutes, stirring occasionally. Gradually add the sherry and stock and cook on HIGH for 3 minutes, stirring occasionally. Add the grapes and cream and cook on HIGH for 1 minute. Serve hot with brown rice.

CHICKEN LIVERS IN SHERRY CREAM SAUCE. Extremely quick to make, this is an ideal – and very tasty – supper dish.

flour, the stock, red wine, tomato purée, lemon rind and bay leaves and season well. Bring to the boil and replace the meat. Cover and simmer for 3 hours, then skim well.

3. Stir the carrots and parsnips into the casserole. Re-cover the casserole and simmer for a further ½ hour, until the meat is quite tender.

4. Skim all fat off the surface of the casserole, adjust seasoning and garnish with parsley. Accompany with plain boiled or mashed potatoes and crisply cooked winter cabbage.

STUFFED HEARTS

THE NORTH

This traditional recipe for lambs' hearts was originally called Love in Disguise, one of the many fancy names given to offal dishes to mask their origins. The fresh, zesty stuffing ingredients complement the meaty taste of their casings.

SERVES 4

| 4 lambs' hearts |
| 40 g (1½ oz) butter |
| 1 small onion, skinned and chopped |
| 50 g (2 oz) fresh wholemeal breadcrumbs |
| finely grated rind of 1 lemon |
| 15 ml (1 tbsp) chopped fresh sage or 2.5 ml (½ tsp) dried |
| pinch of freshly grated nutmeg |
| salt and pepper |
| 1 egg yolk |
| 30 ml (2 tbsp) plain flour |
| 450 ml (¾ pint) chicken stock |
| 45 ml (3 tbsp) dry sherry |
| chopped fresh sage and grated lemon rind, to garnish |

1. Wash the hearts thoroughly under running cold water. Trim and remove any ducts.
2. Melt 15 g (½ oz) of the butter in a large frying pan and lightly fry the onion for about 5 minutes, until softened. Remove from the heat and stir in the breadcrumbs, lemon rind, sage and nutmeg. Season to taste. Bind with the egg yolk and mix well.
3. Fill the hearts with the stuffing and sew up neatly with strong cotton or fine string. Coat them in the flour.
4. Heat the remaining butter in a flameproof casserole and brown the hearts well. Pour over the stock and sherry, season well and bring to the boil.
5. Cover and bake at 150°C (300°F) mark 2 for about 2 hours or until tender. Serve the hearts sliced and pour the skimmed juices over. Garnish with the sage and lemon rind. Accompany with mashed potatoes and red cabbage with pears (see recipe, page 228).

TO MICROWAVE

Complete steps 1, 2, 3 and 4. Transfer to a large bowl, cover and cook on MEDIUM for 1 hour or until tender. Complete the remainder of step 5.

BRAISED OXTAIL. The meat has a flavour all its own that's unbeatable. A really sustaining casserole, best served in the coldest months to keep the chill at bay.

BRAISED OXTAIL

COUNTRYWIDE

Cook long and cook slow – that's the rule for oxtail. And all those hours spent simmering will be amply repaid when you taste the rich tender meat and juices. If you cook it the day before, the cooled fat is much easier to remove.

SERVES 4

| 2 small oxtails, total weight about 1.4 kg (3 lb), trimmed and cut into pieces |
| 30 ml (2 tbsp) plain flour |
| salt and pepper |
| 15 g (½ oz) butter |
| 15 ml (1 tbsp) vegetable oil |
| 2 large onions, skinned and sliced |
| 900 ml (1½ pints) beef stock |
| 150 ml (¼ pint) dry red wine |
| 15 ml (1 tbsp) tomato purée |
| finely grated rind of ½ lemon |
| 2 bay leaves |
| 225 g (8 oz) carrots, thickly sliced |
| 450 g (1 lb) parsnips, peeled and cut into chunks |
| chopped fresh parsley, to garnish |

1. Coat the oxtail pieces in the flour, seasoned with salt and pepper. Heat the butter and oil in a large flameproof casserole and brown the oxtail pieces, a few at a time. Remove with a slotted spoon.
2. Add the onions to the casserole and fry for 5 minutes, until lightly brown. Stir in any remaining

CREAMED SWEETBREADS

COUNTRYWIDE

Sweetbreads, although considered a great delicacy, are not always readily available, so you may have to order them from your butcher. Soaking helps to keep them white. The sauce is deliberately kept fairly mild, so that the delicate flavour of the sweetbreads can be enjoyed to the full.

SERVES 4

450 g (1 lb) sweetbreads
1 small onion, skinned and chopped
1 medium carrot, chopped
few fresh parsley stalks
1 bay leaf
salt and pepper
40 g (1½ oz) butter
60 ml (4 tbsp) plain flour
300 ml (½ pint) fresh milk
squeeze of lemon juice
chopped fresh parsley, to garnish

1. Rinse and soak the sweetbreads in cold water for 2 hours. Drain and remove any fat attached.
2. Put the sweetbreads, vegetables, herbs and salt and pepper in a saucepan with water to cover, then simmer gently for about 15 minutes, until the sweetbreads are tender. Drain, reserving 300 ml (½ pint) of the cooking liquid, and keep hot.
3. Put the butter, flour, milk and reserved stock in a saucepan. Heat, whisking continuously, until the sauce thickens, boils and is smooth. Simmer for 1–2 minutes. Season to taste and add the lemon juice.
4. Add the sweetbreads to the sauce and simmer gently for 5–10 minutes. Garnish with parsley and serve at once with new potatoes and a green vegetable.

TO MICROWAVE

Put the sweetbreads, vegetables, herbs and salt and pepper in a medium bowl with 300 ml (½ pint) water. Cover and cook on HIGH for 8–10 minutes or until cooked. Remove the sweetbreads and vegetables with a slotted spoon and set aside while cooking the sauce. Add the butter, flour and milk to the cooking liquid and cook on HIGH for 5–6 minutes, until boiling, whisking frequently. Add the sweetbreads and vegetables, cover and cook on HIGH for 2–3 minutes to reheat. Add lemon juice and salt and pepper to taste. Complete step 4.

CREAMED SWEETBREADS. Beautifully tender and served in a simple sauce, sweetbreads make an appetising and unusual dish.

TRIPE AND ONIONS
THE NORTH

Lancashire claims to be the home of tripe and onions, an inexpensive and filling dish. Tripe is the stomach linings of an ox; the first stomach's lining is called blanket, the second honeycomb and the third thick seam. They all taste the same, only the appearance is different. Tripe is always sold dressed and parboiled.

SERVES 4

✳

450 g (1 lb) dressed tripe, washed

3 medium onions, skinned and sliced

568 ml (1 pint) fresh milk

pinch of grated nutmeg

1 bay leaf (optional)

salt and pepper

25 g (1 oz) butter

45 ml (3 tbsp) plain flour

chopped fresh parsley, to garnish

1. Put the tripe in a saucepan and cover with cold water. Bring to the boil, then drain and rinse under running cold water. Cut into 2.5 cm (1 inch) pieces.
2. Put the tripe, onions, milk, nutmeg, bay leaf (if using) and salt and pepper into the rinsed out pan. Bring to the boil, cover and simmer for about 2 hours, until tender. Strain off the liquid and reserve 600 ml (1 pint).
3. Melt the butter in a saucepan, stir in the flour and cook gently for 1 minute, stirring. Remove pan from the heat and gradually stir in the reserved cooking liquid. Bring to the boil and continue to cook, stirring, until the sauce thickens.
4. Add the tripe and onions and reheat. Adjust the seasoning and serve sprinkled with parsley.

BRAISED KIDNEYS IN PORT
COUNTRYWIDE

Tender lambs' kidneys are quick to cook and at their best when served in a richly flavoured sauce.

SERVES 3

✳ ▨

8 lambs' kidneys

25 g (1 oz) butter

1 medium onion, skinned and sliced

100 g (4 oz) mushrooms, sliced

45 ml (3 tbsp) plain flour

150 ml (¼ pint) port

150 ml (¼ pint) chicken stock

15 ml (1 tbsp) chopped fresh parsley

bouquet garni

salt and pepper

1. Skin the kidneys, then cut each one in half lengthways. Snip out the cores with scissors.
2. Heat the butter in a large frying pan or flameproof casserole and fry the onion for 3–4 minutes, until softened. Add the mushrooms and fry for a further 3–4 minutes.
3. Stir in the kidneys and cook for 5 minutes, stirring occasionally.
4. Stir in the flour, then gradually stir in the port and stock. Slowly bring to the boil. Stir in the parsley and bouquet garni. Season to taste.
5. Cover and simmer for 15 minutes, stirring occasionally. Remove the bouquet garni and serve hot with boiled rice or mashed potatoes and a mixed salad.

TO MICROWAVE

▨ Put the butter and onion in a large bowl. Cover and cook on HIGH for 5–7 minutes, until the onion is softened, stirring occasionally. Meanwhile, complete step 1. Stir in the mushrooms and the kidneys to the softened onion, re-cover and cook on HIGH for 3–4 minutes, until the kidneys just change colour. Sprinkle in the flour, then gradually add the port, stock, parsley, bouquet garni and salt and pepper. Re-cover and cook on HIGH for 7–8 minutes or until the kidneys are tender, stirring occasionally. Complete the remainder of step 5.

TONGUE AND MUSHROOM SUPPER
COUNTRYWIDE

Don't think of tongue just as a cold meat – it's delicious in hot dishes, too. Choose cooked sliced ox tongue for this recipe, in which onions and mushrooms, plus a creamy egg mixture, keep the meat from drying out during cooking.

SERVES 4

▨

15 g (½ oz) butter

30 ml (2 tbsp) chopped fresh parsley

1 small onion, skinned and chopped

100 g (4 oz) mushrooms, sliced

15 ml (1 tbsp) chopped gherkins

100 g (4 oz) sliced tongue, quartered

salt and pepper

15 ml (1 tbsp) plain flour

2 eggs, beaten

150 ml (¼ pint) fresh milk

65 ml (2½ fl oz) fresh single cream

1. Melt the butter in a saucepan and lightly fry the parsley, onion and mushrooms for 3 minutes, then stir in the gherkin.
2. Grease a 20.5 cm (8 inch) flan dish and put the tongue in the base. Cover with the onion and mushroom mixture, then season to taste.

BRAISED KIDNEYS
IN PORT
Cut kidneys in half, then use sharp knife to cut out the core.

CREAMED KIDNEYS IN WINE. Use wine and cream to add flavour and a silky texture to inexpensive kidneys, and the result is a dish that's in a class of its own.

3. Blend the flour with the eggs and beat in the milk and cream. Pour into the dish.
4. Bake at 190°C (375°F) mark 5 for 40 minutes. Serve hot or cold with mashed potatoes and sliced beetroot.

TO MICROWAVE

 Melt the butter in a small bowl on HIGH for 30 seconds. Add the parsley, onion and mushrooms and cook on HIGH for 4 minutes. Put the gherkins and tongue in a 20.5 cm (8 inch) glass flan dish and add the mushroom mixture. Complete step 3. Cook on HIGH for 15 minutes, then stand, covered, for 5 minutes. Complete the remainder of step 4.

CREAMED KIDNEYS
IN WINE

COUNTRYWIDE

Use lambs' kidneys, which are the smallest available and always juicy and tender, in this very speedy dish.

SERVES 4

25 g (1 oz) butter
12 lambs' kidneys, cored and halved
225 g (8 oz) mushrooms, sliced
3 celery sticks, diced
1 medium onion, skinned and finely chopped
25 g (1 oz) plain flour
300 ml (½ pint) dry red wine
5 ml (1 tsp) mustard powder
salt and pepper
150 ml (5 fl oz) fresh double cream

1. Melt the butter in a medium saucepan. Add the kidneys, mushrooms, celery and onion and fry gently for 10 minutes, until tender.
2. Stir in the flour and cook for 1–2 minutes. Gradually stir in the wine, mustard and salt and pepper. Cook for a further 5 minutes. Stir in the cream and gently reheat. Serve on a bed of boiled rice with a green vegetable.

TO MICROWAVE

 Melt the butter in a large bowl on HIGH for 45 seconds. Add the kidneys, mushrooms, celery and onion. Cook, covered, on HIGH for 10 minutes. Stir in the flour and cook on HIGH for 1 minute. Gradually stir in the wine, mustard and salt and pepper. Cook on HIGH for 3 minutes until boiling and thickened, stirring occasionally. Stir in the cream and cook on HIGH for 30 seconds. Complete the remainder of step 2.

FISH & SHELLFISH

COD IN A SPICY YOGURT CRUST
COUNTRYWIDE

Everyday cod takes on a touch of the Middle East in this recipe. A delicious mixture of herbs and spices is added to the yogurt marinade, which forms a crisp coating to the fish when grilled. Haddock could be used instead of cod, and either steaks or fillets would be equally suitable in this dish.

SERVES 4

30 ml (2 tbsp) chopped fresh mint
1 medium onion, or 2 large spring onions, skinned and roughly chopped
2 garlic cloves, skinned and crushed
5 ml (1 tsp) paprika
30 ml (2 tbsp) coriander seeds
10 ml (2 tsp) ground cumin
10 ml (2 tsp) dried dill
150 g (5 oz) natural yogurt
salt and pepper
4 thick cod or haddock steaks or fillets, each weighing about 225 g (8 oz)

1. First make the marinade mixture. Put the mint, onion, garlic, paprika, coriander, cumin, dill and yogurt in a blender or food processor and process until a thick paste is formed. Season the mixture to taste with salt and pepper.
2. Place the fish in a single layer in a shallow dish.
3. Spread the paste all over the top of the fish and leave in a cool place to marinate for 2–3 hours.
4. Cook under a hot grill, basting occasionally, until the fish is cooked and the yogurt mixture has formed a crust. Serve straight away with rice and chutney, accompanied by a green salad.

CREAMED FISH PIE

COUNTRYWIDE

Firm, juicy cod is used for the filling of this warming pie. Caraway seeds add interest and flavour to the sauce, and the dish has a creamy topping of mashed potato which is baked until well browned and appetising. Coley could be used for a more economical version.

SERVES 4

 before step 6

450 g (1 lb) cod fillets, skinned
100 g (4 oz) button mushrooms
1 bay leaf
300 ml (½ pint) fresh milk, plus 60 ml (4 tbsp)
25 g (1 oz) butter
25 g (1 oz) plain flour
2.5 ml (½ tsp) caraway seeds
salt and pepper
700 g (1½ lb) potatoes, peeled and diced
1 egg

1. Place the cod, mushrooms and bay leaf in a saucepan. Pour over the 300 ml (½ pint) milk and bring to the boil. Cover lightly and simmer for 15–20 minutes or until the fish is just cooked. Drain, reserving the cooking liquor. Discard the bay leaf and flake the fish, discarding any bones. Set the fish aside while making the sauce.
2. Melt the butter in a saucepan. Add the flour and cook gently, stirring, for 1–2 minutes. Remove from the heat and gradually stir in the reserved milk. Bring to the boil, stirring continuously, until the sauce thickens, boils and is smooth. Stir in the caraway seeds. Simmer for 1–2 minutes.
3. Add the flaked fish and mushrooms to the sauce. Season to taste. Spoon into a shallow 1.4 litre (2½ pint) ovenproof serving dish. Set aside.
4. Cook the potatoes in boiling salted water for 20–30 minutes or until very tender. Drain the potatoes thoroughly.
5. Mash the potatoes and remaining milk with a potato masher. Beat in the egg and season to taste. Spoon evenly over the fish mixture.
6. Bake at 200°C (400°F) mark 6 for about 35 minutes, until golden brown.

TO MICROWAVE

 Put the cod, mushrooms and bay leaf in a shallow dish. Pour over the milk, cover and cook on HIGH for 3–4 minutes or until the fish is cooked. Complete the remainder of step 1. Put the butter, flour, reserved milk and caraway seeds in a medium bowl and cook on HIGH for 3–4 minutes, until the sauce has boiled and thickened, whisking frequently. Complete the remainder of step 3. Put the potatoes in a medium bowl with 30 ml (2 tbsp) water. Cover and cook on HIGH for 10–12 minutes or until very tender. Drain well. Complete step 5. Cook on HIGH for 4–5 minutes to heat through, then brown under a hot grill.

FISH CAKES WITH HERBS

THE NORTH

Fish cakes are an economical way of making fish go further. You can, if necessary, replace some of the fish with more breadcrumbs but check the seasoning carefully to make sure the finished cakes don't taste too bland. The addition of herbs gives flavour and also produces attractive green flecks.

SERVES 4

275 g (10 oz) haddock, skinned and boned
15 ml (1 tbsp) lemon juice
15 ml (1 tbsp) Worcestershire sauce
15 ml (1 tbsp) creamed horseradish
100 ml (4 fl oz) fresh milk
15 ml (1 tbsp) snipped fresh chives
15 ml (1 tbsp) chopped fresh parsley
350 g (12 oz) potatoes, cooked and mashed
50 g (2 oz) fresh wholemeal breadcrumbs

1. Purée the fish in a blender or food processor with the lemon juice, Worcestershire sauce and horseradish. Stir in the milk, chives, parsley and potatoes.
2. Shape the mixture into 4 fish cakes and coat with breadcrumbs.
3. Grill under a moderate heat for 5 minutes on each side, until browned. Serve with a tomato sauce and salad.

ABOVE
FISH CAKES WITH HERBS. Everyday favourites, that taste all the better for the clever use of flavouring. Horseradish, Worcestershire sauce, lemon juice and herbs each add their own distinctive note.

OPPOSITE
COD IN A SPICY YOGURT CRUST. A sensational way to add a little something extra to cod, by cooking it in a thick coating of beautifully spiced yogurt.

ROUND WHITE FISH

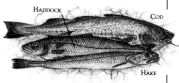

HADDOCK   COD

HAKE

COD

Season June to February. Good baked, braised, poached, shallow-fried or grilled – especially in kebabs, as the firm flesh cubes well. Goes well with strong accompanying flavours like garlic and herbs (see recipe, page 184) and various sauces. Also available smoked, as is the roe (see Cod's Roe Ramekins, page 90).

HADDOCK

Season May to February. Good flavour and flakes well, so excellent in kedgeree (see recipe, page 198). Delicious fried in batter with chips or baked with egg sauce. Smoked haddock is sold in fillets (these make a lovely soufflé) or on the bone as Finnan haddies (see Cullen Skink, page 84) or the smaller Arbroath smokies.

HAKE

Season June to March. Very firm white flesh, shown to advantage in a fish salad, perhaps accompanied by a garlicky mayonnaise.

POLLACK

Season May to September. May be cooked like cod, to which it is related, though has less delicate flavour. Excellent in mixed fish chowder.

WHITING

Season June to February. Abundant and cheap most of the year. Sold whole or in fillets. Good shallow-fried or in mousses.

COLEY

Season August to February. Member of the cod family. Flesh darkish grey but turns white when cooked. Good choice for fish pie or casserole (see recipe, page 186).

COLEY

POLLACK

WHITING

HOT FISH LOAF
COUNTRYWIDE

Hake, a cousin of cod, is available all year round. It has a good, flaky texture and is ideally suited to this recipe, where the flavour is sparked up with prawns, garlic and anchovy essence to make a tasty loaf, served with a cheese sauce.

SERVES 4–6

65 g (2½ oz) butter

1 garlic clove, skinned and crushed

75 ml (5 tbsp) plain flour

750 ml (1¼ pints) fresh milk

550 g (1¼ lb) hake fillets, skinned and chopped

150 ml (5 fl oz) fresh whipping cream

10 ml (2 tsp) anchovy essence

3 eggs

1 egg yolk

salt and pepper

30 ml (2 tbsp) chopped fresh parsley

100 g (4 oz) shelled prawns, chopped

50 g (2 oz) mature Cheddar cheese, grated

watercress sprigs and 6 whole prawns, to garnish

1. Lightly butter and base line a 1.6 litre (2¾ pint) loaf tin or terrine.
2. Melt 40 g (1½ oz) of the butter in a saucepan. Add the garlic. Stir in 45 ml (3 tbsp) of the flour and cook gently, stirring, for 2 minutes. Remove from the heat and gradually stir in 450 ml (¾ pint) of the milk. Bring to the boil, stirring constantly, then simmer for 2 minutes until thick and smooth.
3. In a blender or food processor, purée the sauce, raw chopped fish, cream, anchovy essence, eggs and yolk. Season lightly.
4. Spoon half the fish mixture into the tin. Sprinkle with parsley and half the prawns. Spoon in the rest of the fish mixture. Cover tightly with buttered greaseproof paper.
5. Place in a roasting tin with hot water to come halfway up the sides of the terrine. Cook in the oven at 150°C (300°F) mark 2 for about 1¾ hours.
6. Just before the terrine is cooked, make the sauce. Put the remaining 25 g (1 oz) butter, 30 ml (2 tbsp) flour and remaining milk in a saucepan. Heat, whisking continuously, until the sauce thickens, boils and is smooth. Simmer for 1–2 minutes. Stir in the grated cheese and remaining prawns. Season to taste.
7. Invert the loaf on to a warm serving dish and tilt slightly to drain off juice. Remove cooking container. Spoon a little sauce over terrine and garnish with watercress and prawns. Serve the rest separately.

TO MICROWAVE

Put 40 g (1½ oz) of the butter, garlic, flour and 450 ml (¾ pint) milk in a large bowl and cook on HIGH for 5–6 minutes, whisking frequently until boiling and thickened. Complete step 3. Complete step 4,

spooning the mixture into a 1.7 litre (3 pint) microwave loaf dish. Stand the loaf dish on a roasting rack and cook on MEDIUM for 20 minutes until firm to the touch. Complete the recipe.

SOMERSET FISH CASSEROLE
THE WEST

Cider is a flavoursome – and British – alternative to white wine when cooking fish. Its robust taste makes it a good partner for the stronger brill or coley suggested in the recipe. For a more pronounced cider flavour use slightly more than suggested and boil it down to the required quantity.

SERVES 4

900 g (2 lb) brill or coley fillets, skinned

50 g (2 oz) plain flour

salt and pepper

65 g (2½ oz) butter

1 medium onion, skinned and finely chopped

300 ml (½ pint) dry cider

10 ml (2 tsp) anchovy essence

15 ml (1 tbsp) lemon juice

1 eating apple

chopped fresh parsley, to garnish

1. Cut the fish into 5 cm (2 inch) chunks, then coat the chunks in 25 g (1 oz) of the flour, seasoned with salt and pepper.
2. Melt 25 g (1 oz) of the butter in a medium saucepan and cook the onion gently for 5 minutes, until softened. Add the fish and cook for a further 3 minutes or until lightly browned on all sides. Remove the fish and onion to a buttered ovenproof serving dish.
3. To make the sauce, add 25 g (1 oz) of the butter to that remaining in the pan, then add the remaining flour and cook, stirring, for 1 minute. Gradually stir in the cider, anchovy essence and lemon juice. Bring to the boil, stirring continuously, then simmer for 2–3 minutes, until thick and smooth.
4. Pour the sauce over the fish and cook in the oven at 180°C (350°F) mark 4 for 20 minutes.
5. Meanwhile, peel, core and slice the apple into rings, then fry the apple rings in the remaining butter for 1–2 minutes. Drain on kitchen paper and use to top the fish. Serve garnished with chopped parsley.

TO MICROWAVE

Put the onion and butter in a large bowl. Cover and cook on HIGH for 5–7 minutes, until softened. Sprinkle in the flour, then add the cider, anchovy essence and lemon juice and cook on HIGH for 4–5 minutes, until the sauce has boiled and thickened, whisking frequently. Stir in the fish, cover and cook on HIGH for 5–6 minutes, until the fish is tender, stirring occasionally. Meanwhile complete step 5.

SKATE WITH CAPERS

COUNTRYWIDE

Skate has a soft, pinkish tinge. The wings may look bony but in fact the bones are soft and gelatinous, and the flesh is easily picked off them when the fish is cooked. The delicacy of the flavour is perfectly complemented by the sharp piquancy of capers.

SERVES 4

2 skate wings, each weighing about 550 g (1¼ lb), halved

salt

50 g (2 oz) butter

45 ml (3 tbsp) drained capers

30 ml (2 tbsp) vinegar from the capers

1. Put the skate in a roasting tin and cover with salted water. Bring to the boil, then simmer for 10–15 minutes, until tender.
2. Meanwhile, melt the butter in a small saucepan and cook until it turns golden brown. Add the capers and vinegar and cook until bubbling.
3. Drain the fish and place on serving plates. Pour over the sauce and serve at once, accompanied with boiled new potatoes and peas.

SKATE WITH CAPERS.
This buttery, pleasantly acidic sauce is an ideal complement to the flavour of skate.

MONKFISH AND MUSSEL SKEWERS

COUNTRYWIDE

The bright ochre of mussels adds a dash of colour to the barbecue, and monkfish has a firm texture and a delicious flavour that lend themselves well to a simple cooking method. Keep the skewers well brushed with butter while grilling to prevent them from drying out.

SERVES 6

MONKFISH AND MUSSEL SKEWERS. Bacon goes surprisingly well with the lovely fishy flavours of these tasty kebabs.

12 streaky bacon rashers, rinded and halved

900 g (2 lb) monkfish, skinned, boned and cut into 2.5 cm (1 inch) cubes

36 frozen cooked mussels, thawed

25 g (1 oz) butter

60 ml (4 tbsp) chopped fresh parsley

finely grated rind and juice of 1 large lemon

4 garlic cloves, skinned and crushed

salt and pepper

shredded lettuce and lemon slices, to garnish

1. Roll the bacon rashers up neatly. Thread the cubed fish, mussels and bacon alternately on to 12 oiled skewers.

2. Melt the butter in a saucepan, remove from the heat, then add the parsley, lemon rind and juice and garlic. Season to taste. (Take care when adding salt as both the mussels and the bacon are naturally salty.)

3. Place the skewers on an oiled grill. Brush with the

butter mixture, then grill under a moderate grill for 15 minutes. Turn the skewers frequently during cooking and brush with the butter mixture with each turn. Alternatively, cook over hot coals on a barbecue rack.

4. Arrange the hot skewers on a serving platter lined with shredded lettuce. Garnish with lemon slices and serve at once with any remaining flavoured butter and saffron rice, if liked.

HADDOCK IN BUTTER SAUCE
COUNTRYWIDE

You can usually find haddock on the fishmonger's slab all year round but it is at its best during the winter. If you want to use a slightly cheaper fish, cod, coley or pollack are all good substitutes, and to make a change you can use orange instead of lemon in the simple sauce.

SERVES 4

700 g (1½ lb) haddock fillets, skinned and cut into 4 portions

300 ml (½ pint) fresh milk plus 30 ml (2 tbsp) finely grated rind of 1 lemon

salt and pepper

15 ml (1 tbsp) cornflour

25 g (1 oz) butter

lemon slices and fresh parsley sprigs, to garnish

1. Place the haddock in a large frying pan with 300 ml (½ pint) milk and the lemon rind. Season to taste. Gently simmer for 8 minutes, until the fish is tender. Transfer to a serving dish with a fish slice and keep warm.
2. Blend the cornflour with the 30 ml (2 tbsp) milk, then stir into the poaching liquid with the butter. Heat, whisking continuously, until the sauce thickens, boils and is smooth.
3. Spoon the sauce over the fish. Serve at once, garnished with lemon slices and fresh parsley sprigs.

TO MICROWAVE

Place the haddock in a large shallow dish with half the milk, lemon rind and seasonings. Cook on HIGH for 7 minutes. Remove fish and keep warm. Blend the cornflour with the remaining milk, then stir into the poaching liquid with the butter. Cook on HIGH for 4–5 minutes, until boiling and thickened, whisking frequently. Complete step 3.

PLAICE IN CREAM
THE EASTERN COUNTIES

Top-quality fish abounds off the East Anglian coast and plaice often features in the catch. It is a flat white fish with a delicate flavour. The skin on one side is brownish, with orange spots, and on the other is pearly white. Plaice is best enjoyed in a simple recipe.

SERVES 4

15 g (½ oz) butter

1 small onion, skinned and finely chopped

150 ml (5 fl oz) fresh double cream

150 ml (¼ pint) fish or vegetable stock

blade of mace

salt and pepper

8 single plaice fillets, each weighing 75 g (3 oz), skinned

fresh parsley sprigs and lemon twists, to garnish

1. Melt the butter in a large frying pan, add the onion and cook for about 3 minutes, stirring occasionally, until softened.
2. Stir in the cream and stock and bring to the boil. Lower the heat, add the mace and season lightly to taste. Gently add the fish to the pan, loosely folded in half. Spoon the cream over the fish. Cover and poach gently for about 5 minutes, until the fish is tender and just flakes.
3. Carefully transfer the fish to a warmed plate, using a fish slice, cover and keep warm. Boil the cooking liquor until slightly thickened.
4. Spoon the sauce over 4 warmed plates, discarding the mace. Arrange the fish on top and garnish with parsley sprigs and lemon twists.

TO MICROWAVE

Put the butter and the onion in a large shallow dish. Cover and cook on HIGH for 4–5 minutes, until softened. Stir in the cream, stock and mace. Season to taste. Fold the fish loosely in half, then arrange around the edge of the dish. Re-cover and cook on HIGH for 4–5 minutes, until the fish is tender. Carefully transfer the fish to a warmed plate, then cover and keep warm. Cook the cooking juices, uncovered, on HIGH for 5 minutes or until slightly thickened. Complete step 4.

RED MULLET BAKED IN PAPER

THE WEST

Red mullet is known as the woodcock of the sea because you can eat it all – there's no need to remove the insides. Cooking in paper conserves all the juices, and the parcels, when opened at table, show the attractive red colour to advantage as well as allowing diners to enjoy the delicious smell as the paper is opened.

SERVES 2

2 red mullet, each weighing about 225 g (8 oz)
15 ml (1 tbsp) chopped fresh parsley
1 small onion, skinned and sliced
50 g (2 oz) mushrooms, chopped
finely grated rind and juice of 1 lemon
salt and pepper

1. Cut two squares of greaseproof paper large enough to wrap the fish. Place the fish on top, then add the remaining ingredients. Fold the paper to make a secure parcel.
2. Place the parcels on a baking sheet and bake at 180°C (350°F) mark 4 for 30 minutes, until the fish is tender. Serve the fish in their parcels accompanied with boiled potatoes and broccoli.

TO MICROWAVE

Slash the fish twice on each side, then complete step 1. Place the parcels in a large shallow dish and cook on HIGH for 5–7 minutes, until the fish is tender.

FLAT WHITE FISH

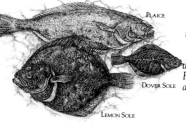

This group includes three of the aristocrats of the fish world – Dover sole, halibut and turbot – as well as the humbler plaice and flounder. Flat fish cooks specially quickly, and as with all fish, care must be taken to avoid over-cooking.

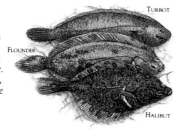

DOVER SOLE

Season May to February. Firm texture and fine flavour. Best grilled on bone and served simply topped with pats of herb or citrus butter.

LEMON SOLE

Season May to March. Considerably cheaper than Dover sole, much softer flesh but with good flavour. May be cooked in the same ways.

PLAICE

Season May to February. Too often neglected and deserving a better reputation. Small plaice may be grilled whole; fillets are delicious fried and served with sauce tartare, lightly poached in a creamy sauce (see recipe, page 189) or rolled round a savoury stuffing mixture and baked.

FLOUNDER

Season March to November. May be cooked as plaice.

HALIBUT

Season June to March. Largest of the flat fish, sold in steaks or fillets. Tail end can be a good buy. A real luxury fish, delicious poached with hollandaise.

TURBOT

Season April to February. Sold whole or as steaks or fillets. May be poached, baked, grilled or shallow-fried. A simple butter sauce brings out its superb flavour best.

SOLES IN COFFINS

THE WEST

Our church-going Victorian forebears named this dish with a play on the words 'souls' and 'soles'. Any kind of sole can be used. Dover sole has the best flavour and is the most expensive but lemon sole and witch or Torbay sole are more widely available; either would be good in this dish.

SERVES 4

4 large potatoes, each weighing about 225 g (8 oz), pricked with a fork
salt and white pepper
8 small sole fillets, each about 75 g (3 oz), skinned
1 small onion, skinned and finely chopped
200 ml (7 fl oz) dry white wine
75 g (3 oz) butter
100 g (4 oz) mushrooms, sliced
50 g (2 oz) plain flour
300 ml (½ pint) fresh milk
pinch of ground mace
100 g (4 oz) peeled cooked prawns, thawed if frozen
fresh parsley sprigs, to garnish

1. Bake the potatoes at 200°C (400°F) mark 6 for about 1½ hours, until soft.
2. Season the fillets, then roll them up, skinned side inwards. Scatter the onion over the bottom of a heavy-based frying pan or shallow flameproof casserole that is just large enough to hold the fish. Place the fish on the onion, pour over the wine, cover and poach for 4–5 minutes, until the fish is tender and just flakes – it is important not to overcook them. Carefully remove the fish rolls from the pan, reserving the cooking liquor.
3. Put 50 g (2 oz) of the butter in a saucepan. Add the mushrooms and cook for 2 minutes. Add the flour and cook gently for 1 minute, stirring. Remove from the heat and gradually stir in 225 ml (8 fl oz) of the milk and strain in the reserved cooking liquor. Heat, stirring continuously, until the sauce thickens, boils and is smooth. Simmer for 2 minutes. Add the mace and prawns. Season to taste and remove from the heat.
4. Cut a slice from each potato, then, using a teaspoon, carefully scoop out the centres and put in a serving dish. Mash the potato flesh with the remaining butter and milk. Season to taste.
5. Place the potato shells on a baking sheet and place 2 rolls of sole in each potato. Divide the sauce between the potatoes and replace the slices of potato.
6. Bake the stuffed potatoes and the mashed potato at 200°C (400°F) mark 6 for 10 minutes. Serve hot, garnished with parsley sprigs.

TO MICROWAVE

Prick the potatoes all over with a fork. Arrange in a circle in the oven and cook on HIGH for 15 minutes or until tender, turning over halfway through cooking. Meanwhile, complete steps 2 and 3. When the potatoes are cooked, complete steps 4–6.

SALMON WITH FENNEL SAUCE

COUNTRYWIDE

Cleaner rivers and controls of fishing have meant that wild salmon is gradually returning to Britain's rivers. Farmed salmon is increasing in number too and comes at lower prices than the wild kind.

SERVES 4

4 salmon steaks, each weighing about 175 g (6 oz)
2 shallots, skinned and chopped
1 small fennel bulb, finely chopped
1 bay leaf
2 stalks fresh parsley, crushed
150 ml (¼ pint) dry white wine
2 egg yolks
100 g (4 oz) butter, softened
salt and pepper
lemon juice, to taste
fresh fennel sprigs, to garnish

1. Place the salmon steaks in a shallow ovenproof dish. Scatter the shallots, fennel, bay leaf and parsley over the top. Pour in the wine, cover tightly and bake at 180°C (350°F) mark 4 for 15 minutes, until fish is tender.

2. Strain off 100 ml (4 fl oz) of the cooking liquor. Turn off oven, re-cover the salmon and keep warm.

3. Boil the strained liquor until reduced to 15 ml (1 tbsp). Beat the egg yolks together in a medium heatproof bowl, then stir in the reduced liquor and work in half of the butter.

4. Place the bowl over a saucepan of hot water and whisk with a balloon whisk until the butter has melted. Gradually whisk in the remaining butter, whisking well after each addition, to make a thick, fluffy sauce. Remove the pan from the heat.

5. Add 10 ml (2 tsp) of the cooked fennel to the sauce and season to taste, adding a little lemon juice, if necessary.

6. Transfer the salmon to a warmed plate. Spoon the sauce over and garnish with fennel sprigs.

TO MICROWAVE

Cook the salmon in the microwave oven. Arrange the salmon in a single layer in a shallow dish and scatter the shallots, fennel, bay leaf and parsley over the top. Pour over the wine, cover and cook on HIGH for 5–8 minutes or until tender and easily flaked. Complete the recipe.

SALMON WITH FENNEL SAUCE. The unmistakable flavours of the two main ingredients make a perfect marriage in this appetising dish.

2. Seal the foil, weigh the fish and place on a baking sheet. Calculate the cooking time at 10 minutes per 450 g (1 lb). Bake at 180°C (350°F) mark 4 until tender.
3. Remove the fish from the foil, reserving the cooking liquor, then carefully remove the skin while still warm. Arrange the fish on a serving dish and leave to cool.
4. To make the sauce, put the cooking liquor and the remaining 25 g (1 oz) butter in a saucepan and heat gently. Add the watercress, spinach, parsley, chervil and dill, then cook for 2–3 minutes, until softened.
5. Put the sauce in a food processor or blender and work until smooth. Transfer to a bowl and add the remaining lemon juice and season to taste. Leave to cool, then fold in the mayonnaise. Turn into a small serving bowl and refrigerate until required.
6. When the fish is cold, garnish with fresh herbs and whole prawns, if liked. Serve with the herb sauce.

TO MICROWAVE

 Cut the head and tail off the fish and discard. Weigh the fish, wrap in a double sheet of greaseproof paper, then place in a large shallow dish or on the oven turntable. Cook on HIGH for 4 minutes per 450 g (1 lb) or until the fish is tender, turning the fish over once halfway through the cooking time. Complete the recipe from step 3.

SEA TROUT WITH HERB SAUCE. Stunning to look at, and easier than you might think to prepare. Go to town on the decoration to make the finished dish as pretty as a picture.

SEA TROUT WITH HERB SAUCE

WALES

The Welsh call sea trout sewin and they come mainly from the fast-flowing rivers of Wales. Their pink flesh and delicate flavour are admirably complemented by the pretty green sauce. If you can't get the herbs specified use other ones but beware of those like thyme with an overpowering flavour.

SERVES 4

900 g (2 lb) sea trout, cleaned

45 ml (3 tbsp) lemon juice

50 g (2 oz) butter

salt and pepper

1 bunch watercress, trimmed and roughly chopped

100 g (4 oz) fresh spinach leaves, roughly chopped

45 ml (3 tbsp) chopped fresh parsley

30 ml (2 tbsp) chopped fresh chervil

5 ml (1 tsp) chopped fresh dill

150 ml (¼ pint) mayonnaise

fresh herbs and whole unpeeled cooked prawns, to garnish

1. Place the fish in the centre of a large piece of foil. Add 30 ml (2 tbsp) of the lemon juice, then dot with 25 g (1 oz) of the butter. Season to taste.

BAKED TROUT WITH CUCUMBER SAUCE

COUNTRYWIDE

A cold dish that would be ideal for a summer gathering. Use freshwater trout, that is, river, lake or rainbow trout. These are now increasingly easy to find at supermarkets. Shiny, slippery skin and bright eyes are the hallmarks of freshness to look for in fresh fish, although frozen can also be used in this recipe.

SERVES 4

4 trout, each weighing about 275 g (10 oz), cleaned

salt and pepper

300 ml (½ pint) fish or vegetable stock

½ small cucumber

300 ml (10 fl oz) fresh soured cream

5 ml (1 tsp) tarragon vinegar

5 ml (1 tsp) chopped fresh tarragon

fresh tarragon, to garnish

1. Arrange the trout in a single layer in a shallow dish. Season to taste. Pour over the stock.
2. Cover and bake at 180°C (350°F) mark 4 for about 25 minutes, until the trout are tender.
3. Remove the fish from the cooking liquor and carefully peel off the skin, leaving the head and tail intact. Leave to cool.

4. Just before serving, make the sauce. Coarsely grate the cucumber, then add the cream, vinegar and tarragon. Season to taste.

5. Coat the trout in some of the sauce, leaving the head and tail exposed. Garnish with tarragon. Serve the remaining sauce separately in a bowl. Accompany with potatoes and a green vegetable.

TO MICROWAVE

 Cook 2 trout at a time. Arrange in a shallow dish. Cover and cook on HIGH for 5–7 minutes or until tender. Repeat with the remaining 2 trout. Complete the recipe.

STUFFED TROUT IN A WINE SAUCE
COUNTRYWIDE

An old recipe which originally called for 'savoury herbs' in the stuffing. This term covered all the common garden herbs, so although thyme and rosemary are specified here, you could equally well substitute marjoram, dill, tarragon or chervil. Use wild trout if you are able to buy them.

SERVES 4

100 g (4 oz) fresh wholemeal breadcrumbs
15 ml (1 tbsp) chopped fresh mixed herbs, such as parsley, thyme, rosemary
finely grated rind and juice of ½ lemon

pinch of freshly grated nutmeg
salt and pepper
1 egg, beaten
4 trout, each weighing about 275 g (10 oz), cleaned
25 g (1 oz) butter
30 ml (2 tbsp) plain flour
150 ml (¼ pint) dry white wine
150 ml (¼ pint) vegetable stock
60 ml (4 tbsp) fresh double cream

1. Put the breadcrumbs, herbs, grated lemon rind and juice and nutmeg in a bowl. Season to taste. Add the egg and mix together well.

2. Fill the cavities of the trout with the stuffing. Wrap the fish in greased foil. Place the parcels on a baking sheet and bake at 180°C (350°F) mark 4 for 30–35 minutes, until tender.

3. Meanwhile, put the butter, flour, wine and stock in a saucepan and heat, whisking continuously, until the sauce thickens, boils and is smooth. Simmer for 1–2 minutes. Stir in the cream and season to taste.

4. Pour a little sauce over the trout and serve the remaining sauce in a warmed sauceboat or jug.

TO MICROWAVE

 Complete step 1. Slash the fish twice on each side. Fill the cavities of the trout with the stuffing. Place the fish side-by-side in a large shallow dish. Add the lemon juice. Cover and cook on HIGH for 10–12 minutes or until the fish is tender, rearranging once during cooking. Meanwhile, complete steps 3 and 4.

BAKED TROUT WITH CUCUMBER SAUCE.
Soured cream makes a memorably piquant sauce, packed with texture and flavour, that sets off the simple baked fish superbly.

GREY MULLET COOKED
IN LEMON AND RED
WINE. An unexpectedly
fruity stuffing is packed into
each fish. Lemon slices are
tucked in to give more
flavour.

GREY MULLET COOKED IN LEMON AND RED WINE

THE WEST

If you can find it when in season (June to August) Cornish grey mullet is a real delicacy. Otherwise use wild or farmed trout. Cox's apples give a distinctive flavour but another English eating apple could be substituted. Cornish instead of double cream would add a real touch of luxury.

SERVES 4

15 g (½ oz) butter

450 g (1 lb) Cox's apples, peeled, cored and sliced

6 spring onions, sliced

finely grated rind and juice of 1 lemon

1–2 garlic cloves, skinned and crushed

salt and pepper

4 grey mullets, each weighing about 275 g (10 oz)

2 lemons, sliced

300 ml (½ pint) dry red wine

60 ml (4 tbsp) fresh double cream

1. To make the stuffing, melt the butter in a medium saucepan and lightly fry the apples, spring onions, lemon rind, 30 ml (2 tbsp) of the lemon juice and the garlic. Season to taste.
2. Make 3 slashes across both sides of each grey mullet and insert the lemon slices. Sprinkle the cavity of each fish with remaining lemon juice and fill with the stuffing. Put into a large ovenproof dish.
3. Pour over the red wine and bake at 180°C (350°F) mark 4 for 20–30 minutes, until the fish is tender.
4. Remove the fish from the dish and place on a warmed serving dish. Keep hot.
5. Pour the cooking liquid into a small saucepan, stir in the cream and reheat gently. Serve poured over the fish.

TO MICROWAVE

Melt the butter in a medium bowl on HIGH for 30 seconds. Add the apples, spring onions, lemon rind, 30 ml (2 tbsp) of the lemon juice and the garlic. Cook on HIGH for 8 minutes. Complete step 2. Put the fish into a shallow dish and pour over the red wine. Cook on HIGH for 10 minutes, rearranging once, until tender. Complete step 4. Stir the cream into the cooking liquid and cook on HIGH for 1 minute. Serve poured over the fish.

TROUT WRAPPED IN BACON

WALES

Welsh farmers with their abundance of home-cured bacon have long enjoyed this dish where the bacon is wrapped round freshly caught trout from their rivers. The combination of flavours and textures is delicious and you can, of course, use any smoked British bacon and wild or farmed trout, which are increasingly widely available.

SERVES 4

4 trout, each weighing about 275 g (10 oz), cleaned
salt and pepper
8 thin streaky bacon rashers, rinded
chopped fresh parsley, to garnish

1. Season the cavity of each fish with salt and pepper. Wind 2 bacon rashers in a spiral round each fish, then arrange them in a shallow ovenproof dish with the loose ends underneath so they cannot unwind.
2. Bake at 200°C (400°F) mark 6 for 15–20 minutes, until tender. Serve garnished with chopped parsley.

TO MICROWAVE

Slash the fish once on each side. Complete step 1. Cover with absorbent kitchen paper. Cook on HIGH for 8–10 minutes or until the fish is tender, rearranging once during cooking. Serve garnished with parsley.

BAKED MACKEREL WITH GOOSEBERRY SAUCE

THE WEST

This delicious summer dish (available all year round if you freeze gooseberry purée) offers an interesting contrast in flavours – rich oily mackerel is offset by sharp tangy gooseberries. Be sure to sieve the gooseberries if you want to get rid of all the pips; a food processor will break them down to some degree but won't remove them.

SERVES 4

15 g (½ oz) butter
225 g (8 oz) gooseberries, topped and tailed
4 mackerel, each weighing about 350 g (12 oz), cleaned and heads removed
salt and pepper
lemon juice, to taste
1 egg, beaten

1. Melt the butter in a medium saucepan and add the gooseberries. Cover tightly and cook over a low heat, shaking the pan occasionally, until the gooseberries are tender.
2. Meanwhile, season the mackerel inside and out with salt, plenty of pepper and lemon juice. Make two or three slashes in the skin on each side of the fish, then grill for 15–20 minutes, depending on size, turning once, until tender.
3. Purée the gooseberries in a blender or food processor or press through a sieve. Pour the purée into a clean pan, beat in the egg, then reheat gently, stirring. Season to taste. Place the mackerel on warmed serving plates and spoon the sauce beside the fish.

TO MICROWAVE

Put the butter and gooseberries in a medium bowl, cover and cook on HIGH for 6–7 minutes, stirring once, until the gooseberries are tender. Purée in a blender or food processor or pass through a sieve. Return to the bowl. Prepare the mackerel as step 2. Arrange in a single layer in a shallow dish. Cover and cook on HIGH for 12 minutes or until the fish is tender, rearranging once during cooking. Reheat the sauce on HIGH for 2 minutes, then stir in the egg and season to taste. Cook on MEDIUM for 30 seconds–1 minute, stirring once. Serve as step 3.

SMOKED MACKEREL SOUFFLE. A very moreish recipe, that bakes to an attractive, crusty brown top, but stays light and moist inside. Serve speedily!

SMOKED MACKEREL SOUFFLE

THE WEST

Although the soufflé was originally a French speciality it made an impact on English cooking in the mid-19th century when cheese soufflé became a spectacular and popular party piece. Smoked fish makes a good soufflé base and you can replace the mackerel with trout or other smoked fish – even smoked salmon offcuts.

SERVES 4

200 ml (7 fl oz) fresh milk
a few onion and carrot slices
1 bay leaf
6 black peppercorns
30 ml (2 tbsp) plain flour
25 g (1 oz) butter
salt and pepper
75 g (3 oz) cooked smoked mackerel, skinned, boned and finely flaked
4 eggs, separated
1 extra egg white

1. Grease a 1.3 litre (2¼ pint) soufflé dish.
2. Put the milk in a medium saucepan with the onion and carrot slices, bay leaf and peppercorns. Slowly bring to the boil, remove from the heat, cover and leave to infuse for 30 minutes. Strain and reserve the milk.
3. Put the flour, butter and reserved milk in a medium saucepan. Heat, whisking continuously, until the sauce thickens, boils and is smooth. Simmer for 1–2 minutes. Season to taste. Leave to cool slightly.
4. Beat the yolks into the cooled sauce, 1 at a time. Sprinkle the fish over the sauce. (At this stage the mixture can be left to stand for several hours if necessary.)
5. Stir in the fish until evenly blended. Whisk the egg whites until stiff.
6. Mix one large spoonful of egg white into the sauce to lighten its texture. Gently pour the sauce over the remaining egg whites and cut and fold the ingredients together. Do not overmix; fold lightly, using a metal spoon or plastic spatula, until the egg whites are just incorporated.
7. Pour the soufflé mixture gently into the prepared dish. The mixture should come about three-quarters up the side of the dish. Smooth the surface of the soufflé.
8. Place the soufflé on a baking sheet and bake at 180°C (350°F) mark 4 for about 30 minutes. It should be golden brown on the top, well risen and just firm to the touch with a hint of softness in the centre.

STUFFED HERRINGS

WALES

Although the Welsh herring catch is not as large as in former days this fish is now widely available throughout the country and makes filling and economical dishes. It is a good idea to get your fishmonger to prepare the fish for you. Mackerel can be substituted if herrings are not available.

SERVES 4

---

65 g (2½ oz) butter

1 medium onion, skinned and finely chopped

50 g (2 oz) fresh wholemeal breadcrumbs

50 g (2 oz) shelled walnut pieces, roughly chopped

15 ml (1 tbsp) prepared English mustard

finely grated rind and juice of 1 lemon

45 ml (3 tbsp) chopped fresh mixed herbs, such as chives, parsley, rosemary, thyme

salt and pepper

4 medium herrings, each weighing about 275 g (10 oz), cleaned, boned and heads and tails removed

---

1. Melt 15 g (½ oz) of the butter in a saucepan, add the onion and fry gently for about 5 minutes, until softened, stirring occasionally.
2. Meanwhile, mix together the breadcrumbs, walnuts, mustard, lemon rind, 15 ml (1 tbsp) lemon juice and mixed herbs. Season to taste. Add the onion and mix together well.
3. Open the herring fillets and lay skin side down. Press the stuffing mixture evenly over each fillet. Fold the herring fillets back in half and slash the skin several times.
4. Melt the remaining butter in a large frying pan, add the fish and fry for about 10 minutes, turning them once, until they are tender and browned on each side.

CUMBERLAND STUFFED HERRINGS WITH MUSTARD SAUCE

THE NORTH

Mustard sauce makes a good accompaniment to the oily flesh of herrings and English mustard has the 'bite' needed to make a good contrast with the rich fish. If herrings are unobtainable, you can use small mackerel or if only large fish of either type are available, serve each person a half.

SERVES 4

---

4 herrings with roe or small mackerel, each weighing about 225 g (8 oz), head and fins removed and cleaned

---

300 ml (½ pint) fresh milk

25 g (1 oz) fresh breadcrumbs

1 small onion, skinned and finely chopped

salt and pepper

25 g (1 oz) butter

45 ml (3 tbsp) plain flour

5 ml (1 tsp) prepared English mustard

5 ml (1 tsp) white wine vinegar

---

1. Put the roes in a small saucepan with the milk. Bring to the boil and simmer gently for 5 minutes. Drain, reserving the milk. Finely chop the roes.
2. Open out the fish on a board, inner side down, and press lightly down the middle to loosen the backbone. Gently ease the backbone away.
3. Mix together the breadcrumbs and onion and add the chopped roes. Season to taste and spread on open herrings. Fold herrings over to enclose the stuffing.
4. Cover and bake at 180°C (350°F) mark 4 for 20 minutes, until tender.
5. Meanwhile, put the butter, the flour and the reserved milk in a saucepan. Heat, whisking continuously, until the sauce thickens, boils and is smooth. Simmer for 1–2 minutes. Stir in mustard and vinegar, adjust seasoning and serve with herrings.

TO MICROWAVE

 Complete steps 1, 2 and 3. Arrange the herrings in a single layer in a large dish. Dot with half of the butter, cover and cook on HIGH for 8–10 minutes or until the fish is tender. Meanwhile, complete step 5.

STUFFED HERRINGS. These richly oily fish pour their delicious juices into the stuffing as they cook. Serve piping hot for a mouthwatering, and inexpensive, supper dish.

SMOKED FINNAN HADDOCK WITH EGG SAUCE

SCOTLAND

True Finnan haddocks are smoked in Findon (corrupted to Finnan), near Aberdeen, but any properly smoked haddock – brownish not bright yellow in colour – will do for this dish.

SERVES 4

2 Finnan haddocks, each weighing about 275 g (10 oz)

1 bay leaf

pepper

300 ml (½ pint) fresh milk

25 g (1 oz) butter

25 g (1 oz) plain flour

2 eggs, hard-boiled and finely chopped

15 ml (1 tbsp) chopped fresh parsley

1. Put the haddock, skin side down, in a large frying pan. Add the bay leaf and pepper to taste, then pour over the milk. Bring to the boil, then gently simmer for 10–15 minutes, until tender.
2. Transfer the fish to a warmed serving dish with a fish slice, reserving the milk. Cover and keep warm.
3. Melt the butter in a saucepan. Add the flour and cook gently, stirring, for 1–2 minutes. Remove from the heat and gradually stir in the reserved milk. Bring to the boil, stirring constantly, then simmer for 2–3 minutes until thick and smooth. Stir in the eggs and parsley. Pour the sauce into a sauceboat or jug and serve with the fish. Accompany with boiled potatoes.

TO MICROWAVE

Put the haddock, bay leaf, milk and pepper to taste in a large shallow dish. Cover and cook on HIGH for 10 minutes, until tender. Complete step 2. Put the butter, flour and reserved milk in a medium bowl and cook on HIGH for 4–5 minutes, until boiled and thickened. Complete remainder of step 3.

SMOKED HADDOCK BAKE

COUNTRYWIDE

An excellent variation on Italian lasagne, now an accepted part of British cooking. Smoked cod or coley would be just as good as haddock, but do try to include the Red Leicester cheese, which gives a mellow flavour as well as a lovely colour.

SERVES 4

450 g (1 lb) smoked haddock fillets, skinned

750 ml (1¼ pints) fresh milk

25 g (1 oz) butter

40 g (1½ oz) plain wholemeal flour

100 g (4 oz) Red Leicester cheese, grated

pepper

100 g (4 oz) oven-ready wholewheat lasagne

1. Put the haddock in a large saucepan with the milk. Bring to the simmering point, cover, then simmer for 10–15 minutes, until tender. Drain, reserving the milk, then flake the fish, discarding any bones. Set aside while making the sauce.
2. Put the butter, flour and reserved milk in a saucepan. Heat, whisking continuously, until the sauce thickens, boils and is smooth. Simmer for 1–2 minutes. Remove the pan from the heat and add 50 g (2 oz) of the Red Leicester, the haddock and pepper. Stir carefully to mix.
3. Layer the sauce and lasagne sheets in an ovenproof serving dish, starting and finishing with the sauce. Sprinkle the remaining cheese on top. Bake at 190°C (375°F) mark 5 for 30–35 minutes until golden brown.

TO MICROWAVE

Put the haddock in a shallow dish with a little of the milk and cook, covered, on HIGH for 4 minutes. Drain, reserving the milk, then flake the fish, discarding any bones. Put the flour, butter, reserved and remaining milk in a large bowl and cook on HIGH for 8 minutes, whisking frequently until boiling and thickened. Complete the recipe.

KEDGEREE

COUNTRYWIDE

Kitchri was originally a spicy Indian dish containing onions and lentils. The British brought the recipe back from India and Anglicised it, leaving out the stronger flavourings and lentils, while adding flaked smoked fish to the rice and eggs. All the ingredients can be prepared in advance and put together when needed. It makes an excellent supper dish and is also delicious for brunch.

SERVES 4

175 g (6 oz) long-grain rice

salt and pepper

450 g (1 lb) smoked haddock fillets

2 eggs, hard-boiled and shelled

50 g (2 oz) butter

chopped fresh parsley, to garnish

1. Cook the rice in a saucepan of fast-boiling salted water until tender. Drain well and rinse under cold water. Drain again and spread out to dry – this prevents the kedgeree from becoming stodgy.

2. Meanwhile, put the haddock in a large frying pan with just enough water to cover. Bring to simmering point, then simmer for 10–15 minutes, until tender. Drain, skin and flake the haddock, discarding any bones.

3. Chop one egg and slice the other into rings. Melt the butter in a saucepan, add the cooked rice, fish and chopped egg. Season to taste and stir over a moderate heat for about 5 minutes, until hot. Pile on to a warmed serving dish and garnish with chopped parsley and the sliced egg.

TO MICROWAVE

☑ Complete step 1. Meanwhile put the haddock in a large shallow dish with 30 ml (2 tbsp) water. Cover and cook on HIGH for 3–4 minutes or until tender. Drain, skin and flake the fish, discarding any bones. Chop one egg and slice the other into rings. Cut the butter into small pieces and melt in a large bowl on HIGH for 1½ minutes. Add the cooked rice and chopped egg. Season to taste. Cover and cook on HIGH for 2–3 minutes or until hot, stirring. Complete step 3.

KEDGEREE. For a truly indulgent, old-fashioned British breakfast, you can't beat a dish of savoury kedgeree. And, of course, it tastes just as good at suppertime, too.

SCALLOP AND
MUSHROOM PIE. Lightly
browned mashed potatoes
form the topping for this
variation on fish pie. Serve
with a mixed salad.

SCALLOP AND MUSHROOM PIE

NORTHERN IRELAND

Scallops have a delicate flavour and pleasant texture which blend well with the haddock. The sliced corals add colour to the dish, which in Ireland is usually baked and served in the individual scallop shells. However, here an ovenproof dish is used.

SERVES 4

4 scallops
450 g (1 lb) haddock fillet, skinned, any bones discarded and cut into chunks
1 bay leaf
6 black peppercorns
1 small onion, skinned and finely chopped
450 ml (¾ pint) fresh milk
700 g (1½ lb) potatoes, cooked
65 g (2½ oz) butter
salt and pepper
100 g (4 oz) mushrooms, sliced
25 g (1 oz) plain flour
60 ml (4 tbsp) dry sherry
30 ml (2 tbsp) fresh single cream
chopped fresh parsley, to garnish

1. If necessary, remove and discard the tough white 'muscle' from each scallop. Separate the red corals from the scallops, then cut the white part into fairly thick slices.
2. Put the sliced scallops and the haddock in a medium saucepan with the bay leaf, peppercorns, onion and 300 ml (½ pint) of the milk. Simmer gently for 10–15 minutes, until tender. Five minutes before the end of the cooking time, add the corals.
3. Meanwhile, mash the potatoes with the rest of the milk and 25 g (1 oz) of the butter. Season to taste. Drain the haddock and scallops, reserving the milk.
4. Melt 25 g (1 oz) of the butter in another medium saucepan and fry the mushrooms for 2 minutes. Stir in

the flour and cook for 1 minute. Remove from the heat and gradually stir in the reserved milk. Bring to the boil, stirring constantly, then simmer for 2–3 minutes, until thick and smooth. Add the sherry, cream and the haddock and scallops and mix well. Season to taste.
5. Turn into an ovenproof serving dish, cover with the mashed potatoes and dot with the remaining butter. Bake at 180°C (350°F) mark 4 for 20 minutes, or until the top is brown. Sprinkle with parsley to garnish.

TO MICROWAVE

 Complete step 1. Put the scallops, haddock, bay leaf, peppercorns, onion and 300 ml (½ pint) of the milk in a large shallow dish. Cover and cook on HIGH for 4 minutes. Add the corals, re-cover and cook on HIGH for 2 minutes or until all of the fish is tender. Complete steps 3 and 4. Turn into an ovenproof serving dish, cover with the mashed potatoes and dot with the remaining butter. Cook on HIGH for 3–4 minutes to reheat, then brown under a hot grill.

WELSH COCKLE PIE
WALES

Cooked fresh cockles have a flavour quite unlike those which have been doused in vinegar – a real taste of the sea. In Wales, for centuries the 'cockle women' have gathered them in strong baskets at low tide. They are taken to co-operative factories where they are boiled before being sold from vans and market stalls.

SERVES 4

25 g (1 oz) butter
225 g (8 oz) streaky bacon, rinded and chopped
1 medium onion, skinned and chopped
50 g (2 oz) plain flour
568 ml (1 pint) fresh milk
900 ml (1½ pints) cooked cockles
60 ml (4 tbsp) dry white wine
45 ml (3 tbsp) snipped fresh chives
salt and pepper
100 g (4 oz) fresh wholemeal breadcrumbs
75 g (3 oz) Caerphilly cheese, grated

1. Melt the butter in a medium saucepan, add the bacon and onion and cook for 5 minutes, until softened.
2. Add the flour and cook for a further minute, stirring. Remove from the heat and gradually stir in the milk. Bring to the boil, stirring continuously, until the sauce thickens, boils and is smooth.
3. Add the cockles, wine and chives. Season to taste and simmer for 2–3 minutes.
4. Turn the mixture into a pie dish. Mix together the breadcrumbs and grated cheese. Sprinkle on top of the mixture.
5. Cook under a hot grill for 5 minutes, until golden brown. Accompany with a salad.

TO MICROWAVE

Cut the butter into small pieces, then melt in a large bowl on HIGH for 1 minute. Add the bacon and the onion, cover and cook on HIGH for 5–7 minutes, until softened. Add the flour and cook on HIGH for 30 seconds. Stir in the milk and the wine and cook on HIGH for 5–6 minutes, stirring frequently, until the sauce has boiled and thickened. Add the cockles and chives and season to taste. Cook on HIGH for 1 minute. Complete steps 4 and 5.

OYSTER LOAVES
THE EASTERN COUNTIES

Whitstable in Essex was once renowned for its oysters, although the beds are no longer farmed extensively. This recipe dates back to when oysters were exceedingly cheap. For a budget version, substitute mussels or lightly cooked baby scallops or clams, with a drop of fish stock in place of the oyster juices.

SERVES 2

2 miniature brioches, baby cottage loaves or other small rolls
50 g (2 oz) butter, melted
6 large oysters
60 ml (4 tbsp) fresh soured cream
cayenne pepper and white pepper
finely grated lemon rind and parsley sprigs, to garnish

1. Remove the top knobs from the brioches, loaves or rolls. Carefully scoop out all the inside, leaving just a wall of crust and taking care not to pierce the crust.
2. Brush the crust shells, inside and out, with half of the melted butter, place on a baking sheet and bake at 220°C (425°F) mark 7 for 5–10 minutes, until they are crisp.
3. Meanwhile, scrub the oysters, then, holding each one in a cloth, flat side uppermost, prise open the shells at the hinge. Loosen the oysters, reserving their liquor for the sauce.
4. Add the liquor to the remaining melted butter in a small saucepan, bring to the boil and boil for a few minutes to reduce the liquid.
5. Stir in the cream and heat gently. Do not boil or the mixture will curdle. Season to taste with cayenne and white pepper.
6. Put the oysters into the crust shells and spoon over the sauce. Garnish with lemon rind and parsley. Accompany with a green salad.

TO MICROWAVE

Complete steps 1, 2 and 3. Put the remaining melted butter and oyster liquor in a medium bowl and cook on HIGH for 3 minutes, until reduced. Stir in the cream and cook on HIGH for 1 minute, until hot. Complete the remainder of step 5 and step 6.

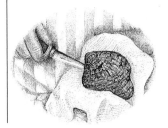

OYSTER LOAVES
To open oysters, insert point of small, strong knife at hinge end and prise open shells.

CRAB SALAD. Only a simple dressing is needed to bring out the full flavour of crabmeat in this very light and appetising summer salad.

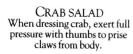

CRAB SALAD
When dressing crab, exert full pressure with thumbs to prise claws from body.

CRAB SALAD

THE WEST

You can buy fresh or frozen cooked crab meat (if the latter, thaw thoroughly before use) in a mixture of dark and light meat. If buying freshly cooked crabs in their shells you'll need one large crab to produce about the weight specified. If you have them, garnish the dish with crab claws.

SERVES 2

15 ml (1 tbsp) lemon juice
15 ml (1 tbsp) mayonnaise
15 ml (1 tbsp) natural yogurt
225 g (8 oz) crab meat
½ cucumber, diced
2 tomatoes, skinned and cubed
50 g (2 oz) pasta shells, cooked
pepper
lettuce, shredded
cucumber and lemon slices, to garnish

1. Mix together the lemon juice, mayonnaise and yogurt.
2. Combine the dressing with remaining ingredients, except the lettuce. Serve the crab salad on a bed of shredded lettuce, garnished with cucumber and lemon slices, accompanied by brown bread and butter if liked.

CORNISH BUTTERED LOBSTER

THE WEST

The long coast of Cornwall is touched by the Gulf Stream, making its warmer waters ideal for lobsters and other shellfish to flourish. A good-quality lobster deserves to be served simply, as in this recipe, so that the full flavour of the flesh can be enjoyed.

SERVES 4

2 lobsters, each weighing about 700 g (1½ lb), split into halves
lemon juice
75 g (3 oz) butter
60 ml (4 tbsp) fresh breadcrumbs
45 ml (3 tbsp) brandy
45 ml (3 tbsp) fresh double cream
salt and pepper
pinch of cayenne pepper
cucumber twists, lemon slices and fresh dill sprigs, to garnish

1. Discard the stomach, the dark vein that runs through the body, and the spongy gills from each lobster. Remove the tail meat. Crack open the claws

and remove the meat. Scrape the meat from the legs with a skewer.

2. Cut the meat into chunks, then sprinkle with lemon juice. Remove and reserve the coral, if present. Remove and reserve the soft pink flesh and liver separately.

3. Scrub the shells and place in a low oven to warm. Melt 25 g (1 oz) of the butter in a small frying pan, add the breadcrumbs and cook until browned and crisp.

4. Meanwhile, melt the remaining butter in a medium saucepan, add the lobster flesh and gently stir until heated through.

5. Warm the brandy in a ladle, ignite with a taper and pour, still flaming, over the lobster. When the flames have subsided, transfer the lobster to the warmed shells, using a slotted spoon, and keep warm in a low oven.

6. Pound the liver and pink flesh. Stir into the cooking juices with the cream, a little salt and cayenne pepper and plenty of black pepper. Boil briefly until thickened, then spoon over the lobster.

7. Sprinkle the fried breadcrumbs over the top. Quickly garnish with the reserved coral, if available, cucumber twists, lemon slices and dill sprigs.

MUSSEL AND ONION STEW

THE WEST

Mussels fresh from the rocks of the West Country make this substantial stew an unusual main course. Good-quality mussels are widely available and, so long as you discard the dead ones, should not cause digestive trouble. This stew is easier to eat than mussel dishes where the shells are not removed.

SERVES 4

2 kg (4½ lb) fresh mussels
150 ml (¼ pint) dry white wine
25 g (1 oz) butter
2 large onions, skinned and chopped
25 g (1 oz) plain wholemeal flour
300 ml (½ pint) fresh milk
30 ml (2 tbsp) chopped fresh parsley
30 ml (2 tbsp) fresh single cream

1. To prepare the mussels, wash them thoroughly under running cold water, then scrape off any barnacles with a small sharp knife. Cut off the fibrous beards that protrude from between the shells. Wash in several changes of water. Discard any that are cracked or do not close when tapped sharply with a knife.

2. Put the wine in a large saucepan and bring to the boil. Add the mussels, cover and cook over a high heat for 3–4 minutes or until the mussels open, shaking the pan occasionally. Discard any mussels that have not opened.

3. Drain the mussels, reserving the juice. Remove mussels from the shells.

4. Melt the butter in a saucepan and lightly fry the onions for about 5 minutes, until soft but not coloured. Stir in the flour and cook for a minute.

5. Gradually add the milk and the mussel cooking liquid, stirring, until the sauce thickens, boils and is smooth. Simmer for 1–2 minutes.

6. Return mussels to the pan with the parsley and cream. Reheat gently. Serve with crusty bread.

TO MICROWAVE

Complete step 1. Put the wine in a large bowl and cook on HIGH for 2–3 minutes, until boiling. Add the mussels, cover and cook on HIGH for 3–5 minutes or until all of the mussels have opened, removing those on the top as they open and shaking the bowl occasionally. Discard any mussels that have not opened. Complete step 3. Melt the butter in a large bowl on HIGH for 45 seconds. Add the onions, cover and cook on HIGH for 7 minutes. Stir in the flour, milk and 50 ml (2 fl oz) of the cooking liquid. Cook on HIGH for 5–6 minutes until boiling and thickened, stirring frequently. Stir in the parsley, cream and mussels, cook on HIGH for 2 minutes.

MUSSEL AND ONION STEW. It's well worth going to the trouble of preparing mussels, when they are so delicious, served swimming in creamy white wine sauce. Have plenty of bread for mopping up the juices.

MUSSELS AND CLAMS WITH TOMATOES. Don't forget the napkins when you serve this dish, since you need to use your fingers to get each fishy morsel out of its shell.

MUSSELS AND CLAMS WITH TOMATOES

THE EASTERN COUNTIES

Mussels and clams are surprisingly good value and their flavour goes well with the acid touch from the tomatoes. Cooked this way the shellfish flavours are fairly similar although textures are different. If you can't get clams, add extra mussels and vice versa.

SERVES 2–3

900 g (2 lb) fresh mussels	
450 g (1 lb) small clams, such as venus clams	
25 g (1 oz) butter	
1–2 large garlic cloves, skinned and crushed	
1 small onion, skinned and finely chopped	
150 ml (¼ pint) dry white wine	
225 g (8 oz) ripe tomatoes, chopped	
finely grated rind of 1 lemon	
30 ml (2 tsp) chopped fresh parsley	
salt and pepper	

1. To prepare the mussels, wash them thoroughly under running cold water, then scrape off any barnacles with a small sharp knife. Cut off the fibrous beards that protrude from between the shells. Wash in several changes of water. Discard any cracked mussels, or any that do not close when tapped sharply with a knife.
2. Scrub the clams thoroughly and discard any that are cracked or open.
3. Melt the butter in a large pan, add the garlic and onion and cook gently for a few minutes, until the onion is softened. Add the wine, tomatoes, lemon rind and half of the parsley. Bring to the boil.
4. Add the mussels and the clams to the pan, cover and cook over a high heat for 3–4 minutes or until the mussels and clams are open, shaking the pan occasionally. Discard any mussels or clams that have not opened.
5. Season to taste. Transfer to two large bowls or soup plates and sprinkle with the remaining parsley. Serve with lots of crusty bread.

TO MICROWAVE

Complete steps 1 and 2. Melt the butter on HIGH for 45 seconds in a very large bowl. Add the garlic and the onion, cover and cook on HIGH for 4–5 minutes, until softened. Add the wine, tomatoes, lemon rind and half of the parsley. Re-cover and cook on HIGH for 3–4 minutes or until boiling. Add the mussels and the clams, re-cover and cook on HIGH for 4–6 minutes or until all of the mussels and clams have opened, removing those on the top as they open and shaking the bowl occasionally. Discard any mussels or clams that have not opened. Complete step 5.

VEGETARIAN

CHEESY POTATO PIE

COUNTRYWIDE

Buy maincrop potatoes rather than new for this recipe. Maris Piper is particularly good for mashing, or you could use Desirée, recognisable by its red skin. Cotswold cheese, a mixture of Double Gloucester cheese and chives, gives a lovely flavour to the crispy potato topping.

SERVES 4

❄ ✎

900 g (2 lb) potatoes, peeled and cut into chunks
45 ml (3 tbsp) fresh milk
100 g (4 oz) Cotswold or Cheddar cheese, grated
50 g (2 oz) butter
salt and pepper
450 g (1 lb) leeks, trimmed, sliced and washed
1 large red pepper, seeded and roughly chopped
450 g (1 lb) courgettes, thickly sliced
225 g (8 oz) button mushrooms
10 ml (2 tsp) mild paprika
25 g (1 oz) plain wholemeal flour
300 ml (½ pint) vegetable stock

1. Cook the potatoes in boiling salted water for 15–20 minutes or until tender. Drain and mash with the milk, half the cheese and half the butter. Season to taste.
2. Meanwhile, heat the remaining butter in a large saucepan and fry the leeks and pepper for 4–5 minutes, until softened. Add the courgettes, mushrooms and paprika and fry for a further 2 minutes.
3. Sprinkle in the flour, then gradually add the stock and bring to the boil, stirring continuously. Cover and simmer for 5 minutes.
4. Spoon the vegetable mixture into an ovenproof serving dish and cover evenly with the cheesy potato. Sprinkle with the remaining cheese. Bake at 200°C (400°F) mark 6 for 20–25 minutes or until the top is crisp and golden brown.

TO MICROWAVE

✎ Complete steps 1, 2 and 3. Spoon the vegetable mixture into a flameproof dish and cover evenly with the cheesy potato. Mark the top in a decorative pattern with a fork. Cook the completed dish on HIGH for 4–5 minutes until hot, then brown under a hot grill.

SQUASH

SPAGHETTI SQUASH

VEGETABLE MARROW   COURGETTE

Many supermarkets now stock excitingly shaped and coloured squash as well as more familiar marrow and courgettes, in response to increasing interest in lesser known vegetables. Squash are well worth trying, especially in vegetarian cooking.

VEGETABLE MARROW

Popular garden vegetable, best in August. Lends itself well to stuffing (see recipe, page 213); can be bland so good flavoured as in the recipe on page 227, or with herb sauce. Best steamed or braised, not boiled, as can be watery.

COURGETTE

Miniature yellow or green marrow, available all year. Grated courgettes make a pretty green-speckled soufflé; they also look attractive sliced in a flan. Delicious steamed with herb butter, stir-fried as in the recipe on page 161, dipped in light batter and fried.

PUMPKIN

Nationwide pumpkin contests yield some staggering results – the winner of a recent British National Championship at Ashby de la Zouch weighed in at 284.2 lb! As well as featuring as lanterns at Hallowe'en parties, pumpkins (October to November) make smooth golden soup and irresistible pie, well flavoured with warm spices. Also very nice baked as gratin.

SPAGHETTI SQUASH

Boil this in the skin and when cut open you'll find the flesh resembles strands of spaghetti! Pull them out and serve with butter and grated cheese or tomato sauce, like real spaghetti.

BUTTERNUT SQUASH

Increasingly familiar in our shops. Use like pumpkin.

GOLDEN NUGGET SQUASH

Try serving this as a change from potatoes; fried like chips or mashed with butter and milk.

PUMPKIN   BUTTERNUT SQUASH

GOLDEN NUGGET SQUASH

BROAD BEAN BAKE

COUNTRYWIDE

Broad beans were eaten by the Egyptians and Romans, and have been cultivated in Britain for hundreds of years. They were often served at feasts in the sixteenth and seventeenth centuries. Although savory is not one of the most widely used herbs in cooking, it is worth seeking it out especially for this recipe, as it was traditionally used to flavour beans.

SERVES 2

700 g (1½ lb) fresh broad beans or 225 g (8 oz) frozen broad beans

2 medium carrots, cut into chunks

2 medium parsnips, peeled and cut into chunks

25 g (1 oz) butter

25 g (1 oz) plain wholemeal flour

300 ml (½ pint) fresh milk

30 ml (2 tbsp) chopped fresh mixed herbs, such as savory, chives, parsley, thyme

5 ml (1 tsp) prepared English mild mustard

salt and pepper

30 ml (2 tbsp) porridge oats

50 g (2 oz) Double Gloucester cheese, grated

25 g (1 oz) chopped mixed nuts

1. Shell the fresh broad beans, if using, then cook in boiling salted water for 5 minutes.
2. Add the carrots and parsnips to the beans and continue to cook for 10–15 minutes or until the vegetables are tender. If using frozen beans, add for the last 5 minutes of cooking. Drain well.
3. Put the butter, flour and milk in a small saucepan. Heat, whisking continuously, until the sauce thickens, boils and is smooth. Simmer the sauce for 1–2 minutes.
4. Stir in the herbs, mustard and the vegetables, and season to taste. Simmer for 2–3 minutes, until heated through, then divide between two individual flameproof dishes.
5. Mix the oats, cheese and nuts together and sprinkle on top of the vegetable mixture. Brown for 2–3 minutes under a hot grill.

TO MICROWAVE

Put the shelled broad beans and 30 ml (2 tbsp) water in a large bowl. Cover and cook on HIGH for 4 minutes. Add the carrots and parsnips to the broad beans, re-cover and cook on HIGH for 5–7 minutes or until all the vegetables are tender. Put the butter, flour and milk in a medium bowl. Cook on HIGH for 4–5 minutes, until boiling and thickened, whisking frequently. Stir in the herbs, mustard and vegetables, and season with salt and pepper to taste. Re-cover and cook on HIGH for 2–3 minutes or until hot. Divide the mixture between two individual flameproof dishes. Complete step 5.

EGG AND ARTICHOKE WITH NOODLES

COUNTRYWIDE

Jerusalem artichokes have a pleasant and distinctive flavour and texture. The small, brown, knobbly tubers are tricky to peel, so bear this in mind when shopping and don't choose any that are too small or lumpy. The flavour is said to be best in early spring, although they are available all winter as well. Jerusalem artichokes are also delicious with chicken and fish, and they make a fine soup with a subtle flavour. Tagliatelle or pasta noodles are now as popular in Britain as in their native Italy. This recipe uses dried noodles; freshly made noodles are also increasingly widely available from supermarkets – if you use them instead of dried, remember their cooking time is considerably shorter.

SERVES 4

450 g (1 lb) Jerusalem artichokes, peeled and cut into large chunks

150 ml (5 fl oz) fresh soured cream

salt and pepper

450 g (1 lb) ribbon noodles

6 eggs, hard-boiled

1. Put the artichokes into a medium saucepan, cover with water, bring to the boil, then simmer for 15–20 minutes or until they are very tender. Drain the artichokes well. Purée in a blender or food processor until smooth.
2. Add the soured cream and season to taste.
3. Cook the noodles in plenty of boiling salted water for about 7 minutes until just tender. Drain well. Cover the base of four shallow, lightly greased flameproof dishes with the pasta.
4. Shell and quarter the eggs, then arrange over the pasta. Spoon the artichoke sauce evenly over each dish.
5. Place under a hot grill for 3–4 minutes, until golden. Serve at once.

TO MICROWAVE

Put the artichokes in a medium bowl with 60 ml (4 tbsp) water. Cover and cook on HIGH for 6–8 minutes, until tender. Complete step 1 and the remaining recipe.

VEGETARIAN ROAST

COUNTRYWIDE

This recipe makes a 'loaf' which slices well and can be served hot or cold. Any type of chopped nuts can be used for this dish, such as almonds, brazils or unsalted peanuts, but it's worth buying mature Cheddar specially, as it adds a mouthwatering depth of flavour.

SERVES 4–6

175 g (6 oz) long-grain brown rice

15 g (½ oz) butter

1 medium onion, skinned and chopped

1 garlic clove, skinned and crushed

2 carrots, grated

100 g (4 oz) button mushrooms, finely chopped

100 g (4 oz) fresh wholemeal breadcrumbs

100 g (4 oz) nuts, finely chopped

100 g (4 oz) mature Cheddar cheese, grated

2 eggs

salt and pepper

1. Cook the rice in boiling salted water for

30–35 minutes or until tender. Drain well.

2. Meanwhile, heat the butter in a medium frying pan and fry the onion, garlic, carrots and mushrooms, stirring frequently, until softened. Stir in the breadcrumbs, nuts, cooked rice, cheese and the eggs. Season to taste with salt and pepper and mix thoroughly together.

3. Pack the mixture into a greased 1.7 litre (3 pint) loaf tin and bake at 180°C (350°F) mark 4 for 1–1¼ hours or until firm to the touch and brown on top. Serve the Vegetarian Roast sliced, hot or cold, with tomato sauce or chutney.

VEGETARIAN ROAST.
Brown rice is the base of this tasty picnic idea. Onion and garlic add interest to the well-seasoned mixture.

2. Meanwhile, melt the butter in a large frying pan and cook the garlic and mushrooms, stirring frequently, until just softened. Crumble in the Stilton cheese and cook for a couple of minutes, stirring continuously. Stir in the cream and season to taste.

3. Drain the pasta and season with lots of pepper. Mix into the mushroom sauce. Stir in the egg and mix together thoroughly.

4. Turn the mixture into a buttered ovenproof dish and grate the mozzarella on top. Cover with foil and bake at 180°C (350°F) mark 4 for 10 minutes, then remove the foil and bake at 220°C (425°F) mark 7 for a further 10–15 minutes, until brown and crusty on top. Serve with a green salad.

TO MICROWAVE

Complete step 1. Meanwhile, put the butter, garlic and mushrooms in a large bowl, cover and cook on HIGH for 3–4 minutes, until the mushrooms are softened, stirring occasionally. Stir in the Stilton cheese and the cream and cook on HIGH for 2 minutes, stirring once. Complete step 3. Turn the mixture into a buttered flameproof dish and grate the mozzarella on top. Cook on HIGH for 3–4 minutes or until heated through. Brown the top under a hot grill.

PARSNIP AND LENTIL POTS

COUNTRYWIDE

Like all vegetables, parsnips should be used as fresh as possible. If you do need to keep them for a day or two, buy them unwashed and store in a cool, dry place. Always buy firm parsnips that have a good creamy colour, with no brown patches.

SERVES 4

 before step 5

900 g (2 lb) parsnips, peeled and thinly sliced
75 g (3 oz) green lentils
75 g (3 oz) long-grain brown rice
salt and pepper
40 g (1½ oz) butter
1 small onion, skinned and finely chopped
30 ml (2 tbsp) plain flour
568 ml (1 pint) fresh milk
pinch of grated nutmeg

1. Place the parsnips in a large saucepan. Cover with cold water and bring to the boil for 2 minutes, then drain immediately.

2. Put the lentils and rice together in a large saucepan. Cover with cold water, bring to the boil and simmer for 35–40 minutes, until just cooked. Drain well and season to taste.

3. Melt 25 g (1 oz) of the butter in a medium saucepan. Add the onion and cook for 2–3 minutes, until

PASTA AND MUSHROOMS BAKED WITH TWO CHEESES

COUNTRYWIDE

Stilton cheese is marvellous for cooking, and gives a very distinctive flavour to the mushroom sauce in this pasta dish. Mozzarella, used here for the topping, is a famous Italian cheese, which is now also being made in Britain. It is deliciously creamy when melted.

SERVES 2–3

225 g (8 oz) ribbon noodles
25 g (1 oz) butter
1 garlic clove, skinned and crushed
225 g (8 oz) mushrooms, thinly sliced
50 g (2 oz) Stilton cheese
60 ml (4 tbsp) fresh double cream
salt and pepper
1 egg, lightly beaten
100 g (4 oz) mozzarella cheese

1. Cook the noodles in boiling salted water for about 7 minutes, until just tender.

beginning to soften. Stir in the flour and cook for a further 1–2 minutes. Remove from the heat and gradually stir in the milk. Slowly bring to the boil and continue to cook, stirring all the time, until the sauce comes to the boil and thickens. Simmer for a further 2–3 minutes. Season with nutmeg and salt and pepper.

4. Lightly grease four 450 ml (¾ pint) deep ovenproof dishes or one 1.7 litre (3 pint) dish. Reserve some parsnip slices for garnish. Spoon alternate layers of parsnip, lentils and brown rice and onion sauce into each dish. Finish with a layer of onion sauce and the reserved parsnip slices. Melt the remaining butter and brush over the tops.

5. Place on a baking sheet and bake at 190°C (375°F) mark 5 for about 1–1¼ hours, until golden brown. Serve hot.

TO MICROWAVE

 The sauce, in step 3, can be prepared in the microwave. Put 25 g (1 oz) of the butter in a medium bowl and cook on HIGH for 45 seconds, until melted. Add the onion and cook on HIGH for 4–5 minutes, until softened, stirring occasionally. Stir in the flour and cook on HIGH for 30 seconds. Gradually stir in the milk and cook on HIGH for 5–6 minutes until the sauce has boiled and thickened, whisking frequently. Season with nutmeg and salt and pepper.

CHILLED SPINACH STUFFED SHELLS

COUNTRYWIDE

Don't buy tiny pasta shells for this recipe, as you'll need extra large ones to hold the cheesy spinach filling, which is well seasoned with garlic and nutmeg. As the shells are served cold, you can cook the pasta and prepare the stuffing ahead of time and assemble the dish when you are ready to serve.

SERVES 2

10 large pasta shells
450 g (1 lb) fresh spinach, trimmed, or 225 g (8 oz) frozen spinach
1–2 garlic cloves, skinned and crushed
100 g (4 oz) low-fat soft cheese
freshly grated nutmeg
salt and pepper
150 g (5 oz) natural yogurt
15 ml (1 tbsp) tomato purée
finely grated rind and juice of ½ lemon

1. Cook the pasta in a large saucepanful of boiling salted water for 8–10 minutes or until tender.

2. Meanwhile, wash the fresh spinach in several changes of water and roughly chop. Cook with just the water clinging to the leaves for 3–4 minutes or until just wilted. If using frozen spinach, cook for about 10 minutes or until thawed. Drain the spinach and finely chop.

3. Mix the spinach with the garlic and cheese and season generously with nutmeg and salt and pepper. Leave to cool.

4. Drain the pasta and rinse with cold water, then drain again. When the spinach mixture is cold, use to stuff the shells. Arrange on two plates.

5. Mix the yogurt, tomato purée and lemon rind and juice together and season with salt and pepper to taste. Pour over the stuffed shells. Cover and chill until ready to serve.

TO MICROWAVE

 Complete step 1. Meanwhile, prepare the fresh spinach and put in a large bowl with just the water clinging to the leaves. Cover and cook on HIGH for 2–3 minutes or until just wilted. If using frozen spinach, cook on HIGH for 5–7 minutes or until thawed, stirring occasionally. Complete the recipe.

CHILLED SPINACH STUFFED SHELLS. An attractive and unusual way with pasta, that could be served as a starter or main course. The light yogurt sauce is coloured pale pink with tomato purée.

VEGETARIAN MEDLEY

COUNTRYWIDE

Protein-rich pulses combine with fresh vegetables, fresh and dried fruit, nuts and dairy products to make an exceptionally well-balanced, nutritious vegetarian meal, perfect for a warming winter supper.

SERVES 4

25 g (1 oz) butter
2 carrots, sliced
1 large onion, skinned and chopped
1 green pepper, seeded and sliced
2 tomatoes, skinned and chopped
1 large cooking apple, peeled and chopped
1 clove garlic, skinned and crushed
15 ml (1 tbsp) chopped fresh sage or 5 ml (1 tsp) dried
100 g (4 oz) lentils, cooked
15 ml (1 tbsp) raisins
30 ml (2 tbsp) unsalted peanuts
salt and pepper
300 g (10 oz) natural yogurt
25 g (1 oz) cream cheese

1. Melt the butter in a large frying pan. Lightly fry the carrots, onion, green pepper, tomatoes, apple, garlic and sage for 15 minutes, until softened.
2. Add the lentils, raisins and peanuts. Season to taste. Stir the yogurt into the cream cheese and mix well to blend. Stir into the mixture. Reheat gently for 5 minutes. Serve at once.

TO MICROWAVE

 Melt the butter in a large bowl on HIGH for 45 seconds. Add the carrots, onion, green pepper, tomatoes, apple, garlic and sage and cook on HIGH for 7 minutes, stirring occasionally. Add the remaining ingredients as in step 2 and cook on HIGH for 2 minutes. Serve at once.

VEGETARIAN MEDLEY. Colourful and tasty, a chunky mixture of pulses, fruit, nuts and vegetables is combined in a yogurt and cream cheese sauce. Fresh sage adds its distinctive bite.

LYMESWOLD AND WATERCRESS FLAN

THE MIDLANDS

Lymeswold is a full-fat soft blue cheese with a white rind, the texture of which varies as it ages. Watercress is available all year round now that it is specially cultivated, and its strong distinctive taste gives a nice zest to this flan.

SERVES 4

✳

100 g (4 oz) plain wholemeal flour
salt and pepper
50 g (2 oz) butter, diced
150 g (5 oz) Lymeswold cheese, rinded and sliced
2 eggs, beaten
150 ml (¼ pint) fresh milk
1 small onion, skinned and chopped
50 g (2 oz) watercress, trimmed and chopped

1. Put the flour and salt in a bowl. Rub in the butter until the mixture resembles fine breadcrumbs. Add 30–45 ml (2–3 tbsp) cold water and mix to form a dough.
2. Roll out on a lightly floured work surface and use to line an 18 cm (7 inch) flan dish. Bake blind at 200°C (400°F) mark 6 for 10–15 minutes, until set but not too brown.
3. Put the Lymeswold on the base of the flan case. Mix together the eggs and milk, and season to taste. Add the onion and watercress and pour into the flan case.
4. Bake at 190°C (375°F) mark 5 for 40–45 minutes. Serve warm.

BACK
LEEK AND PEA FLAN.
There's Cheddar in the
pastry, as well as on top, to
bring out the flavours of the
vegetables.

FRONT
BROCCOLI FLAN. Florets
of broccoli give the filling an
appetising finish.

LEEK AND PEA FLAN

WALES

This attractive green flan makes excellent use of traditional Welsh leek. Frozen peas taste just as good in it as fresh but don't use canned ones or the flavour will be altered.

SERVES 4–6

450 g (1 lb) leeks, trimmed, sliced and washed
100 g (4 oz) fresh or frozen shelled peas
salt and pepper
150 ml (¼ pint) fresh milk
150 g (5 oz) natural yogurt
3 eggs
175 g (6 oz) plain wholemeal flour
100 g (4 oz) Cheddar cheese, grated
75 g (3 oz) butter

1. Cook the leeks and peas in a little salted water in a tightly covered medium saucepan until tender. Drain well.
2. Purée together the leeks, peas, milk and yogurt in a blender or food processor.
3. Beat 2 of the eggs into the purée and season to taste. Lightly beat the remaining egg in a small bowl.
4. Put the flour and half the cheese in a bowl. Rub in the butter until the mixture resembles fine breadcrumbs, then bind together with the remaining egg.
5. Roll out the pastry on a lightly floured surface and use to line a 23 cm (9 inch) flan dish. Pour in the leek mixture.
6. Sprinkle over the remaining cheese. Bake at 190°C (375°F) mark 5 for 50–55 minutes, until golden.

BROCCOLI FLAN

THE SOUTH-EAST

As well as heads of green broccoli, often sold prepacked, you will sometimes find purple sprouting broccoli in the shops. Whichever variety you choose, buy the freshest possible, with no yellowing leaves, and eat within a couple of days. The pastry in this recipe uses rolled oats for an unusual texture.

SERVES 4–6

175 g (6 oz) plain wholemeal flour
50 g (2 oz) porridge oats
salt and pepper
100 g (4 oz) butter
350 g (12 oz) broccoli, trimmed
3 eggs
300 ml (½ pint) fresh milk

1. Put the flour, oats and 2.5 ml (½ tsp) salt into a bowl. Rub in the butter until the mixture resembles fine breadcrumbs. Add enough cold water to bind the mixture together and form a firm dough.
2. Roll out the pastry on a lightly floured surface and use to line a 23 cm (9 inch) flan dish. Bake blind at 200°C (400°F) mark 6 for 10–15 minutes, until set but not too brown.
3. Roughly chop the broccoli, then cook in boiling, salted water until just tender. Drain well. Arrange in the flan case.
4. Whisk together the eggs, milk and season to taste. Pour into the flan case, making sure the broccoli is covered.
5. Bake at 190°C (375°F) mark 5 for about 40 minutes, until lightly set. Serve warm.

GOAT'S CHEESE WITH PEAR AND WALNUT SALAD. The strong, salty flavour of goat's cheese is complemented by the sweet pears and sharp lemon dressing.

SPINACH ROLL
When rolling up Spinach Roll use a sheet of greaseproof to help you.

SPINACH ROLL
COUNTRYWIDE

Fromage frais is an unripened, soft fresh cheese. Many different types are stocked by supermarkets and delicatessens, and they all have one thing in common – their light, fresh taste. The fat content, however, varies widely, so check the labels before buying.

SERVES 3–4

900 g (2 lb) fresh spinach, trimmed, or 450 g (1 lb) packet frozen chopped spinach
4 eggs, separated
pinch of freshly grated nutmeg
salt and pepper
15 g (½ oz) butter
1 medium onion, skinned and finely chopped
100 g (4 oz) fromage frais
50 g (2 oz) Cheddar cheese, grated
30 ml (2 tbsp) fresh soured cream

1. Grease a 33×23 cm (13×9 inch) Swiss roll tin and line with non-stick baking parchment. Set aside.
2. Wash the fresh spinach in several changes of cold water. Place in a saucepan with only the water that clings to the leaves and cook gently, covered, for about 5 minutes, until wilted. If using frozen spinach cook for 7–10 minutes, until thawed.
3. Drain the spinach well and chop finely. Turn into a bowl and cool slightly for about 5 minutes, then beat in the egg yolks and nutmeg, and season with salt and pepper to taste.
4. Whisk the egg whites until stiff, then fold into the spinach mixture with a large metal spoon until they are evenly incorporated.
5. Spread the mixture in the prepared tin. Bake at 200°C (400°F) mark 6 for 15–20 minutes, until firm.
6. Meanwhile, prepare the filling. Melt the butter in a saucepan. Add the onion and fry gently for about 5 minutes, until soft and lightly coloured. Remove from the heat and stir in the fromage frais, cheese and soured cream. Season to taste.
7. Turn the roll out on to greaseproof paper, peel off the lining paper and spread immediately and quickly with the cheese mixture.
8. Roll up by gently lifting the greaseproof paper. Serve hot, cut into thick slices. Accompany with boiled new potatoes.

TO MICROWAVE

Complete step 1. If using fresh spinach, place in a large bowl with only the water that clings to the leaves. Cover and cook on HIGH for 4–5 minutes, until just wilted. If using frozen spinach, cover and cook on HIGH for 7–10 minutes, until thawed. Complete steps 3, 4 and 5. Meanwhile, put the butter and onion in a medium bowl, cover and cook on HIGH for 5 minutes, until softened. Complete the remainder of step 6 and steps 7 and 8.

GOAT'S CHEESE WITH PEAR AND WALNUT SALAD
THE WEST

Goat's cheese has a distinctive taste which is, for some people, acquired. It is produced in much smaller quantities than cow's milk cheese, often on individual farms. The flavour will vary according to the time of year and the type of feed. If you prefer, use another white variety such as Caerphilly, Lancashire, Wensleydale or white Stilton.

SERVES 2

a few lettuce leaves, such as Webbs and radicchio, torn into pieces
100 g (4 oz) goat's cheese, halved into 2 discs
2 ripe pears, cored and chunked
50 g (2 oz) walnuts, chopped
½ bunch watercress, trimmed
30 ml (2 tbsp) lemon juice
45 ml (3 tbsp) vegetable oil

1. Arrange the lettuce on 2 plates and top with the goat's cheese. Mix together the pears, walnuts and watercress.
2. Blend the lemon juice and oil together, then toss into the salad ingredients. Serve on top of the cheese.

SAVOURY NUT BURGERS

COUNTRYWIDE

The nut mixture is quite sticky, so coat your hands with flour to make shaping the burgers easier. Buy a ready chopped mixture of nuts, or a selection of whole nuts to chop yourself.

SERVES 4

25 g (1 oz) butter
1 large onion, skinned and chopped
15 ml (1 tbsp) chopped fresh parsley
15 g (½ oz) plain wholemeal flour
150 ml (¼ pint) fresh milk
225 g (8 oz) chopped mixed nuts
15 ml (1 tbsp) soy sauce
15 ml (1 tbsp) tomato purée
175 g (6 oz) fresh wholemeal breadcrumbs
1 egg, beaten
pepper

1. Melt the butter in a medium saucepan and lightly fry the onion and parsley until soft. Stir in the flour and cook for 2 minutes.
2. Remove from heat, gradually add the milk, bring back to boil, stirring until the sauce thickens, boils and is smooth. Simmer for 1–2 minutes.
3. Add the nuts, soy sauce, tomato purée, breadcrumbs, eggs and pepper to taste. Mix well.
4. Divide into 8 and shape into rounds. Place under a grill for 4 minutes, then turn and grill for 4 minutes more. Serve with cheese sauce, tomatoes and parsley.

TO MICROWAVE

Melt the butter in a large bowl on HIGH for 45 seconds. Add the onion, cook on HIGH for 5 minutes. Add the flour, cook on HIGH for 1 minute. Gradually add the milk, cook on HIGH for 3 minutes until boiling and thickened, whisking frequently. Complete step 3. Divide mixture into 8 and shape into rounds. Preheat a browning dish on HIGH for 8–10 minutes or according to manufacturer's instructions. Quickly put the burgers in the browning dish and cook on HIGH for 2 minutes, turn over and cook for a further 2 minutes.

STUFFED MARROW

COUNTRYWIDE

This recipe makes the most of English root vegetables. Autumn is the time to make it, when supplies are plentiful. The skin should be shiny and pressing it with the thumb should leave an impression.

SERVES 4

SAVOURY NUT BURGERS. Moist and nutty inside, crispy and well browned outside, these tempting burgers will be just as popular with non-vegetarians.

550 g (1¼ lb) marrow, peeled and halved lengthways
25 g (1 oz) butter
175 g (6 oz) aubergine, cubed
2 parsnips, peeled and diced
2 carrots, diced
100 g (4 oz) swede, peeled and diced
100 g (4 oz) turnip, peeled and diced
15 ml (1 tbsp) chopped fresh parsley
15 ml (1 tbsp) tomato purée
150 ml (¼ pint) vegetable stock
salt and pepper
natural yogurt, to serve

1. Scoop the seeds out of the marrow.
2. Melt the butter in a large frying pan and lightly fry the vegetables for 10 minutes.
3. Add the parsley, tomato purée and stock. Season to taste. Simmer gently for 15 minutes.
4. Fill one half of the marrow with the mixture. Top with the other half of marrow and wrap in foil. Bake at 190°C (375°F) mark 5 for about 45 minutes, until tender. Serve at once, in slices, with natural yogurt.

TO MICROWAVE

Complete step 1. Melt the butter in a large bowl on HIGH for 45 seconds. Add the vegetables and cook on HIGH for 10 minutes. Add the parsley, tomato purée and stock and cook on HIGH for 20 minutes, stirring occasionally. Fill one half of the marrow, top with the other half and put into a large shallow dish. Cook on HIGH for 10–12 minutes, until tender. Serve at once, in slices, with natural yogurt.

VEGETABLE CURRY. A
subtle blend of spices gives
this curry its flavour. Adjust
the amount of chilli powder
according to how much heat
you like, and vary the
vegetables according to what's
in season.

VEGETABLE CURRY

COUNTRYWIDE

Spices were very costly until the 16th century, because they had to be brought to Britain overland from the East. We have to thank great explorers like Drake and Raleigh for first making these vital ingredients of good cooking more readily available. Buy your spices freshly and in small amounts, as they lose their strength quickly when stored.

SERVES 4

30 ml (2 tbsp) vegetable oil
10 ml (2 tsp) ground coriander
5 ml (1 tsp) ground cumin
2.5–5 ml (½–1 tsp) chilli powder
2.5 ml (½ tsp) ground turmeric
2 garlic cloves, skinned and crushed
1 medium onion, skinned and chopped
1 small cauliflower, cut into small florets
2 potatoes, roughly chopped
2 carrots, sliced
1 green pepper, seeded and chopped
225 g (8 oz) tomatoes, roughly chopped
150 g (5 oz) natural yogurt
salt and pepper

1. Heat the oil in a large saucepan, then add the coriander, cumin, chilli, turmeric, garlic and onion and fry for 2–3 minutes, stirring continuously.
2. Add the cauliflower, potatoes, carrots and green pepper and stir to coat in the spices. Stir in the tomatoes and 150 ml (¼ pint) water. Bring to the boil, cover and gently simmer for 25–30 minutes or until the vegetables are tender.
3. Remove from the heat, stir in the yogurt and season to taste. Serve with rice and chutney.

TO MICROWAVE

Put the oil, coriander, cumin, chilli, turmeric, garlic and onion in a large bowl and cook on HIGH for 2 minutes, stirring once. Add the cauliflower, potatoes, carrots and green pepper and stir to coat in the spices. Stir in the tomatoes and 150 ml (¼ pint) water. Cover and cook on HIGH for 20 minutes or until the vegetables are tender, stirring occasionally. Complete step 3.

WHOLEMEAL VEGETABLE AND HERB PIE

COUNTRYWIDE

The herb used here is fresh parsley, which is often found in supermarkets. If you grow your own, sow some in spring and again in late summer to keep a supply going all year round. Wholemeal pastry needs gentle handling, as it tears easily, but the nutty-flavoured, crumbly result is worth the extra care.

SERVES 4

90 g (3½ oz) butter
3 carrots, sliced
40 g (1½ oz) plain flour
300 ml (½ pint) fresh milk
salt and pepper
1 small cauliflower, broken into florets
100 g (4 oz) broccoli
50 g (2 oz) pearl barley, cooked
30 ml (2 tbsp) chopped fresh parsley
100 g (4 oz) plain wholemeal flour
fresh milk, to glaze

1. Melt 40 g (1½ oz) of the butter in a medium saucepan. Lightly fry the carrots for 7 minutes. Stir in the plain flour and cook for 1 minute. Gradually add the milk, whisking continuously, until the sauce thickens, boils and is smooth. Simmer for 1–2 minutes. Season to taste.
2. Blanch the cauliflower and broccoli in boiling salted water for 5 minutes. Drain.
3. Mix the sauce with the cauliflower, broccoli, pearl barley and parsley. Spoon into a 1.1 litre (2 pint) pie dish.

4. Put the plain wholemeal flour and salt in a bowl. Rub in the remaining butter until the mixture resembles fine breadcrumbs. Add 75 ml (3 tbsp) cold water to mix to form a dough. Roll out on a lightly floured work surface to 5 cm (2 inch) wider than the pie dish. Cut a 2.5 cm (1 inch) wide strip from the outer edge and place on the dampened rim of the dish. Brush the strip with water. Cover with the pastry lid, press lightly to seal the edges. Trim off excess pastry. Knock the edges back to seal and crimp. Garnish with pastry leaves and brush with milk.

5. Bake at 200°C (400°F) mark 6 for 30 minutes, until golden.

TO MICROWAVE

Dice 40 g (1½ oz) of the butter, place in a large bowl and cook on HIGH for 1 minute. Add the carrots and cook on HIGH for 2 minutes. Stir in the flour and cook on HIGH for 1 minute. Stir in the milk and cook on HIGH for 4–5 minutes, until boiling and thickened, stirring frequently. Blanch the cauliflower and broccoli in boiling water from the kettle on HIGH for 3 minutes. Complete steps 3, 4, 5 and 6.

MIXED VEGETABLE RING

COUNTRYWIDE

Cotswold cheese is a tangy blend of Double Gloucester with chopped chives and onions. Here it is used to make a light pastry ring, filled with a delicious mixture of colourful vegetables. Serve as a lunch or supper dish with salad.

SERVES 4

100 g (4 oz) butter
1 large onion, skinned and sliced
50 g (2 oz) mushrooms, wiped
2 courgettes, sliced
175 g (6 oz) aubergine, quartered and sliced
1 red pepper, seeded and sliced
3 tomatoes, skinned and chopped
salt and pepper
215 ml (7½ oz) fresh milk
100 g (4 oz) plain flour
3 eggs, beaten
40 g (1½ oz) walnut pieces, chopped
100 g (4 oz) Cotswold cheese, grated

1. Melt 25 g (1 oz) of the butter in a large saucepan. Lightly fry the onion and mushrooms for 5 minutes, until softened.

2. Add the courgettes, aubergines and red pepper and cook for 5 minutes, stirring occasionally. Add the tomatoes and season to taste.

3. Melt the remaining butter in a medium saucepan with the milk, then bring to the boil. Remove the pan

from the heat, tip in all the flour and beat thoroughly with a wooden spoon. Allow to cool slightly, then beat in the eggs, a little at a time. Stir in the walnuts. Pipe or spoon around the edge of a well-greased 900 ml (1½ pint) ovenproof serving dish.

4. Fill the centre with vegetables. Bake at 200°C (400°F) mark 6 for 35–40 minutes, until the pastry is risen and golden. Sprinkle with the cheese, return to the oven until the cheese has melted. Serve at once.

TO MICROWAVE

Melt 25 g (1 oz) of the butter in a large shallow dish on HIGH for 45 seconds. Add the onions and mushrooms and cook on HIGH for 3 minutes. Add the courgettes, aubergine and red pepper and cook on HIGH for 5 minutes, stirring occasionally. Add the tomatoes and season to taste. Cook on HIGH for 1 minute. Complete steps 3 and 4.

MIXED VEGETABLE RING. Everyone gets a piece of the cheesy ring and a generous helping of the filling, made from juicy Mediterranean vegetables.

FARMHOUSE
CAULIFLOWER
SOUFFLES. The mellowness
of Farmhouse Cheddar can be
enjoyed at its best in these
light and airy soufflés.

FARMHOUSE CAULIFLOWER SOUFFLES

THE WEST

The distinctive flavour of cauliflower lends itself to soufflé treatment. This dish, like all soufflés, can be started and left before finishing off. If the sauce base is allowed to cool, allow about 10 minutes extra cooking time. Ensure people are ready to eat the soufflé as soon as it is done.

SERVES 8

225 g (8 oz) small cauliflower florets	
salt and pepper	
40 g (1½ oz) butter	
45 ml (3 tbsp) plain flour	
200 ml (7 fl oz) fresh milk	
15 ml (1 tbsp) wholegrain mustard	
100 g (4 oz) mature Farmhouse Cheddar cheese, grated	
4 eggs, separated	

1. Grease eight individual ramekin dishes.
2. Put the cauliflower in a saucepan and just cover with boiling salted water. Cover and simmer until tender, then drain.
3. Meanwhile, prepare a white sauce. Put the butter, flour and milk in a saucepan. Heat, whisking continuously, until the sauce thickens, boils and is smooth. Simmer for 1–2 minutes. Add the mustard and season to taste.
4. Turn the sauce into a blender or food processor. Add the cauliflower and work to an almost smooth purée.
5. Turn into a large bowl and leave to cool slightly. Stir in the cheese with the egg yolks.
6. Whisk the egg whites until stiff but not dry and fold into the sauce mixture. Spoon into the dishes.
7. Bake at 180°C (350°F) mark 4 for 25 minutes or until browned and firm to the touch. Serve at once.

TO MICROWAVE

The sauce can be prepared in the microwave. Put the butter, flour and milk in a medium bowl. Cook on HIGH for 4–5 minutes, until boiling and thickened, whisking frequently. Add the mustard and season to taste.

RED KIDNEY BEAN HOT-POT

COUNTRYWIDE

Make this dish in the late summer or early autumn, when runner beans, courgettes and celery are all in season together. Ensure that the dried beans are simmered for the full time given in the recipe. Substitute a 397 g (14 oz) can kidney beans to speed things up, if you prefer.

SERVES 2

100 g (4 oz) dried red kidney beans, soaked overnight
25 g (1 oz) butter
1 medium onion, skinned and roughly chopped
100 g (4 oz) celery, sliced
100 g (4 oz) carrots, sliced
15 ml (1 tbsp) plain flour
300 ml (½ pint) vegetable stock
salt and pepper
100 g (4 oz) runner beans, topped and tailed
100 g (4 oz) courgettes, sliced
25 g (1 oz) fresh wholemeal breadcrumbs
75 g (3 oz) Cheddar cheese, grated

1. Drain the kidney beans and rinse well under running cold water. Put in a large saucepan, cover with plenty of fresh cold water and slowly bring to the boil.
2. Skim off the surface with a slotted spoon, then boil rapidly for 10 minutes. Half cover the pan and simmer for about 1½ hours, until tender.
3. Melt the butter in a large saucepan, add the onion and gently fry for about 5 minutes, until softened. Add the celery and carrots, cover and gently cook for 5 minutes.
4. Add the flour and gently cook, stirring, for 1–2 minutes. Remove from the heat and gradually blend in the stock. Bring to the boil, stirring constantly, then simmer for 5 minutes. Season to taste.
5. Add the runner beans and simmer for a further 5 minutes, then add the courgettes. Cook for a further 5–10 minutes, until the vegetables are tender but still with a bite to them.
6. Drain the kidney beans, add to the vegetables and heat through for about 5 minutes. Taste and adjust seasoning, then turn into a deep flameproof dish.
7. Mix the breadcrumbs and cheese together. Sprinkle on top of the bean mixture, then brown under a hot grill until crisp and crusty. Serve hot, accompanied with wholemeal bread and a green salad.

TO MICROWAVE

 Complete steps 1 and 2. Put the butter, onion, celery and carrot in a large bowl. Cover and cook on HIGH for 10–12 minutes, until softened. Sprinkle in the flour and cook on HIGH for 30 seconds. Gradually add the stock, then cook on HIGH for 3–4 minutes, until boiling and thickened, stirring occasionally. Add the

runner beans, cover and cook on HIGH for 2 minutes. Stir in the courgettes and drained kidney beans and season to taste. Re-cover and cook on HIGH for 4–5 minutes, until the courgettes are just tender. Complete step 7.

BAKED ONIONS WITH NUT STUFFING

COUNTRYWIDE

Choose onions that are hard, with no obvious soft spots, and avoid any that are showing signs of sprouting. Although raw onions are known for their pungent smell, when cooked they have a mild, sweet flavour which contrasts well with the cheesy stuffing.

SERVES 4

4 large onions, each weighing 225–275 g (8–10 oz)
150 g (5 oz) long-grain brown rice
salt and pepper
50 g (2 oz) hazelnuts
50 g (2 oz) salted peanuts
225 g (8 oz) tomatoes, roughly chopped
100 g (4 oz) Cheddar cheese, grated
2.5 ml (½ tsp) dried basil
1.25 ml (¼ tsp) dried oregano
5 ml (1 tsp) turmeric

1. Boil the onions in their skins for 45–50 minutes, until very tender. Drain and leave to cool.
2. Meanwhile, cook the rice in plenty of boiling salted water for about 30 minutes, until tender. Drain well.
3. Put the hazelnuts and peanuts on a sheet of foil and cook under a grill until brown, turning frequently. Leave the skins on the hazelnuts and finely chop with the peanuts.
4. Mix the tomatoes with the rice, cheese, nuts, herbs and turmeric and season to taste.
5. Slice off the tip and root of each onion, but leave on the coloured outer skin. Down one side of each onion cut through to the centre from tip to root. Ease the onions open.
6. Divide the stuffing between each onion, pressing it well into the centre.
7. Place in a roasting tin, cover and bake at 200°C (400°F) mark 6 for about 40 minutes. Serve hot.

TO MICROWAVE

 Prick the onions with a fork (do not skin), then put the onions and 300 ml (½ pint) boiling water in a large bowl. Cover and cook on HIGH for 20–25 minutes, until tender. Meanwhile, complete steps 2, 3 and 4. Drain the onions and complete steps 5, 6 and 7.

CABBAGE AND
HAZELNUT ROLLS. Deep-
fried until crisply golden,
these nutty croquettes have a
simple filling of mashed
potato and cabbage.

CABBAGE AND HAZELNUT ROLLS

THE SOUTH-EAST

Hazelnuts, also called filberts or cob nuts, are grown in Kent. You'll sometimes see them with their leafy outer covering still in place, fitting closely over the nut. The three varieties are not exactly the same, but are interchangeable in most recipes.

MAKES 16

✳ ⚡

450 g (1 lb) potatoes
salt and pepper
900 g (2 lb) green cabbage, roughly chopped
45 ml (3 tbsp) fresh milk, if necessary
50 g (2 oz) butter
50 g (2 oz) plain flour
50 g (2 oz) hazelnuts, chopped and toasted
2 eggs, beaten
100 g (4 oz) dry breadcrumbs
vegetable oil for deep-frying
lemon twists, to garnish

1. Boil the potatoes in salted water for 20 minutes or until tender. Drain and mash without adding liquid.
2. Cook the cabbage in boiling salted water for 5–10 minutes or until just tender. Drain well. Purée in a blender or food processor, adding the milk if necessary – you should have 450 ml (¾ pint) purée.
3. Melt the butter in a saucepan, add the flour and cook gently, stirring, for 1–2 minutes. Gradually blend in the cabbage purée and milk, if necessary. Bring to the boil, then simmer for 5 minutes.
4. Stir the mashed potatoes and hazelnuts into the sauce, season to taste and mix well. Transfer to a bowl, cool, cover and chill for at least 1½ hours or until firm.
5. With dampened hands, shape the mixture into 16 rolls. Place on a greased baking sheet and chill again for at least 20 minutes.
6. Coat the croquettes in the beaten eggs, then the breadcrumbs. Heat the oil to 180°C (350°F) in a deep-fat fryer. Deep-fry the rolls in batches for about 4 minutes, until crisp and golden. Remove with a slotted spoon and drain on absorbent kitchen paper while frying the remainder. Serve hot, garnished with lemon twists. Accompany with a crisp salad.

TO MICROWAVE

 Cut the potatoes into small pieces and put in a medium bowl with 30 ml (2 tbsp) water. Cover and cook on HIGH for 7–10 minutes or until tender. Complete remainder of step 1. Put the cabbage in a large bowl with 30 ml (2 tbsp) water. Cover and cook on HIGH for 7–10 minutes or until just tender, stirring once. Complete the remainder of step 2 and the recipe.

SPICY CHICK-PEAS AND SWEDE

COUNTRYWIDE

Swedes are a variety of turnip originally introduced to this country from Sweden. They have a delicate flavour and good colour which is useful in stews or makes a delicious purée.

SERVES 4

✳ ⚡

225 g (8 oz) dried chick-peas, soaked overnight
225 g (8 oz) swede, peeled and roughly chopped
salt and pepper
25 g (1 oz) butter
1 medium onion, skinned and roughly chopped
5 ml (1 tsp) cumin seeds
2.5 ml (½ tsp) dried oregano
10 ml (2 tsp) paprika
15 ml (1 tbsp) plain flour
450 g (1 lb) tomatoes, roughly chopped
50 g (2 oz) Cheddar cheese, grated
wholemeal bread, to serve

1. Drain the chick-peas and rinse under running cold water. Put in a large saucepan, cover with plenty of fresh cold water and slowly bring to the boil. Cover and simmer for 45 minutes or until just tender. Drain well.
2. Put the swede in a saucepan and cover with cold salted water. Bring to the boil, then simmer for 15–20

minutes or until tender. Drain, reserving 150 ml
(¼ pint) cooking liquor.

3. Heat the butter in a medium saucepan, add the onion, cumin, oregano and paprika and fry for 1–2 minutes.

4. Stir in the flour. Cook, stirring, for 1–2 minutes, then gradually stir in the reserved liquor. Bring to boil, stir in tomatoes. Cover and simmer for 2–3 minutes.

5. Add the chick-peas and swede and stir over a gentle heat for a few minutes until hot. Season to taste and serve, topped with a sprinkling of Cheddar cheese and accompanied by wholemeal bread.

TO MICROWAVE

Complete step 1. Meanwhile, peel and finely chop the swede and put into a medium bowl with 150 ml (¼ pint) water. Cover and cook on HIGH for 4 minutes or until tender. Drain, reserving the cooking liquor. Put the butter, onion, cumin, oregano and paprika in a large bowl. Cook on HIGH for 2 minutes, then stir in the flour and cook on HIGH for 30 seconds. Stir in the reserved liquor, tomatoes, swede and chick-peas and mix well. Cover and cook on HIGH for 5–6 minutes, until thickened and heated through, stirring occasionally. Serve as step 5.

CELERIAC WITH TOMATO SAUCE

COUNTRYWIDE

Celeriac tastes much like celery, but is a knobbly vegetable that looks like a rough turnip and can vary from about the size of a large apple to as big as a coconut.

SERVES 3

25 g (1 oz) butter
1 large onion, skinned and finely chopped
3 garlic cloves, skinned and crushed
350 g (12 oz) ripe tomatoes, skinned and finely chopped
15 ml (1 tbsp) tomato purée
30 ml (2 tbsp) red wine or red wine vinegar
60 ml (4 tbsp) chopped fresh parsley
5 ml (1 tsp) ground cinnamon
1 bay leaf
salt and pepper
2 heads celeriac, total weight about 900 g (2 lb)
5 ml (1 tsp) lemon juice
50 g (2 oz) fresh wholemeal breadcrumbs
50 g (2 oz) Cheddar cheese, grated
fresh parsley, to garnish

1. To prepare the tomato sauce, heat the butter in a large heavy-based saucepan, add the onion and garlic and fry gently for about 10 minutes, until very soft and lightly coloured.

2. Add the tomatoes, tomato purée, wine, parsley, cinnamon and bay leaf. Season to taste. Add 450 ml (¾ pint) hot water and bring to the boil, stirring with a wooden spoon to break up the tomatoes.

3. Lower the heat, cover and simmer for 30 minutes, stirring occasionally.

4. Meanwhile, peel the celeriac, then cut into chunky pieces. As you prepare the celeriac, place the pieces in a bowl of water to which the lemon juice has been added, to prevent discoloration.

5. Drain the celeriac, then plunge quickly into a large pan of boiling salted water. Return to the boil and blanch for 10 minutes.

6. Drain the celeriac well, then put in an ovenproof serving dish or 3 individual dishes. Pour over the tomato sauce, discarding the bay leaf, then sprinkle the breadcrumbs and cheese evenly over the top.

7. Bake at 190°C (375°F) mark 5 for 30 minutes, until the celeriac is tender when pierced with a skewer and the topping is golden brown. Garnish with parsley and serve hot, straight from the dish. Accompany with boiled rice.

TO MICROWAVE

Make the tomato sauce. Put the butter, onion and garlic in a large bowl, cover and cook on HIGH for 7 minutes or until softened, stirring occasionally. Add the tomatoes, tomato purée, wine, parsley, cinnamon and bay leaf. Season to taste and add 300 ml (½ pint) hot water. Re-cover and cook on HIGH for 15 minutes, stirring occasionally. Complete step 4. Drain the celeriac and put into a large flameproof dish. Pour over the tomato sauce. Cover and cook on HIGH for 25 minutes or until tender, stirring occasionally. Sprinkle with the breadcrumbs and cheese, then brown under a hot grill.

CELERIAC WITH TOMATO SAUCE. An unusual vegetable that's well worth trying. This recipe pairs it with a full-bodied tomato sauce, lightly flavoured with cinnamon.

ACCOMPANYING
VEGETABLES
& SALADS

The great variety and quality of fresh vegetables and salad ingredients now available from all over the country is wonderful. Vegetable accompaniments so often get forgotten, and yet they are a vital part of any main course. This chapter will fire your imagination and turn your vegetable accompaniments and salads into dishes to be savoured in their own right.

POTATOES

Endlessly adaptable, potatoes are one of the cheapest and most substantial vegetables. They are also highly nutritious, being full of vitamins, minerals and fibre. Always delicious with the traditional 'meat and veg' of Sunday lunch, they are also excellent as the basic ingredient in a wide variety of snacks and supper dishes. Always store potatoes in a cool, dry, dark place.

Maincrop potatoes are available September to May. These are the five most common varieties:

PENTLAND CROWN   PENTLAND SQUIRE

DESIREE

KING EDWARD   MARIS PIPER

DESIREE

Pale yellow, firm but soft textured flesh, particularly popular in the south and east. Excellent all-round potato that does not disintegrate when cooked. Particularly good boiled, baked or chipped, or in dishes such as Pan Haggerty (see recipe, page 101).

MARIS PIPER

Most popular maincrop variety, cream-coloured flesh with soft floury texture. Excellent mashed (see recipe, page 205), baked, chipped or roast.

PENTLAND CROWN

White flesh, less floury than other maincrop varieties, and wetter when cooked. Best mashed, baked or roast.

KING EDWARD

The most widely known variety named after King Edward VII. Creamy flesh with dry, floury texture ideal for mashing or roasting.

PENTLAND SQUIRE

Very white flesh with soft dry powdery texture. Tends to be larger than other maincrop varieties, so especially good baked (see recipes, page 108).

CAULIFLOWER AND POTATO BAKE

COUNTRYWIDE

Cauliflower is available all year round and is often eaten with a rich creamy sauce, as in this recipe. Freshly grated nutmeg and garlic add flavour to the sauce, which is soaked up deliciously by the potatoes.

SERVES 4

450 g (1 lb) new potatoes, thinly sliced
salt and pepper
1 small cauliflower, broken into florettes
1 garlic clove, skinned and crushed
pinch of freshly grated nutmeg
150 ml (5 fl oz) fresh single cream or buttermilk
50 g (2 oz) Cheddar cheese, grated

1. Cook the potatoes in boiling salted water for 5 minutes. Drain well.
2. Layer the potatoes and cauliflower in a lightly buttered 1.1 litre (2 pint) ovenproof serving dish. Stir the garlic and nutmeg into the cream and pour over the potatoes and cauliflower.
3. Sprinkle the cheese, cover and bake at 180°C (350°F) mark 4 for 45–50 minutes, until the vegetables are tender. Uncover and place under a medium grill until lightly browned. Serve at once, straight from the casserole.

TO MICROWAVE

 Place the potatoes in a large bowl with enough boiling water to cover and cook on HIGH for 5 minutes. Complete step 2. Cook on HIGH for 10 minutes. Sprinkle with the cheese and grill until golden.

BUTTERED BROCCOLI WITH ALMONDS

COUNTRYWIDE

The delicious crunch of almonds makes broccoli into something quite special. Broccoli does not keep well, so buy it as fresh as possible, without any signs of yellowing. Beware of overcooking it – some crispness should be retained.

SERVES 4

700 g (1½ lb) broccoli florets, trimmed
salt and pepper
25 g (1 oz) butter
50 g (2 oz) flaked almonds
juice of ½ lemon

1. Cook the broccoli in boiling salted water for 10–15 minutes, until just tender.
2. Meanwhile, melt the butter in a small saucepan and cook the almonds over a gentle heat until golden brown. Stir in the lemon juice and season with pepper to taste.

3. Drain the broccoli well, then toss with the almonds and butter. Serve at once.

TO MICROWAVE

 Put the broccoli in a large bowl with 45 ml (3 tbsp) water. Cover and cook on HIGH for about 10 minutes or until just tender. Meanwhile, complete steps 2 and 3.

LEEK MOUSSES
WALES

Delicious and impressive looking, these pale green mousses go well with fish dishes, or can be served as a starter or light lunch dish on their own. Because leeks harbour dirt it is best to slice them before washing thoroughly in a colander.

MAKES 8

450 g (1 lb) leeks, trimmed, thinly sliced and washed
salt and pepper
25 g (1 oz) butter
30 ml (2 tbsp) plain wholemeal flour
300 ml (½ pint) fresh milk
150 g (5 oz) soft cheese with garlic and herbs
2 eggs
25 g (1 oz) fresh wholemeal breadcrumbs

1. Place the leeks in a medium saucepan of boiling salted water and cook for about 5 minutes until tender. Drain well and rinse with cold water.
2. Meanwhile, put the butter, the flour and milk in a medium saucepan. Heat, whisking continuously, until the sauce thickens, boils and is smooth. Simmer for 2–3 minutes. Add half the cooked leeks and leave to cool.
3. Place the cooled sauce, soft cheese, eggs and breadcrumbs in a blender or food processor and process until almost smooth. Season to taste.
4. Lightly grease eight 100 ml (4 fl oz) ramekin dishes and scatter a few of the reserved leeks in the bottom of each. Carefully pour the sauce on top of the leeks.
5. Place the ramekins in a roasting tin. Add enough hot water to come halfway up the sides of the dishes. Cover the roasting tin tightly with foil.
6. Bake at 180°C (350°F) mark 4 for about 1 hour or until just firm to the touch. Stand for 4–5 minutes before turning out.

TO MICROWAVE

 Place the leeks in a large bowl with 45 ml (3 tbsp) water, cover and cook on HIGH for 4–6 minutes, until softened. Drain well and rinse with cold water. Put the butter, flour and milk in a medium bowl and cook on HIGH for 4–5 minutes, until boiling and thickened, whisking frequently. Complete the remainder of steps 2, 3 and 4. Arrange the ramekins in a circle in the oven and cook on MEDIUM for about 13 minutes or until just firm to the touch. Then complete the remainder of step 6.

CLAPSHOT
SCOTLAND

This hearty, root vegetable dish is often eaten as an accompaniment to haggis. It is a combination of potatoes and the coarse-skinned root vegetable with orange flesh known as turnip in Scotland and the North but swede in the South.

SERVES 6

700 g (1½ lb) potatoes, roughly chopped
700 g (1½ lb) turnips, roughly chopped
salt and pepper
25 g (1 oz) butter
30 ml (2 tbsp) snipped fresh chives

1. Cook the potatoes and turnips in boiling salted water until tender, then drain well. Mash together until smooth.
2. Beat in the butter and the snipped chives, then season to taste. Serve hot.

TO MICROWAVE

 Put the potatoes and turnips in a large bowl with 90 ml (6 tbsp) water, cover and cook on HIGH for 15–20 minutes, until tender, stirring occasionally. Drain well. Mash together, then beat in the butter and the snipped chives, then season to taste. Serve hot.

LEEK MOUSSES. Pretty little mousses to liven up any meal and add a dash of pastel colour to the plate.

OPPOSITE

LEFT
CAULIFLOWER AND POTATO BAKE. A simple and very tasty variation on the theme of cauliflower cheese. Easy to prepare, it makes a good supper.

RIGHT
BUTTERED BROCCOLI WITH ALMONDS. An easy and appetising way with broccoli, to serve as an accompaniment with meat or fish.

MUSHROOMS

Mushrooms enhance the flavour of any dish, blending deliciously with most types of foods. They are a source of vitamins and vegetable protein and are quick and easy to prepare. Keep them in a paper bag within a plastic bag in the salad drawer of the refrigerator. Wipe with a clean damp cloth just before use, never wash. Here are five common types of mushroom:

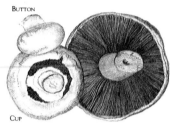

BUTTON

CUP

OPEN AND FLAT

BUTTON

The least mature, with firm, tightly-closed caps. Ideal for sauces, as in the Mushrooms in White Wine recipe featured opposite. Take care not to overcook.

CUPS

More mature with a fuller flavour. Use in casseroles, soups or pies, or as a stuffing (see recipe, page 128).

OPEN AND FLAT

Fully mature with a rich flavour. Best grilled, fried or stuffed.

OYSTER

Less widely known. They have a stronger flavour and are good fried, grilled or stewed lightly with butter, parsley and garlic.

CHESTNUT

Similar in shape to cup mushrooms, but firmer and with a stronger taste. Available in a few main supermarkets. Use as for cups.

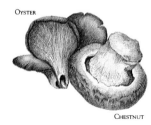

OYSTER

CHESTNUT

STUMP
THE NORTH

This tasty vegetable purée combines three of the best of Britain's traditional root vegetables. It is a particularly good method of using up older carrots and swede, which tend to be tough unless cooked well. You can vary the quantities if you prefer one vegetable to predominate but do include enough carrots to give an attractive colour.

SERVES 4

225 g (8 oz) carrots, peeled and sliced

225 g (8 oz) swede, peeled and sliced

225 g (8 oz) potatoes, peeled and sliced

15 g (½ oz) butter

150 ml (¼ pint) fresh milk

salt and pepper

1. Simmer the vegetables in lightly salted water in a medium saucepan for 30 minutes or until soft. Drain well.
2. Mash the vegetables with the butter and milk. Reheat gently and season to taste. Serve hot.

TO MICROWAVE

Cook the vegetables in 150 ml (¼ pint) water in a large bowl, covered, on HIGH for 15 minutes. Complete step 2.

CREAMED PARSNIPS
COUNTRYWIDE

This smooth purée is an excellent accompaniment to roast meats, poultry and game, and makes a pleasant change from roast parsnips. This was a popular dish in the 16th and 17th centuries, when food with a sweet flavour, such as parsnips, was often served as a complement to savoury dishes.

SERVES 4

900 g (2 lb) parsnips, peeled and roughly chopped

salt and pepper

150 ml (5 fl oz) fresh single cream

chopped fresh parsley, to garnish

1. Cook the parsnips in boiling salted water for 35–40 minutes, until very tender.
2. Drain thoroughly then return to the pan and mash, using a potato masher. Stir in the cream and season to taste. Heat gently, then serve hot, garnished with parsley.

TO MICROWAVE

Put the parsnips and 120 ml (8 tbsp) water in a large bowl. Cover and cook on HIGH for 25–30 minutes, until very tender. Drain thoroughly and mash with a

potato masher. Add the cream and season to taste. Cook on HIGH for 2–3 minutes or until hot. Serve hot, garnished with parsley.

MUSHROOMS IN WHITE WINE
THE WEST

Firm, whole button mushrooms are the best choice for this recipe as they keep their shape when cooked. The dish also makes a good starter or an appetising snack.

SERVES 4

225 g (8 oz) button mushrooms

300 ml (½ pint) dry white wine

1 garlic clove, skinned and crushed

1 medium onion, skinned and finely chopped

15 ml (1 tbsp) chopped fresh parsley

60 ml (4 tbsp) fresh soured cream

1. Put the mushrooms in a small saucepan with the wine, garlic, onion and parsley. Simmer gently for 20 minutes.
2. Remove the pan from the heat and stir in the soured cream. Serve at once.

TO MICROWAVE

Use only 200 ml (7 fl oz) white wine. Put the mushrooms, wine, garlic, onion and parsley in a large bowl. Cover and cook on HIGH for 15–20 minutes, until the onions and mushrooms are softened. Stir in the cream and serve.

BAKED BEETROOT
COUNTRYWIDE

Beetroot is usually served cold in salads, but it is also delicious served hot. Be careful when preparing the beetroots for cooking in a conventional oven – if the skin is damaged the colour will 'bleed' during baking. For the same reason, do not prod them with a fork to see if they are done, but instead test whether the skin slides off easily.

SERVES 4

4 raw beetroots, each weighing about 225 g (8 oz)

butter or fresh soured cream, to serve

salt and pepper

1. Wash the beetroots, but do not trim. Wrap them in greased foil or place in a greased ovenproof dish.
2. Cover tightly and bake at 180°C (350°F) mark 4 for 2–3 hours. When the beetroots are cooked the skin will slide off easily. Serve with a slice cut off the top, but not skinned, topped with the butter or soured cream and seasoned to taste.

TO MICROWAVE

 Prick the beetroot skins with a fork. Arrange in a circle in a shallow dish and pour over 45 ml (3 tbsp) water. Cover and cook on HIGH for 20–25 minutes or until tender. Drain, then serve with a slice cut off the top, but not skinned, topped with the butter and seasoned to taste.

CABBAGE WITH JUNIPER BERRIES

THE EASTERN COUNTIES

You can use any type of cabbage that happens to be in season for this delicious recipe. Juniper berries are wrinkled and black and, when crushed, release their delightful aroma. The flavour is reminiscent of gin, since juniper is a basic ingredient of the spirit. As a faint background hint, married with garlic, it adds a very special touch to cabbage.

SERVES 4

25 g (1 oz) butter	
1 medium onion, skinned and chopped	
1 garlic clove, skinned and crushed	
6 juniper berries, crushed	
450 g (1 lb) cabbage, shredded	
salt and pepper	

1. Melt the butter in a large saucepan. Add the onion, garlic and juniper berries and lightly cook for 5 minutes, until the onion is soft.
2. Add the cabbage and stir until well coated in butter. Season to taste. Cover and cook the cabbage in its own juice for 10 minutes, stirring occasionally. The cabbage should still be slightly crunchy and not soft. Serve hot.

TO MICROWAVE

 Melt the butter on HIGH for 45 seconds. Add the onion, garlic and juniper berries. Cook on HIGH for 5 minutes, until the onion is softened. Add the cabbage and season to taste. Cook, covered, on HIGH for 7–8 minutes, stirring occasionally.

LEFT
CABBAGE WITH JUNIPER BERRIES. A lovely, warming way to prepare cabbage, that gives it an extra special tang. Good with sausages or bacon.

RIGHT
BAKED BEETROOT. Soured cream and beetroot is a classic combination that works wonders in this unusual recipe.

CELERY BAKED IN
CREAM. A little cream is a
delicious way of bringing out
the full superb flavour of
celery. Serve with plain
grilled meat or fish.

CELERY BAKED
IN CREAM

THE EASTERN COUNTIES

Celery grows well in the rich black soil of the fen country surrounding Ely in Cambridgeshire, where more than half the British outdoor crop comes from. Both white and green celery are available and either variety can be used for this recipe.

SERVES 4

1 large head of celery, trimmed
1.25 ml (¼ tsp) ground allspice
2 garlic cloves, skinned and crushed
300 ml (10 fl oz) fresh single cream
salt and pepper
25 g (1 oz) fresh wholemeal breadcrumbs

1. Reserve a few celery leaves to garnish, then cut the sticks lengthways into thin strips. Cut each strip into 5 cm (2 inch) lengths and put into an ovenproof serving dish.

2. Mix the allspice, garlic and cream together and season to taste. Pour over the celery. Sprinkle with the breadcrumbs.

3. Bake at 200°C (400°F) mark 6 for about 1¼ hours or until the celery is tender. Serve hot, garnished with the reserved celery leaves.

TO MICROWAVE

☑ Complete steps 1 and 2, omitting the breadcrumbs. Cover and cook on HIGH for about 20 minutes, until tender, stirring occasionally. Sprinkle with the breadcrumbs, then brown under a hot grill. Serve hot, garnished with the reserved celery leaves.

BRUSSELS SPROUTS
WITH CHESTNUTS

COUNTRYWIDE

Brussels sprouts and chestnuts are a delicious combination, traditionally served at Christmas to accompany the turkey. Buy Brussels sprouts on the day they are needed if possible, as they will only keep for a day or two before starting to turn yellow even if in the refrigerator. If you have to store them, prepare them for cooking and keep in the fridge in a polythene bag. Peeling the chestnuts is a fiddly job, which can be done in advance. Take care when peeling the hot chestnuts not to burn the tips of your fingers.

SERVES 4–6

350 g (12 oz) fresh chestnuts
salt and pepper
700 g (1½ lb) Brussels sprouts, trimmed
25 g (1 oz) butter

1. With the point of a small sharp knife make a small cut on the flat side of each chestnut.

2. Bake the nuts in their skins in the oven at 200°C (400°F) mark 6 for 20 minutes, then peel off the outer shell and the inner skin. (They are easier to peel while hot.)

3. Meanwhile, cook the Brussels sprouts in boiling salted water for 8–10 minutes, until just tender. Drain.

4. Over a high heat, toss the chestnuts and Brussels sprouts with the butter and pepper to taste, until the butter is melted. Serve at once.

TO MICROWAVE

☑ With the point of a small sharp knife cut a lengthways slash in each chestnut. Spread out half of the chestnuts on a large plate and cook on LOW for 3–4 minutes, until the shells can easily be removed. Repeat with the remaining chestnuts. Complete step 2. Put the Brussels sprouts and 45 ml (3 tbsp) water in a large bowl, cover and cook on HIGH for 10–12 minutes, until just tender. Drain. Add the cooked chestnuts, butter, salt and pepper to taste and cook on HIGH for 1–2 minutes or until hot and the butter is melted. Serve at once.

MARROW WITH TOMATO AND ONION

COUNTRYWIDE

Use well-flavoured English tomatoes for this recipe. Marrows are excellent cooked in a tasty sauce, as they happily absorb all the delicious herby juices.

SERVES 4–6

25 g (1 oz) butter

2 medium onions, skinned and chopped

1 garlic clove, skinned and crushed

1 medium marrow, peeled, seeded and cubed

6 large tomatoes, skinned and chopped

30 ml (2 tbsp) tomato purée

30 ml (2 tbsp) chopped fresh mixed herbs or 10 ml (2 tsp) dried mixed herbs

salt and pepper

1. Melt the butter in a large saucepan and gently fry the onions and garlic for 5 minutes, until soft. Add the marrow and cook for a further 5 minutes.
2. Stir in remaining ingredients, cover and simmer for 30 minutes, until the vegetables are tender. Season to taste. Serve at once.

TO MICROWAVE

 Melt the butter in a large bowl on HIGH for 45 seconds. Cook the onions and garlic on HIGH for 4 minutes, then add the marrow and continue cooking on HIGH for a further 4 minutes. Add remaining ingredients, cover and cook on HIGH for 30 minutes, until the vegetables are tender. Serve at once.

MARROW WITH TOMATO AND ONION. A lively way to make the most of marrows. The colourful mixture tastes as good as it looks.

CARROTS WITH MINT AND LEMON

THE EASTERN COUNTIES

Tender young carrots, in the shops during spring and early summer, have a lovely sweet flavour which is brought out to the full by the sugar and lemon juice in this recipe. Unwashed carrots, which sometimes still have their feathery foliage, keep better than those sold washed and prepacked.

SERVES 4

700 g (1½ lb) small new carrots, trimmed and scrubbed

salt and pepper

finely grated rind and juice of ½ lemon

5 ml (1 tsp) light soft brown sugar

15 g (½ oz) butter

30 ml (2 tbsp) chopped fresh mint

1. Cook the carrots in boiling salted water for about 10 minutes, until just tender. Drain.
2. Return the carrots to the pan with the remaining ingredients and toss together over a high heat until the butter melts. Serve at once.

TO MICROWAVE

Put the carrots in a large bowl with the lemon rind and juice, sugar and the butter. Cover and cook on HIGH for about 10 minutes or until just tender. Stir in the mint and serve at once.

CARROTS WITH MINT AND LEMON. A mouthwatering mix of flavours in a simple and attractive dish which takes only a few minutes to prepare.

RED CABBAGE WITH PEARS

COUNTRYWIDE

This recipe rings the changes on the old favourite, cabbage with apples, using pears instead. All varieties of dessert pears can be used successfully in this dish, which has a gentle, mellow flavour after long, slow cooking. It's a perfect accompaniment for bacon.

SERVES 4–6

1 garlic clove, skinned and crushed

900 g (2 lb) red cabbage, finely shredded

2 large firm pears, peeled, cored and thickly sliced

salt and pepper

150 ml (¼ pint) vegetable or chicken stock

30 ml (2 tbsp) lemon juice

1. Rub the garlic round the sides of a 3.4 litre (6 pint) casserole. Spoon half of the cabbage into the dish, followed by a layer of pears. Season to taste and repeat the layers. Pour over the stock and lemon juice.
2. Cover tightly and bake at 170°C (325°F) mark 3 for about 2 hours or until the cabbage is just tender. Adjust the seasoning and stir gently to mix together before serving.

TO MICROWAVE

Complete step 1 (substituting a large bowl or microwave casserole). Cover and cook on HIGH for 20–25 minutes or until the cabbage is tender. Adjust the seasoning and stir gently to mix together before serving.

GLAZED SHALLOTS

COUNTRYWIDE

Shallots are smaller than onions and have a milder flavour. They keep well, so it's worth buying a supply when you see them. Store them in a cool, dry place and use them up as soon as they show any signs of sprouting.

SERVES 4

700 g (1½ lb) shallots, skinned

40 g (1½ oz) butter

salt and pepper

chopped fresh parsley, to garnish

1. Put the shallots in a medium saucepan, cover with water and bring to the boil and cook for 5 minutes. Drain.
2. Melt the butter in a medium frying pan, add the shallots and season to taste. Cover and cook for about 10 minutes, until the shallots are tender and well glazed. Turn into a warm serving dish and sprinkle with parsley.

TO MICROWAVE

 Put the shallots in a medium bowl, add 45 ml (3 tbsp) water and cook on HIGH for 4 minutes. Melt the butter in a medium bowl on HIGH for 1 minute. Add the shallots and cook on HIGH for 10 minutes. Turn into a warm serving dish and sprinkle with parsley.

RUNNER BEANS WITH ONIONS AND TOMATOES

COUNTRYWIDE

Runner beans used to be grown for their attractive red flowers and have only been produced for food since the last century. They are grown mainly in the south of England.

SERVES 4–6

15 g (½ oz) butter

1 medium onion, skinned and chopped

1 garlic clove, skinned and crushed

397 g (14 oz) can chopped tomatoes

700 g (1½ lb) young runner beans, topped and tailed and cut into 1 cm (½ inch) lengths

15 ml (1 tbsp) chopped fresh basil or 5 ml (1 tsp) dried

salt and pepper

1. Melt the butter in a large saucepan and cook the onion and garlic gently for 3–5 minutes, until softened but not browned. Add the tomatoes with their juice, bring to the boil and simmer for 10–15 minutes, until reduced.
2. Stir the beans into the sauce with the dried basil, if using, cover tightly and cook for 10–15 minutes, until the beans are tender but still crisp. Stir in the fresh basil, if using, and season to taste. Serve hot or cold.

TO MICROWAVE

Put the butter, onion and garlic in a large bowl, cover and cook on HIGH for 5–7 minutes, until softened. Add the tomatoes and their juice and cook, uncovered, on HIGH for 8–10 minutes, until reduced and thickened. Stir the beans into the sauce with the dried basil, if using, re-cover and cook on HIGH for 10–12 minutes or until the beans are tender but still crisp, stirring occasionally. Stir in the fresh basil, if using, and season to taste. Serve hot or cold.

LEFT
GLAZED SHALLOTS.
Their buttery sheen and sprinkling of parsley give these sweet-tasting little shallots plenty of eye-appeal.

RIGHT
RUNNER BEANS WITH ONIONS AND TOMATOES. An interesting way to serve one of the best summer vegetables. Garlic and basil make this a deliciously aromatic dish.

CABBAGE

Cabbage has always been one of Britain's most popular vegetables and is available all year round in seasonal varieties. The main growing areas are Lincolnshire, Lancashire and Kent.

ROUNDHEAD SPRING CABBAGE

RED CABBAGE   WHITE CABBAGE

ROUNDHEADED SPRING CABBAGE

Looser, with a smaller heart, than other types. Don't overcook – it's delicious steamed until tender but still crunchy, then tossed in butter. Strong flavours like caraway seeds or juniper berries (see recipe, page 225) go well with cabbage.

RED CABBAGE

Popular in autumn and winter, this is often cooked with apple and vinegar (see recipe, page 228 for an interesting variation with pears), and served with game or pork. Also good raw in salads.

WHITE CABBAGE

Very firm, with densely packed leaves, and stores well. Good raw, grated or shredded in winter salads and coleslaw (see recipe, page 231). An autumn and winter vegetable.

SAVOY CABBAGE

Distinctive for its crinkly, curly leaves. The whole head or individual leaves are good for stuffing. Available all year.

CHINESE LEAF

This cabbage originally from Asia is crunchy with a mild celery flavour. Good raw in salads and cooked in stir-fries. Available from spring to autumn.

SAVOY CABBAGE

CHINESE LEAF

NEW POTATO SALAD

THE WEST

The warm climate of Cornwall produces tender young vegetables earlier than other parts of the UK. Buy the smallest freshest potatoes you can find and cook them the same day. For a luxury touch use clotted instead of double cream. Dress the potatoes while still warm, even if you are serving them cold, as this allows the flavours to be absorbed.

SERVES 4–6

700 g (1½ lb) small new potatoes
2 hard-boiled egg yolks
large pinch of cayenne pepper
5 ml (1 tsp) caster sugar
1.25 ml (¼ tsp) anchovy essence
15 ml (1 tbsp) herb vinegar
150 ml (5 fl oz) fresh double cream
snipped fresh chives, to garnish

1. Cook the potatoes in their skins, in boiling salted water for 10–15 minutes, until tender.
2. Meanwhile, make the dressing. Mash the egg yolks, cayenne pepper and sugar to a paste with the anchovy essence, the vinegar and 5 ml (1 tsp) cold water. Stir in the cream.
3. When the potatoes are cooked, drain thoroughly and toss with the dressing. Serve warm or cold, garnished with snipped chives.

VARIATION
Replace the fresh cream with fresh soured cream or natural yogurt and substitute the anchovy essence for 15 ml (1 tbsp) chopped fresh herbs such as tarragon, chives, mint or parsley.

TO MICROWAVE

Put the potatoes and 90 ml (6 tbsp) water in a large bowl. Cover and cook on HIGH for 9–12 minutes, until tender, stirring occasionally. Complete the recipe.

ENDIVE, ORANGE AND HAZELNUT SALAD

COUNTRYWIDE

Endive is rather like a lettuce with very crinkly leaves, ranging through shades of green to yellow. It is sometimes sold as 'frissée'. Endive wilts quickly, so buy it fresh when needed and don't store for more than a day.

SERVES 4–6

4 large oranges
1 head of endive, torn into small pieces

1 bunch of watercress, trimmed, torn into sprigs and washed

1 small red pepper, seeded and cut into thin strips

150 g (5 oz) natural yogurt

salt and pepper

25 g (1 oz) hazelnuts

1. Remove all of the peel and the white pith from 3 of the oranges, then segment them. Mix the orange segments with the endive, watercress and pepper in a large salad bowl.
2. To make the dressing, finely grate the rind from the remaining orange into a small bowl, then squeeze in the juice. Whisk in the yogurt and season to taste with salt and pepper.
3. Spread the hazelnuts out on a baking sheet and toast lightly under a hot grill. Turn the nuts on to a clean tea-towel and rub off the loose skins. Roughly chop the nuts.
4. Just before serving, drizzle the dressing over the salad and sprinkle with the nuts. Serve at once while the nuts are still crunchy.

COLESLAW SALAD WITH BLUE CHEESE DRESSING

COUNTRYWIDE

Lymeswold was the first new English cheese to appear for 200 years, when it was launched on the market in 1982. It quickly became popular for its creamy texture and rich flavour, with an added tang from the blue veining. Somerset Blue is a similar style, full-fat, soft cheese. Use either to make the tasty dressing for this salad, which is ideal to serve in winter.

SERVES 4

50 g (2 oz) Lymeswold or Somerset Blue cheese, rinded

30 ml (2 tbsp) mayonnaise

15 ml (1 tbsp) lemon juice

150 g (5 oz) natural yogurt

salt and pepper

225 g (8 oz) white cabbage, very finely shredded

225 g (8 oz) red cabbage, very finely shredded

1 eating apple, unpeeled, cored and cut into matchstick strips

50 g (2 oz) sultanas

1. To make the dressing, put the cheese, mayonnaise and lemon juice in a food processor and work until smooth. Gradually beat in the yogurt and season to taste.
2. Put the cabbages, apple and sultanas in a salad bowl. Pour over the dressing and toss together until well coated in the dressing. Cover and chill until ready to serve.

WINTER SALAD

COUNTRYWIDE

A crunchy combination of colourful fresh vegetables. British chicory is available from mid-April to mid-November. It has a distinctive, bitter flavour and comes as tightly packed heads of white leaves, with yellow tips. Store it in the salad drawer of the fridge, where it will keep well for up to one week.

SERVES 4–6

1 eating apple, cored and chopped

1 head of celery, sliced

1 cooked beetroot, peeled and sliced

2 heads of chicory, sliced

1 punnet of mustard and cress, trimmed

2.5 ml (½ tsp) prepared English mustard

2.5 ml (½ tsp) sugar

60 ml (4 tbsp) fresh single cream

10 ml (2 tsp) white wine vinegar

salt and pepper

3 eggs, hard-boiled and cut into wedges

1. Lightly mix the apple, celery, beetroot and chicory together with the cress in a large salad bowl.
2. To make the dressing, whisk the mustard, sugar, cream and vinegar together. Season to taste. Pour over the salad and toss together so that everything is coated in the dressing. Add the eggs, then serve at once.

WINTER SALAD. An attractively arranged dish, that can be served either alone, for a light lunch or supper, or as a main course accompaniment.

OPPOSITE

LEFT
ENDIVE, ORANGE AND HAZELNUT SALAD. A glorious mixture of flavours and textures, combined to make a bright and colourful salad.

RIGHT
NEW POTATO SALAD. Tiny potatoes, coated in a rich, piquant dressing, for a tempting early summer salad.

PUDDINGS
& DESSERTS

For over three centuries puddings from Britain have had a great and well deserved reputation. Substantial, or light and delicate, there's much to be said for rounding off a meal with one of these fabulous dishes. They range from traditional puddings to dinner party desserts. Choose from fresh fruit puddings, pies, milk, custard and cream puddings, cheesecakes and ice creams.

OSBORNE PUDDING

COUNTRYWIDE

*A delicious variation on that much-loved nursery favourite,
bread and butter pudding, which uses brown bread, spread
with marmalade. The recipe has been round for centuries
and has always been popular, partly because it is such a good
way to use up day-old bread. But, of course, there's nothing
to stop you cutting a few slices specially to make it.*

SERVES 4

4 thin slices day-old wholemeal bread
butter for spreading
orange marmalade for spreading
50 g (2 oz) currants or sultanas
450 ml (¾ pint) fresh milk
2 eggs
15 ml (1 tbsp) brandy or rum (optional)
finely grated rind of 1 orange
15 ml (1 tbsp) light soft brown sugar
grated nutmeg

OSBORNE PUDDING.
Mellow orange flavours
permeate this pudding with its
crisp and buttery topping.

1. Spread the bread with butter and marmalade, then
cut into triangles. Arrange, buttered side up, in a
buttered ovenproof serving dish, sprinkling the layers
with the fruit.
2. Heat the milk, but do not boil. Beat the eggs with
the brandy, if using, and the orange rind, then gradually
pour on the warm milk, stirring continuously. Pour over
the bread and leave to stand for at least 15 minutes to
allow the bread to absorb the milk.
3. Sprinkle the sugar and nutmeg on top of the pudding
and bake at 180°C (350°F) mark 4 for 30–40 minutes,
until set and lightly browned. Serve hot with custard or
fresh cream.

TO MICROWAVE

Complete step 1. Put the milk in a heatproof jug
and cook on HIGH for 2 minutes or until hot but not
boiling. Complete the remainder of step 2. Cook the
pudding on LOW for 15–20 minutes or until just set.
Sprinkle with the sugar and nutmeg, then brown under
a hot grill. Serve hot with custard or fresh cream.

MILK PUDDING

COUNTRYWIDE

*There's nothing nicer than a lovingly made milk pudding – do
use creamy, fresh milk though, and don't omit the butter or
spice. Opt for rice, tapioca, sago or semolina, whichever you
have. The method's easy for them all.*

SERVES 4

50 g (2 oz) short-grain white or brown pudding rice, flaked rice or tapioca, or 40 g (1½ oz) semolina or sago
568–900 ml (1–1½ pints) fresh milk
30 ml (2 tbsp) sugar
15 g (½ oz) butter
1.25 ml (¼ tsp) ground cinnamon, ground mixed spice or grated nutmeg

1. If using rice, flaked rice or tapioca, put it in a
buttered 1.1 litre (2 pint) ovenproof serving dish. Pour
in 568 ml (1 pint) milk. If using brown rice, add an
extra 300 ml (½ pint) milk. Add the sugar and butter.
Sprinkle top with cinnamon, mixed spice or nutmeg.
2. If using semolina or sago, heat the milk in a
saucepan until lukewarm, then gradually sprinkle in the
semolina or sago, stirring continuously. Add the sugar
and butter and continue to cook for 10 minutes, until
thickened, stirring frequently. Pour into a buttered
1.1 litre (2 pint) ovenproof serving dish and sprinkle
the top with the cinnamon, mixed spice or nutmeg.
3. Bake the rice, flaked rice or tapioca pudding in the
oven at 170°C (325°F) mark 3 for 2–2½ hours (brown
rice for an extra 30 minutes). Stir the pudding 2 or 3
times during the first hour, but leave for the remaining
time to form a crust.
4. Bake the semolina or sago pudding at 180°C (350°F)
mark 4 for 30 minutes, without stirring.
5. Serve milk puddings hot or cold, plain or topped with
fresh fruit, chopped nuts, or thick natural yogurt.

CHRISTMAS PUDDING

COUNTRYWIDE

Plum pudding only took on its connections with Christmas when it was introduced to the Victorians by Prince Albert. Burying a silver coin in the pudding mixture is said to bring good fortune to whoever finds it in their portion and all the family should make a wish while stirring the mixture on Stir Up Sunday, the Sunday before Advent. Keep an eye on the pudding during the long steaming, and be sure to keep the pan topped up with boiling water.

SERVES 6–8

50 g (2 oz) plain flour

2.5 ml (½ tsp) ground mixed spice

2.5 ml (½ tsp) grated nutmeg

2.5 ml (½ tsp) ground cinnamon

50 g (2 oz) shredded beef suet

50 g (2 oz) fresh breadcrumbs

50 g (2 oz) soft light brown sugar

175 g (6 oz) raisins

175 g (6 oz) sultanas

25 g (1 oz) mixed peel, chopped

1 eating apple, grated

1 carrot, peeled and grated

25 g (1 oz) blanched almonds, chopped

grated rind and juice of ½ lemon

grated rind ½ orange

10 ml (2 tsp) treacle

65 ml (2½ fl oz) barley wine

15 ml (1 tbsp) brandy

1. Grease a 1.1 litre (2 pint) ovenproof pudding basin. Mix all the ingredients together, cover and leave overnight in the refrigerator.
2. Spoon the mixture into the prepared basin, cover with pleated greaseproof paper and foil and secure with string. Steam for 6 hours. Cool, then remove the covers.
3. Turn out of the basin and cover the pudding tightly with greaseproof paper. Store for at least 1 month in a cool place.
4. To serve, uncover, place in a basin, re-cover and steam for 2 hours. Or, reheat in a pressure cooker, following the manufacturer's instructions. Serve with brandy butter, fresh cream or custard.

MILK

Milk is a highly nutritious food and a major source of protein and calcium. A cool refreshing drink in summer, or a warming one in winter, milk is one of the most versatile ingredients in the kitchen. It is vital for making a wide range of dishes – sauces, soups, batters, pancakes and many delicious desserts.

Five different types of pasteurised milk are available, each classified according to fat content. Use the foil caps on milk bottles as a guide to each type.

CHANNEL ISLAND
(gold top)

This is the richest, creamiest milk, with 4.8% fat content.

WHOLE MILK
(silver top)

Most of the cream rises to the surface to give a visible cream line. It contains 3.8% fat.

HOMOGENISED
(red top)

Whole milk (3.8% fat) in which cream has been evenly distributed throughout.

SEMI-SKIMMED
(silver and red striped top)

A little over half the cream has been removed to give between 1.5 and 1.8% fat.

SKIMMED
(silver and blue checked top)

Almost all the cream has been removed to give 0.1% fat.

Other types of whole, semi-skimmed and skimmed milk widely available are:

STERILIZED

This has been heated to boiling point or above to ensure a sterile product and will keep for several weeks without refrigeration, provided it is not opened. Refrigerate after opening.

ULTRA-HEAT
TREATED

Known as UHT or long-life milk, this has been ultra-heated and aseptically packaged in foil-lined containers. It keeps unopened without refrigeration until expiry of date-stamp. Refrigerate after opening.

STEAMED SYRUP PUDDING. Ideal food for chilly days, steamed puddings are a childhood favourite which deserve to be made more often. This variation is served in a sticky pool of warm golden syrup, which also soaks into the top during cooking.

STEAMED AND BAKED PUDDINGS

COUNTRYWIDE

There are dozens of variations on the basic steamed pudding, and by adding ingredients to the mixture, or using different preserves for the topping, you can ring the changes almost indefinitely. But whichever version you go for, remember that no pudding is complete without a jug of creamy custard.

SERVES 4

175 g (6 oz) self-raising flour
pinch of salt
75 g (3 oz) shredded beef suet or softened butter
50 g (2 oz) caster sugar
1 egg
about 90 ml (6 tbsp) fresh milk

1. Grease a 1.1 litre (2 pint) pudding basin if making a steamed pudding, or a deep pie dish if baking the pudding. Spoon the flavouring of your choice into the bottom (see below).
2. Mix together the flour, salt, suet or softened butter and sugar. Make a well in the centre and add the egg and enough milk to give a soft dropping consistency. Pour into the prepared dish.
3. If steaming the pudding, cover with pleated greaseproof paper or foil and secure with string. Steam for 1½–2 hours.
4. If baking, cook, uncovered, at 180°C (350°F) mark 4 for about 1 hour, until well risen. Serve hot with custard.

VARIATIONS

CHOCOLATE PUDDING
Add 45 ml (3 tbsp) cocoa, sifted with the flour, or stir 25 g (1 oz) chocolate dots or chips into the basic mixture.

COCONUT PUDDING
Replace 25 g (1 oz) of the flour with 25 g (1 oz) desiccated coconut.

BLACK CAP PUDDING
Spoon 45 ml (3 tbsp) blackcurrant jam into the bottom of the basin.

MARMALADE PUDDING
Spoon 45 ml (3 tbsp) marmalade into the bottom of the basin.

TREACLE OR SYRUP PUDDING
Spoon 30 ml (2 tbsp) treacle or golden syrup into the bottom of the basin.

LEMON OR ORANGE PUDDING
Add the finely grated rind of 1 lemon or orange to the basic mixture.

CASTLE PUDDING
Divide lemon pudding mixture between 8 dariole moulds, then cover and steam for 30–40 minutes.

FRUIT PUDDING
Add 75 g (3 oz) no-soak mixed dried fruit to the basic mixture.

CANTERBURY PUDDING
Replace half of the flour with fresh breadcrumbs. Add the finely grated rind and juice of 1 lemon and replace half the milk with brandy.

GINGER PUDDING
Add 5 ml (1 tsp) ground ginger and 25 g (1 oz) chopped stem ginger to the basic mixture. Spoon 30 ml (2 tbsp) golden syrup into the bottom of the basin, if liked.

CANARY PUDDING
Replace half of the flour with fresh breadcrumbs. Add the finely grated rind of 1 lemon and 30 ml (2 tbsp) Madeira or sweet sherry instead of some of the milk.

COLLEGE PUDDING
Replace the flour with 100 g (4 oz) fresh breadcrumbs. Add 100 g (4 oz) mixed sultanas and raisins, 2.5 ml (½ tsp) baking powder and a large pinch each of ground cinnamon, ground cloves and grated nutmeg. Spoon into 6 greased dariole moulds, cover with foil and bake at 180°C (350°F) mark 4 for 45 minutes.

EVE'S PUDDING
Put 450 g (1 lb) peeled, cored and thickly sliced eating apples in the bottom of a deep pie dish. Make the mixture using butter and bake as above.

TO MICROWAVE

 Complete steps 1, 2 and 3, covering with greaseproof paper. Cook on HIGH for 5–7 minutes, until well risen and firm to the touch. Serve hot with custard.

HASTY PUDDING
COUNTRYWIDE

All you need for this surprisingly good stand-by pudding are milk, flour, butter, sugar and a little spice. It takes just a few minutes to make, hence its name, and can be eaten hot or cold. It is particularly good served with poached fruit.

SERVES 2–4

50 g (2 oz) butter
30 ml (2 tbsp) plain flour
450 ml (¾ pint) fresh milk
1 egg
Freshly grated nutmeg or ground cinnamon
40 g (1½ oz) light soft brown sugar

1. Put 25 g (1 oz) of the butter, the flour and milk in a saucepan. Heat, whisking continuously, until the sauce thickens, boils and is smooth. Simmer for 1–2 minutes. Stir in the egg, then pour into a flameproof serving dish.
2. Dot with the remaining butter and sprinkle generously with nutmeg or cinnamon and the sugar. Brown quickly under a hot grill. Serve hot on its own or with poached fruit such as apples, pears or rhubarb.

ROLY-POLY PUDDINGS
COUNTRYWIDE

The same basic suet pastry is used for jam roly-poly and all its variations. It is fast and easy to make and, if mixed quickly and deftly, has a light, spongy texture – a far cry from the hefty steamed puds of schooldays. Steam or boil the puddings or, if less time is available, bake them instead.

SERVES 4

175 g (6 oz) self-raising flour
pinch of salt
75 g (3 oz) shredded beef suet

1. Mix the flour, salt and suet together in a bowl.
2. Using a round-bladed knife, stir in enough water to give a light, elastic dough. Knead very lightly until smooth.
3. Roll out to an oblong about 23 × 25 cm (9 × 11 inches) and use as required. (See variations below.)
4. Make a 5 cm (2 inch) pleat across a clean tea-towel or pudding cloth. Or pleat together sheets of greased greaseproof paper and strong foil. Wrap the roll loosely, to allow for expansion, in the cloth or foil, pleating the open edges tightly together. Tie the ends securely with string to form a cracker shape. Make a string handle across the top. Lower the suet roll into a roasting tin or large pan of boiling water, cover and boil for 1½ hours depending on filling and size. Lift the pudding out of the water using the string handle. Place on a wire rack standing over a plate and allow excess moisture to drain off. Snip the string and gently roll the pudding out of the cloth or foil on to a warmed serving plate. Roly-poly puddings can also be baked, uncovered at 200°C (400°F) mark 6 for about 40 minutes. Serve sliced with custard.

VARIATIONS
JAM ROLY-POLY
Spread the pastry with 60–90 ml (4–6 tbsp) jam. Brush the edges with milk and roll up, starting from the short end. Steam or bake as above.
SYRUP ROLY-POLY
Spread the pastry with 60 ml (4 tbsp) golden syrup mixed with 30–45 ml (2–3 tbsp) fresh white bread-crumbs. Steam or bake as above.
LEMON ROLY-POLY
Add the finely grated rind of 1 lemon to the pastry. Roll out and spread with 60–90 ml (4–6 tbsp) lemon curd. Steam or bake as above.
MINCEMEAT ROLY-POLY
Add the finely grated rind of 1 orange to the dough. Roll out and spread with 60–90 ml (4–6 tbsp) mincemeat. Steam or bake as above.
SPOTTED DICK OR DOG
Replace half of the flour with 100 g (4 oz) fresh breadcrumbs. Add 50 g (2 oz) caster sugar, 175 g (6 oz) currants, finely grated rind of 1 lemon and 75 ml (5 tbsp) milk. Mix everything together. Shape into a neat roll about 15 cm (6 inches) long. Boil as above.

TO MICROWAVE

 Complete steps 1, 2 and 3. Wrap the pudding in pleated greaseproof paper and cook on HIGH for 4–5 minutes.

BUTTER

Butter is a delicious and versatile ingredient. Excellent as a spread on biscuits or bread, it also transforms any recipe, making extra tasty sauces, vegetables and mouthwatering cakes, pastries and biscuits. It is made by churning fresh cream, and is a valuable source of vitamin A.

Butter is available salted, slightly salted or unsalted. Slightly salted is the most popular and most widely available type and is suited to all kinds of cooking and baking (though unsalted butter is particularly good for pastries and sweets). For a change try flavoured butters using garlic or herbs for a savoury spread, or add a touch of brandy or rum butter to accompany Christmas pudding.

Butter is produced countrywide but there are distinct differences of colour and flavour in every region, owing to the richness of the grass and the amount of salt added. Welsh butter has a distinctive salty taste, while butter from the Channel Islands is much creamier.

Store butter in the refrigerator, or in a cool dark place, well wrapped or covered to keep it from picking up other flavours. In these conditions butter will keep for 2–3 weeks (or until 'best before' date on the package). Can be frozen for up to 6 months.

BAKED APPLE AND COCONUT PUDDING

THE SOUTH-EAST

Eating apples are sweeter than cookers and many varieties – especially Cox's – hold their shape well when cooked. Juicy slices are baked on top of a light and airy pudding mixture, and a topping of toasted coconut completes the dish.

SERVES 6

finely grated rind and juice of 1 lemon

100 g (4 oz) soft light brown sugar, plus 30 ml (2 tbsp)

6 medium eating apples, each weighing about 100 g (4 oz), peeled, cored and sliced

100 g (4 oz) butter

2 eggs, separated

100 g (4 oz) plain wholemeal flour

7.5 ml (1½ tsp) baking powder

25 g (1 oz) desiccated coconut

about 60 ml (4 tbsp) apricot jam, warmed

shredded coconut, toasted, to decorate

1. Pour the lemon juice into a large bowl; stir in the 30 ml (2 tbsp) sugar and add the apples, making sure they are well coated.

2. Gradually beat the 100 g (4 oz) sugar into the butter until well blended. Add the lemon rind, then beat in

BAKED APPLE AND COCONUT PUDDING. Thin slices of apple sunk into the meltingly light base and arranged in patterns make for a very attractive dish that tastes wonderful too.

the egg yolks one at a time. Stir in the flour, baking powder and desiccated coconut.

3. Whisk the egg whites until stiff but not dry, then fold into the creamed ingredients. Spoon into a lightly greased 24–25.5 cm (9½–10 inch) fluted flan dish. Press the apples into the mixture, spooning any juices over them.

4. Stand the dish on a baking sheet and bake at 170°C (325°F) mark 3 for 1–1¼ hours or until well browned and firm to the touch, covering lightly with greaseproof paper if necessary.

5. Cool for about 15 minutes, then brush with the apricot jam and scatter over the toasted shredded coconut. Serve while still warm with custard.

APPLE CHARLOTTE

COUNTRYWIDE

There is much doubt surrounding the origin of the name 'charlotte'. Meat dishes called 'charlets' were around in the 15th century, but some say that the sweet dish took its name much later, from Queen Charlotte, wife of George III. Whatever the truth of the matter, this is a delicious dessert, with a crisp golden crust and a filling of apples.

SERVES 6

900 g (2 lb) cooking apples, peeled, cored and sliced
2.5 ml (½ tsp) ground cinnamon
finely grated rind and juice of 1 lemon
light soft brown sugar, to taste
75 g (3 oz) butter, melted
8 thin slices brown bread, crusts removed

1. Put the apples, cinnamon, lemon rind and juice and sugar in a heavy-based saucepan. Cover and simmer gently until pulpy, stirring occasionally.

2. Beat thoroughly with a wooden spoon, then cook, uncovered, over a high heat, stirring continuously, until any excess liquid has evaporated and the purée is very thick.

3. Brush the butter all over the slices of bread. Line the base and sides of a greased 15 cm (6 inch) Charlotte mould or deep cake tin with the slices of bread, making sure that they overlap.

4. Spoon in the apple purée and cover with more overlapping slices of bread. Bake at 190°C (375°F) mark 5 for about 30 minutes, until the top is golden brown. Serve at once, turned out and accompanied with custard or fresh cream.

TO MICROWAVE

To melt the butter, cut into small pieces, put in a small bowl and cook on HIGH for 1 minute. Put the apples, cinnamon, lemon rind and juice and sugar in a large bowl. Cover and cook on HIGH for 6–8 minutes, until the apple is soft, stirring occasionally. Uncover and cook on HIGH for 5 minutes, until any excess liquid has evaporated and the purée is very thick, stirring occasionally. Complete the recipe.

APPLE AND ORANGE CRUMBLE

COUNTRYWIDE

The beauty of crumbles is that they are very easy to make, and good-tempered enough to have their cooking time and temperature adjusted a little to fit in with the rest of the menu. The only thing to make sure of is that the top is nicely golden, but not too brown. The recipe here uses apple and orange but any type of fruit can be used.

SERVES 4–6

700 g (1½ lb) cooking apples, peeled, cored and sliced
grated rind and juice of 1 orange
25 g (1 oz) light soft brown sugar
100 g (4 oz) plain flour
50 g (2 oz) plain wholemeal flour
75 g (3 oz) butter
40 g (1½ oz) icing sugar, sieved
1.25 ml (¼ tsp) ground cinnamon

1. Put the apples, orange rind and juice and sugar into a 1.4 litre (2½ pint) ovenproof serving dish.

2. Put the flours into a mixing bowl and rub in the butter until the mixture resembles fine breadcrumbs. Stir in the icing sugar and cinnamon, making sure all the ingredients are thoroughly combined.

3. Sprinkle the crumble topping over the apple. Bake at 200°C (400°F) mark 6 for 30–40 minutes, until the topping is crisp and golden. Serve hot with fresh cream or custard.

VARIATIONS

1. Use any type of fresh fruit such as pears, rhubarb, plums, apricots, damsons or gooseberries.

2. Add the grated rind of an orange or lemon to the crumb mixture before sprinkling it over the fruit.

3. Replace 75 g (3 oz) of the flour with rolled oats, bran flakes or oatmeal.

4. Add 25 g (1 oz) chopped nuts such as almonds, walnuts or brazils to the crumble topping mixture.

5. Replace the cinnamon with mixed spice or ginger and add to the flour before rubbing in the butter.

BANBURY APPLE PIE. A spicy fruit filling, light, short pastry and a thick dredging of sugar on top make this apple pie extra special.

DAIRY ICE CREAM

Ice cream made with dairy cream can now bear a special logo that is a mark of high-quality. It will contain at least 10% butterfat, half of which must come from Welsh or English Double Cream. Choose from a wide variety of flavours, including vanilla, butter pecan, creamy toffee, almond, and many more.

BANBURY APPLE PIE

THE SOUTH-EAST

A traditional recipe which uses a pie dish with pastry on the top and bottom. Use wholemeal flour instead of white if you prefer a nuttier taste. Cooking apples have been used here, but if you like, you can substitute eating apples – they will not need extra sugar.

SERVES 6

✳

350 g (12 oz) plain flour
pinch of salt
150 g (6 oz) butter
15 ml (1 tbsp) caster sugar
1 egg, lightly beaten
700 g (1½ lb) cooking apples
juice of ½ lemon
100 g (4 oz) sultanas
75 g (3 oz) soft light brown sugar
pinch of ground cinnamon
pinch of freshly grated nutmeg
grated rind and juice of 1 orange
fresh milk, to glaze
caster sugar for sprinkling

1. To make the pastry, put the flour and salt in a bowl and rub in the butter until the mixture resembles fine breadcrumbs. Stir in the caster sugar, then stir in the egg and enough water to bind the mixture together.
2. Knead lightly on a lightly floured surface, then roll out two-thirds of the pastry and use to line a shallow 900 ml (1½ pint) pie dish.
3. Peel, core and thinly slice the apples. Put in a bowl and sprinkle with lemon juice.
4. Layer the apples, sultanas, brown sugar, spices and orange rind in the pie dish. Sprinkle with the orange juice.
5. Roll out the remaining pastry to form a lid, pressing the edges together. Scallop the edges, then make a slit in the centre of the pie.
6. Brush the top with milk to glaze, then bake at 200°C (400°F) mark 6 for 30 minutes, until golden brown. Sprinkle the top with caster sugar and serve hot or cold. Accompany with dairy ice cream.

CUMBERLAND RUM NICKY

THE NORTH

This rich and sticky tart is a northern speciality incorporating several of the exotic imports which came from Cumberland's trade with the West Indies. Dates, ginger and rum feature widely in many local dishes. This version also includes dried apricots and is made with wholemeal flour, making it a dish high in fibre.

SERVES 6

✳

225 g (8 oz) stoned dates, chopped
100 g (4 oz) no-soak dried apricots
50 g (2 oz) stem ginger, chopped
45 ml (3 tbsp) light rum
30 ml (2 tbsp) soft light brown sugar
225 g (8 oz) plain wholemeal flour
pinch of salt
115 g (4½ oz) butter
1 egg yolk, lightly beaten
demerara sugar, to decorate (optional)

1. Mix together the dates, apricots, ginger, rum and half of the sugar. Leave to soak while making the pastry.
2. Put the flour and salt in a bowl and rub in 100 g (4 oz) of the butter until the mixture resembles fine breadcrumbs. Add the remaining sugar, then the egg yolk and enough water to bind. Knead lightly on a floured surface.
3. Roll out half of the pastry and use to line a greased 25.5 cm (10 inch) flat pie plate.
4. Spread the pastry with the soaked dried fruit. Dot with the remaining butter.
5. Roll out the remaining pastry and use to cover the pie. Cut any pastry trimmings into leaves and use to decorate the pie. Brush with milk and bake at 200°C (400°F) mark 6 for 30–35 minutes until golden brown. Sprinkle with demerara sugar, if liked. Serve hot with natural yogurt.

BAKEWELL PUDDING

THE MIDLANDS

A buttery mixture, flavoured with ground almonds and baked in a light, flaky pastry case, is the basis of this traditional Derbyshire recipe, sometimes known as Bakewell tart, the origin of which is still secret.

SERVES 6

✳

212 g (7½ oz) frozen packet puff pastry, thawed
60 ml (4 tbsp) red jam
100 g (4 oz) ground almonds
100 g (4 oz) caster sugar
50 g (2 oz) butter
3 eggs, beaten
1.25 ml (¼ tsp) almond essence

1. Roll out the pastry on a floured surface and use to line a 900 ml (1½ pint) shallow pie dish.
2. Knock up the edge of the pastry in the pie dish with the back of a knife.
3. Mark the rim with the prongs of a fork. Brush the jam over the base. Chill in the refrigerator while making the filling.
4. Make the filling. Beat the almonds with the sugar, butter, eggs and almond essence.
5. Pour the filling over the jam and spread it evenly. Bake in the oven at 200°C (400°F) mark 6 for 30 minutes or until the filling is set. Serve warm or cold, with fresh cream or custard.

RIPE TART

THE SOUTH-EAST

The name comes from the village of Ripe in the Sussex South Downs, where a pie feast celebrated the cherry harvest.

SERVES 8

225 g (8 oz) plain flour
pinch of salt
25 g (1 oz) cornflour
100 g (4 oz), plus 10 ml (2 tsp) icing sugar
100 g (4 oz) butter
1 egg yolk
450 g (1 lb) cherries, stoned
2 eggs
75 g (3 oz) ground almonds
few drops of almond essence

1. Sift the flour, salt, cornflour and 10 ml (2 tsp) icing sugar into a bowl, then rub in the butter until the mixture resembles fine breadcrumbs. Add the egg yolk and 30 ml (2 tbsp) cold water and stir to bind together.
2. Knead lightly on a lightly floured surface, roll out. Use to line a 23 cm (9 inch) fluted flan tin. Bake blind at 200°C (400°F) mark 6 for 10–15 minutes, until set.
3. Arrange cherries in flan case. Mix 100 g (4 oz) icing sugar, eggs, almonds and essence, pour over cherries.
4. Bake at 170°C (325°F) mark 3 for 50–60 minutes, until the top is firm and golden. Serve hot or cold.

RIPE TART. Cherries and almonds are a great combination, and both are used in the mouthwateringly moist filling.

WALNUT AND HONEY TART

THE WEST

Walnuts were formerly grown far more widely in Britain than they are today and used in both sweet and savoury dishes. This West Country speciality combines them with local honey in a very rich tart which should be served in small portions only.

SERVES 6

175 g (6 oz) plain wholemeal flour
pinch of salt
75 g (3 oz) butter
finely grated rind and juice of 1 orange
60 ml (4 tbsp) clear honey
75 g (3 oz) fresh wholemeal breadcrumbs
45 ml (3 tbsp) dark soft brown sugar
3 eggs
100 g (4 oz) walnut pieces, roughly chopped

1. To make the pastry, put the flour and salt in a bowl and rub in the butter until the mixture resembles fine breadcrumbs. Stir in the orange rind and enough orange juice to bind the mixture together.
2. Roll out the pastry on a lightly floured surface and use to line a 20.5 cm (8 inch) fluted flan dish or tin. Bake blind at 200°C (400°F) mark 6 for 10–15 minutes, until set.
3. Mix the honey, breadcrumbs and the sugar together. Gradually beat in the eggs, one at a time, and any remaining orange juice.
4. Sprinkle the walnuts in the bottom of the pastry case and pour over the filling. Bake at 200°C (400°F) mark 6 for 20–25 minutes, until set. Cover the tart with greaseproof paper if it browns too quickly. Serve warm or cold with clotted or fresh double cream.

WALNUT AND HONEY TART. Chopped walnuts add crunch to the gooey honey and orange mixture inside this irresistible tart.

KENT LENT PIE

THE SOUTH-EAST

In the days when Lent was strictly observed, many cooks became very ingenious at thinking up new dishes to break the monotony of their abstemious diet. This recipe, sometimes called Kentish Pudding Pie, is rather like a baked cheesecake and made a pleasant change; it was particularly popular in the area round Folkestone.

SERVES 4–6

175 g (6 oz) plain wholemeal flour
pinch of salt
150 g (5 oz) butter
300 ml (½ pint) fresh milk
25 g (1 oz) ground rice
50 g (2 oz) sugar
2 eggs
finely grated rind of 1 lemon
1.25 ml (¼ tsp) grated nutmeg
25 g (1 oz) currants

1. To make the pastry, put the flour and salt in a bowl and rub in 75 g (3 oz) of the butter until the mixture resembles fine breadcrumbs. Stir in 45–60 ml (3–4 tbsp) cold water to bind the mixture together into a dough.
2. Roll out the pastry on a lightly floured surface and use to line a greased 20.5 cm (8 inch) fluted flan dish or tin. Bake blind at 200°C (400°F) mark 6 for 10–15 minutes, until set.
3. Meanwhile, put the milk and rice in a pan and bring to the boil, stirring continuously, until the mixture thickens. Remove the pan from the heat and leave to cool.
4. When the mixture is cold, cream the remaining butter and sugar together until pale and fluffy. Beat in the eggs, one at a time, then add the lemon rind, salt, nutmeg and the rice mixture. Mix thoroughly together and pour into the flan case. Sprinkle the currants on top.
5. Bake at 190°C (375°F) mark 5 for 40–45 minutes, until firm to the touch and golden brown. Serve the pie warm.

SQUIDGY CHOCOLATE ROLL

COUNTRYWIDE

Chocoholics will love this rich recipe, which uses cocoa powder to flavour a moist sponge, rolled and filled with fresh cream. It is an ideal dinner party dessert.

SERVES 6–8

60 ml (4 tbsp) cocoa powder
150 ml (¼ pint) fresh milk
4 eggs, separated
100 g (4 oz) caster sugar
225 ml (8 fl oz) fresh double cream
fresh strawberries and grated chocolate, to decorate

1. Grease and line a 20.5 × 30.5 cm (8 × 12 inch) Swiss roll tin. Mix the cocoa powder and milk in a small saucepan and heat gently until the cocoa powder has dissolved. Remove the pan from the heat and set aside to cool.
2. Whisk the egg yolks and sugar together until pale and fluffy. Whisk the cooled milk mixture into the egg yolk mixture.
3. Whisk the egg whites until stiff, then fold into the cocoa mixture. Spread the mixture evenly into the prepared tin and bake at 180°C (350°F) mark 4 for about 20 minutes until the sponge has risen and is just firm to the touch.
4. Turn out on to a sheet of greaseproof paper and cover with a warm, damp tea-towel to prevent the sponge from drying out. Leave the sponge to cool for 20 minutes.
5. Meanwhile, whip the cream until stiff. Spread over the sponge, reserving half for decorating and then roll it up carefully. Do not roll it up too tightly and do not worry if it cracks slightly. Pipe the reserved cream on top and decorate with strawberries and grated chocolate. Serve chilled.

GREENGAGE TART

THE EASTERN COUNTIES

Back in the 18th century, Sir William Gage planted some French plum trees at Hengrave Hall, near Bury St Edmunds, without knowing exactly what type of fruit to expect. The plums turned out to be green and became known as the green Gage's plum, which eventually became shortened to greengage. They are sweet, oval and yellowy-green with a good flavour and are in season late August and early September.

SERVES 4–6

175 g (6 oz) plain wholemeal flour
pinch of salt

75 g (3 oz) butter
25 g (1 oz) toasted hazelnuts, very finely chopped
15 ml (1 tbsp) soft light brown sugar
450 g (1 lb) greengages or plums, halved and stoned
2 eggs
300 ml (10 fl oz) fresh single cream
caster sugar (optional)

1. To make the pastry, put the flour and salt in a bowl and rub in the butter until the mixture resembles fine breadcrumbs. Stir in the hazelnuts and sugar and enough water to bind the mixture together.
2. Knead lightly on a lightly greased floured surface, then roll out and use to line a greased 20.5 cm (8 inch) fluted flan dish or tin. Bake blind at 200°C (400°F) mark 6 for 10–15 minutes, until set.
3. Arrange the fruit, cut side down, in the pastry case. Beat the eggs with the cream and a little sugar, if liked, and pour over the fruit. Bake at 200°C (400°F) mark 6 for 30–40 minutes, until golden and puffy. Serve warm.

SQUIDGY CHOCOLATE ROLL. Here's a dish that really lives up to its name. Topped with fresh strawberries and cream, it has everything you could want from a special occasion dessert.

243

RICH PANCAKES
COUNTRYWIDE

An outrageously extravagant version of an everyday dish, this recipe produces wickedly rich pancakes which melt in the mouth.

SERVES 4

✳

3 eggs

30 ml (2 tbsp) plain flour

15 ml (1 tbsp) brandy or sherry

5 ml (1 tsp) orange flower water

300 ml (10 fl oz) fresh single cream

50 g (2 oz) butter, melted and cooled

extra butter for frying

caster sugar and lemon or orange wedges, to serve

1. Put the eggs, flour, brandy or sherry, orange flower water and cream in a bowl and whisk together. Whisk in the melted butter.
2. Heat a little butter in a small frying pan. When hot, pour in 45 ml (3 tbsp) batter, tilting the pan to cover the base. Cook until the pancake moves freely, then turn over and cook the underside until golden.
3. Transfer the pancake to an ovenproof plate, cover and keep hot in a warm oven. Repeat with the remaining batter to make 8 pancakes. Pile the cooked pancakes on top of each other with a piece of greaseproof paper in between each one. Serve as soon as they are all cooked with sugar and orange or lemon wedges.

OATEN HONEYCOMB
NORTHERN IRELAND

An unusual steamed pudding, which uses porridge oats instead of flour. Honey, both in the mixture and poured over the finished pudding, adds its own distinctive sweetness, which is very pleasant without being cloying.

SERVES 4–6

450 ml (¾ pint) fresh milk

175 g (6 oz) porridge oats

50 g (2 oz) caster sugar

30 ml (2 tbsp) clear honey

25 g (1 oz) butter

finely grated rind of 1 orange

2.5 ml (½ tsp) ground cinnamon

3 eggs, separated

1. Put the milk into a heavy-based saucepan and bring to the boil. Sprinkle in the oats and cook gently, stirring constantly, for 5 minutes.
2. Beat in the sugar, honey, butter, orange rind and cinnamon and mix well. Remove from the heat and beat in the egg yolks.

3. Whisk the egg whites until stiff and carefully fold into the mixture. Turn into a greased 1.2 litre (2 pint) pudding basin, cover with pleated greased greaseproof paper or foil and secure with string.
4. Steam for about 2 hours. Turn out on to a dish and serve with warm honey and single cream.

DAMSON AND APPLE TANSY
THE NORTH

Tansies originally always included the bitter-sweet herb called tansy, which still lends its name to many custard and omelette-type puddings. This sweet/tart combination with Cox's apples traditionally used the Witherslack damsons which grow south of Lake Windermere.

SERVES 4

2 large Cox's apples, peeled, cored and thinly sliced

225 g (8 oz) damsons, halved, stoned and quartered

15 g (½ oz) butter

40 g (1½ oz) sugar

pinch of ground cloves

pinch of ground cinnamon

4 eggs, separated

45 ml (3 tbsp) fresh soured cream or natural yogurt

1. Put the apples, damsons, butter and half of the sugar in a large frying pan.
2. Cook over a gentle heat, until the fruit is softened, stirring continuously. Stir in the cloves and cinnamon, then remove from the heat.
3. Beat the egg yolks with the cream and stir into the fruit. Whisk the egg whites until stiff, then carefully fold in.
4. Cook over a low heat until the mixture has set. Sprinkle the top with the remaining sugar, then brown under a hot grill. Serve immediately, straight from the pan, with soured cream or natural yogurt.

RHUBARB AND ORANGE FLAN
THE NORTH

The use of orange juice in this flan offsets the natural tartness of the rhubarb, while the ginger adds a touch of spice. Rhubarb flourishes in the north of England and 81 per cent of the forced early crop is from there, though rhubarb is grown outdoors throughout other parts of the country.

SERVES 4

75 g (3 oz) butter

150 g (6 oz) digestive biscuits, crushed

450 g (1 lb) fresh rhubarb, trimmed and cut into 2.5 cm (1 inch) lengths

finely grated rind and juice of 1 large orange

2 eggs, separated

50 g (2 oz) caster sugar

30 ml (2 tbsp) cornflour

2.5 ml (½ tsp) ground ginger

orange slices, to decorate

1. Melt the butter in a saucepan, then mix in the biscuit crumbs.
2. Press the mixture over the base and sides of a 20.5 cm (8 inch) fluted flan dish or tin. Chill in the refrigerator while preparing the filling.
3. Put the rhubarb in a saucepan with 45 ml (3 tbsp) water. Cover and simmer gently until the fruit is soft and pulpy. Stir occasionally to prevent the rhubarb

sticking to the pan. Work the rhubarb to a purée in a blender or food processor.
4. Put the orange rind and juice into a heavy-based saucepan. Add the egg yolks, caster sugar, cornflour and ginger. Heat gently, stirring constantly, until thick. Stir into the rhubarb purée.
5. Whisk the egg whites until stiff. Fold into the rhubarb custard, then spoon the mixture into the biscuit crust. Refrigerate for at least 4 hours or overnight. Decorate with orange slices just before serving.

TO MICROWAVE

☑ Complete steps 1 and 2. Put the rhubarb and the water in a bowl. Cover and cook on HIGH for 5–6 minutes until tender, stirring occasionally. Complete the recipe.

DAMSON AND APPLE TANSY. Spices and fruit sunk in a deep, rich custard make a deliciously filling supper dish for winter evenings.

RED BERRY FOOL

THE MIDLANDS

The word 'fool' was used to describe a light and airy blend of cream and fresh fruit purée. Depending on the season, choose from any of the soft, juicy fruits that flourish in the Vale of Evesham. Raspberries, strawberries, red- or blackcurrants are all excellent.

SERVES 4

15–30 ml (1–2 tbsp) caster sugar
225 g (8 oz) raspberries
225 g (8 oz) redcurrants
225 g (8 oz) blackcurrants
15 ml (1 tbsp) custard powder
15 ml (1 tbsp) sugar
300 ml (½ pint) fresh milk
150 ml (5 fl oz) fresh whipping cream

1. Put the sugar to taste and 90 ml (6 tbsp) water in a saucepan large enough to hold the fruit and heat gently until the sugar dissolves. Reserve a little of each fruit to decorate and poach the remaining fruit for about 10 minutes, until soft.
2. Remove the pan from the heat and sieve the fruit into a large bowl, then set aside to cool.

3. Blend the custard powder and sugar with 30 ml (2 tbsp) milk. Bring the remaining milk to the boil and pour on to the mixture, stirring well. Return to a clean saucepan, bring to the boil, stirring continuously. Leave to cool completely.
4. Whip the cream until stiff. Fold the custard and most of the cream into the sieved fruit.
5. Spoon the fool into individual glasses. Pipe each dessert with a rosette of remaining cream and top with the reserved fruit to decorate. Serve with crisp biscuits.

TO MICROWAVE

Put most of the fruit and sugar to taste in a medium bowl with 45 ml (3 tbsp) of water. Cook on HIGH for 4–5 minutes. Complete step 2. Blend the custard powder, sugar and milk together in a medium bowl. Cook on HIGH for 4–5 minutes, until boiling and thickened, whisking frequently. Complete the recipe.

OLDE ENGLISH TRIFLE

COUNTRYWIDE

A perfect trifle should be a rich confection of fruit, light sponge, alcohol, real egg custard and whipped cream. The recipe has altered little over the centuries – at one time the custard was topped with syllabub, and fruit has not always been included.

SERVES 6–8

4 trifle sponges
60 ml (4 tbsp) cherry jam
15 ratafia biscuits
60 ml (4 tbsp) sherry
2 bananas, peeled and sliced
grated rind and juice of ½ lemon
225 g (8 oz) cherries, stoned
450 ml (¾ pint) fresh milk
3 eggs
50 g (2 oz) caster sugar
150 ml (5 fl oz) fresh double cream
glacé cherries, to decorate
25 g (1 oz) chopped nuts, toasted, to decorate

1. Cut the trifle sponges in half and spread with jam, then sandwich together. Arrange in the base of a glass serving dish.
2. Cover with ratafias and sprinkle with sherry. Coat the bananas in lemon juice. Arrange the bananas and cherries on top of the ratafias.
3. Heat the milk in a medium saucepan until almost boiling. In a large bowl, whisk together the eggs, lemon rind and sugar until pale, then pour on the hot milk, stirring continuously.
4. Return to the saucepan and heat gently, stirring continuously, until the custard thickens enough to coat

OLDE ENGLISH TRIFLE. Use a clear glass dish to show off this moreish dessert. Nuts and cherries are used to decorate the thick topping of whipped cream.

AUTUMN PUDDING.
Always a pleasure to eat, at
any time of year. The bread
soaks up the ruby red juices
beautifully.

the back of a wooden spoon. Do not allow to boil. This
takes about 20 minutes. Set aside to cool.
5. Pour the custard over the trifle and leave until cold.
6. Whip the cream until stiff and pipe on the top of the
trifle and decorate with glacé cherries and nuts.

TO MICROWAVE

 Complete steps 1 and 2. Put the milk into a medium
bowl, cook on HIGH for 5 minutes. Complete remaining
part of step 3. Cook the custard on MEDIUM for 7–8
minutes, whisking frequently. Complete the recipe.

AUTUMN PUDDING

COUNTRYWIDE

*Exactly the same as summer pudding, but this time the
bread-lined basin is filled with a juicy mixture of the finest
fruits of autumn. Keep any left-over juice to 'top up' any dry
patches of bread.*

SERVES 4–6

❄ ⚡

700 g (1½ lb) mixed autumn fruit, such as apples,
blackberries, plums, prepared

about 25 g (1 oz) light soft brown sugar

8–10 thin slices of day-old bread, crusts removed

fresh fruit and mint sprigs, to decorate

1. Stew the fruit gently with 60–90 ml (4–6 tbsp)
water and the sugar until soft but still retaining their
shape. The exact amounts of water and sugar depend on
the ripeness and sweetness of the fruit.
2. Meanwhile, cut a round from one slice of bread to
neatly fit the bottom of a 1.1 litre (2 pint) pudding basin
and cut 6–8 slices of the bread into fingers about 5 cm
(2 inches) wide. Put the round at the bottom of the
basin and arrange the fingers around the sides,
overlapping them so there are no spaces.
3. When the fruit is cooked, and still hot, pour it
gently into the basin, being careful not to disturb the
bread framework. Reserve about 45 ml (3 tbsp) of the
juice. When the basin is full, cut the remaining bread
and use to cover the fruit so a lid is formed.
4. Cover with foil, then a plate or saucer which fits just
inside the bowl and put a weight on top. Leave the
pudding until cold, then put into the refrigerator and
chill overnight.
5. To serve, run a knife carefully round the edge to
loosen, then invert the pudding on to a serving dish.
Pour the reserved juice over the top. Serve cold with
cream. Decorate with fruit and mint sprigs.

TO MICROWAVE

 Put the fruit, water and sugar in a large bowl, cover
and cook on HIGH for 4–8 minutes, stirring
occasionally. The time will depend on the type of fruit
used. Complete the recipe.

BARNSTAPLE FAIR PEARS

THE WEST

The pear orchards of Devon used to supply stalls at the annual Barnstaple Fair and these pears would originally have been simmered in local cider or scrumpy. This dessert makes the perfect end to a meal with its spicy flavour and rich syrupy liquid complemented by clotted cream.

SERVES 4

4 large firm Comice pears
25 g (1 oz) blanched almonds, split in half
50 g (2 oz) caster sugar
300 ml (½ pint) red wine
2 cloves

1. Peel the pears, leaving the stalks on. Spike the pears with the almond halves.

2. Put the sugar, wine and the cloves in a saucepan just large enough to hold the pears and heat gently until the sugar has dissolved. Add the pears, standing them upright in the pan, cover and simmer gently for about 15 minutes, until the pears are just tender, basting from time to time with the liquid.

3. Using a slotted spoon transfer the pears to a serving dish. Remove the lid from the pan of syrup, increase the heat and boil fast until the liquid is reduced by half. Pour over the pears and serve hot or cold with thick natural yogurt or clotted cream.

TO MICROWAVE

 Complete step 1. Put the sugar, wine and the cloves in a large bowl and cook on HIGH for 3–4 minutes, until boiling, stirring occasionally. Add the pears, cover and cook on HIGH for 8–10 minutes, until the pears are tender. Using a slotted spoon transfer the pears to a serving dish. Uncover the syrup and cook on HIGH for about 10 minutes, until reduced by half. Pour over the pears and serve hot or cold with thick natural yogurt or clotted cream.

RASPBERRY AND WALNUT SHORTBREAD

SCOTLAND

Two of Scotland's most celebrated foods – shortbread and raspberries – come together in this recipe to make a truly mouth-watering dessert that tastes even better than it looks. The walnuts are ground and added to the shortbread mixture for a subtle nutty flavour. The shortbread could also be made with strawberries.

SERVES 8

100 g (4 oz) walnut pieces
100 g (4 oz) butter
75 g (3 oz) caster sugar
175 g (6 oz) plain flour
450 g (1 lb) fresh raspberries
50 g (2 oz) icing sugar
30 ml (2 tbsp) raspberry-flavoured liqueur or kirsch (optional)
300 ml (10 fl oz) fresh whipping cream

1. Draw three 20.5 (8 inch) circles on non-stick baking parchment. Place the parchment circles on baking sheets.
2. Grind the walnuts finely in a blender or food processor.
3. Cream the butter and sugar together in a mixing bowl until pale and fluffy, then beat in the walnuts and flour. Divide the dough into 3 shortbread portions.
4. Put a portion of shortbread dough in the centre of each parchment circle and press out with the heel of your hand until the dough is the same size as the circle.
5. Cut one of the circles into eight triangles with a sharp knife and ease them slightly apart. Refrigerate the circles and triangles for 30 minutes. Bake at 190°C (375°F) mark 5 for 15–20 minutes, swapping over the sheets to ensure the pastries brown evenly. Leave to cool and harden for 10 minutes on the paper, then transfer to wire racks to cool completely.
6. Meanwhile, reserve one-third of the raspberries for decoration. Put the rest in a bowl with the icing sugar and liqueur, if using. Crush the raspberries with a fork, then leave them to macerate while the pastry rounds are cooling.
7. Assemble the shortbread just before serving, to ensure that the pastry remains crisp. Whip the cream until thick, then fold in the crushed raspberries and juice. Stand one round of pastry on a flat serving plate and spread with half of the cream mixture. Top with the remaining round of pastry, then the remaining cream mixture.
8. Arrange the triangles of pastry on top of the cream, wedging them in at an angle. Scatter the reserved whole raspberries in between. Serve the shortbread as soon as possible.

ETON MESS

THE SOUTH-EAST

When the annual prize-giving is held at Eton College, one of Britain's most famous public schools, parents and pupils have a picnic on the playing fields. Among the dishes then served is this marvellously boozy mixture of strawberries, cream and crushed meringues, to which the school has lent its name.

SERVES 4–6

450 g (1 lb) strawberries, hulled
75 ml (3 fl oz) kirsch
375 ml (12 fl oz) fresh double or whipping cream
6 small meringues, crushed

1. Reserve a few small strawberries for the decoration. Chop the remainder and place in a bowl. Sprinkle with the kirsch, cover and chill for 2–3 hours.
2. Whip the cream until it just holds its shape, then gently fold in the strawberries and their juices and the crushed meringues. Spoon into a glass serving dish, decorate with the reserved strawberries and serve immediately.

WHIM WHAM

SCOTLAND

This is a very simple recipe for a delicious and swiftly made trifle. It originates from the 18th century, when the word whim-wham was used to describe something light and fanciful.

SERVES 6

25 g (1 oz) butter
50 g (2 oz) blanched almonds
25 g (1 oz) sugar
30 trifle sponge fingers
150 ml (¼ pint) sweet sherry
60 ml (4 tbsp) brandy
finely grated rind and juice of 1 large orange
300 ml (10 fl oz) fresh double cream
300 g (10 oz) natural yogurt

1. Melt the butter in a heavy-based frying pan and fry the almonds until golden brown. Stir in the sugar and cook for 1 minute, stirring continuously, until the sugar dissolves and the almonds are well coated. Tip on to a greased baking sheet and leave to cool.
2. About 30 minutes before ready to serve, break the sponge fingers in half and put into a serving bowl. Pour the sherry, brandy and orange rind and juice over and leave to soak for 30 minutes.
3. Whip the cream until it just holds its shape, then carefully fold in the yogurt. Spoon it on top of the sponge. Roughly chop the almonds, sprinkle on top and serve immediately.

CREAM

Cream lends a special touch to all kinds of dishes. Different types are most easily distinguished by butterfat content.

HALF CREAM

For pouring only, like top of milk. Good in coffee or on porridge and cereal. 12% butterfat.

SINGLE CREAM

Will not whip. Ideal for soups and sauces; in casseroles, omelettes and batter; or poured over desserts. 18% butterfat.

SOURED CREAM

Single cream treated with bacterial culture, with a rich tangy taste and thicker texture. Use in dressings, goulash or cheese cakes (see recipe, page 253). 18% butterfat.

WHIPPING CREAM

Doubles in volume when whipped. Ideal for cake fillings and light-textured fools, mousses and syllabubs. 35% butterfat.

WHIPPED CREAM

Whipping cream sold ready-whipped and sweetened.

CREME FRAICHE

May be whipped. Treated with bacterial culture. Has a distinctive, slight sharp taste. 35% butterfat.

DOUBLE CREAM

May be whipped stiffly, almost doubling in volume. Excellent all-purpose cream. 48% butterfat.

EXTRA THICK DOUBLE CREAM

For spooning only; will not whip.

CLOTTED CREAM

Thick, straw-coloured with a strong flavour. Spreads well; serve with scones for Devon tea. 55% butterfat.

EVERLASTING SYLLABUB

COUNTRYWIDE

The first syllabubs were made centuries ago by dairy maids, who would direct the warm milk straight from the cow into a pail containing sherry or cider. The froth was then skimmed off and served for breakfast. These days, syllabub is thicker and richer, and so called "everlasting" because it can be kept in the glass for several hours before serving.

SERVES 4

finely grated rind and juice of 1 lemon

75 g (3 oz) caster sugar

15–30 ml (1–2 tbsp) brandy

30 ml (2 tbsp) sweet sherry

300 ml (10 fl oz) fresh double cream

lemon twists, to decorate

1. Soak the lemon rind in the juice for 2–3 hours, then mix with sugar, brandy and sherry. Stir until dissolved.
2. Whip the cream lightly until it is just beginning to hold its shape, then gradually add the liquid, whipping continuously. Take care not to over-beat. Chill before serving in glasses, decorated with lemon twists.

BOODLES ORANGE FOOL. Plan this recipe in advance, so that the sponge cakes in the base have time to soak up all the citrus flavour.

LONGER LIFE CREAMS

UHT CREAM

Long life cream treated at high temperature. Unlike pasteurised cream, UHT (available in half, single, double and whipping varieties) may be stored unopened without refrigeration.

AEROSOL CREAM

UHT cream in aerosol cans. Collapses quickly after use.

FROZEN CREAM

Single, double, whipping and clotted creams are commercially available ready-frozen.

CANNED CREAM

Sterilised, with a slight caramel taste. Good for spooning on desserts; will not whip. 23% butterfat.

BOODLES ORANGE FOOL

THE SOUTH-EAST

Boodle's Club, in London's St. James's Street, was founded in 1764 and this luscious fool has been a speciality on the menu for many years. It's a bit like a trifle, with a sponge-cake base which sops up the creamy, fruit-flavoured mixture on top.

SERVES 6

4–6 trifle sponges, cut into 1 cm (½ inch) thick slices

grated rind and juice of 2 oranges

grated rind and juice of 1 lemon

25–50 g (1–2 oz) sugar

300 ml (10 fl oz) fresh double cream

orange slices or segments, to decorate

1. Use the sponge slices to line the bottom and halfway up the sides of a deep serving dish or bowl.
2. Mix the orange and lemon rinds and juice with the sugar and stir until the sugar has completely dissolved.
3. In another bowl, whip the cream until it just starts to thicken, then slowly add the sweetened fruit juice, whipping the cream as you do so. Whip until the cream is light and thickened and all the juice absorbed.
4. Pour the mixture over the sponge and refrigerate for at least 2 hours, longer if possible, so that the juice can soak into the sponge and the cream thicken. Serve decorated with segments or slices of fresh orange.

COMPOTE OF FRUIT WITH ELDERFLOWER CREAM

COUNTRYWIDE

The mixture of fruit, which can include any varieties in season, is here poached in fruit juice rather than the sugary syrup preferred by the Victorians. Elderflowers are beautifully aromatic and grow abundantly in the hedgerows. You can find dried elderflowers in health food shops.

SERVES 4

25 g (1 oz) sugar

6 large heads of fresh elderflowers or 25 g (1 oz) dried elderflowers

150 ml (5 fl oz) fresh double cream

900 g (2 lb) mixed fresh fruit, such as gooseberries, rhubarb, pears, strawberries, cherries, prepared

300 ml (½ pint) unsweetened orange or apple juice

1 cinnamon stick

2 strips of lemon rind

clear honey, to taste (optional)

1. To make the elderflower cream, put the sugar and 150 ml (¼ pint) water in a saucepan and heat gently until the sugar has dissolved, then boil rapidly until the liquid is reduced by half. Take off the heat and submerge the fresh or dried flowers in the syrup.

2. Leave to infuse for at least 2 hours, then press the syrup through a sieve, discarding the elderflowers. Whip the cream until it just holds its shape, then fold in the elderflower syrup. Chill until ready to serve.

3. Put the fruit, fruit juice, cinnamon and lemon rind in a large saucepan and simmer gently for 3–5 minutes until the fruits are softened, but still retain their shape. Serve the compote warm or cold with the elderflower cream.

TO MICROWAVE

⬚ Put the sugar and 150 ml (¼ pint) water in a medium bowl. Cook on HIGH for 5–6 minutes until the liquid is reduced by half, stirring occasionally. Complete steps 1 and 2. Put the fruit, fruit juice, cinnamon and lemon rind in a large bowl. Cover and cook on HIGH for about 5 minutes, until the fruit is tender, but still retains its shape. The time will depend on the type of fruit used. Serve warm or cold with the elderflower cream.

WINE JELLY CREAM

COUNTRYWIDE

A pretty pudding with a lovely flavour. The wine jelly glows enticingly from beneath the topping of rich and creamy custard. Propping the glasses at an angle as the jelly sets is a simple trick that gives an unusual effect.

SERVES 4

300 ml (½ pint) white wine
45 ml (3 tbsp) sugar
15 g (½ oz) gelatine
450 ml (¾ pint) fresh milk
2 egg yolks
15 ml (1 tbsp) cornflour
2.5 ml (½ tsp) vanilla flavouring
150 ml (5 fl oz) fresh whipping cream
fresh strawberries, to decorate

1. Heat half the wine, 30 ml (2 tbsp) of the sugar and the gelatine in a small saucepan. Dissolve over a gentle heat, then mix with remaining wine and set aside to cool.

2. Pour into 4 wine glasses. Place in the refrigerator to set at a 45° angle.

3. Pour the milk into a medium saucepan and heat almost to the boiling point. In a medium bowl, blend together the egg yolks, cornflour, remaining sugar and vanilla flavouring until pale, then pour on the hot milk, stirring continuously.

4. Strain the mixture into a medium heavy-based or double saucepan and stir over a gentle heat until the custard thickens enough to coat the back of a wooden spoon. This takes about 20 minutes. Cool, then whip the cream until stiff, then fold into the custard.

5. When the wine jelly is set, stand the glasses upright and pour in the custard. Return to the refrigerator to chill. Decorate with strawberries and serve with finger biscuits.

WINE JELLY CREAM. The jelly is clear and golden and the smooth topping flavoured with a touch of vanilla.

LEFT

TEA CREAM. Simple to make, this attractive dessert is good served with a few sweet grapes and some crisp little biscuits.

RIGHT

DAMASK CREAM. Fresh picked rose petals make a charming and original decoration for this fragrant dessert.

TEA CREAM

THE SOUTH-EAST

Many different types of tea are available, each giving a different, very subtle and intriguing taste to this dish. For special elegance make it in an old-fashioned, elaborate jelly mould.

SERVES 4

15 g (½ oz) loose aromatic tea, such as Earl Grey, jasmine or lapsang souchong
300 ml (½ pint) fresh milk
2 eggs, separated
30 ml (2 tbsp) sugar
15 ml (1 tbsp) gelatine
150 ml (5 fl oz) fresh double cream
fresh fruit, to decorate

1. Put the tea and the milk into a saucepan and bring slowly to the boil. Remove from the heat and leave to infuse for 10–15 minutes.
2. Beat the egg yolks with the sugar, then strain in the milk and mix well.
3. Sprinkle the gelatine over 45 ml (3 tbsp) water in a small bowl and leave to soak for 5 minutes. Place the bowl over a pan of simmering water and stir until dissolved. Stir into the tea mixture. Whip the cream until it just holds its shape, then fold in. Finally whisk the egg whites until stiff and fold in.
4. Pour into a dampened 568 ml (1 pint) mould and refrigerate for 2–3 hours, until set. Turn out and decorate with fresh fruit. Serve with crisp biscuits.

TO MICROWAVE

Put the tea and the milk in a large heatproof jug and cook on HIGH for 2–3 minutes, until just boiling. Complete the remainder of step 1 and step 2. Sprinkle the gelatine over 45 ml (3 tbsp) water in a small bowl and leave to soak for 5 minutes, then cook on HIGH for 30 seconds, until hot but not boiling. Stir until dissolved. Complete the recipe.

DAMASK CREAM

THE WEST

This subtly flavoured dish, also known as Devonshire junket, is a far cry from a junket that comes from a packet. Do not serve it until you are ready to eat, as once it is cut the shape will disintegrate.

SERVES 4

568 ml (1 pint) fresh single cream
45 ml (3 tbsp) caster sugar
10 ml (2 tsp) rennet essence
large pinch of freshly grated nutmeg
15 ml (1 tbsp) brandy
60 ml (4 tbsp) fresh clotted or double cream
5 ml (1 tsp) rosewater
rose petals, to decorate (optional)

1. Put the cream and 30 ml (2 tbsp) of the sugar in a saucepan. Heat gently until tepid, stirring so the sugar dissolves. (When the mixture is tepid it will register

36.9°C (98.4°F) on a sugar thermometer, or not feel hot or cold if you put your finger in it.) Stir in the rennet, nutmeg and brandy, then pour into a serving dish.
2. Leave for 2–3 hours, until set. Do not disturb the junket during this time or it will not set.
3. When the junket is set, mix the remaining sugar, cream and rose water together and spoon carefully over the top. Decorate with rose petals, if liked.

BAKED STRAWBERRY CHEESECAKE

COUNTRYWIDE

Cheesecakes have long been enjoyed in British cookery and many variations exist. Keep curd cheese in the fridge and use within a couple of days. For a real treat, make this cake in June, when the first sweet red berries appear in the shops.

SERVES 6–8

✳

75 g (3 oz) self-raising flour
25 g (1 oz) cornflour
75 g (3 oz) butter
fresh milk for mixing
100 g (4 oz) fresh strawberries, hulled and sliced
225 g (8 oz) medium-fat curd cheese
50 g (2 oz) caster sugar
2 eggs, separated
150 ml (5 fl oz) fresh soured cream

1. Put the flour and cornflour in a bowl. Rub in the butter until the mixture resembles fine breadcrumbs, then add a little milk to mix.
2. Roll out on a lightly floured work surface and use to line a 23 cm (9 inch) spring form tin. Bake blind at 200°C (400°F) mark 6 for 10 minutes, until set.
3. Arrange the strawberries on top of the pastry case.
4. Blend together the cheese, sugar, egg yolks and soured cream. Whisk the egg whites until stiff and gently fold into the mixture. Pour on top of the strawberries and bake at 180°C (350°F) mark 4 for 40–45 minutes, until firm. Serve hot or cold.

REDCURRANT CHEESECAKE

COUNTRYWIDE

Fresh redcurrants are only to be had during the height of summer but their sharpness does go very well with the sweet cheesecake base. Substituting a fruit-flavoured yogurt for natural gives more fruit flavour and a hint of extra colour.

SERVES 4–6

📈

65 g (2½ oz) butter, melted
150 g (5 oz) wheatmeal biscuits, finely crushed
175 g (6 oz) redcurrants
15 ml (1 tbsp) gelatine
100 g (4 oz) cottage cheese
1 egg, separated
40 g (1½ oz) caster sugar
150 g (5 oz) natural yogurt
150 ml (5 fl oz) fresh double cream
15 ml (1 tbsp) redcurrant jelly
redcurrants, to decorate

1. Mix together the butter and biscuit crumbs. Press the mixture into a loose bottomed 20.5 cm (8 inch) cake tin so it lines the base and sides.
2. Put the redcurrants in a medium saucepan with 45 ml (3 tbsp) water and simmer gently for 5–6 minutes, until soft. Allow to cool.
3. Sprinkle the gelatine in 45ml (3 tbsp) water in a small bowl and leave to soak. Place the bowl over a saucepan of simmering water and stir until dissolved. Leave until lukewarm.
4. Put the cheese, egg yolk, sugar and yogurt in a food processor or blender and work together until smooth. Whip the cream until it just holds its shape. Fold the cooked redcurrants, redcurrant jelly, gelatine and most of the cream into the cheese mixture. Whisk the egg white until stiff and fold into the mixture.
5. Pour on to the biscuit base and chill until set. Remove from the tin and decorate with the remaining cream and redcurrants.

TO MICROWAVE

📈 Cut the butter into cubes and melt on HIGH for 1½ minutes. Complete step 1. Put the redcurrants in a medium bowl with 45 ml (3 tbsp) water. Cook on HIGH for 3–4 minutes. Allow to cool. Put the gelatine and 45 ml (3 tbsp) water in a small bowl. Cook on HIGH for 1 minute, until hot but not boiling. Stir until dissolved. Complete steps 4 and 5.

REDCURRANT CHEESECAKE. A buttery base of crushed wheatmeal biscuits complements the rich and fruity topping.

CHRISTMAS PUDDING
ICE CREAM
COUNTRYWIDE

All the nicest things that go into the Christmas pud – dried fruit, rum, port and spices – are used in this unusual recipe. The ice cream mixture of eggs, sugar and cream is very luxurious and needs to be beaten twice while freezing to prevent ice crystals from spoiling the smoothness.

SERVES 4–6

100 g (4 oz) mixed no-soak dried fruit
60 ml (4 tbsp) light or dark rum
30 ml (2 tbsp) port
grated rind and juice of 1 orange
450 ml (15 fl oz) fresh single cream
3 egg yolks
100 g (4 oz) caster sugar
150 ml (5 fl oz) fresh whipping cream
5 ml (1 tsp) ground mixed spice

1. Mix the dried fruit, rum, port and orange rind and juice together, then set aside to marinate overnight.

2. Gently heat the single cream in a small saucepan to simmering point.

3. Whisk the egg yolks and sugar together in a medium bowl until pale and thick. Gradually pour on the hot cream, stirring continuously.

4. Strain the mixture into a medium heavy-based or double saucepan and cook over a gentle heat, stirring continuously, until it coats the back of a wooden spoon. Do not boil. This takes about 20 minutes. Set aside to cool.

5. Whip the cream until stiff, then fold into the cold custard with the dried fruit mixture and mixed spice.

6. Pour into a shallow freezer container, then cover and freeze for about 3 hours until mushy.

7. Turn into a chilled bowl and beat well. Return to the freezer container and freeze for a further 2 hours.

8. Beat the mixture again, then turn into a 1.1 litre (2 pint) bombe mould, cover and freeze for a further 2 hours until firm.

9. Transfer to the refrigerator to soften for 30 minutes before serving. Turn out on to a cold serving plate.

TO MICROWAVE

 Complete step 1. Put the cream in a medium bowl and cook on HIGH for 5 minutes. Complete step 3. Strain the mixture into a large bowl and cook on MEDIUM for 7–8 minutes, whisking frequently. Cool, then complete steps 5–9.

LEMON GERANIUM
ICE CREAM
COUNTRYWIDE

Not only do lemon-scented geraniums provide a marvellous display of colour all through the summer, but their leaves can be used to add a deliciously aromatic flavour to this unusual dessert.

SERVES 4–6

300 ml (½ pint) fresh milk
10–12 lemon-scented geranium leaves, crushed
3 egg yolks
100 g (4 oz) icing sugar
300 ml (10 fl oz) fresh whipping cream
lemon-scented geranium leaves, to decorate

1. Bring the milk and geranium leaves almost to the boil. Remove from the heat and leave to infuse for 30 minutes. Remove the geranium leaves.

2. Whisk the egg yolks and sugar together in a medium bowl until pale and frothy. Stir in the milk, then strain back into the pan.

3. Cook the custard gently over a low heat, stirring continuously, until it coats the back of a wooden spoon. Do not boil. This takes about 20 minutes.

4. Pour into a shallow freezer container, cool, then cover and freeze for 2 hours, until mushy.

5. Whip the cream until stiff, then fold into the

CHRISTMAS PUDDING ICE CREAM. The rich ice cream is flecked with red, green and gold of dried fruit and well laced with alcohol.

mixture. Return to the freezer container and freeze for a further 2 hours.

6. Turn into a chilled bowl and beat well again. Return to the freezer and freeze until firm.

7. Transfer to the refrigerator to soften for 30 minutes before serving. Decorate with geranium leaves.

TO MICROWAVE

 Put the milk and geranium leaves in a large bowl and cook on HIGH for 2–3 minutes, until the milk boils. Complete the remainder of step 1 and step 2. Cook the custard on MEDIUM for 3–4 minutes, stirring frequently, until the custard coats the back of a wooden spoon. Do not boil. Complete the recipe.

GOOSEBERRY YOGURT SORBET

THE MIDLANDS

A light and refreshing way to use gooseberries in which yogurt gives a pleasant sharpness to the smooth sorbet. You can make it a day or two ahead for a dinner party and transfer it from freezer to fridge 30 minutes before serving.

SERVES 4–6

✳ ⬙

700 g (1½ lb) fresh or frozen gooseberries, topped and tailed

100 g (4 oz) granulated sugar

15 ml (1 tbsp) gelatine

300 g (10 oz) natural yogurt

2 egg whites

1. Put the gooseberries in a saucepan with the sugar and 50 ml (2 fl oz) water. Cook gently, covered, until the fruit is soft. Purée in a blender or food processor, then push through a nylon sieve and leave until cool.

2. Sprinkle the gelatine in 45 ml (3 tbsp) cold water in a small bowl and leave to soak for 2–3 minutes. Place the bowl over a saucepan of simmering water and stir until dissolved. Leave until lukewarm, then stir into the gooseberry purée with the yogurt.

3. Whisk the egg whites until stiff but not dry. Fold into the purée.

4. Pour into a rigid freezer container and freeze for about 2½ hours or until almost frozen. Remove from the freezer and beat or whisk well, or blend in a food processor. Return to the freezer and freeze for at least 4 hours, until firm.

5. Before serving, transfer to the refrigerator for about 30 minutes to soften slightly.

TO MICROWAVE

 Put the gooseberries, sugar and 50 ml (2 fl oz) water in a bowl. Cover and cook on HIGH for 8–10 minutes, stirring occasionally. Complete the remainder of step 1. Sprinkle the gelatine over 45 ml (3 tbsp) water in a small bowl and leave to soak for 2–3 minutes. Cook on HIGH for 30 seconds–1 minute. Do not boil. Stir until dissolved. Complete the remainder of step 2 and the recipe.

YOGURT

To make yogurt, whole or skimmed milk is thickened by the action of a special bacterial culture, which also gives yogurt its characteristic tangy taste. Yogurt can be successfully used in a variety of dishes – in sauces and dressings, savoury dishes, cakes and desserts, and as a topping for cereal and fruit. There are a number of different varieties which can vary from brand to brand so always check the label:

VERY LOW FAT

Based on skimmed milk, this contains less than 0.5% fat and is often sweetened artificially for slimmers.

LOW FAT

Contains 0.5–2.0% fat.

CREAMY YOGURT

Made with whole milk, this may be enriched with cream.

GREEK-STYLE

Made with whole milk (may be cows' or ewes'), and has a very thick, creamy consistency.

SET YOGURT

This is inoculated, packaged and incubated in the container in which it is sold.

NATURAL YOGURT

Contains no colour, preservatives, stabilisers or thickeners.

FRUIT YOGURT

Contains at least 5% of the whole fruit as pieces or purée.

FLAVOURED YOGURT

Honey and chocolate are the most common flavourings for yogurt.

LEMON GERANIUM ICE CREAM. The leaves are infused in warm milk for the subtle taste which makes this dessert so interesting. Use a few leaves as a decoration, too, as a clue to the flavouring.

STRAWBERRY YOGURT MOULD

THE MIDLANDS

A light mousse made in a ring mould always looks pretty filled with fresh fruit, and strawberries are probably the most decorative of all the soft summer berries. The delicately flavoured mould has a very light set, just firm enough to turn it out. Substitute buttermilk for the yogurt if you prefer.

SERVES 6

3 eggs

50 g (2 oz) caster sugar

finely grated rind and juice of 1 lemon

450 g (1 lb) strawberries

20 ml (4 tsp) gelatine

150 g (5 oz) natural yogurt

150 g (5 oz) strawberry yogurt

STRAWBERRY YOGURT MOULD. A hint of lemon brings out the flavour of strawberries to the full, in this prettily fluted ring.

1. Put the eggs, sugar and lemon rind in a large bowl. Using an electric mixer, whisk together until the mixture is pale, thick and creamy and leaves a trail when the whisk is lifted from the bowl.

2. Hull half of the strawberries and place in a blender or food processor with half of the lemon juice. Purée until smooth.

3. Gradually whisk the purée into the mousse mixture, whisking well to keep the bulk.

4. Sprinkle the gelatine over the remaining lemon juice in a small bowl and leave to soak for 5 minutes. Place the bowl over a saucepan of simmering water and stir until dissolved. Leave until lukewarm, then gradually add to the mousse mixture with the natural and strawberry yogurts. Stir carefully but thoroughly to mix. Pour into a greased 1.7 litre (3 pint) ring mould and chill for 4–5 hours or until set.

5. To serve, dip the mould briefly in hot water, then invert on to a serving plate. Hull most of the remaining strawberries, but leave a few of the green hulls on for decoration. Fill the centre of the ring with the fruit. Serve with extra natural yogurt, if liked.

TO MICROWAVE

Complete steps 1, 2 and 3. Sprinkle the gelatine over the remaining lemon juice and leave to soak for 5 minutes. Cook on HIGH for 30–45 seconds. Do not boil. Stir until dissolved. Complete the recipe.

CHOCOLATE ORANGE SOUFFLE

COUNTRYWIDE

Dark plain chocolate is the best kind to use for mouth-watering desserts like this one, which call for a good depth of flavour. Cold soufflés and mousses, concocted from whipped cream and egg whites, have been popular puddings since the 17th century.

SERVES 6–8

450 ml (¾ pint) fresh milk

175 g (6 oz) plain chocolate

3 eggs, separated, plus 1 egg white

75 g (3 oz) sugar

15 ml (1 tbsp) gelatine

grated rind and juice of 1 orange

300 ml (10 fl oz) fresh whipping cream

15 ml (1 tbsp) chocolate liqueur

1. Line a 900 ml (1½ pint) soufflé dish with greaseproof paper to make a collar.
2. Put the milk in a saucepan and break 150 g (5 oz) chocolate into it. Heat gently until the chocolate melts, then cook over a high heat until almost boiling.
3. Whisk the egg yolks and sugar together until pale and thick. Gradually pour on the chocolate milk, stirring. Return to the saucepan and cook, stirring continuously, until it coats the back of a wooden spoon. This takes about 20 minutes. Do not boil.
4. Sprinkle the gelatine in 45 ml (3 tbsp) water in a small bowl and leave to soak. Place the bowl over a saucepan of simmering water and stir until dissolved. Stir into the custard with the orange rind and juice. Cool.
5. Whip the cream until it just holds its shape, then fold most of the cream into the cold mixture. Whisk the egg whites until stiff and fold into the mixture.
6. Pour the mixture into the prepared dish and leave to set. Remove paper collar.
7. Stir the liqueur into the remaining cream and use to decorate the soufflé. Grate the remaining chocolate and sprinkle on top.

DOUBLE CHOCOLATE ICE CREAM

COUNTRYWIDE

This recipe uses bitter plain chocolate to flavour the smooth ice cream base and is then given added bite with chocolate chips. Home-made ice cream is in a class of its own, and well worth taking a little time and trouble over.

SERVES 4–6

300 ml (½ pint) fresh milk

100 g (4 oz) plain chocolate

3 egg yolks

50 g (2 oz) sugar

300 ml (10 fl oz) fresh whipping cream

50 g (2 oz) chocolate chips

1. Put the milk in a saucepan and break the plain chocolate into it. Heat gently over a low heat until the chocolate melts, then cook over a high heat until almost boiling.
2. Whisk the egg yolks and sugar together until pale and thick. Gradually pour on the chocolate milk, stirring. Return to the saucepan and cook over a gentle heat, stirring continuously, until it coats the back of a spoon. Do not boil. This takes about 20 minutes.
3. Pour into a shallow freezer container and leave to cool. When the mixture is cool, cover and freeze for 2 hours, until mushy.
4. Turn into a large bowl and beat with a fork or whisk to break down any large ice crystals. Whip the cream until it just holds its shape, then fold into the frozen custard with the chocolate chips. Return the mixture to the freezer container and freeze for 2 hours.
5. Beat the mixture again, to break down any large ice crystals, then freeze until firm.
6. Transfer to the refrigerator to soften for 30 minutes before serving.

TO MICROWAVE

⚡ Put the milk and chocolate in a large bowl and cook on HIGH for 2–3 minutes, until the chocolate melts, stirring occasionally, then cook on HIGH for 1 minute, until almost boiling. Beat the egg yolks and sugar together, stir in the milk, then pour back into the bowl. Cook on MEDIUM for 3–4 minutes, stirring frequently, until the custard coats the back of a spoon. Do not boil. Complete the recipe.

CHOCOLATE ORANGE SOUFFLE. Grated chocolate curls and liqueur-flavoured cream whirls are used to decorate this handsome dessert.

APPLE AND HAZELNUT LAYER. To make serving easy, the meltingly short pastry is cut into portions before being placed on the fruity centre.

APPLE AND
HAZELNUT LAYER

THE SOUTH-EAST

If you make this pudding during the autumn, look out for Kentish hazelnuts to add a nutty crunch to the layers.

SERVES 8

75 g (3 oz) hazelnuts, shelled

75 g (3 oz) butter

45 ml (3 tbsp) caster sugar

115 g (4½ oz) plain flour

pinch of salt

450 g (1 lb) Cox's apples, peeled, cored and sliced

15 ml (1 tbsp) apricot jam or marmalade

grated rind of 1 lemon

15 ml (1 tbsp) candied peel, chopped

30 ml (2 tbsp) currants

30 ml (2 tbsp) sultanas

icing sugar, whipped fresh cream and hazelnuts, to decorate

1. Cut out two 20.5 cm (8 inch) circles of greaseproof paper.

2. Reserve 8 nuts and finely chop the remainder. Cream the butter and sugar until pale and fluffy. Stir in the flour, salt and chopped nuts, then form into a ball and chill for 30 minutes.

3. Put the apple in a saucepan with the jam and lemon rind and cook over a low heat for 5 minutes, until soft. Add the candied peel and dried fruit and simmer for 5 minutes.

4. Divide the pastry in half, place on the sheets of greaseproof paper and roll out into two circles. Transfer to greased baking sheets.

5. Bake at 190°C (375°F) mark 5 for 7–10 minutes, until light brown. Cut one circle into 8 triangles while warm. Leave to cool.

6. Just before serving, place the complete circle on a serving plate and cover with the apple mixture. Arrange the triangles on top. Dust with icing sugar, pipe cream on top and decorate the apple layer with hazelnuts.

YOGURT AND
BANANA DESSERT

COUNTRYWIDE

Any type of yogurt can be used for this very quick and easy recipe, and there are many varieties to choose from.

SERVES 4

300 g (10 oz) natural yogurt

150 ml (5 fl oz) fresh double cream

3 ripe bananas, mashed

grated rind and juice of 1 lemon

15–30 ml (1–2 tbsp) caster sugar

1 egg white

grated lemon rind and fresh mint leaves, to decorate

1. In a large bowl, whisk the yogurt and cream together until lightly stiff, then stir in the bananas, lemon rind and juice and sugar to taste.

2. In a medium bowl, whisk the egg white until stiff, then fold gently into the mixture. Chill until ready to serve.

3. Pour into 4 glass dishes, and serve, decorated with lemon rind and fresh mint leaves.

VARIATION

Replace the bananas with 450 g (1 lb) raspberries, 2 medium mangoes or 4 ripe, skinned nectarines or peaches.

CHERRIES IN BRANDY

THE SOUTH-EAST

A simple way to serve cherries, which shows them off at their best, steeped in a spicy alcoholic syrup and accompanied by a light orange cream. For easy eating, stone the cherries first, using a special cherry stoner or a skewer.

SERVES 6

900 g (2 lb) cherries, stoned

15 g (½ oz) sugar

1 cinnamon stick

finely grated rind and juice of 2 oranges

30 ml (2 tbsp) redcurrant jelly

60 ml (4 tbsp) cherry brandy or brandy

150 ml (5 fl oz) fresh double cream

150 g (5 oz) natural yogurt

1. Place the cherries in a saucepan with the sugar, cinnamon, half of the orange rind and the juice of both oranges. Cover and cook over a low heat for about 10 minutes or until the cherries are soft and the juice runs.

2. Stir in the redcurrant jelly and the brandy and cook gently until the jelly melts. Cool, then chill.

3. Mix the remaining orange rind and the cream together in a bowl. Whip until the cream just holds its shape, then fold in the yogurt. Serve the cherries in brandy, with the orange cream handed separately.

TO MICROWAVE

Put the stoned cherries, sugar, cinnamon, half of the orange rind and the juice of both oranges in a large bowl. Cover and cook on HIGH for 4–6 minutes or until the cherries are soft and the juice runs. Stir in the redcurrant jelly and the brandy and cook on HIGH for 1 minute. Complete the recipe.

CHILLED BLACKBERRY SNOW

THE SOUTH-EAST

The swirled layers of iced fruit purée and creamy egg white are very effective in this recipe but do finish it off just before it is needed and serve immediately. If really necessary, it can be kept refrigerated for a couple of hours, but it will start to lose some volume.

SERVES 6

450 g (1 lb) blackberries, fresh or frozen, thawed

2 egg whites

50 g (2 oz) caster sugar

300 ml (10 fl oz) fresh double cream

1. Rub the blackberries through a nylon sieve. Pour the purée into a rigid container and freeze for about 2 hours or until mushy.

2. Whisk the egg whites until stiff, then add the sugar gradually, whisking until the mixture stands in soft peaks. Whip the cream until it just holds its shape.

3. Remove the frozen blackberry purée from the freezer and mash to break down the large ice crystals, being careful not to break it down completely.

4. Fold the cream and whites together, then quickly fold in the semi-frozen blackberry purée to form a 'swirled' effect. Spoon into tall glasses and serve immediately.

CHILLED BLACKBERRY SNOW. A lovely, marbled dessert to serve in individual tall glasses. Place one fresh berry on top of each one to finish.

CAKES, PASTRIES, BISCUITS & SWEETS

Few can resist a freshly baked home-made cake or a batch of biscuits for tea. In this chapter you'll find lots to inspire you. There are cakes and bakes for every taste and occasion. Fruit, chocolate and cream cakes, flaky pastries, melt-in-the-mouth biscuits and sweets too – they're all here for you to make for your family or friends.

CHOCOLATE AND ORANGE CAKE. Fresh fruit segments on top and a thick layer of liqueur-flavoured cream in the middle makes this cake quite irresistible.

CHOCOLATE AND ORANGE CAKE

COUNTRYWIDE

This chocolate sponge is quick and easy to make. Chocolate and orange are natural partners.

SERVES 6–8

※

100 g (4 oz) butter
100 g (4 oz) sugar
1 egg, beaten
175 g (6 oz) self-raising flour
30 ml (2 tbsp) cocoa powder
5 ml (1 tsp) bicarbonate of soda
175 ml (6 fl oz) fresh milk
300 ml (10 fl oz) fresh whipping cream
10 ml (2 tsp) orange-flavoured liqueur
grated rind and segments of 1 orange

1. Lightly grease two 15 cm (6 inch) cake tins. Melt the butter and sugar in a saucepan over a low heat. Leave to cool for 2 minutes. Add the egg and beat well. Fold in the flour and cocoa powder. Mix the bicarbonate of soda and milk, add slowly to mixture.
2. Pour into the prepared cake tins and bake at 180°C (350°F) mark 4 for 25 minutes, until cooked and risen.
3. Leave in the tins for 2 minutes, then turn out and leave to cool on a wire rack.
4. Whip the cream stiffly. Fold in the liqueur and most of the orange rind. Use to sandwich the cakes together, reserving a little for the top.
5. Decorate with the remaining cream mixture, orange rind and the segments.

TO MICROWAVE

 Melt the butter and sugar in a large bowl on HIGH for 3 minutes. Cool for 2 minutes. Complete remaining part of step 1. Pour into a deep 18 cm (7 inch) cake dish, base lined with greaseproof paper. Cook on HIGH for 6–7 minutes, until the cake looks risen but still looks slightly moist on the surface. Leave to stand for 10 minutes. Complete step 3. Cut the cake in half, then complete steps 4 and 5.

DUNDEE CAKE

SCOTLAND

A classic rich and buttery fruit cake, with a characteristic pattern of blanched almonds on top, named after the town where it originated. Dundee was famous first and foremost for its marmalade, which used to feature in the recipe.

MAKES ABOUT 16 SLICES

※

100 g (4 oz) currants
100 g (4 oz) seedless raisins
100 g (4 oz) sultanas

100 g (4 oz) chopped candied orange peel

25 g (1 oz) blanched almonds, chopped

275 g (10 oz) plain flour

225 g (8 oz) butter

225 g (8 oz) light soft brown sugar

finely grated rind of 1 orange

finely grated rind of 1 lemon

4 eggs

whole blanched almonds, to decorate

1. Grease and line a deep 20.5 cm (8 inch) round cake tin with greaseproof paper.
2. Mix fruit, peel and chopped almonds with flour.
3. Cream the butter, sugar and orange and lemon rinds together until pale and fluffy. Gradually beat in eggs.
4. Fold in the fruit and flour mixture, then spoon into the prepared tin. Make a slight hollow in the centre of the top. Arrange whole almonds in circles to decorate.
5. Bake at 170°C (325°F) mark 3 for 2½–3 hours or until firm to the touch. If the top gets too brown, cover with paper. Leave to cool in the tin for 30 minutes, then turn on to a wire rack to cool completely.

CARROT CAKE

COUNTRYWIDE

Root vegetables were often used to lend sweetness to 18th-century cakes and puddings. Beetroots, parsnips and carrots were all common ingredients, but of these, only carrot is still favoured today. It makes a very pleasant, moist cake, without any hint of carrot in the taste.

SERVES 8

225 g (8 oz) butter

225 g (8 oz) light soft brown sugar

4 eggs, separated

finely grated rind of ½ orange

20 ml (4 tsp) lemon juice

175 g (6 oz) self-raising flour

5 ml (1 tsp) baking powder

50 g (2 oz) ground almonds

125 g (5 oz) walnut pieces, chopped

350 g (12 oz) young carrots, peeled and grated

225 g (8 oz) cream cheese

10 ml (2 tsp) clear honey

1. Grease and line a deep 20.5 cm (8 inch) round cake tin.
2. Cream the butter and sugar together in a bowl until pale and fluffy. Beat in the egg yolks, then stir in the orange rind and 15 ml (3 tsp) of the lemon juice.
3. Sift in the flour and baking powder, then stir in the ground almonds and 100 g (4 oz) of the walnuts.
4. Whisk the egg whites until stiff, then fold into the cake mixture with the carrots. Pour into the prepared tin and hollow the centre slightly.
5. Bake at 180°C (350°F) mark 4 for about 1½ hours. Cover top with foil after 1 hour if it starts to brown.

6. Leave to cool slightly, then turn out on to a wire rack and remove the lining paper. Leave to cool.
7. To make the topping, beat together the cheese, honey and remaining lemon juice and spread over the top of the cake. Sprinkle the topping with the remaining walnuts.

TO MICROWAVE

Grease a 20.5 cm (8 inch) round dish and line the base with greaseproof paper. Follow the recipe to step 5, stirring in 30 ml (2 tbsp) fresh milk. Stand the dish on a roasting rack, cover with kitchen paper and microwave on HIGH for 9–10 minutes, until risen, firm, but still looking slightly moist on the surface. Uncover and leave to stand for 10 minutes. Complete steps 6 and 7.

CARROT CAKE. The topping of cream cheese, honey and lemon juice gives a tangy flavour, and makes an interesting change from icing.

HALF POUND CAKE

COUNTRYWIDE

So named because the main items are added in 225 g (8 oz) quantities, this is a version of old English plum cake, although no plums or prunes were ever used.

MAKES ABOUT 16 SLICES

225 g (8 oz) butter
225 g (8 oz) caster sugar
4 eggs, beaten
225 g (8 oz) plain flour, sifted
225 g (8 oz) seedless raisins
225 g (8 oz) mixed currants and sultanas
100 g (4 oz) glacé cherries
pinch of salt
2.5 ml (½ tsp) ground mixed spice
15 ml (1 tbsp) brandy
walnut halves, to decorate

1. Grease and line a deep 20.5 cm (8 inch) round cake tin with greaseproof paper.

2. Cream the butter and sugar together until pale and fluffy. Gradually add the eggs, beating well after each addition. Fold in the flour, fruit, salt and spice, then add the brandy and mix in well to make a soft dropping consistency.

3. Turn into the prepared tin, level the top and decorate with the halved walnuts. Bake at 150°C (300°F) mark 2 for about 2½ hours. If the top gets too brown, cover with paper. Leave to cool in the tin for 30 minutes, then turn out on to a wire rack to cool.

MADEIRA CAKE

COUNTRYWIDE

This cake does not itself contain Madeira wine but was originally made to eat accompanied by a glass of the fortified wine. It has a firm, even but light texture. Seed cake is a variation that has, unaccountably, fallen from favour. Caraway seeds lend a slightly aniseed flavour.

MAKES ABOUT 12 SLICES

175 g (6 oz) butter
175 g (6 oz) caster sugar

5 ml (1 tsp) vanilla essence

3 eggs

100 g (4 oz) plain flour

100 g (4 oz) self-raising flour

about 15–30 ml (1–2 tbsp) fresh milk

2–3 thin slices of citron peel

1. Grease and line a deep 18 cm (7 inch) round cake tin.
2. Cream the butter and sugar with the vanilla essence until pale and fluffy, then gradually beat in the eggs. Sift the two flours together and fold into the creamed mixture, adding a little milk if necessary to give a dropping consistency.
3. Turn into the prepared tin and bake at 180°C (350°F) mark 4 for 20 minutes. Arrange the citron slices across the top of the cake and return it to the oven for a further 40 minutes or until well risen and firm to the touch. Turn out and cool on a wire rack.

SEED CAKE
Make as the Madeira cake but omit the citron peel and add 10 ml (2 tsp) caraway seeds, 5 ml (1 tsp) ground cinnamon and a large pinch of ground cloves to the flour.

SOMERSET APPLE CAKE
THE WEST

Both Somerset and Dorset lay claim to this deliciously moist cake which is equally good served with cream and eaten warm as a pudding. It is best consumed within two days of being made.

MAKES ABOUT 10 SLICES

100 g (4 oz) butter

175 g (6 oz) dark soft brown sugar

2 eggs, beaten

225 g (8 oz) plain wholemeal flour

5 ml (1 tsp) ground mixed spice

5 ml (1 tsp) ground cinnamon

10 ml (2 tsp) baking powder

450 g (1 lb) cooking apples, peeled, cored and chopped

45–60 ml (3–4 tbsp) fresh milk

15 ml (1 tbsp) clear honey

15 ml (1 tbsp) light demerara sugar

1. Grease and line a deep 18 cm (7 inch) round cake tin with greaseproof paper.
2. Cream the butter and sugar together until pale and fluffy. Add the eggs, a little at a time, beating well after each addition. Add the flour, spices and baking powder and mix well. Fold in the apples and enough milk to make a soft dropping consistency.
3. Turn the mixture into the prepared tin and bake at 170°C (325°F) mark 3 for 1½ hours, until well risen and firm to the touch. Turn out on to a wire rack to cool.

4. When the cake is cold, brush with the honey and sprinkle with the demerara sugar to decorate.

TO MICROWAVE

Grease a 1.6 litre (2¾ pint) ring mould. Complete step 2. Turn the mixture into the prepared mould and level the surface. Cook on HIGH for 8–9 minutes or until well risen and firm to the touch. Leave to cool in the dish, then turn out, brush with the honey and sprinkle with the sugar.

VINEGAR CAKE
COUNTRYWIDE

This fruit cake recipe is lighter and less rich than those made with eggs because the bicarbonate of soda and vinegar act as raising agents. When cooked, the vinegar loses its acidity and provides just a hint of tartness. This cake is sometimes sliced and served with cheese.

MAKES ABOUT 16 SLICES

225 g (8 oz) butter

450 g (1 lb) plain flour

450 g (1 lb) mixed dried fruit

225 g (8 oz) light soft brown sugar

5 ml (1 tsp) bicarbonate of soda

300 ml (½ pint) fresh milk

45 ml (3 tbsp) malt vinegar

1. Grease a deep 23 cm (9 inch) round cake tin.
2. Rub the butter into the flour until the mixture resembles fine breadcrumbs, then add the fruit and sugar. Sprinkle the bicarbonate of soda into the milk, then add the vinegar. This will froth up. While it is still foaming, add it to the dry ingredients and mix in well.
3. Turn the mixture into the prepared tin and bake at 200°C (400°F) mark 6 for 30 minutes, then reduce the oven temperature to 170°C (325°F) mark 3 and bake for another 1½ hours or until firm to the touch. If the top gets too brown, cover with paper. Leave to cool in the tin for 30 minutes, then turn out on to a wire rack to cool completely.

CIDER CAKE

THE WEST

This fruited cake uses cider as its liquid, which produces a subtle flavour with more than a hint of apple. Recipes from this part of the world use cider in many imaginative ways to flavour both sweet and savoury dishes.

MAKES 16 SQUARES

150 ml (¼ pint) dry cider

225 g (8 oz) sultanas

100 g (4 oz) butter

100 g (4 oz) light soft brown sugar

2 eggs, beaten

225 g (8 oz) plain flour

5 ml (1 tsp) bicarbonate of soda

1. Grease an 18 cm (7 inch) square cake tin.
2. Put the cider and fruit in a bowl and leave to soak for 12 hours or overnight.
3. Cream the butter and the sugar together until pale and fluffy. Gradually beat in the eggs, a little at a time, beating well after each addition. Add half of the flour and the bicarbonate of soda and beat thoroughly together.
4. Pour over the sultanas and the cider and mix well together. Fold in the remaining flour, then pour quickly into the prepared tin.
5. Bake at 180°C (350°F) mark 4 for about 1 hour, until well risen and firm to the touch. Leave to cool in the tin for 30 minutes, then turn out on to a wire rack and leave to cool completely. Serve cut into squares.

CIDER CAKE. Sultanas are soaked in cider overnight to give this cake its moist finish and delicious flavour.

PORTER CAKE

NORTHERN IRELAND

A rich, dark fruit-cake, which keeps very well. The original recipe used porter, a weaker variety of stout, which used to be a very popular working man's pint. However, as porter died out with the advent of bitter and is no longer produced, stout makes an admirable substitute.

MAKES 10 SLICES

225 g (8 oz) self-raising wholemeal flour

2.5 ml (½ tsp) baking powder

100 g (4 oz) butter, softened

100 g (4 oz) soft light brown sugar

5 ml (1 tsp) ground mixed spice

finely grated rind of 1 lemon

150 ml (¼ pint) stout

2 eggs

350 g (12 oz) mixed dried fruit

1. Grease and line a deep 18 cm (7 inch) cake tin.
2. Put the flour, baking powder, butter, sugar, spice, lemon rind, stout and eggs in a bowl and beat for 2–3 minutes, until well mixed. Stir in the dried fruit.
3. Pour into the prepared tin and bake at 170°C (325°F) mark 3 for about 1½ hours or until risen and firm to the touch. Leave to cool in the tin. When the cake is cold wrap it in greaseproof paper and foil and store for 1 week before eating.

WESTMORLAND PEPPER CAKE

THE NORTH

If you've never tried adding pepper to a sweet dish before now you'll be pleasantly surprised by its effect. It adds unusual spiciness to what is otherwise a fairly standard fruit-cake and is just one example of the huge variety of fruit-cake recipes that come from this part of the world.

MAKES 8 SLICES

75 g (3 oz) raisins

75 g (3 oz) currants

100 g (4 oz) caster sugar

75 g (3 oz) butter

225 g (8 oz) self-raising flour

pinch of salt

2.5 ml (½ tsp) ground ginger

large pinch of ground cloves

2.5 ml (½ tsp) finely ground black pepper

60 ml (4 tbsp) fresh milk

1 egg, beaten

1. Grease the base of a deep 18 cm (7 inch) round cake tin and line the base with greaseproof paper.

2. Put the fruit, sugar, butter and 150 ml (¼ pint) water in a saucepan and bring to the boil. Simmer for 10 minutes, then leave to cool slightly. Put the flour, salt, spices and pepper in a large bowl and gently stir in the fruit mixture, milk and the egg. Mix thoroughly together without beating.

3. Turn the mixture into the prepared tin and bake at 180°C (350°F) mark 4 for about 50 minutes or until firm to the touch and golden brown. Turn out and leave to cool on a wire rack.

COURTING CAKE

THE NORTH

This is a real summer treat and a good way of using up slightly bruised or over-ripe strawberries or making just a few go further. It was originally made in the North by young girls for their betrotheds, hence the name.

MAKES ABOUT 16 SLICES

225 g (8 oz) butter

225 g (8 oz) caster sugar

4 eggs, beaten

350 g (12 oz) self-raising flour

30–45 ml (2–3 tbsp) fresh milk

300 ml (10 fl oz) fresh double cream

225 g (8 oz) strawberries, sliced

icing sugar, to decorate

1. Grease and line the bases of three 18 cm (7 inch) round cake tins.

2. Cream the butter and the sugar together until pale and fluffy. Gradually add the eggs, a little at a time, beating well after each addition. Fold in the flour, then add enough milk to give a soft dropping consistency.

3. Divide the mixture evenly between the prepared tins and bake at 190°C (375°F) mark 5 for 25–30 minutes, until well risen and firm to the touch, swapping the position of the top and bottom cakes halfway through cooking. Turn out and leave to cool on a wire rack.

4. Whip the cream until it just holds its shape. Sandwich the cakes together with the cream and the strawberries, reserving a few for decoration. Dredge the top with icing sugar and decorate with the reserved strawberries.

COURTING CAKE. Strawberries and cream are made for summer days, and in this tempting, tantalising cake they come together to perfection. More strawberries to decorate add the finishing touches to this lavish tea-time treat.

SCOTTISH GINGER CAKE. Lovely and dark, this teatime treat is flavoured with mixed spice as well as ginger.

SCOTTISH GINGER CAKE

SCOTLAND

A truly delicious, sticky cake containing stem ginger as well as sultanas and mixed peel. The flavour will be even better if the cake is wrapped first in greaseproof paper and then in foil and stored for 2 to 3 days before eating.

MAKES 12 SQUARES

225 g (8 oz) plain flour
pinch of salt
2.5 ml (½ tsp) bicarbonate of soda
15 ml (1 tbsp) ground ginger
10 ml (2 tsp) ground mixed spice
25 g (1 oz) medium oatmeal
50 g (2 oz) sultanas
100 g (4 oz) chopped mixed peel
50 g (2 oz) preserved stem ginger, chopped
100 g (4 oz) treacle
150 g (5 oz) golden syrup
175 g (6 oz) butter
50 g (2 oz) soft dark brown sugar
150 ml (¼ pint) fresh milk
2 eggs

1. Grease and line an 18 cm (7 inch) square cake tin.
2. Sift the dry ingredients together, then add the oatmeal, sultanas, chopped peel and preserved ginger.

3. Put the treacle, golden syrup, butter, sugar and milk in a saucepan and heat gently until melted. Make a well in the centre of the dry ingredients, then break in eggs, pour in treacle mixture and beat well together.
4. Pour into the prepared tin and bake at 140°C (275°F) mark 1 for about 2¼ hours, until well risen and firm to the touch. Turn out on to a wire rack to cool.

COFFEE AND WALNUT LOG

COUNTRYWIDE

It was in Victorian times that tea really came into its own as a meal, with an array of delicious sandwiches and cakes being served. This is a variation on a whisked sponge, flavoured with coffee and walnuts, with a coffee cream filling.

SERVES 6–8

3 eggs
75 g (3 oz) caster sugar
40 g (1½ oz) self-raising flour
40 g (1½ oz) wholemeal self-raising flour
30 ml (2 tbsp) coffee essence
50 g (2 oz) walnut pieces, finely chopped
150 ml (5 fl oz) fresh double cream
icing sugar, to dredge

1. Grease and line an 18×28 cm (7×11 inch) Swiss roll tin.

2. Put the eggs and sugar in a large bowl and stand it over a pan of hot water. Whisk together until doubled in volume and thick enough to leave a thin trail on the surface when the whisk is lifted.

3. Fold in 15 ml (1 tbsp) of the coffee essence and the walnuts.

4. Pour the mixture into the prepared tin and bake at 200°C (400°F) mark 6 for 8–10 minutes until risen and firm to the touch.

5. Meanwhile, place a sheet of greaseproof paper over a damp tea-towel.

6. Quickly turn out the cake on to the paper and trim the edges. Roll up the cake with the paper inside. Leave to cool for about 30 minutes, covered with the damp tea-towel.

7. To make the filling, whisk the cream until stiff, then fold in the remaining coffee essence.

8. When cold, unroll the coffee log and remove the paper. Gently spread with the filling and re-roll. Do not worry if it cracks slightly. Dust with icing sugar before serving.

HONEY CAKE

COUNTRYWIDE

The Greeks were very fond of honey, and believed that they would have a longer, healthier life if they ate it; the Romans, too, ate honey cake. By the 18th century it was popular in Britain, where it was made in different regions using the local honey.

MAKES 12–16 SQUARES

225 ml (8 fl oz) clear honey plus 45 ml (3 tbsp)
75 g (3 oz) butter
350 g (12 oz) plain wholemeal flour
pinch of salt
5 ml (1 tsp) ground mixed spice
5 ml (1 tsp) bicarbonate of soda
50 g (2 oz) glacé cherries, halved
50 g (2 oz) chopped mixed peel
3 eggs
45 ml (3 tbsp) fresh milk
grated rind of 1 large lemon
25 g (1 oz) flaked almonds

1. Grease a 20.5 cm (8 inch) square cake tin and line the base and sides with greaseproof paper.

2. Pour 225 ml (8 fl oz) honey into a saucepan, add the butter and heat gently, stirring, until blended.

3. Sift the flour, salt, spice and bicarbonate of soda into a large bowl, stirring in any bran left in the sieve. Add the cherries and peel.

4. Beat the eggs and the milk together and stir into the honey mixture with the lemon rind. Pour gradually on to the dry ingredients, beating well after each addition, until well blended.

5. Turn the mixture into the prepared tin and sprinkle with flaked almonds. Bake at 170°C (325°F) mark 3 for about 1¼ hours, until the cake is firm to the touch or a

skewer inserted in the centre of the cake comes out clean.

6. Using a skewer, prick the top of the cake and spoon over the remaining honey. Turn out and leave to cool on a wire rack. Do not remove the lining paper until the cake is cold.

TO MICROWAVE

Grease a 23 cm (9 inch) square dish and line the base with greaseproof paper. Put 225 ml (8 fl oz) honey and the butter in a medium bowl and cook on HIGH for 2 minutes or until the butter has melted. Complete steps 3 and 4, adding an extra 30 ml (2 tbsp) fresh milk. Pour into the prepared dish, sprinkle with the almonds and cover with kitchen paper. Stand the dish on a roasting rack and cook on HIGH for 4–5 minutes, until risen but slightly moist on the surface. Complete step 6.

HONEY CAKE. Nice and moist, with glacé cherries and mixed peel to add texture, lemon and mixed spice for flavour.

TWELFTH-NIGHT CAKE

COUNTRYWIDE

Twelfth night was celebrated, in some places, with far more feasting and festivity than Christmas itself. Traditionally, a special cake containing a dried bean was served, and whoever found it would have good luck in the coming year. This is a rich fruit-cake, which could be made for any special occasion.

MAKES ABOUT 25–30 SLICES

350 g (12 oz) butter

350 g (12 oz) caster sugar

6 eggs, beaten

75 ml (5 tbsp) brandy

350 g (12 oz) plain flour

5 ml (1 tsp) ground allspice

5 ml (1 tsp) ground ginger

5 ml (1 tsp) ground coriander

5 ml (1 tsp) ground cinnamon

700 g (1½ lb) mixed dried fruit

50 g (2 oz) blanched almonds, chopped

45 ml (3 tbsp) apricot conserve

900 g (2 lb) almond paste

4 egg whites

900 g (2 lb) icing sugar

15 ml (1 tbsp) lemon juice

10 ml (2 tsp) glycerine

glacé fruit, angelica and silver balls, to decorate

TWELFTH-NIGHT CAKE. A swag of shiny glacé fruit makes an unusual and very attractive decoration. A good party cake, for post-Christmas festivities.

1. Grease a deep 25 cm (10 inch) round cake tin and line the base and side with greaseproof paper.
2. Cream the butter and sugar together until pale and fluffy. Gradually add the eggs and then the brandy, beating well after each addition. Fold in the flour, spices, fruit and nuts.
3. Turn into the prepared tin and level the surface. Bake at 150°C (300°F) mark 2 for 2½ hours or until firm to the touch. Cover with paper halfway through cooking if the cake browns too quickly.
4. Leave to cool in the tin for 30 minutes, then turn out and cool completely on a wire rack.
5. When the cake is cold, heat the apricot conserve in a small saucepan until just melted, then brush over the top and sides of the cake.
6. Measure around the cake with a piece of string. Dust the working surface with icing sugar and roll out two-thirds of the almond paste to a rectangle, half the length of the string by twice the depth of the cake.
7. Trim the edges, then cut in half lengthways with a sharp knife. Gently lift the almond paste and place it firmly in position around the cake. Smooth the joins with a palette knife and keep the top and bottom edges square. Roll a jam jar lightly around the cake to help the paste stick more firmly.
8. Roll out the remaining almond paste to fit the top of the cake. With the help of the rolling pin, lift it on to the cake. Lightly roll with the rolling pin, then smooth the join and leave to dry for up to 4 days before starting to ice.
9. Make the icing 3 days after covering the cake with almond paste. Whisk the egg whites until slightly frothy. Then sift and stir in about one quarter of the icing sugar with a wooden spoon. Continue adding more sugar gradually, beating well after each addition, until about three-quarters of the sugar has been added. Beat in the lemon juice and continue beating, until the icing is smooth.
10. Beat in the remaining sugar. Finally, stir in the glycerine to prevent the icing becoming too hard. Cover and keep for 1 day to allow any air bubbles to rise to the surface.
11. The next day, use two-thirds of the icing to roughly flat ice the top and sides of the cake. Leave to dry for 24 hours.
12. Spoon the remaining icing on top of the flat icing and roughly smooth over it with a palette knife. Using the palette knife or back of a teaspoon, pull the icing to make rough peaks. Decorate lavishly with the glacé fruit, angelica and silver balls, then leave to dry completely.

CHERRY AND ALMOND CAKE

THE SOUTH-EAST

Ground almonds give an unbeatably moist texture and delicate flavour to this cake, and juicy glacé cherries make it even more tempting. Don't buy too large a quantity of ground almonds at a time, as they quickly lose flavour once the pack is opened.

MAKES ABOUT 12 SLICES

275 g (10 oz) glacé cherries
225 g (8 oz) butter, softened
225 g (8 oz) caster sugar
6 eggs, beaten
65 g (2½ oz) self-raising flour
pinch of salt
175 g (6 oz) ground almonds
2.5 ml (½ tsp) almond essence
icing sugar, to decorate

1. Grease a deep 23 cm (9 inch) loose-bottomed round cake tin and line the base and sides with greaseproof paper. Grease the paper.
2. Arrange the cherries in the bottom of the tin.
3. Cream the butter and sugar together until pale and fluffy. Beat in the eggs a little at a time, adding a little of the flour if the mixture shows signs of curdling.
4. Sift in the remaining flour and salt, then add the ground almonds and almond flavouring.
5. Turn the mixture into the prepared tin and bake at 180°C (350°F) mark 4 for 1 hour, until firm to the touch. Cover with greaseproof paper if browning too quickly. Leave in the tin to cool. When the cake is cold, remove from the tin and dredge the top with icing sugar to decorate.

QUEEN CAKES

THE SOUTH-EAST

These individual sponge cakes, enriched with sultanas, are very easy to prepare. Children enjoy piling the mixture into the paper cases – and licking the spoon! In the past, the mixture would sometimes be baked in heart-shaped tins and would then be called heart-cakes, which were eaten accompanied by a glass of wine or cider.

MAKES 16

100 g (4 oz) butter
100 g (4 oz) caster sugar
2 eggs, beaten
100 g (4 oz) self-raising flour
50 g (2 oz) sultanas

1. Spread out 16 paper cases on baking sheets, or put them into patty tins.

2. Cream the butter and sugar together until pale and fluffy. Gradually beat in the egg, a little at a time, beating well after each addition. Fold in the flour, then the fruit.
3. Fill the paper cases half full. Bake at 190°C (375°F) mark 5 for 15–20 minutes, until golden brown. Transfer to a wire rack to cool.

VARIATIONS
Replace the sultanas with one of the following:
50 g (2 oz) chopped dates
50 g (2 oz) chopped glacé cherries
50 g (2 oz) chocolate chips

TO MICROWAVE

Omit step 1. Complete step 2. Arrange 6 double layers of paper cases in a microwave muffin tray. Fill the paper cases half full and cook on HIGH for 1 minute, until risen but still slightly moist on the surface. Transfer to a wire rack to cool. Repeat twice with the remaining mixture to make 16 cakes. (Cook the last batch of 4 cakes for 30–45 seconds only.)

LEFT
CHERRY AND ALMOND CAKE. The cherries make a pretty stripe across the bottom of each slice from this sugar-dredged cake.

RIGHT
QUEEN CAKES. There are lots of variations to choose from to ring the changes with these appetising little cakes.

271

PASTRIES

ECCLES CAKES

THE NORTH

Baked originally at Eccles in Lancashire, but now available countrywide, these cakes are pastries with a sweet spicy mixture enclosed in a puff pastry case. They should have a shiny coating and are best eaten warm.

MAKES 8

25 g (1 oz) butter

100 g (4 oz) currants

25 g (1 oz) chopped mixed peel

50 g (2 oz) demerara sugar

2.5 ml (½ tsp) ground mixed spice

212 g (7½ oz) packet frozen puff pastry, thawed

1 egg white

caster sugar for sprinkling

1. Melt the butter in a saucepan, then stir in the currants, peel, sugar and spice and mix thoroughly together.
2. On a lightly floured surface, roll out the pastry very thinly and cut out eight 12.5 cm (5 inch) circles using a saucer as a guide. Divide the fruit mixture between the circles, damp the edges of the pastry and draw them to the centre, sealing well together.
3. Turn the cakes over and roll gently into circles with a rolling pin. Brush with egg white and sprinkle with caster sugar. Make 3 diagonal cuts across the top of each.
4. Place on dampened baking sheets and bake at 220°C (425°F) mark 7 for about 15 minutes, until light golden brown. Eccles cakes are best eaten while still slightly warm.

APPLE CREAM BUNS

THE WEST

These delicious choux pastry buns conceal a traditional mixture of apples and cream, and make a soft and surprising tea-time treat. Make sure the apples are completely cool before folding them into the cream or it will separate.

MAKES 16 BUNS

50 g (2 oz) butter

65 g (2½ oz) plain flour, sifted

pinch of salt

2 eggs, beaten

450 g (1 lb) Bramley apples, peeled, cored and sliced

25 g (1 oz) sugar

150 ml (5 fl oz) fresh double cream

icing sugar

1. Put 150 ml (¼ pint) water and the butter into a medium saucepan. Heat slowly until the butter melts, then bring to a brisk boil. Lower the heat and tip in all the flour and salt at once.
2. Stir briskly until the mixture forms a soft ball and leaves the side of the pan.
3. Remove from the heat and cool slightly. Gradually add the eggs, a little at a time, beating until the mixture is smooth and shiny.
4. Pipe or spoon 16 buns of the mixture on to a buttered baking sheet. Bake the buns at 200°C (400°F) mark 6 for 10 minutes.
5. Remove from the oven and make a slit in the side of each. Return to the oven for a further 5 minutes. Cool on a wire rack.
6. Poach the apple slices in 150 ml (¼ pint) water with the sugar for 15 minutes, until soft. Cool.
7. Whip the cream until stiff peaks form. Remove the apple slices from the syrup with a slotted spoon, then fold them into the whipped cream. Split the buns, fill with the apple mixture and dust with sifted icing sugar.

TO MICROWAVE

Put 150 ml (¼ pint) water and butter into a large bowl and cook on HIGH for 3 minutes. Complete steps 2 through 5. Put the apples and 65 ml (2½ fl oz) water and sugar in a large bowl and cook on HIGH for 6–7 minutes. Cool and complete step 7.

HAZELNUT CARTWHEEL

THE SOUTH-EAST

Hazelnuts are found in many parts of the world and are also called cob nuts or filberts. In Britain, the crop comes from Kent and is famous for the sweetness of the nuts. As well as being useful for lending crunch and flavour to recipes like this, hazelnuts are good on their own, as a healthy snack, or as an accompaniment to wine and cheese.

SERVES 8

212 g (7½ oz) packet frozen puff pastry, thawed

25 g (1 oz) butter

25 g (1 oz) soft light brown sugar

1 egg, beaten

75 g (3 oz) plain cake crumbs

75 g (3 oz) hazelnuts, chopped

50 g (2 oz) raisins

finely grated rind of 1 lemon

1 egg, beaten, to glaze

caster sugar, to dredge

1. Roll out the pastry to a rectangle about 40.5×25.5 cm (16×10 inches). Cream the butter and sugar together until pale and fluffy, then beat in the egg and stir in the cake crumbs, hazelnuts, raisins and lemon rind. Spread the mixture over the pastry to within 0.5 cm (¼ inch) of the edges.
2. Roll up like a Swiss roll starting from the narrow end. Trim the ends, if necessary.
3. Place on a dampened baking sheet and curl round into a circle. Seal the ends together.
4. Snip all round the ring at 4 cm (1½ inch) intervals so the cuts come to within about 2 cm (¾ inch) of the ring's inner edge. Brush with beaten egg to glaze. Bake at 220°C (425°F) mark 7 for 25–30 minutes, until golden brown. Dredge with caster sugar and serve warm.

HAZELNUT CARTWHEEL. Puff pastry is spread with a nutty, lemon mixture before being rolled up to bake. Best eaten warm.

YORKSHIRE CURD TARTS

THE NORTH

Perhaps a forerunner of today's cheesecakes, these small, rich tarts combine the savoury flavour of curd cheese with the sweetness of currants and peel, plus a kick from spices and a spoonful of brandy. Don't leave out the latter unless you have to – the dash of spirits makes all the difference to the taste.

MAKES ABOUT 24

100 g (4 oz) butter, diced
225 g (8 oz) plain flour
100 g (4 oz) caster sugar
1 egg yolk
225 g (8 oz) curd cheese
50 g (2 oz) currants
2 eggs, beaten
finely grated rind of 1 lemon
5 ml (1 tsp) finely chopped mixed peel
15 ml (1 tbsp) brandy
nutmeg

1. To make the pastry, rub the butter into the flour until the mixture resembles fine breadcrumbs. Stir in 25 g (1 oz) of the sugar, then mix with the egg yolk and about 45 ml (3 tbsp) water to make a firm dough.
2. Knead lightly, then roll out on a lightly floured surface and use to line 24 greased patty tins.
3. To make the filling, mash the curd cheese, then add the remaining sugar, currants, eggs, lemon rind, mixed peel and brandy and mix thoroughly together. Spoon into the patty cases. Grate a little nutmeg over the tops.
4. Bake at 180°C (350°F) mark 4 for 35–45 minutes, until the pastry is lightly browned and the filling set and golden brown. Serve warm or cold.

FIG SLY CAKES

COUNTRYWIDE

Sly cakes, or 'cheats', as they were sometimes called, got their name because of their deceptive appearance. On the outside they look plain and uninteresting. But concealed inside is a rich filling of figs, currants, nuts and raisins.

MAKES 12

✳

275 g (10 oz) plain flour
pinch of salt
100 g (4 oz) butter, diced
75 g (3 oz) lard, diced
50 g (2 oz) caster sugar
225 g (8 oz) dried figs, chopped
75 g (3 oz) walnut pieces, chopped
50 g (2 oz) currants
50 g (2 oz) raisins
fresh milk, to glaze

1. To make the pastry, put the flour and salt into a bowl, then rub in the butter and lard until the mixture resembles fine breadcrumbs. Stir in the sugar and enough water to bind the mixture together. Chill while preparing the filling.
2. Put the figs, walnuts, currants and raisins into a saucepan with 150 ml (¼ pint) water and cook, uncovered, stirring continuously, until the water has evaporated and the fruit mixture is soft and thick. Leave to cool.
3. Divide the dough into two, and roll out one half to fit a shallow 18×28 cm (7×11 inch) tin. Spread the fruit mixture over the dough, then roll out the remaining dough and use to cover the filling. Seal the edges well and mark into 12 squares. Brush the top with a little milk to glaze.
4. Bake at 190°C (375°F) mark 5 for about 40 minutes, until golden brown. Leave to cool, then cut into the marked squares.

BISCUITS

SHREWSBURY BISCUITS

THE MIDLANDS

Light, lemony biscuits, which need to be stored in an airtight container to keep their crispness. In other traditional recipes for Shrewsbury biscuits, caraway seeds or currants were added to the basic mixture, to make pleasant variations.

MAKES ABOUT 24

100 g (4 oz) butter
150 g (5 oz) caster sugar
2 egg yolks
225 g (8 oz) plain flour
finely grated rind of 1 lemon

1. Cream the butter and sugar together until pale and fluffy. Add the egg yolks and beat in well. Stir in the flour and lemon rind and mix to a fairly firm dough.
2. Knead lightly on a lightly floured surface and roll out until about 0.5 cm (¼ inch) thick. Cut out 6.5 cm (2½ inch) rounds with a fluted cutter, and put on greased baking sheets.
3. Bake at 180°C (350°F) mark 4 for about 15 minutes, until lightly browned and firm to the touch. Transfer to wire racks to cool. Store in an airtight container.

VARIATIONS

SPICE BISCUITS
Omit the lemon rind and add 5 ml (1 tsp) mixed spice and 5 ml (1 tsp) ground cinnamon, sifted with the flour.

FRUIT BISCUITS
Add 50 g (2 oz) chopped dried fruit to the mixture with the flour.

FRUIT SQUARES
Make up the mixture and divide in half. Roll out both portions into oblongs and sprinkle 100 g (4 oz) chopped dried fruit over one piece. Cover with the other piece and roll out the mixture 0.5 cm (¼ inch) thick. Cut into squares.

TONBRIDGE BISCUITS

THE SOUTH-EAST

Home-made biscuits are a real treat and they only take a few minutes to make. These are wafer-thin and, with caraway seeds sprinkled on top, have their own distinctive flavour.

MAKES ABOUT 24

✳

75 g (3 oz) butter, diced
225 g (8 oz) plain flour
75 g (3 oz) caster sugar
1 egg, beaten
1 egg white, beaten, to glaze
caraway seeds, for sprinkling

1. Rub the butter into the flour until the mixture resembles fine breadcrumbs, then stir in the sugar. Add the egg and mix to a stiff paste.

2. Roll out on a lightly floured surface, until about 0.5 cm (¼ inch) thick, prick the top with a fork and cut into rounds with a 5 cm (2 inch) plain cutter. Brush with egg white and sprinkle on a few caraway seeds.
3. Put on to greased baking sheets and bake at 180°C (350°F) mark 4 for about 10 minutes or until light brown. Transfer to wire racks to cool. Store in an airtight container.

INVERNESS GINGERNUTS

SCOTLAND

These favourite biscuits are good and gingery with an extra treacle flavour and a crisp texture.

MAKES ABOUT 36

✳

225 g (8 oz) plain flour
10 ml (2 tsp) ground ginger
5 ml (1 tsp) ground mixed spice
75 g (3 oz) fine oatmeal
75 g (3 oz) caster sugar
2.5 ml (½ tsp) bicarbonate of soda
175 g (6 oz) treacle
50 g (2 oz) butter

1. Put the flour, ginger, spice, oatmeal, sugar and bicarbonate of soda in a bowl and mix together.
2. Heat the treacle and butter in a small pan until melted. Pour on to dry ingredients and mix to make a smooth dough. Knead well.
3. Roll the dough out until about 0.5 cm (¼ inch) thick. Prick with a fork and cut out 6.5 cm (2½ inch) rounds with a plain cutter. Place on greased baking sheets and bake at 170°C (325°F) mark 3 for 20–25 minutes, until firm to the touch. Transfer to wire racks to cool.

BRANDY SNAPS

THE NORTH

Brandy snaps can be kept, unfilled, in an airtight container for up to a week.

MAKES ABOUT 12

50 g (2 oz) butter
50 g (2 oz) caster sugar
30 ml (2 tbsp) golden syrup
50 g (2 oz) plain flour
2.5 ml (½ tsp) ground ginger
5 ml (1 tsp) brandy
finely grated rind of ½ lemon
150 ml (5 fl oz) fresh double cream

1. Line 2 or 3 large baking sheets with non-stick baking paper.

ABOVE
INVERNESS
GINGERNUTS. These crisp gingery rounds are perfect dipped in coffee, with tea, or just as a snack at any time of day.

BELOW
TONBRIDGE BISCUITS.
Delicious, mouth-melting morsels. The sprinkling of caraway seeds adds an interesting contrast of flavour.

BRANDY SNAPS. These crisp gingery curls can be eaten as an accompaniment to mousse or ice cream, or overflowing with whipped cream, as shown here.

Roll each biscuit around the buttered handle of a wooden spoon.

2. Gently heat butter, sugar and syrup until butter has melted and sugar dissolved. Remove from heat.

3. Sift the flour and ginger together, then stir into the melted mixture with the brandy and lemon rind.

4. Drop teaspoons of mixture on to baking sheets, leaving 10 cm (4 inches) between them. Bake at 180°C (350°F) mark 4 for 7 minutes, until cooked.

5. Quickly remove from baking sheets using a palette knife. Roll each one around the buttered handle of a wooden spoon. Leave on handles until set, then gently twist to remove. Cool on a wire rack.

6. If the biscuits set before they have been shaped, return them to the oven for a few minutes to soften. Store in an airtight container until required.

7. Just before serving, whip the cream until it just holds its shape. Spoon into a piping bag fitted with a star nozzle and pipe cream into snaps. Serve immediately.

GINGERBREAD MEN

THE NORTH

Gingerbread has always been popular in the North. Children love these shapes.

MAKES ABOUT 16

350 g (12 oz) plain flour
5 ml (1 tsp) bicarbonate of soda
10 ml (2 tsp) ground ginger
100 g (4 oz) butter, diced
175 g (6 oz) soft light brown sugar
60 ml (4 tbsp) golden syrup
1 egg, beaten
currants, to decorate

1. Sift the flour, bicarbonate of soda and ginger into a mixing bowl. Rub in the butter until the mixture resembles fine breadcrumbs, then stir in the sugar. Beat the syrup into the egg, then stir into flour mixture. Mix together to make a smooth dough.

2. Knead the dough until smooth, then divide in half. Roll out, half at a time, on a floured surface until about 0.5 cm (¼ inch) thick.

3. Using a gingerbread man cutter, cut out gingerbread men until all of the dough has been used, re-rolling and cutting the trimmings. Repeat with the second half of dough. Place the gingerbread men on greased baking sheets and decorate them with currants, to represent eyes and buttons.

4. Bake at 190°C (375°F) mark 5 for 12–15 minutes, until golden brown. Leave on the baking sheets to cool slightly, then transfer carefully to wire racks and leave to cool completely. Store the gingerbread men in an airtight container.

WALNUT CLUSTERS

COUNTRYWIDE

In this recipe walnuts are combined with chocolate to produce small, crunchy, mounded biscuits. The walnuts can be replaced by other nuts, such as almonds or hazelnuts, to vary the flavour.

MAKES ABOUT 36

40 g (1½ oz) plain chocolate
50 g (2 oz) butter
100 g (4 oz) caster sugar
1 egg, beaten
7.5 ml (1½ tsp) vanilla flavouring
50 g (2 oz) plain flour
2.5 ml (½ tsp) salt
1.25 ml (¼ tsp) baking powder
175 g (6 oz) walnut pieces, chopped
icing sugar for dredging

1. Grease and line three baking sheets with rice paper. Break the chocolate into pieces and put in a bowl over a saucepan of simmering water. Heat gently until the chocolate has melted. Leave to cool slightly.
2. Cream the butter with the sugar and chocolate until fluffy. Beat in the egg and vanilla flavouring. Sift in the flour, salt and baking powder and fold into the butter mixture with the walnuts.
3. Drop heaped teaspoonfuls of the mixture well apart on to the baking sheets.
4. Bake at 180°C (350°F) mark 4 for 10 minutes. Transfer to a wire rack and leave to cool. Dredge with icing sugar. Store in an airtight container.

DEVON FLATS

THE WEST

These delicious creamy biscuits are very easy to make and are not as rich as their list of ingredients might indicate.

MAKES ABOUT 24

225 g (8 oz) self-raising flour
pinch of salt
100 g (4 oz) caster sugar
100 ml (4 fl oz) clotted or double cream
1 egg, beaten
about 15 ml (1 tbsp) fresh milk

1. Mix the flour, salt and sugar together. Stir in the cream, egg and enough milk to make a stiff dough. If the dough feels at all sticky, cover it and place in the refrigerator to firm up.
2. Roll the dough out on a lightly floured surface until about 0.75 cm (⅓ inch) thick, then cut out circles using a 7.5 cm (3 inch) cutter.
3. Transfer to greased baking sheets and bake at 220°C

(425°F) mark 7 for 8–10 minutes, until a light golden brown. Carefully transfer to wire racks and leave to cool. Store in an airtight container.

MAIDSTONE BISCUITS

THE SOUTH-EAST

Crisp and light, these crunchy little biscuits include almond pieces to give a pleasant bite. Scented rose water is an unusual flavouring which was popular with the Tudors.

MAKES ABOUT 18

100 g (4 oz) butter
100 g (4 oz) caster sugar
150 g (5 oz) plain flour
5 ml (1 tsp) rose water
50 g (2 oz) blanched almonds, chopped

1. Cream the butter and sugar together until pale and fluffy. Fold in the flour, rose water and almonds, and mix to make a stiff dough.
2. Place in small heaps on a floured baking sheet. Bake at 180°C (350°F) mark 4 for 12–15 minutes, until golden brown. Cool on a wire rack. Store in an airtight container.

TOASTED OAT AND RAISIN BISCUITS

COUNTRYWIDE

These toasted oat biscuits can be varied according to your taste. Replace the raisins with sultanas, stoned chopped dates or chocolate chips, if you prefer.

MAKES ABOUT 48

75 g (3 oz) rolled oats
100 g (4 oz) butter
50 g (2 oz) caster sugar
50 g (2 oz) soft dark brown sugar
1 egg, beaten
175 g (6 oz) plain flour
2.5 ml (½ tsp) salt
2.5 ml (½ tsp) bicarbonate of soda
2.5 ml (½ tsp) vanilla flavouring
75 g (3 oz) seedless raisins
50 g (2 oz) shelled unsalted peanuts, roughly chopped

1. Grease three baking sheets. Toast the oats for a few minutes under the grill, until golden brown.
2. Cream the butter and sugars together until light and fluffy. Beat in the egg. Sift in the flour, salt and bicarbonate of soda and fold into the creamed mixture with the remaining ingredients.
3. Drop heaped teaspoonfuls of the mixture, about

OPPOSITE
TOP RIGHT
MAIDSTONE BISCUITS. The almonds add an extra richness to these little biscuits that makes them impossible to resist.

TOP LEFT
EASTER BISCUITS. The serrated edges and crisply toasted sprinkled sugar make these pretty biscuits a treat for any occasion.

BELOW
DUNDEE BISCUITS. These short biscuits gain a crunch and a richness from the sprinkled almonds.

5 cm (2 inches) apart on to the baking sheets, flattening them lightly with the back of the spoon.
4. Bake at 180°C (350°F) mark 4 for 12–15 minutes until lightly browned. Transfer from the baking sheets on to a wire rack and leave to cool. Store in an airtight container.

DUNDEE BISCUITS
SCOTLAND

Scotland is famous for rich, mouth-wateringly short biscuits, and these are no exception. A scattering of almonds on top adds interest but otherwise the biscuits rely on good, simple ingredients, like butter and egg, for their wholesome flavour.

MAKES ABOUT 25

✳

225 g (8 oz) plain flour

100 g (4 oz) butter, diced

50 g (2 oz) caster sugar

1 egg, separated

50 g (2 oz) flaked almonds, chopped

1. Put the flour in a bowl and rub in the butter until the mixture resembles fine breadcrumbs. Stir in the sugar and mix well, then stir in the egg yolk to bind the mixture together.
2. Knead lightly, then roll out on a lightly floured surface until about 0.5 cm (¼ inch) thick. Prick with a fork, then cut out 5 cm (2 inch) rounds with a plain cutter.
3. Place the rounds on greased baking sheets, brush with the egg white and sprinkle with the almonds. Bake at 170°C (325°F) mark 3 for 25–30 minutes, until pale golden brown. Transfer to wire racks to cool. Store in an airtight container.

EASTER BISCUITS
THE WEST

These spicy, fruited biscuits were originally baked and eaten around Easter, particularly in the West Country, but are too good to be restricted to such a short period. They keep well in an airtight tin.

MAKES ABOUT 30

✳

100 g (4 oz) butter

75 g (3 oz) caster sugar

1 egg, separated

200 g (7 oz) plain flour

pinch of salt

2.5 ml (½ tsp) ground mixed spice

2.5 ml (½ tsp) ground cinnamon

50 g (2 oz) currants

15 ml (1 tbsp) chopped mixed peel

15–30 ml (1–2 tbsp) brandy or milk

caster sugar for sprinkling

1. Cream the butter and sugar together until pale and fluffy, then beat in the egg yolk. Sift in the flour, salt and spices and mix well. Add the fruit and peel and enough brandy or milk to give a fairly soft dough.
2. Knead lightly on a lightly floured surface and roll out until about 0.5 cm (¼ inch) thick. Cut into 6 cm (2 inch) rounds using a fluted cutter. Place on to greased baking sheets and bake at 200°C (400°F) mark 6 for 10 minutes.
3. Remove from the oven, brush with the lightly beaten egg white, sprinkle with a little caster sugar and return to the oven to bake for about 5 minutes longer, until the tops are golden brown. Transfer to a wire rack to cool. Store in an airtight container.

SCOTTISH OATCAKES.
Can be served lightly buttered
with cheese, or are equally
good spread with jam, honey
or marmalade.

SCOTTISH OATCAKES

SCOTLAND

The climate of Scotland is well suited to growing oats, which don't mind the cold or a drop of rain. These griddle cakes are very simple but quite delicious.

MAKES ABOUT 12

100 g (4 oz) fine oatmeal
pinch of salt
pinch of bicarbonate of soda
15 g (½ oz) lard
oatmeal for rolling

1. Put the oatmeal, salt and bicarbonate of soda in a bowl.
2. Gently heat the lard and 150 ml (¼ pint) water until the lard is melted, then quickly pour enough of it on to the dry ingredients to make a firm dough.
3. Roll out the dough on a work surface sprinkled with oatmeal until about 0.3 cm (⅛ inch) thick. Using a plain 7.5 cm (3 inch) round cutter, cut out 12 rounds, re-rolling as necessary. Or, cut into triangles, if preferred.
4. Cook the oatcakes on a hot griddle, on one side only for about 5–8 minutes, until they curl and are firm. Or place on a greased baking sheet and bake at 170°C (325°F) mark 3 for 30 minutes or until crisp.

TO MICROWAVE

Follow steps 1 and 2. Roll out the dough on a work surface sprinkled with oatmeal until about 0.3 cm (⅛ inch) thick. Using a plain 6.5 cm (2½ inch) round cutter, cut out 18 rounds, re-rolling as necessary. Place 6 oatcakes in a circle on a microwave baking tray and cook on HIGH for 1½ minutes. Turn over and cook on HIGH for 2 minutes. Repeat with the remaining oatcakes.

PETTICOAT TAILS

SCOTLAND

These traditional Scottish shortbread biscuits date back beyond the 12th century. The triangles fit together into a circle and were the same shape as the pieces of fabric used to make a full-gored petticoat in Elizabethan times. The biscuits got their name because in those days the word for a pattern was a 'tally', and so the biscuits became known as 'petticote tallis'.

MAKES 8

---

100 g (4 oz) butter, softened

50 g (2 oz) caster sugar, plus extra for dredging

150 g (5 oz) plain flour

50 g (2 oz) ground rice

---

1. In a medium bowl, cream the butter and sugar together until pale and fluffy.
2. Gradually stir in the flour and ground rice. Draw the mixture together and press into an 18 cm (7 inch) round sandwich tin.
3. Prick well all over, pinch up the edges with a finger and thumb. Mark into 8 triangles with a sharp knife. Bake at 170°C (325°F) mark 3 for about 40 minutes, until pale straw in colour.
4. Leave in the tin for 5 minutes, cut into 8 triangles, then dredge with caster sugar. Remove from the tin when cold. Store in an airtight container.

MELTING MOMENTS

COUNTRYWIDE

These crisp, crunchy biscuits melt in the mouth – hence their name. A freshly baked batch will soon disappear.

MAKES ABOUT 24

---

100 g (4 oz) butter

75 g (3 oz) caster sugar

1 egg yolk

few drops of vanilla flavouring

150 g (5 oz) self-raising flour

crushed cornflakes

---

1. Grease two baking sheets.
2. Cream the butter and sugar together until pale and fluffy. Beat in the egg yolk.
3. Add the vanilla flavouring, stir in the flour to give a smooth dough and divide into about 24 portions.
4. Form each piece into a ball and roll in crushed cornflakes.
5. Place the balls on the baking sheets and bake in the oven at 190°C (375°F) mark 5 for 15–20 minutes.
6. Cool on the baking sheets for a few moments before lifting on to a wire rack.

VARIATION
Instead of cornflakes, use 50 g (2 oz) rolled oats. Press half a glacé cherry in the centre of each biscuit.

PETTICOAT TAILS. Rich shortbread triangles, with an unmistakable flavour of butter and meltingly short texture.

FUDGE. Homemade sweets make a treat for the family, or a lovely gift for sweet-toothed friends. There are several variations on the basic recipe, using coffee, walnuts, vanilla or cherry.

COFFEE FUDGE

COUNTRYWIDE

Fudge is a creamy sweet, made from milk, sugar and butter, with different flavourings. Coffee became popular in England in the 18th century, when it arrived here from Turkey, via Europe.

MAKES 50 SQUARES

300 ml (½ pint) fresh milk
550 g (4 oz) sugar
100 g (4 oz) butter
45 ml (3 tbsp) coffee essence

1. Pour the milk into a medium heavy-based saucepan, with a sugar thermometer attached, and bring slowly to the boil. Add the sugar and butter. Heat slowly, stirring continuously, until the sugar dissolves and the butter melts. Bring to the boil, cover and boil for 2 minutes.
2. Uncover and continue to boil steadily, stirring occasionally, for 15–20 minutes, until the temperature reaches the soft ball stage 116°C (270°F), when a little of the mixture, dropped into a cup of cold water, forms a soft ball when rolled between finger and thumb.
3. Remove from the heat. Stir in the coffee flavouring and leave to cool for 5 minutes.
4. Beat the fudge until it just begins to lose its gloss and is thick.
5. Transfer to a greased 18 cm (7 inch) square tin. Mark into 50 squares when almost set. When firm and set, cut along the marked lines. Store in an airtight container.

VARIATIONS

WALNUT AND COFFEE FUDGE
Add 50 g (2 oz) chopped walnut pieces with the coffee flavouring.

VANILLA FUDGE
Omit the coffee essence and add 10 ml (2 tsp) vanilla flavouring.

CHERRY FUDGE
Omit the coffee essence and add 50 g (2 oz) chopped glacé cherries.

BUTTERSCOTCH

SCOTLAND

Real butterscotch is made from the simplest ingredients but has no equal for rich, smooth flavour. It's easiest to use a sugar thermometer so you know that the syrup has reached the right stage before adding the butter.

MAKES ABOUT 450 g (1 lb)

450 g (1 lb) demerara sugar
50 g (2 oz) unsalted butter

1. Put the sugar and 150 ml (¼ pint) water in a large heavy-based saucepan, with a sugar thermometer attached, and heat gently until dissolved.
2. Bring to the boil, then boil until the temperature reaches the soft crack stage 132°C (270°F), when a little of the syrup dropped into cold water separates into hard but not brittle threads. Brush down the sides of the pan occasionally with a pastry brush dipped in cold water.
3. Add the butter a little at a time, stirring until dissolved before adding more. Pour into a greased 18 cm (7 inch) square tin. Mark into squares when almost set. When set, break along the marked lines. Store in an airtight container.

TREACLE TOFFEE

THE NORTH

Many areas of the North have their own recipes for toffee, ranging from the dark, sticky Harrogate variety to the lighter, lemon-flavoured Everton version. When making this recipe keep brushing the sides of the pan with water to stop sugar crystals forming. Do not stir the mixture or it will crystallise.

MAKES ABOUT 800 g (1¾ lb)

450 g (1 lb) demerara sugar
75 g (3 oz) butter
1.25 ml (¼ tsp) cream of tartar
100 g (4 oz) black treacle
100 g (4 oz) golden syrup

1. Put the sugar and 150 ml (¼ pint) water in a large heavy-based saucepan, with a sugar thermometer attached, and heat gently until dissolved. Add the remaining ingredients and bring to the boil.
2. Boil until the temperature reaches the soft crack stage 132°C (270°F), when a little of the syrup dropped in cold water separates into hard but not brittle threads. Brush down the sides of the pan occasionally with a pastry brush dipped in water. Do not stir.
3. Pour into a greased 18 cm (7 inch) square tin. Cool for 5 minutes and mark into squares with an oiled knife when almost set. When set, break the toffee into squares and wrap in waxed papers or foil. Store in an airtight container.

VARIATION

TOFFEE APPLES
1. Wipe 6–8 medium eating apples and push a wooden cocktail stick into each core, making sure they are secure.
2. Make the Treacle Toffee, completing steps 1 and 2, and boiling until the temperature reaches 143°C (290°F).
3. Dip the apples into the toffee, twirl around for a few seconds to allow excess toffee to drip off, then leave to cool and set on a buttered baking sheet or waxed paper. Do not keep for more than 1 day.

ABOVE
BUTTERSCOTCH. Glossy brown squares for sucking slowly to enjoy the full flavour.

BELOW
TREACLE TOFFEE. A mixture of golden syrup and treacle makes a slightly paler toffee than usual.

BREADS &
TEABREADS

There's nothing quite like the aroma of baked bread to whet the appetite. Loaves come in all shapes and sizes, are plain or fancy and are surprisingly easy to make at home. There is a vast selection from which to choose, from Barm Brack and the traditional British cottage loaf to marmalade teabread and potato scones.

COTTAGE LOAF

COUNTRYWIDE

Bread-making is soothing and enjoyable, although you do need a lot of time to allow for the rising process. This loaf can be made with wholemeal or plain flour and, as it is baked in the traditional cottage loaf shape, you will not need a loaf tin but just a baking sheet.

MAKES 1 LARGE LOAF

15 g (½ oz) fresh yeast or 7.5 ml (1½ tsp) dried

300 ml (½ pint) warm fresh milk

450 g (1 lb) malted brown flour, strong wholemeal flour or strong white flour

5 ml (1 tsp) salt

beaten egg, to glaze

poppy or sesame seeds for sprinkling (optional)

1. Dissolve the fresh yeast in the milk. If using dried yeast, sprinkle it into the milk and leave in a warm place for 15 minutes, until frothy.
2. Put the flour and salt in a bowl. Make a well in the centre, then pour in the yeast liquid. Beat well together until the dough leaves the sides of the bowl clean.
3. Turn on to a lightly floured surface and knead for about 10 minutes, until smooth and elastic. Place in a clean bowl. Cover with a clean tea-towel and leave in a warm place for about 1 hour, until doubled in size.
4. Turn the dough on to a floured surface and knead lightly. Cut off one-third of the dough and shape into a round. Shape the remaining dough into a round. Place the larger round on to a greased baking sheet and brush with a little water. Place the smaller round on top.
5. Push the lightly floured handle of a wooden spoon down through the centre of the loaf right to the bottom. Using a sharp knife, slash the dough at 5 cm (2 inch) intervals around the top and bottom edges to make a decorative pattern. Cover and leave in a warm place for about 30 minutes, until doubled in size.
6. Brush with a little beaten egg to glaze and sprinkle with poppy or sesame seeds, if liked. Bake at 230°C (450°F) mark 8 for 10 minutes, then reduce the oven temperature to 200°C (400°F) mark 6 and bake for a further 20–25 minutes, until the loaf sounds hollow when tapped on the bottom. Transfer to a wire rack to cool.

COTTAGE ROLLS

Makes 6

Complete steps 1, 2 and 3. Divide the dough into 6, then cut off one-third of each piece. Shape the rolls as in steps 4 and 5. Complete the recipe, baking the rolls at 230°C (450°F) mark 8 for 10 minutes, then at 200°C (400°F) mark 6 for about 10 minutes. Transfer to a wire rack to cool.

PLAITS

Makes 6

Complete steps 1, 2 and 3. Divide the dough into 6, then divide each piece into 3. Shape them into 3 long rolls about 30.5 cm (12 inches) long. Pinch the ends together and plait loosely, then pinch the other ends together. Complete steps 5 and 6, baking the rolls at 230°C (450°F) mark 8 for 10 minutes, then at 200°C (400°F) mark 6 for about 10 minutes. Transfer to a wire rack to cool.

KNOTS

Makes 6

Complete steps 1, 2 and 3. Divide the dough into 6. Shape each piece into a thin roll and tie into a knot. Complete steps 5 and 6, baking the rolls at 230°C (450°F) mark 8 for 10 minutes, then at 200°C (400°F) mark 6 for about 10 minutes. Transfer to a wire rack to cool.

TREFOILS

Makes 6

Complete steps 1, 2 and 3. Divide the dough into 6, then divide each piece into 3. Roll each into a ball and place the 3 balls grouped together. Complete steps 5 and 6, baking the rolls at 230°C (450°F) mark 8 for 10 minutes, then 200°C (400°F) mark 6 for about 10 minutes. Transfer to a wire rack to cool.

BARM BRACK

NORTHERN IRELAND

Similar breads, using a fruity yeast dough, are made in other parts of Britain. Scotland has its Selkirk bannock and Wales has bara brith, which means speckled bread, a reference to the fruit in the mixture. In Ireland, barm brack was traditionally eaten at Hallowe'en.

MAKES 1 LARGE LOAF

15 g (½ oz) fresh yeast or 7.5 ml (1½ tsp) dried and a pinch of sugar
25 g (1 oz) butter
450 g (1 lb) strong white flour
60 ml (4 tbsp) caster sugar
2.5 ml (½ tsp) ground ginger
freshly grated nutmeg
175 g (6 oz) sultanas
175 g (6 oz) currants
50 g (2 oz) chopped candied peel

1. Blend the fresh yeast with 300 ml (½ pint) warm water. If using dried yeast, sprinkle it into 300 ml (½ pint) warm water with the pinch of sugar and leave in a warm place for 15 minutes, until frothy.
2. Rub the butter into the flour, then stir in half of the sugar, the ginger and nutmeg to taste. Stir in the fruit and peel and mix well together. Make a well in the centre and stir in the yeast liquid.
3. Beat well together until the dough leaves the sides of the bowl clean. Turn on to a lightly floured surface and knead well for about 10 minutes, until smooth and elastic. Place in a clean bowl. Cover with a clean tea-towel and leave in a warm place for about 1 hour, until doubled in size.
4. Turn the dough on to a floured surface and knead lightly. Shape the dough into a large round or oval and

place on a greased baking sheet. Cover and leave in a warm place for about 30 minutes, until doubled in size.
5. Bake at 230°C (450°F) mark 8 for 15 minutes, then reduce the oven temperature to 200°C (400°F) mark 6 and bake for a further 20–30 minutes, until the bread sounds hollow when tapped on the bottom.
6. Dissolve the remaining sugar in 15 ml (1 tbsp) hot water and brush over the loaf to glaze. Return to the oven for 2–3 minutes, then transfer to a wire rack to cool.

KENTISH HUFFKINS

THE SOUTH-EAST

These are oval, flat loaves, with a deep indentation in the centre and a soft crust. The recipe is traditional to Kent, and is softer, with a more open texture than ordinary bread. Eat them sliced and buttered at tea time.

MAKES 12

✳

15 g (½ oz) fresh yeast or 7.5 ml (1½ tsp) dried and a pinch of sugar
about 225 ml (8 fl oz) warm fresh milk and water mixed
450 g (1 lb) plain flour
5 ml (1 tsp) salt
10 ml (2 tsp) sugar
50 g (2 oz) butter, diced

1. Blend the fresh yeast with the milk and water. If using dried yeast, sprinkle it into the milk and water with the sugar and leave for 15 minutes, until frothy.
2. Put the flour, salt and sugar in a bowl and rub in the butter. Make a well in the centre, then pour in the yeast liquid. Beat well together to form a dough that leaves the sides of the bowl clean.
3. Turn on to a floured surface and knead well for about 10 minutes, until smooth and elastic. Place in a clean bowl. Cover with a clean tea-towel and leave to rise in a warm place for 1 hour, until doubled in size.
4. Divide the dough in 12, then roll into oval cakes about 1 cm (½ inch) thick. Place on 2 greased baking sheets, cover and leave for about 30 minutes, until doubled in size. Before baking make a deep thumb mark in the centre. Bake at 220°C (425°F) mark 7 for 15–20 minutes, until golden brown. Wrap in a warm tea-towel and leave to cool. (This will keep the crust soft.)

VARIATION

Huffkin – In step 4, shape the dough into one large oval cake. Complete step 4, baking for 20–25 minutes.

LEFT
BREAD ROLLS. A delightful basketful of shaped rolls, made with strong white, wholemeal and malted brown flours. Plump, shiny plaits, pretty knots and chubby little cottage rolls. A sprinkling of poppy seeds or sesame seeds adds a decorative touch.

SAGE AND ONION BREAD

COUNTRYWIDE

This is a mouth-watering savoury bread that fills the kitchen with an aroma of herbs as it bakes. Serve it warm with soup, or well buttered with cheese or pâté and salad, for a simple lunch. Using dried sage will still give good results.

MAKES 2 SMALL LOAVES

SAGE AND ONION BREAD. The cracked wheat topping gives an appetising crunch to this deliciously flavoured, close-textured loaf.

15 g (½ oz) fresh yeast or 7.5 ml (1½ tsp) dried

300 ml (½ pint) warm fresh milk

1 large onion, skinned and finely chopped

25 g (1 oz) butter

225 g (8 oz) strong white flour

225 g (8 oz) strong wholemeal flour

5 ml (1 tsp) salt

pepper

30 ml (2 tbsp) chopped fresh sage or 5 ml (1 tsp) dried

cracked wheat for sprinkling

1. Blend the fresh yeast with the milk. If using dried yeast, sprinkle it into the milk and leave in a warm place for 15 minutes, until frothy.
2. Meanwhile, put the onion and the butter in a small saucepan, cover and cook gently for about 5 minutes, until the onion is soft and transparent but not browned.
3. Put the flours, salt, pepper and sage in a large bowl and mix together. Make a well in the centre, then pour in the softened onion and the butter and the yeast liquid. Beat well together until the dough leaves the sides of the bowl clean.
4. Turn on to a lightly floured surface and knead well for about 10 minutes, until smooth and elastic. Place in a clean bowl. Cover with a clean tea-towel and leave in a warm place for about 1 hour, until doubled in size.
5. Turn the dough on to a floured surface and knead lightly. Divide into two, shape into rounds and place on a large greased baking sheet.
6. Brush with a little milk and sprinkle with cracked wheat. Cover and leave in a warm place for about 30 minutes, until doubled in size. Bake at 230°C (450°F) mark 8 for 15 minutes, then reduce the oven temperature to 200°C (400°F) mark 6 and bake for a further 15 minutes. When cooked the loaves will be well risen and golden brown, and sound hollow if tapped on the bottom. Cool slightly and serve warm, or turn on to a wire rack and leave to cool completely.

SODA BREAD

NORTHERN IRELAND

Round loaves of soda bread were traditionally baked on a hot griddle over the fire and had a lovely crisp crust. The bread is moist, close-textured and delicious, with a distinctive flavour which comes from the soda and buttermilk.

MAKES 1 LARGE LOAF

450 g (1 lb) plain wholemeal flour

100 g (4 oz) plain flour

50 g (2 oz) rolled oats

5 ml (1 tsp) bicarbonate of soda

5 ml (1 tsp) salt

about 450 ml (¾ pint) buttermilk

1. Put the flours, oats, bicarbonate of soda and salt in a large bowl and mix together. Add enough buttermilk to mix to a soft dough.
2. Knead very lightly, then shape into a large round and place on a greased baking sheet. Cut a deep cross in the top. Bake at 230°C (450°F) mark 8 for 15 minutes, then reduce the oven temperature to 200°C (400°F)

mark 6 and bake for a further 20–25 minutes or until the loaf sounds hollow when tapped on the bottom. Eat while still warm.

TO MICROWAVE

 Complete step 1. Knead very lightly, then shape into a large round. Place on a greased microwave baking tray or large flat plate and cut a deep cross in the top. Stand on a microwave roasting rack and cook on HIGH for 9–10 minutes or until the bread is well risen and the surface looks dry, turning 2 or 3 times during cooking. Turn the bread over and cook on HIGH for a further 1–1½ minutes or until the bottom looks dry. Eat while still warm.

HERBED GRANARY BREAD STICK

COUNTRYWIDE

This is one recipe where dried herbs are no substitute for fresh, as they just cannot provide the herby flavour that makes these bread sticks so delicious, especially if they are served warm.

MAKES 1 BREAD STICK

❄

15 g (½ oz) fresh yeast or 7.5 ml (1½ tsp) dried and a pinch of sugar
450 g (1 lb) Granary flour
5 ml (1 tsp) salt
30 ml (2 tbsp) chopped fresh parsley
30 ml (2 tbsp) chopped fresh mixed herbs, such as mint, thyme, marjoram, rosemary, chives
1 garlic clove, skinned and crushed (optional)
10 ml (2 tsp) clear honey
fine oatmeal for sprinkling

1. Blend the fresh yeast with 300 ml (½ pint) warm water. If using dried yeast, sprinkle it into 300 ml (½ pint) warm water with the sugar and leave in a warm place for 15 minutes, until frothy.
2. Put the flour, salt and herbs in a bowl and mix together. Make a well in the centre. Stir the garlic, if using, and the honey into the yeast liquid, then pour into the centre of the dry ingredients. Beat together until the dough leaves the sides of the bowl clean.
3. Turn on to a lightly floured surface and knead well for about 10 minutes, until smooth and elastic. Place in a clean bowl. Cover with a clean tea-towel and leave in a warm place for about 1 hour, until doubled in size.
4. Turn the dough on to a floured surface and knead lightly. Shape into a sausage shape about 40 cm (16 inches) long. Place on a greased baking sheet. Cut several slashes on the top of the loaf. Cover and leave in a warm place for about 30 minutes, until doubled in size.
5. Brush with a little milk and sprinkle with oatmeal. Bake at 230°C (450°F) mark 8 for 10 minutes, then reduce the oven temperature to 200°C (400°F) mark 6 and bake for a further 15–20 minutes. Leave to cool on a wire rack.

HERBED GRANARY BREAD STICK. Perfect for bread-and-cheese lunches, or as a partner for home-made soups, this crusty loaf with its fragrance of herbs is very moreish.

MARMALADE TEABREAD

COUNTRYWIDE

A moist, spicy cake with a fruity flavour. The tradition of making good, plain cakes grew up in the country, where a cake was part of an early supper, eaten at the end of the day in winter or before a last bout of work in summer.

MAKES 8–10 SLICES

200 g (7 oz) plain flour
5 ml (1 tsp) ground ginger
5 ml (1 tsp) baking powder
50 g (2 oz) butter, diced
50 g (2 oz) light soft brown sugar
60 ml (4 tbsp) orange marmalade
1 egg, beaten
75 ml (3 tbsp) fresh milk
25 g (1 oz) candied orange peel, chopped

1. Grease a 750 ml (1½ pint) loaf tin, then line the base with greaseproof paper and grease the paper.
2. Put the flour, ginger and baking powder in a bowl and rub in the butter until the mixture resembles fine breadcrumbs. Stir in the sugar.
3. Mix together the marmalade, egg and most of the milk. Stir into the dry ingredients and mix to a soft dough. Add the rest of the milk, if necessary.
4. Turn the mixture into the prepared tin, level the surface and press the candied orange peel on top. Bake at 170°C (325°F) mark 3 for about 1¼ hours or until golden brown. Turn out on to a wire rack to cool.

TO MICROWAVE

 Grease a 1.7 litre (3 pint) loaf dish and line the base with greaseproof paper. Complete steps 2 and 3, adding an extra 30 ml (2 tbsp) fresh milk. Turn the mixture into the prepared dish, level the surface and press the candied peel on top. Cover with kitchen paper, stand on a roasting rack and cook on HIGH for 6 minutes until well risen and firm to the touch. Complete step 4.

CHEESE AND WALNUT LOAF

THE WEST

This tasty teabread combines two West Country specialities which are now readily available throughout the country: walnuts, which were originally grown in the Vale of Pewsey in Wiltshire, and Cheddar cheese. Use a mature version for a stronger taste.

MAKES 1 LARGE LOAF

15 g (½ oz) fresh yeast or 7.5 ml (1½ tsp) dried and a pinch of sugar

450 g (1 lb) strong wholemeal flour
5 ml (1 tsp) salt
2.5 ml (½ tsp) paprika
7.5 ml (1½ tsp) mustard powder
175 g (6 oz) Cheddar cheese, grated
100 g (4 oz) walnut pieces, finely chopped
45 ml (3 tbsp) chopped fresh mixed herbs or 5 ml (1 tsp) dried

1. Grease a 900 g (2 lb) loaf tin.
2. Blend the fresh yeast with 300 ml (½ pint) warm water. If using dried yeast, sprinkle it into 300 ml (½ pint) warm water with the sugar and leave in a warm place for 15 minutes, until frothy.
3. Put the flour, salt, paprika, mustard powder, 100 g (4 oz) of the cheese, the walnuts and the herbs in a large bowl and mix together. Make a well in the centre, then pour in the yeast liquid. Mix together to make a smooth dough that leaves the sides of the bowl clean.
4. Turn the dough on to a lightly floured surface and knead well for about 10 minutes, until smooth and elastic. Place in a clean bowl. Cover with a clean tea-towel and leave in a warm place for about 1 hour, until doubled in size.
5. Turn the dough on to a floured surface and knead lightly. Shape the dough to fit the prepared tin. Cover and leave in a warm place for 30 minutes, until the dough rises almost to the top of the tin.
6. Sprinkle with the remaining cheese and bake at 190°C (375°F) mark 5 for 45 minutes, until well risen and the loaf sounds hollow when tapped on the bottom. Turn out on to a wire rack to cool.

MARBLED CHOCOLATE TEABREAD

COUNTRYWIDE

The Victorians were very fond of marbled cakes. The recipe is so called because the feathery swirls of chocolate that are revealed when it is sliced make a pattern similar to that of Italian marble.

MAKES ABOUT 10 SLICES

225 g (8 oz) butter
225 g (8 oz) caster sugar
4 eggs, beaten
225 g (8 oz) self-raising flour
finely grated rind of 1 large orange
15 ml (1 tbsp) orange juice
few drops orange flower water (optional)
75 g (3 oz) plain chocolate
15 ml (1 tbsp) cocoa powder

1. Grease a 900 ml (2 pint) loaf tin and line the base and sides with greaseproof paper.
2. Cream the butter and sugar together until pale and

fluffy, then gradually beat in the eggs, beating well after each addition. Fold in the flour.

3. Transfer half of the mixture to another bowl and beat in the orange rind, juice and orange flower water, if using.

4. Break the chocolate into pieces, put into a small bowl and place over a pan of simmering water. Stir until the chocolate melts. Stir into the remaining cake mixture with the cocoa powder.

5. Put alternate spoonfuls of the two mixtures into the prepared tin. Use a knife to swirl through the mixture to make a marbled effect, then level the surface.

6. Bake at 180°C (350°F) mark 4 for 1¼–1½ hours,

until well risen and firm to the touch. Turn out on to a wire rack to cool. Serve cut in slices.

TO MICROWAVE

☑ Grease a 1.7 litre (3 pint) loaf dish and line the base with greaseproof paper. Complete steps 2 and 3, adding an extra 30 ml (2 tbsp) fresh milk. Break the chocolate into a small bowl and cook on LOW for 2–3 minutes until melted. Complete the remainder of step 4, adding 15 ml (1 tbsp) milk, and step 5. Cover with kitchen paper, stand on a roasting rack and cook on HIGH for 10 minutes, until well risen and firm to the touch.

LEFT
MARMALADE
TEABREAD. Serve this plain but well-flavoured bread thickly sliced and generously buttered.

RIGHT
MARBLED CHOCOLATE
TEABREAD. Seen at its best sliced, and arranged on a plate, to show off the intriguing pattern.

FLOUR

*Flour is
the basic ingredient in baking and
bread making. A wide range of
flours is available, each suitable
for specific uses. All contain
fibre and are a valuable source of
B vitamins.*

*Store flour in a cool, dry place in
a container with a tight-fitting
lid. Plain white flour keeps for up
to six months, self-raising for up
to three months. Wholemeal and
brown flour are best eaten within
two months.*

*There are three main types of
wheat flour:*

WHITE

*Most of the bran and wheatgerm
of the grain is removed. It is
available plain, for shortcrust
pastry, biscuits and thickening;
self-raising, with an added
raising agent, for cakes,
puddings and suet crust pastry;
and strong, with a high protein
content, for bread making, all
yeast cookery and puff and flaky
pastry. It can also be used with
wholemeal or brown flours
(below) for variety of colour,
flavour and texture.*

BROWN (also known as WHEATMEAL)

*Some of the bran and wheatgerm
is removed. Bread, pastries and
puddings using brown flour will
have a slightly darker colour and
heavier texture than those using
white. Available plain, self-
raising and strong.*

WHOLEMEAL or WHOLEWHEAT

*This is made from the entire
wheat grain. Bread made
entirely from this has a close
texture and slightly nutty taste.
Available plain, self-raising and
strong.*

*Both brown and wholemeal
flours are available
STONEGROUND. The
wheat is ground between two
stones which heats the flour and
gives it a nutty flavour and
coarser texture. Use as for
brown and wholemeal flours.*

POTATO SCONES
THE NORTH AND SCOTLAND

*These scones need to be made from floury potatoes such as
Pentland Squire or Maris Piper which will mash well without
lumps. You can use leftover cold cooked potatoes, but for the
best and lightest flavour boil them freshly. If using leftovers,
warm them in a conventional or microwave oven before
working in the flour and proceeding with the recipe.*

MAKES ABOUT 12

450 g (1 lb) floury potatoes, peeled
5 ml (1 tsp) salt
25 g (1 oz) butter
about 100 g (4 oz) plain flour

1. Cook the potatoes in boiling salted water for about
20 minutes or until tender. Drain and mash until
smooth. Add the salt and butter while the potatoes are
still hot, then work in enough flour to make a stiff
dough.
2. Turn on to a floured surface, knead lightly and roll
out until 0.5 cm (¼ inch) thick. Cut into 6.5 cm
(2½ inch) rounds.
3. Cook on a greased griddle or heavy-based frying pan
for 4–5 minutes on each side or until golden brown.
Serve hot with butter.

LARDY CAKE
THE WEST

*Warm or cold, this recipe is sweet, filling and delicious.
Lardy cake originates from Wiltshire, and in the West
Country local bakers still make it to their own recipes,
cramming in as much lard, sugar and fruit as they or their
customers choose.*

MAKES ABOUT 12 SLICES

15 g (½ oz) fresh yeast, or 7.5 ml (1½ tsp) dried and a pinch of sugar
450 g (1 lb) strong white flour
5 ml (1 tsp) salt
75 g (3 oz) lard, diced
75 g (3 oz) butter, diced
175 g (6 oz) mixed sultanas and currants
50 g (2 oz) chopped mixed peel
50 g (2 oz) sugar

1. Grease a 20.5 × 25 cm (8 × 10 inch) roasting tin.
2. Blend the fresh yeast with 300 ml (½ pint) warm
water. If using dried yeast, sprinkle it into 300 ml
(½ pint) warm water with the sugar and leave for
15 minutes, until frothy.
3. Put the flour and salt in a bowl and rub in 15 g
(½ oz) of the lard. Make a well in the centre and pour in
the yeast liquid. Beat together to make a dough that
leaves the sides of the bowl clean, adding more water if
necessary.

4. Turn on to a lightly floured surface and knead well
for about 10 minutes, until smooth and elastic. Place in
a clean bowl. Cover with a clean tea-towel and leave in
a warm place for about 1 hour, until doubled in size.
5. Turn the dough on to a floured surface and roll out to
a rectangle about 0.5 cm (¼ inch) thick. Dot one-third
of the remaining lard and the butter over the surface of
the dough. Sprinkle over one-third of the fruit, peel and
sugar. Fold the dough in three, folding the bottom third
up and the top third down. Give a quarter-turn, then
repeat the process twice more.
6. Roll the dough out to fit the prepared tin. Put in the
tin, cover and leave in a warm place for 30 minutes,
until puffy. Score the top in a criss-cross pattern with a
knife, then bake at 220°C (425°F) mark 7 for about
30 minutes, until well risen and golden brown. Turn
out and serve immediately or leave to cool on a wire
rack. Serve plain or with butter.

MALTED FRUIT TEABREAD
COUNTRYWIDE

*Fruit loaves keep well and the flavour actually improves if
they are kept for a day or two before eating. Malt is the raw
material from which beer and malt whisky are made and it's
this that makes this sticky cake particularly moreish. Serve
thinly sliced and spread with butter.*

MAKES 10 SLICES

225 g (8 oz) self-raising flour
pinch of salt
30 ml (2 tbsp) dark soft brown sugar
175 g (6 oz) mixed dried fruit
30 ml (2 tbsp) golden syrup
30 ml (2 tbsp) malt extract
150 ml (¼ pint) fresh milk

1. Grease a 900 ml (2 pint) loaf tin and line the base
and sides with greaseproof paper.
2. Put the flour, salt, sugar and fruit in a bowl and mix
together. Make a well in the centre.
3. Put the syrup, malt extract and milk in a saucepan
and heat gently until melted. Pour into the well in the
centre of the dry ingredients, then beat thoroughly
together. Add a little extra milk, if necessary, to make a
fairly sticky consistency.
4. Turn the mixture into the prepared tin and bake at
170°C (325°F) mark 3 for about 1¼ hours. Turn out and
leave to cool on a wire rack. When completely cold,
wrap in greaseproof paper and foil and store for 1 day
before eating. Serve sliced, spread with butter.

OAST CAKES

THE SOUTH-EAST

Named after the distinctive hop-drying houses that dot the Kent countryside, these cakes were originally eaten after the crop had been gathered. They are like thin, fried scones, and are good served lightly dredged with sugar or with cherry jam.

MAKES 12

✳

225 g (8 oz) plain flour

2.5 ml (½ tsp) salt

2.5 ml (½ tsp) baking powder

50 g (2 oz) lard, diced

40 g (1½ oz) caster sugar

75 g (3 oz) currants

45 ml (3 tbsp) vegetable oil

25 g (1 oz) butter

1. Put the flour, salt and baking powder into a bowl, then rub in the lard until the mixture resembles fine breadcrumbs.
2. Stir in the sugar and currants, then mix with 45–60 ml (3–4 tbsp) water to make a soft dough.
3. Turn out on to a lightly floured surface and roll out until 1 cm (½ inch) thick. Using a 5 cm (2 inch) plain cutter, cut out 12 rounds.
4. Heat the oil and the butter in a heavy-based frying pan and fry the cakes for 2–3 minutes on each side, until golden brown. Drain on kitchen paper. Eat warm or very fresh.

CHEESE AND CHIVE SCONES

THE NORTH

Crumbly Lancashire cheese is ideal in cooking. Combined with the onion flavour of freshly snipped chives, these scones are deliciously savoury. To increase flavour try spreading them with Welsh butter, which has a distinctive flavour.

MAKES 10

✳

225 g (8 oz) self-raising flour

pinch of salt

50 g (2 oz) butter, diced

100 g (4 oz) Lancashire cheese, grated

15 ml (1 tbsp) snipped fresh chives

150 ml (¼ pint) fresh milk and extra for brushing

1. Put the flour and salt into a bowl and rub in the butter until the mixture resembles fine breadcrumbs. Stir in 50 g (2 oz) of the cheese and the chives.
2. Add the milk and mix to form a soft dough, then knead quickly until smooth.
3. Roll out on a floured work surface until 1 cm (½ inch) thick. Cut into 10 rounds with a 5 cm (2 inch) plain cutter and brush the tops with milk. Transfer to baking sheets.
4. Bake at 230°C (450°F) mark 8 for 7–10 minutes, until well risen and golden brown.
5. Immediately put the remaining cheese on top of the scones and allow to melt before serving hot or cold.

CHEESE AND CHIVE SCONES. So simple to make, and so mouthwateringly good, these cheesy scones are the ideal teatime treat.

BOXTY BREAD

NORTHERN IRELAND

A traditional potato bread from Ireland, where potatoes were used to make cakes, dumplings and pancakes as well. Boxty would be served with milk and salt, and children sometimes called it 'dippity'.

MAKES 4 SMALL LOAVES

700 g (1½ lb) old potatoes, peeled
salt and pepper
25 g (1 oz) butter
150 ml (¼ pint) fresh milk
350 g (12 oz) self-raising flour
5 ml (1 tsp) baking powder

BOXTY BREAD. You'd never guess to look at it, that the main ingredient of this enticing loaf is potatoes. The texture and flavour are excellent; it's well worth trying for a change.

1. Roughly chop half the potatoes and cook in boiling salted water until tender, then drain and mash with the butter.

2. Grate the remaining potatoes into a bowl and mix with the milk. Beat in the cooked potato and salt and pepper to taste.

3. Sieve the flour and baking powder on to the potato mixture and beat together to make a dough. If the mixture is too soft, add a little extra flour.

4. Turn out on to a floured surface and knead lightly, then shape into four 10 cm (4 inch) flat round cakes. Put on to a greased baking sheet and mark each with a cross. Bake at 200°C (400°F) mark 6 for about 30 minutes, until well risen and golden brown. Break each loaf into quarters and serve warm spread with butter.

HOT CROSS BUNS

COUNTRYWIDE

A much-loved recipe, hot cross buns were traditionally eaten for breakfast on Good Friday and are still sold widely at Easter time. They were first made in the 18th century, when they were extra rich and spicy, and marked with a cross as a reminder of the festival.

MAKES 12

15 g (½ oz) fresh yeast or 7.5 ml (1½ tsp) dried
300 ml (½ pint) warm milk
450 g (1 lb) strong white flour
5 ml (1 tsp) salt
5 ml (1 tsp) ground mixed spice
5 ml (1 tsp) ground cinnamon
2.5 ml (½ tsp) grated nutmeg
50 g (2 oz) caster sugar
75 g (3 oz) butter
75 g (3 oz) currants
25 g (1 oz) chopped mixed peel
1 egg, beaten
50 g (2 oz) plain flour
For the glaze
60 ml (4 tbsp) fresh milk and water, mixed
45 ml (3 tbsp) caster sugar

1. Dissolve the fresh yeast in the milk. If using dried yeast, sprinkle it into the milk and leave in a warm place for about 15 minutes, until frothy.

2. Put the strong flour, salt, spices and sugar in a bowl. Rub in 50 g (2 oz) of the butter, then stir in the currants and peel. Make a well in the centre and stir in the egg and yeast liquid and beat together to a soft dough.

3. Turn on to a lightly floured surface and knead for about 10 minutes, until smooth and elastic and no longer sticky. Put into a clean bowl, cover with a clean tea-towel and leave to rise in a warm place for about 1 hour, until doubled in size.

4. Turn the dough out on to a floured surface and knead for 2–3 minutes. Divide the dough into 12 pieces and shape into round buns.

5. Place on greased baking sheets, cover and leave in a warm place for about 30 minutes, until doubled in size.

6. Meanwhile, make the pastry for the crosses. Put the plain flour in a bowl and rub in the remaining butter until the mixture resembles fine breadcrumbs. Stir in enough water to bind the mixture together. Knead lightly.

7. Roll out the pastry thinly on a floured surface and cut into thin strips about 9 cm (3½ inches) long. Dampen the pastry strips and lay two on each bun to make a cross.

8. Bake at 190°C (375°F) mark 5 for 15–20 minutes, until golden brown. For the glaze, heat the milk and water with the sugar. Brush the hot buns twice with glaze, then transfer to a wire rack to cool.

CHELSEA BUNS

THE SOUTH-EAST

The shop from which these buns originated would, in its heyday, sell as many as 250,000 buns in one day. The owner, Richard Hand, was known as 'Captain Bun'. The buns are easily recognised, as the dough is baked in a flat coil and given a shiny sugar glaze.

MAKES 12

✳ 〽

15 g (½ oz) fresh yeast or 7.5 ml (1½ tsp) dried
100 ml (4 fl oz) warm fresh milk
225 g (8 oz) strong white flour
2.5 ml (½ tsp) salt
40 g (1½ oz) butter, diced
1 egg, beaten
100 g (4 oz) mixed dried fruit
50 g (2 oz) light soft brown sugar
clear honey, to glaze

1. Grease a 17.5 cm (7 inch) square tin.
2. Blend the fresh yeast with the milk. If using dried yeast, sprinkle it into the milk and leave in a warm place for 15 minutes, until frothy.
3. Put the flour and salt in a bowl, then rub in 25 g (1 oz) of the butter until the mixture resembles fine breadcrumbs. Make a well in the centre, pour in the yeast liquid and the egg, then beat together until the mixture forms a dough that leaves sides of bowl clean.
4. Turn on to a lightly floured surface and knead well for 10 minutes, until smooth and elastic. Cover with a clean tea-towel and leave in a warm place for about 1 hour, until doubled in size.
5. Knead the dough lightly on a floured surface, then roll it out to a large rectangle, measuring about 30×23 cm (12×9 inches). Mix the dried fruit and sugar together. Melt the remaining butter, then brush over the dough. Scatter with the fruit mixture, leaving a 2.5 cm (1 inch) border around the edges.
6. Roll the dough up tightly like a Swiss roll, starting at a long edge. Press the edges together to seal them, then cut the roll into 12 slices. Place the rolls cut side uppermost in a greased 17.5 cm (7 inch) square tin. Cover and leave in a warm place for 30 minutes, until doubled in size.

7. Bake the rolls at 190°C (375°F) mark 5 for 30 minutes, until they are well risen and golden brown. Brush them with the honey while still hot. Leave them to cool slightly in the tin before turning out. Serve the Chelsea Buns warm.

TO MICROWAVE

〽 Complete steps 2, 3, 4, 5 and 6, placing the rolls in a greased 20.5 cm (8 inch) round dish. Complete the remainder of step 6. Stand on a roasting rack and cook on HIGH for 6–8 minutes, until well risen and firm to the touch. Leave to stand for 10 minutes, then turn out, brush all over with honey and brown under a hot grill. Serve warm.

CHELSEA BUNS. Wonderfuly sticky and packed with juicy dried fruit, these buns will disappear as fast as you can bake them.

Cut the rolled Chelsea bun dough into slices.

GRIDDLE PANCAKES.
What could be nicer than
these little pancakes, cooked
while you wait and eaten fresh
and hot, the minute they're
ready.

GRIDDLE PANCAKES

THE NORTH

Today's cookers make cooking on a griddle much less of a hit and miss business than when the griddle or bakestone was perched over the coals of the fire. These pancakes or drop scones should be eaten as soon as they are cooked. They are quick and easy to make but don't reheat well.

MAKES 15–18

100 g (4 oz) self-raising flour
30 ml (2 tbsp) caster sugar

1 egg, beaten
150 ml (¼ pint) fresh milk

1. Mix the flour and sugar. Make a well in the centre and stir in the egg, with enough of the milk to make a batter the consistency of thick cream. The mixing should be done as quickly and lightly as possible.
2. Drop the mixture in spoonfuls on to a greased hot griddle or heavy-based frying pan. For round pancakes, drop it from the point of the spoon, for oval ones, drop from the side.
3. Keep the griddle at a steady heat and when bubbles rise to the surface of the pancakes and burst, after 2–3 minutes, turn the pancakes over with a palette knife. Continue cooking for a further 2–3 minutes,

until golden brown on the other side.
4. Wrap the cooked pancakes in a clean tea-towel to keep them warm. Repeat with the remaining mixture to make 15–18 pancakes. Eat while still warm with butter or with golden syrup or honey.

CINNAMON TOAST

COUNTRYWIDE

Sugar and spice are extremely nice in this old-fashioned nursery tea-time recipe, which still tastes just as good today. You can substitute 2.5 ml (½ tsp) ground mixed spice, ground ginger or coriander, or a little grated nutmeg for the cinnamon.

SERVES 2

4 slices of bread

5 ml (1 tsp) ground cinnamon

30 ml (2 tbsp) caster sugar

butter for spreading

1. Toast the bread on one side only. Meanwhile, mix the cinnamon and sugar together.
2. Generously butter the untoasted side of the bread and sprinkle with the cinnamon sugar.
3. Grill until the mixture begins to melt. Cut into fingers and serve immediately.

MUFFINS

THE SOUTH-EAST

The muffin man hasn't been seen in the streets for many years, but this is an authentic recipe to make yourself. The correct way to toast muffins is not to split them and toast the two halves separately, as this makes them tough. Instead, cut them open, then close together again and toast slowly until warm right through, before opening out and buttering generously.

MAKES ABOUT 12

15 g (½ oz) fresh yeast or 7.5 ml (1½ tsp) dried

300 ml (½ pint) warm fresh milk

450 g (1 lb) strong white flour

5 ml (1 tsp) salt

5 ml (1 tsp) plain flour, for dusting

5 ml (1 tsp) semolina

1. Dissolve the yeast in the milk. If using dried yeast, sprinkle over the milk and leave in a warm place for about 15 minutes, until frothy.
2. Sift the flour and salt together, then make a well in the centre. Pour the yeast liquid into the well, draw in the flour and mix to a smooth dough.
3. Knead the dough on a lightly floured surface for about 10 minutes, until smooth and elastic. Place in a

clean bowl, cover with a tea-towel and leave in a warm place for about 1 hour, until doubled in size.
4. Roll out the dough on a lightly floured surface using a lightly floured rolling pin to about 0.5–1 cm (¼–½ inch) thick. Leave to rest, covered with a tea-towel, for 5 minutes, then cut into rounds with a 7.5 cm (3 inch) plain cutter.
5. Place the muffins on a well-floured baking sheet. Mix together the flour and semolina and use to dust the tops. Cover with a tea-towel and leave in a warm place until doubled in size.
6. Grease a griddle, electric griddle plate or heavy frying pan and heat over a moderate heat, until a cube of bread turns brown in 20 seconds.
7. Cook the muffins on the griddle or frying pan for about 7 minutes each side, until golden brown.

CINNAMON TOAST. The simplest things are often the best, and these buttery fingers, with their melting, sugary topping, are quite irresistible.

PRESERVES

Whether you have bought a quantity of fresh fruit and vegetables cheaply or have an abundance of produce from your garden, if you try the recipes in this chapter you can enjoy them all the year round. There are jams to go with scones, jellies, chutneys and pickles to accompany cooked meat and delicious vinegars to use in your favourite recipes.

STRAWBERRY CONSERVE

COUNTRYWIDE

Conserves are made from whole fruits, suspended in a thick, sweet syrup, and they do not set firmly. Use them as fillings for summer tarts, spread them on scones with cream or serve with custard or milk puddings as a quick dessert. Raspberries and loganberries can be conserved in the same way.

MAKES ABOUT 1.4 kg (3 lb)

1.4 kg (3 lb) strawberries, hulled

1.4 kg (3 lb) sugar

---

1. Place the strawberries in a large bowl in layers with the sugar. Cover and leave for 24 hours.
2. Put into a large saucepan and bring to the boil, stirring until the sugar dissolves. Boil rapidly for 5 minutes.
3. Return the mixture to the bowl, cover and leave in a cool place for a further 2 days.
4. Return to the pan again and boil rapidly for 10 minutes. Leave to cool for 15 minutes, then pot and cover as for jam.

TO MICROWAVE

 Halve the ingredients. Complete step 1. Cook on HIGH for 10 minutes or until the sugar dissolves, stirring frequently, then cook on HIGH for 2 minutes. Cover and leave for 2 days. Cook on HIGH for 10 minutes or until boiling, stirring frequently, then cook on HIGH for 4 minutes. Cool for 15 minutes, then pot and cover as for jam. Makes about 700 g (1½ lb).

RHUBARB AND GINGER JAM

COUNTRYWIDE

Forced, early rhubarb makes its appearance at the beginning of the year and by the late spring it is sprouting in gardens and the main crop is coming into the shops. Preserved ginger, which comes mostly from China, gives a good bite and extra flavour to the jam.

MAKES ABOUT 1.4 kg (3 lb)

1.1 kg (2½ lb) trimmed rhubarb, chopped

1.1 kg (2½ lb) sugar

juice of 2 lemons

25 g (1 oz) fresh root ginger

100 g (4 oz) preserved or crystallised ginger, chopped

---

1. Put the rhubarb in a large bowl in alternate layers with the sugar and lemon juice, cover and leave overnight.
2. Next day, bruise the root ginger slightly with a

weight or rolling pin, and tie it in a piece of muslin. Put the rhubarb mixture into a preserving pan with the muslin bag, bring to the boil and boil rapidly for 15 minutes.
3. Remove the muslin bag, add the preserved or crystallised ginger and boil for a further 5 minutes or until the rhubarb is clear. Test for a set and, when setting point is reached, take the pan off the heat and skim the surface with a slotted spoon. Pot and cover the jam.

TO MICROWAVE

 Halve the ingredients. Complete step 1. Prepare the ginger as in step 2 and add to the bowl with the fruit, juice and sugar. Cover and cook on HIGH for 10 minutes. Uncover and cook on HIGH for 20–25 minutes, stirring occasionally. Remove the muslin bag, add the ginger and cook for 2 minutes. Complete the recipe, cooking for an extra 4–5 minutes, if necessary. Makes about 700 g (1½ lb).

BRAMBLE AND APPLE JAM

COUNTRYWIDE

Wild blackberries, or brambles, have always been in plentiful supply in British hedgerows, and have been gathered and used in many different ways for centuries. Blackberries are also being more widely cultivated commercially and are often available on pick-your-own fruit farms, as well as being in the shops from the end of July until September.

MAKES ABOUT 4.5 kg (10 lb)

1.8 kg (4 lb) blackberries

700 g (1½ lb) peeled, cored and sliced cooking apples

2.7 kg (6 lb) sugar

a knob of butter

---

1. Put the blackberries in a large saucepan with 150 ml (¼ pint) water and simmer gently until soft.
2. Put the apples in a separate preserving pan with 150 ml (¼ pint) water and simmer gently until soft. Pulp with a wooden spoon or potato masher.
3. Add the blackberries and sugar to the apple pulp, stirring until the sugar has dissolved, then add a knob of butter.
4. Bring to the boil and boil rapidly, stirring frequently, for about 10 minutes. Test for a set and, when setting point is reached, take the pan off the heat and skim the surface with a slotted spoon. Pot and cover the jam.

GOOSEBERRY JAM

THE MIDLANDS

Late June is the time to look for the hard, green, early gooseberries this recipe calls for. The jam can also be made later in the season, with riper, sweeter fruit. It will then have a light set and an attractive pale pink colour.

MAKES ABOUT 4.5 kg (10 lb)

2.7 kg (6 lb) gooseberries (slightly under-ripe), topped and tailed

2.7 kg (6 lb) sugar

a knob of butter

---

1. Put the gooseberries in a preserving pan with 1.1 litres (2 pints) water. Simmer gently for about 30 minutes, until the fruit is really soft and reduced, mashing it to a pulp with a wooden spoon and stirring from time to time to prevent sticking.
2. Remove from the heat, add the sugar to the fruit pulp and stir until dissolved, then add a knob of butter.

3. Bring to the boil and boil rapidly for about 10 minutes. Test for a set and, when setting point is reached, take the pan off the heat and skim the surface with a slotted spoon. Pot and cover the jam.

VARIATION
Elderflower gooseberry jam
A delicious and unusual flavour can be given to gooseberry jam by adding 6–8 elderflower heads to each 1 kg (2¼ lb) fruit. Cut off the stems close to the flowers and tie the flowers in a piece of muslin. Add the muslin bag to the jam when it comes to the boil, removing it before the jam is potted.

TO MICROWAVE

Use 900 g (2 lb) gooseberries and 900 g (2 lb) sugar. Put the gooseberries in a large bowl and cook on HIGH for 8–10 minutes, stirring frequently, until really soft. Stir in the sugar until dissolved. Cook on HIGH for 35 minutes, until setting point is reached. Stir twice during cooking. Pot and cover the jam.

ORANGE CURD

COUNTRYWIDE

This luscious preserve makes a change from the more usual lemon curd. It is very simple to prepare, and has a beautifully smooth, rich texture and a fresh flavour. Use it to fill a sandwich cake, or as a tea-time spread for scones, toast or bread.

MAKES ABOUT 450 g (1 lb)

grated rind and juice of 2 large oranges
juice of ½ lemon
225 g (8 oz) caster sugar
100 g (4 oz) butter
3 egg yolks, beaten

1. Put all the ingredients in the top of a double saucepan or in a bowl standing over a pan of simmering water. Heat gently, stirring, for about 20 minutes, until the sugar has dissolved and the mixture is thick enough to coat the back of a spoon.
2. Strain, pot and cover the curd.
Note Home-made orange curd should be made in small quantities as it only keeps for about 1 month. Store in a cool place.

TO MICROWAVE

Put all of the ingredients in a large bowl. Cook on HIGH for 5–6 minutes or until the curd is thick enough to coat the back of a spoon, whisking frequently. Do not let it boil. Follow step 2.

CURRANT AND PORT JELLY

THE SOUTH-EAST

This is a delicious way to use up a glut of red or blackcurrants, and has a richer flavour and deeper colour than usual. The port goes in at the last moment, so none of its flavour is lost through boiling.

The yield will depend on the ripeness of the fruit and the time allowed for dripping.

1.4 kg (3 lb) red or blackcurrants
sugar
45 ml (3 tbsp) port

1. There is no need to remove the currants from their stalks. Put the currants in a preserving pan with 568 ml (1 pint) water and simmer gently for about 30 minutes, until the fruit is really soft and pulpy. Stir from time to time to prevent sticking.
2. Spoon the fruit pulp into a jelly bag or cloth attached to the legs of an upturned stool, and leave to strain into a large bowl for at least 12 hours. Do not squeeze.

3. Discard the pulp remaining in the jelly bag. Measure the extract and return it to the pan with 450 g (1 lb) sugar for each 568 ml (1 pint) extract.
4. Heat gently, stirring, until the sugar has dissolved, then boil rapidly for about 15 minutes. Test for a set and, when setting point is reached, remove the pan from the heat.
5. Stir in the port, skim the surface with a slotted spoon and pot and cover the jelly.

TO MICROWAVE

Put the currants in a large bowl with 300 ml (½ pint) boiling water. Cook on HIGH for 10–15 minutes, until the fruit is really soft and pulpy, stirring frequently. Complete the recipe.

OXFORD MARMALADE

THE SOUTH-EAST

The tradition of making marmalade at home goes back at least 200 years, even though in those times oranges were something of a luxury, as they were expensive to import. Oxford marmalade is characteristically dark and chunky, with a slightly bitter flavour.

MAKES ABOUT 4 kg (9 lb)

1.4 kg (3 lb) Seville oranges
2.7 kg (6 lb) sugar

1. Peel the oranges and cut the peel into strips and the fruit into small pieces, reserving the pips. Put the pips into a small bowl. Put the strips of peel and chopped flesh into a large bowl.
2. Bring 3.4 litres (6 pints) water to the boil and pour 568 ml (1 pint) over the pips and the remainder over the orange peel and flesh. Cover both bowls and leave for several hours or overnight.
3. The next day, the pips will be covered with a soft transparent jelly which must be washed off them into the orange peel and flesh. To do this, lift the pips out of the water with a slotted spoon and put them in a nylon sieve. Pour the water the pips were soaking in over the pips into the large bowl. Repeat the process, using water from the large bowl. Discard the pips.
4. Boil the peel, flesh and water until the peel is very soft – the longer this mixture boils the darker the marmalade will be.
5. When the peel is quite soft, remove the pan from the heat and add the sugar, stirring until it has dissolved.
6. Boil very gently until the marmalade is as dark as you like it, then boil rapidly for about 15 minutes. Test for a set and, when setting point is reached, take the pan off the heat and skim the surface with a slotted spoon.
7. Leave to stand for 15 minutes, then stir to distribute the peel. Pot and cover the marmalade.

MINCEMEAT. Fruity, spicy
and with more than a dash of
alcohol, this is the traditional
filling for mince pies. It can
also be used to fill open tarts,
large or small.

ROSE PETAL JAM
COUNTRYWIDE

An unusual jam, with a strong, distinctive flavour. Deep-red heavily scented roses are the best to use.

MAKES ABOUT 450 g (1 lb)

225 g (8 oz) rose heads
450 g (1 lb) sugar
juice of 2 lemons

1. Pick the roses when they are in full bloom, remove the petals and snip off the white bases.
2. Place the petals in a bowl and add 225 g (8 oz) sugar. Cover and leave overnight. This will extract the scent and darken the petals.
3. Pour 1.1 litres (2 pints) water and the lemon juice into a saucepan and stir in the remaining sugar. Heat gently until the sugar has dissolved, but do not boil.
4. Stir in the rose petals and simmer gently for 20 minutes. Bring to the boil and boil for about 5 minutes, until thick. Pot and cover in the usual way.

TO MICROWAVE

Complete steps 1 and 2. Pour 1.1 litres (2 pints) boiling water into a large bowl. Add the remaining sugar and stir until dissolved. Stir in the rose petals and cook on HIGH for 35–40 minutes, until thick. Pot and cover the jam.

MINCEMEAT
COUNTRYWIDE

The use of beef suet is reminiscent of the days when meat was always included in the recipe – hence its name. It was originally made to preserve meat through the winter.

MAKES ABOUT 2.5 kg (5½ lb)

1.6 kg (3½ lb) dried mixed fruit
225 g (8 oz) cooking apples, peeled, cored and grated
100 g (4 oz) blanched almonds, chopped
450 g (1 lb) dark soft brown sugar
175 g (6 oz) shredded beef suet
5 ml (1 tsp) grated nutmeg
5 ml (1 tsp) ground cinnamon
grated rind and juice of 1 lemon
grated rind and juice of 1 orange
300 ml (½ pint) brandy or sherry

1. Put the dried fruits, apples and almonds in a large bowl. Add the sugar, suet, spices, lemon and orange rinds and juice and brandy or sherry, then mix all the ingredients together thoroughly.
2. Cover the mincemeat and leave to stand for 2 days. Stir well, put into jars and cover. Allow at least 2 weeks to mature before using.
Note For mincemeat that will keep well, use a firm, hard type of apple, such as Wellington; a juicy apple, such as Bramley's Seedling, may make the mixture too moist.

HERBS

Used from earliest times as natural flavourings as well as aids to health and beauty, herbs have recently enjoyed a tremendous revival in Britain. Many specialist herb farms now offer mail order facilities, and fresh as well as frozen and dried herbs are increasingly available from supermarkets. It's a delight to experiment with herbs in cooking, to discover their nuances of flavour, from the robust to the delicate.

BAY

Often used as a flavouring with parsley and thyme sprigs; used to flavour slow-cooked dishes – soups, stocks, pâtés, casseroles, even baked custard in days gone by.

ROSEMARY

Pungent flavour, special affinity with lamb. Can give subtle aroma to scones and breads (see recipe, page 289). The sharp needles must be finely chopped or dried and crumbled.

PARSLEY

Curly and flat-leaved continental types available. Britain's most popular herb, used in stuffings (see recipe, page 166), sauces for fish, ham and eggs (see recipes, pages 151, 104), and as a garnish, both fresh and deep-fried. Loses flavour when dried; freezes well.

CHERVIL

Closely resembles parsley, more delicate flavour. With tarragon, parsley and chives it's a classic flavouring for sauces, herb butters and omelettes.

DILL

The feathery leaves are specially good with fish; seeds are used in pickling mixtures, potato salad, coleslaw.

GREEN TOMATO CHUTNEY

COUNTRYWIDE

The answer to the problem of what to do with tomatoes that refuse to ripen is to make this lightly spiced, smooth chutney, which goes well with cheese and all cold meats.

MAKES ABOUT 1.4 kg (3 lb)

450 g (1 lb) cooking apples, peeled, cored and finely chopped

225 g (8 oz) onions, skinned and finely chopped

1.4 kg (3 lb) green tomatoes, thinly sliced

225 g (8 oz) sultanas

225 g (8 oz) demerara sugar

10 ml (2 tsp) salt

450 ml (¾ pint) malt vinegar

4 small pieces of dried root ginger

2.5 ml (½ tsp) cayenne pepper

5 ml (1 tsp) mustard powder

1. Put all the ingredients in a preserving pan. Bring to the boil, reduce the heat and simmer gently for about 2 hours, stirring occasionally, until the ingredients are tender, reduced to a thick consistency and no excess liquid remains.
2. Remove the ginger, spoon the chutney into preheated jars and cover at once with airtight, vinegar-proof tops.

TO MICROWAVE

Reduce the vinegar to 300 ml (½ pint) and put in a large bowl with all the remaining ingredients. Cook on HIGH for 1 hour until thick and reduced, stirring frequently. Complete the recipe.

MINT JELLY

COUNTRYWIDE

A delicious herb jelly, made in the traditional way, and a pleasant change from mint sauce to go with roast lamb.
The yield will depend on the ripeness of the fruit and the time allowed for dripping.

2.3 kg (5 lb) cooking apples, such as Bramleys

a few large sprigs fresh mint

1.1 litres (2 pints) distilled white vinegar

sugar

90–120 ml (6–8 tbsp) chopped fresh mint

a few drops of green food colouring

1. Remove any bruised or damaged portions from the apples and roughly chop them into thick chunks without peeling or coring. Put them in a preserving pan

with 1.1 litres (2 pints) water and the mint sprigs. Bring to the boil, then simmer gently for about 45 minutes, until soft and pulpy. Stir from time to time to prevent sticking. Add the vinegar and boil for a further 5 minutes.
2. Spoon the apple pulp into a jelly bag or cloth attached to the legs of an upturned stool, and leave to strain into a large bowl for at least 12 hours. Do not squeeze.
3. Discard the pulp remaining in the jelly bag. Measure the extract and return it to the preserving pan with 450 g (1 lb) sugar for each 568 ml (1 pint) extract.
4. Heat gently, stirring, until the sugar has dissolved, then boil rapidly for about 10 minutes. Test for a set and, when setting point is reached, take the pan off the heat and skim the surface with a slotted spoon.
5. Stir in the chopped mint and add a few drops of green food colouring. Allow to cool slightly, then stir well to distribute the mint and pot and cover the jelly.

VARIATION
Herb jellies
Other fresh herbs, such as rosemary, parsley, sage and thyme, can be used equally as well as mint. Serve these herb jellies with roast meats – rosemary jelly with lamb; parsley jelly with gammon; sage jelly with pork; and thyme jelly with poultry.

SPICED CRAB-APPLES

COUNTRYWIDE

Crab-apples were used in medieval times to make verjuice, a kind of vinegar. Their pleasantly tangy acidity makes them well worth using in this recipe for spicy pickled fruits. Serve as an accompaniment to cold meat.
The yield will depend on how tightly the apples are packed and the capacity of the jars.

2.7 g (6 lb) crab-apples, trimmed

2–3 strips lemon rind

450 g (1 lb) sugar

450 ml (¾ pint) red wine vinegar

1 cinnamon stick

1–2 whole cloves

3 peppercorns

1. Put the crab-apples in a preserving pan with 900 ml (1½ pints) water and the strips of lemon rind and simmer gently until just tender.
2. Remove the pan from the heat and strain, reserving the liquid. Put the sugar and vinegar in a pan and add 900 ml (1½ pints) of the liquid from the fruit.
3. Tie the spices in a piece of muslin and add to the liquid. Heat gently, stirring, until the sugar has dissolved, then bring to the boil and boil for 1 minute.
4. Add the crab-apples and simmer gently for 30–40 minutes, until the syrup has reduced to a coating consistency. Remove the muslin bag after 30 minutes.
5. Pack the fruit in small jars, pour over the syrup and cover with airtight and vinegar-proof tops.

TARRAGON

Subtle flavour goes well with fish, chicken, eggs and veal. Makes fine vinegar.

BASIL

Sweet aroma goes superbly with tomatoes – cooked, in pasta sauces, raw in salads. Crushed leaves infused in oil give superb flavour to salads.

THYME

Can be used very successfully dried, to flavour hearty soups and stews.

MARJORAM

Good in meat loaf, shepherd's pie, pasta sauces, pizza toppings and stuffing mixtures.

CHIVES

Best added at end of cooking or as garnish: mild onion flavour lost when cooked. Snip over creamy soups, into salads, mix with cream cheese, use in potato (see recipe, page 230) and egg dishes.

BEET RELISH

THE NORTH

There are two types of beetroot: long and globe shaped. Use either for this spicy pickle, which makes an excellent accompaniment to cold meats. This is a good recipe for using up large, maincrop beetroots, available all year, which are tougher than the younger, small beetroots which are available in early summer and are so good in salads.

MAKES ABOUT 700 g (1½ lb)

| 900 g (2 lb) cooked beetroot, skinned and diced |
| 450 g (1 lb) white cabbage, finely shredded |
| 75 g (3 oz) fresh horseradish, grated |
| 15 ml (1 tbsp) mustard powder |
| 568 ml (1 pint) malt vinegar |
| 225 g (8 oz) sugar |
| pinch of cayenne pepper |
| salt and pepper |

1. Combine all the ingredients in a large saucepan. Bring slowly to the boil, then simmer for 30 minutes, stirring occasionally.
2. Spoon into pre-heated jars and cover at once with airtight, vinegar-proof tops.
3. Store in a cool, dry, dark place and leave to mature for 2–3 months before eating.

TO MICROWAVE

Halve the ingredients. Put all the ingredients in a large bowl and cook on HIGH for about 40 minutes, stirring frequently. Complete the recipe. Makes about 350 g (12 oz).

LEFT
BEET RELISH. Fresh horseradish gives a spark of heat to this spicy relish which is particularly good with cold roast beef.

RIGHT
SPICED CRAB-APPLES. Spices, sugar and red wine vinegar are used to infuse the apples with flavour.

PLUM BUTTER

COUNTRYWIDE

It takes a lot of fruit to make a small amount of butter, so save this recipe for the end of the season, when there is a glut. Fruit butter does not keep very well, so eat it up fairly quickly. It is soft, and can be spread easily.

MAKES ABOUT 1.1 kg (2½ lb)

1.4 kg (3 lb) plums, skinned and stoned
grated rind and juice of 1 lemon
sugar

1. Put the plums, lemon rind and juice in a large saucepan and add about 450 ml (¾ pint) water to cover. Simmer gently for 15–20 minutes, until the fruit is soft and pulpy.
2. Using a wooden spoon, press the fruit pulp through a nylon sieve and measure the purée.
3. Return the purée to the pan and add 350 g (12 oz) sugar for each 568 ml (1 pint) purée.
4. Heat gently, stirring, until the sugar has dissolved, then bring to the boil and boil for 20–25 minutes, stirring frequently, until the mixture thickens and is like jam in consistency.
5. Pot and cover the butter.

TO MICROWAVE

 Put the plums, lemon rind and juice in a large bowl with 300 ml (½ pint) water. Cover and cook on HIGH for 10–15 minutes, until tender, stirring occasionally. Complete the recipe.

DAMSON CHEESE

COUNTRYWIDE

Fruit cheeses are traditional country preserves, with a very thick texture, and are usually served sliced, to accompany meat, poultry or game. They can be potted in small moulds and simply turned out whole when needed.

MAKES ABOUT 1.4 kg (3 lb)

1.4 kg (3 lb) damsons
sugar

1. Put the fruit and 150–300 ml (¼–½ pint) water, to just cover, in a saucepan. Cover and simmer gently for 15–20 minutes, until the fruit is really soft. Scoop out the stones with a slotted spoon as they come to the surface.
2. Using a wooden spoon, press the fruit pulp through a nylon sieve and measure the purée.
3. Return the purée to the pan and add 350 g (12 oz) sugar for each 568 ml (1 pint) purée.
4. Heat gently, stirring, until the sugar has dissolved, then bring to the boil and boil gently, stirring frequently, for 30–40 minutes, until so thick that the wooden spoon leaves a clean line through the mixture when drawn across the bottom of the pan.
5. Pot and cover the cheese or, if preferred, prepare and fill a bowl or several small moulds from which the cheese can be turned out and served whole. Leave to set and cover as for jam. Store in a cool, dry place for 2 months to mature.

TO MICROWAVE

 Put the fruit and 150 ml (¼ pint) water in a large bowl. Cover and cook on HIGH for 10–15 minutes, until tender, stirring occasionally. Discard the stones. Complete the recipe.

BREAD AND BUTTER PICKLE

COUNTRYWIDE

Home-produced cucumbers, grown under glass, are available almost all year round, with just a brief gap from November to February. Choose firm, straight cucumbers that have an even colour to make this sharp-flavoured pickle, which is good with simple dishes such as sandwiches or bread and butter – hence its name.

The yield will depend on how tightly the vegetables are packed and the capacity of the jars.

3 large ridge or smooth-skinned cucumbers
4 large onions, skinned and sliced
45 ml (3 tbsp) salt
450 ml (¾ pint) distilled white vinegar
150 g (5 oz) sugar
5 ml (1 tsp) celery seeds
5 ml (1 tsp) black mustard seeds

1. Thinly slice the cucumbers, then layer the cucumber and onion slices in a large bowl, sprinkling each layer with salt. Leave for 1 hour, then drain and rinse well.
2. Put vinegar, sugar and celery and mustard seeds in a saucepan and heat gently, stirring, until sugar has dissolved. Bring to boil and boil for 3 minutes.
3. Pack the vegetable slices into pre-heated jars and add enough hot vinegar mixture to cover. Cover immediately with airtight, vinegar-proof tops.
4. This pickle must be stored in a dark place or the cucumber will lose its colour. Store for 2 months to mature before eating.

TO MICROWAVE

 Complete step 1. Put the vinegar, sugar and celery and mustard seeds in a large jug and cook on HIGH for 4–5 minutes, until boiling. Stir until the sugar has dissolved. Cook on HIGH for 2 minutes. Complete the recipe.

FRUIT VINEGARS

COUNTRYWIDE

Flavoured vinegars can be used wherever you would use ordinary vinegar, and add a subtle flavour all of their own. You can use one favourite herb by itself, or a mixture of several. The fruit-flavoured versions are unusual and make very successful salad dressings.

raspberries, blackberries or blackcurrants

red or white wine vinegar

sugar

1. Put the fruit in a bowl and break it up slightly with the back of a wooden spoon. For each 450 g (1 lb) fruit, pour in 568 ml (1 pint) red or white wine vinegar. Cover with a cloth and leave to stand for 3–4 days, stirring occasionally.
2. Strain through muslin and add 450 g (1 lb) sugar to each 568 ml (1 pint). Boil for 10 minutes, then cool,

strain again, pour into bottles and seal with airtight and vinegar-proof tops. Add a few whole pieces of fruit to each bottle, if liked. Use when making salad dressings.

HERB VINEGARS

COUNTRYWIDE

sprigs of fresh herbs, such as rosemary, tarragon, mint, thyme, marjoram, basil, dill, sage, parsley

red or white wine vinegar

1. Fill bottles with sprigs of fresh herbs. Use either a mixture of herbs or one variety. Fill with red or white wine vinegar.
2. Seal with vinegar-proof tops and leave in a cool, dry place for about 6 weeks. Use when making salad dressings.

FRUIT AND HERB VINEGARS. Raid the garden to make a stunning array of vinegars in jewel colours to liven up the larder shelf. And they taste every bit as good as they look.

FROM THE SHOP TO THE KITCHEN

BUYING FRESH FOOD

Knowing what to look for and how to select wisely are important factors when buying foods. The following notes will help you in your choice.

CHOOSING MEAT

When choosing meat, it helps to bear in mind the cooking method that you intend using. If you want something to cook quickly by a dry heat method such as grilling or roasting, it must be a lean, tender cut from a prime-quality animal and will inevitably be more expensive. Slower cooking with added moisture is suitable for one of the tougher, probably fattier cuts, which will be cheaper. If in doubt, ask your butcher for advice. Many prepackaged meat cuts carry labels suggesting suitable methods of cooking, and these should be considered. The nutritional quality of the cheaper cuts is the same as that of the dearer cuts and the flavour of both is just as good if cooked properly.

Generally speaking, choose meat which has no undue amount of fat surrounding it; what fat there is should be firm and free from dark marks or discoloration. The colour of fat may vary for a number of reasons, none of which will affect the taste. Lean meat should be finely grained, firm and slightly elastic; a fine marbling, or flecks of fat in the meat, will help to keep the meat moist during cooking and often gives a better flavour. Coarse-grained meat is usually an indication that the meat is suitable only for stewing or

braising. Do not worry about the colour of meat. The redness of meat will vary after cutting and exposure to air, but this need not affect your choice.

Whether you choose fresh or frozen meat is a matter mainly of personal preference, but frozen meat that has been thawed should not be refrozen unless cooked first.

CHOOSING POULTRY AND GAME

If buying *fresh poultry*, choose a bird that looks plump and well rounded. The skin should be free from blemishes and bruising. In a young chicken the tip of the breast bone will be soft and flexible; if it is hard and rigid the bird is probably too old to roast satisfactorily although it will be suitable for steaming or boiling.

Modern poultry production methods ensure a moist, tender-fleshed bird. Prompt freezing also guarantees freshness, so you can expect high quality from any of the well-known brands of frozen poultry. Traditionally reared farmyard birds are inclined to have more flavour.

Larger birds generally give the best value as the proportion of meat to bone is higher and the extra meat, particularly chicken and turkey, left over from the first meal is excellent cold or made up in another dish. Remember that packaged poultry, frozen or fresh, is sold by oven-ready weight, but a fresh bird bought from a traditional poulterer or butcher will probably be sold at 'plucked weight' – plucked but not drawn. The butcher will draw it for you, but after weighing and pricing. You will need to allow for this in estimating the size of bird you require.

Game birds are best eaten young. The plumage is a guide as all young birds have soft even feathers. With pheasants and partridge, the long wing feathers are V-shaped in a young bird, as distinct from the rounded ones of an older bird. Smooth, pliable legs, short spurs and a firm, plump breast are other points to look for. Most game birds need to be hung so check this with your butcher or poulterer. He will probably pluck and draw it for you if you ask. If game is not hung, the flesh will be tough and tasteless. Look out for game in supermarkets too, where the game is ready for the oven.

CHOOSING FISH AND SEAFOOD

Really fresh *whole fish* has clear, bulging eyes and bright red gills. Avoid any with sunken, cloudy eyes and faded pink or grey gills. The body of the fish should be firm and springy to the touch, with shining skin and bright, close-fitting scales. *Fish fillets* and *steaks* should look freshly cut, the flesh moist and firm-textured, showing no signs of dryness or discoloration. The bones should be firmly embedded in the flesh; if they are loose and coming away from the flesh this indicates that the fish has been cut for some time and is past its best.

When buying *frozen fish*, make sure that it is solidly frozen, clear in colour and free of ice crystals. Any smell should be mild and clean, exactly as for fresh fish. Breadcrumbs or batter coatings on frozen fish portions should be crisp and dry looking. Avoid frozen fish that has a brownish tinge or that is in any way damaged.

Shellfish should be very fresh as they are more perishable than other fish. They should have a clean sea smell and clear fresh colour; avoid any that are dull looking. Prawns and shrimps should have tails curled well under them. Look for tightly closed shells where applicable.

While it is unwise to freeze your own shellfish – since the temperature required for satisfactory preservation of shellfish is lower than that normally obtainable in any domestic freezer – commercially *frozen shellfish* are useful when the type you require is out of season. You can also freeze very fresh shellfish in made-up dishes such as soups, fish pies and quiches.

CHOOSING DAIRY PRODUCE

When buying fresh *milk*, *cream* and *yogurt*, look at their date stamps, then keep them cool, clean and covered to ensure they stay fresh.

Cheese can be bought from specialist cheese shops and supermarkets. Freshly cut cheese should look fresh, with no dried or greasy areas on the surface. It is important that the cut surface of cheese is always covered and that a mild-flavoured cheese is not kept alongside a strong cheese. If buying pre-packed cheese, check that it does not look sweaty or excessively runny and that it is within the life of its date stamp. If buying a ripened soft cheese, such as Lymeswold, well before the expiry of the date stamp, you may prefer to keep it to allow it to ripen to your liking.

When buying prepacked *eggs* in shops you can get some idea of how old they are by checking the week number given on the box. Week 1 falls at the end of December or beginning of January.

CHOOSING FRESH FRUIT AND VEGETABLES

When buying fruit and vegetables always choose them carefully and make sure that they are fresh. Fruits should be bought with unblemished skins. Root vegetables, such as potatoes, carrots and swedes, should be bought firm and unwrinkled. Buy little and often to ensure freshness.

STORING FOOD

Storage of perishable foods such as meat, fish, dairy products, soft fruit and vegetables is of vital importance to keep them as fresh as possible. The best place to keep them is in the refrigerator or, failing this, a cool larder. Perishable foods intended for long-term storage can be kept in a freezer.

All foods that are stored in the refrigerator should be covered or well wrapped to prevent the flavours drifting from one to another and to prevent the food from drying out. Store *cheese* in the bottom of the refrigerator, so it does not get too cold, but it's best to remove it from the refrigerator half an hour before serving to allow it to come up to room temperature and regain its flavour. *Milk*, *cream* and *yogurt* will keep for several days, but check date stamps when buying them. The same applies to cartons of fresh fruit juice. UHT milk will keep well even without a refrigerator but is best stored in a cool place.

Put *meat* in the refrigerator as soon as possible after buying. Remove any paper wrappings, rewrap the meat loosely in polythene or foil, leaving an end open for ventilation, and place the package on a plate in case it drips. If the meat is prepackaged in polythene or cling film, just loosen the wrapping to allow air to circulate. When buying meat in vacuum packs or controlled atmospheric packaging, follow the manufacturer's instructions.

Most fresh meat can be stored in the refrigerator for up to 3 or 4 days; minced meat and offal are more perishable and should be used within 24 hours. Cooked meat should be cooled quickly, wrapped in foil or polythene and, if possible, put into the refrigerator within 1½–2 hours of cooking. Store for up to 4 days. Frozen meat should be left in its wrappings and stored in the freezer or frozen food compartment of the refrigerator.

To store fresh *poultry*, remove the giblets from inside the bird as soon as you get it home. Remove any tight packaging, cover the bird loosely with a polythene bag that will allow the air to circulate and store in the refrigerator for 1–2 days. The giblets should preferably be cooked straight away, as they deteriorate more quickly than the rest of the bird, but in any case they should be stored separately. Stuffings can be prepared in advance, but store them separately too and stuff the bird just before cooking.

Fresh *fish*, from the fishmonger, should be loosely wrapped and stored in the refrigerator. Cook it within 24 hours of purchase. Store frozen fish in the freezer or frozen food compartment in its original wrapping.

Eggs are best kept in a rack in a cool place. If you have to store them in a refrigerator, keep them well away from the ice compartment (there is often a special egg storage rack) and away from foods like cheese, fish or onions whose smells may transfer to the eggs.

Store eggs pointed end down and use them at room temperature; eggs that are too cold will crack when boiled and are also difficult to whisk. Fresh eggs can be stored for 2–3 weeks in the refrigerator or 1–2 weeks in a cool place.

Salad ingredients should be kept at the bottom of the refrigerator, loosely wrapped in polythene bags. Unwashed, most will keep for a week. Mushrooms are best kept in a paper bag and then wrapped in a polythene bag. Once washed, dry salad ingredients well before returning to the refrigerator in a polythene bag.

Green leafy vegetables are also best stored at the bottom of the refrigerator. Trim away any damaged parts and wrap the vegetables in paper before refrigerating. *Root vegetables* like onions, potatoes and carrots should be stored in a cool, airy place such as a vegetable rack so that air can circulate around them. If you buy potatoes ready washed in polythene bags it is best to transfer them to a paper bag so that they do not become soft and spongy. *Fruits* such as apples and pears are best kept in a fruit bowl.

COMMERCIAL FREEZING OF BRITISH FRUIT AND VEGETABLES

All fruit and vegetables, from the moment they are picked, begin to lose their nutritional value and flavour.

Freezing is a convenient way of preserving fresh fruit and vegetables and if blanched and frozen with minimal delay, they remain as close to their natural state as possible.

Commercial quick-freezing produces small ice crystals, which means there is little deterioration of the flavour, colour and nutritive value of fruit and vegetables. Frozen produce can thus often be fresher than the fresh fruit and vegetables in the shops.

PICK YOUR OWN

Fruit and vegetable picking can be an enjoyable day out and it's satisfying to come home laden with fresh produce. There is a wide variety of produce available, including soft fruits, green and root vegetables. Don't, however, get so carried away that you have to spend hours freezing, or making jam which you didn't plan to do because you have picked too much to consume. Check with the supplier concerning the suitability of their produce for freezing.

Try to choose a part of the field that hasn't already been well picked – usually the further away from the entrance the better. The best fruit and vegetables tend to grow at the edge of the plant so tread carefully as you walk along the rows.

Select fresh, firm produce and when picking soft fruits don't pile them up so much in your basket that you squash the fruit below. The best way to pick fruits such as strawberries is to pinch the stem and snap it off above the fruit; don't pull the fruit from the plant.

When you get the fruit or vegetables home, use them quickly to avoid them going to waste. If you intend to freeze them, lay them singly on trays and put in the coldest part of the freezer. When solid, pack in polythene bags or rigid containers.

FROM FREEZER TO MICROWAVE

Home freezing is an ideal way of preserving food since you can have a store of produce readily available and you can buy food to preserve at the height of the season when they are cheap. A ✳ symbol beside the recipe in the book indicates which dishes can successfully be frozen.

A freezer and microwave cooker can be ideal companions. The microwave will thaw food in a fraction of the time normally required for complete thawing, which allows you the convenience of being able to select food from the freezer at short notice.

Most foods can be frozen and microwaved without impairing the quality. The thawing process is very fast and because there is a risk that some parts of the food will start to cook while others are still frozen always use the DEFROST or LOW settings.

Pack food in containers suitable for using in both freezer and microwave, never microwave in foil containers and remove metal tags. Open all cartons and remove lids and slit or pierce polythene bags.

To help foods thaw evenly, stir when possible, moving frozen parts to the outside of the dish, separate chunks of food and turn large items over.

Some foods, such as joints of meat, also need to be given a standing time after thawing to ensure that they are completely thawed.

MICROWAVE COOKERS

A microwave cooker can save much time and if used to its best advantage, can be a very useful appliance to have in conjunction with a conventional cooker. Many of the recipes in this book can be prepared and/or cooked in a microwave and instructions are given where appropriate. A ▨ symbol beside the recipe indicates that it is suitable for cooking in a microwave. Microwave instructions are then given at the end of the recipe.

HOW TO USE THE RECIPES IN THIS BOOK WITH YOUR MICROWAVE COOKER SETTINGS

Unlike conventional ovens, the power output and heat controls on microwave cookers do not follow a standard formula. When manufacturers refer to a 700-watt cooker, they are referring to the cooker's POWER OUTPUT; its INPUT, which is indicated on the back of the cooker, is double that figure. The higher the wattage of a cooker, the faster the rate of cooking. Thus food cooked at 700 watts on full power cooks in half the time of food cooked at 350 watts. That said, the actual cooking performance of one 700-watt cooker may vary slightly from another with the same wattage because factors such as cooker cavity size affect cooking performance. The vast majority of microwave cookers sold today are either 600, 650 or 700 watts, but there are many cookers still in use which may be 400 and 500 watts.

IN THIS BOOK

* HIGH refers to 100% full power output of 600–700 watts
* MEDIUM refers to 60% of full power
* LOW is 35% of full power

Whatever the wattage of your cooker, the HIGH/FULL setting will always be 100% of the cooker's output. Thus your highest setting will correspond to HIGH.

However, the MEDIUM and LOW settings used in this book may not be equivalent to the MEDIUM and LOW settings marked on your cooker. As these settings vary according to power input, use the following calculation to estimate the correct setting for a 600–700-watt cooker. This simple calculation should be done before you use the recipes for the first time, to ensure successful results.

Multiply the percentage power required by the total number of settings on your cooker and divide by 100. For example:

MEDIUM (60%) = % Power required
× Total Number of Cooker Settings
÷ 100 = Correct Setting

$$= \frac{60 \times 9}{100} = 5$$

LOW (35%) = % Power required
× Total Number of Cooker Settings
÷ 100 = Correct Setting

$$= \frac{35 \times 9}{100} = 3$$

If your cookery power output is lower than 600 watts, then you must allow a longer cooking time for all recipes in this book.

Add approximately 10–15 seconds per minute for a 500-watt cooker and 15–20 seconds per minute for a 400-watt cooker.

No matter what the wattage of your cooker is, you should always check food before the end of cooking time, to ensure that it does not get overcooked.

Don't forget to allow for standing time.

COMBINATION COOKER OWNERS

Combination cookers combine conventional and microwave methods of cooking so that food browns as well as cooking quickly. If you own a combination cooker you should follow your manufacturer's instructions regarding cooking times.

MICROWAVE COOKERY NOTES

Bowl Sizes
* Small bowl = 900 ml (1½ pints)
* Medium bowl = about 2.3 litres (4 pints)
* Large bowl = about 3.4 litres (6 pints)

Covering
* Cook uncovered unless otherwise stated.
* At the time of going to press, it has been recommended by the Ministry of Agriculture, Fisheries and Food that the use of cling film should be avoided in microwave cooking. When a recipe requires you to cover the container, cover with either a lid or a plate, leaving a gap to let the steam escape.

RECIPE NOTES

* Follow either metric or imperial measures for the recipes in this book. They are not interchangeable.
* All spoon measures are level.
* Sets of measuring spoons are available in both metric and imperial sizes to give accurate measurement of small quantities.
* Size 2 (large) eggs should be used except when otherwise stated.
* Plain or self-raising flour can be used unless otherwise stated.
* Brown or white breadcrumbs can be used unless otherwise stated.

WHEN VEGETABLES ARE IN SEASON
This is to show when British-grown vegetables are available.

	January	February	March	April	May	June	July	August	September	October	November	December
Artichokes – Globe						•	•	•	•			
Jerusalem	•	•	•	•						•	•	•
Asparagus					•	•						
Beans – Broad						•	•					
Runner							•	•	•	•		
Kidney						•	•	•	•			
Beetroot	•	•	•	•	•	•	•	•	•	•	•	•
Broccoli – Calabrese						•	•	•	•	•		
Sprouting			•	•	•							
Brussels – Top	•									•	•	•
Sprouts	•	•	•	•						•	•	•
Cabbage – January King	•	•	•	•						•	•	•
Drum Head								•	•	•	•	
Spring Green	•	•	•									
Red	•	•										•
Carrot	•	•	•	•	•	•	•	•	•	•	•	•
Cauliflower	•	•	•	•	•	•	•	•	•	•	•	•
Celeriac	•	•	•						•	•	•	•
Celery				•	•	•	•	•	•	•	•	•
Chicory	•	•							•	•	•	•
Chinese Leaves				•	•	•	•	•	•	•	•	
Courgettes						•	•	•	•	•		
Cucumbers			•	•	•	•	•	•	•	•		
Endive					•	•	•	•				
Kale	•	•	•	•	•						•	•
Leeks	•	•	•	•				•	•	•	•	•
Lettuce	•	•	•	•	•	•	•	•	•	•	•	•
Marrows						•	•	•	•	•		
Mint				•	•	•	•	•	•	•		
Mushrooms	•	•	•	•	•	•	•	•	•	•	•	•
Mustard and Cress	•	•	•	•	•	•	•	•	•	•	•	•
Onions	•								•	•	•	•
Parsley					•	•	•	•	•	•	•	
Parsnips	•	•	•	•					•	•	•	•
Peppers					•	•	•	•	•	•		
Peas					•	•	•	•	•	•		
Potatoes – New						•	•	•				
Maincrop	•	•	•	•	•					•	•	•
Pumpkin									•	•	•	
Radishes				•	•	•	•	•	•	•		

WHEN VEGETABLES ARE IN SEASON
This is to show when British-grown vegetables are available.

	January	February	March	April	May	June	July	August	September	October	November	December
Seakale	●	●	●									●
Shallots	●								●	●	●	●
Spinach (best Mar/Apr)			●	●	●	●	●	●	●	●		
Spring Onions				●	●	●	●	●				
Swedes	●	●	●	●	●				●	●	●	●
Sweetcorn								●	●	●		
Tomatoes				●	●	●	●	●	●	●		
Turnips	●	●	●			●	●	●	●	●	●	●
Watercress	●	●	●	●	●	●	●	●	●	●	●	●

WHEN FRUITS ARE IN SEASON
This is to show when British-grown fruit is available.

	January	February	March	April	May	June	July	August	September	October	November	December
Apples – cooking	●	●	●	●	●	●				●	●	●
dessert	●	●	●							●	●	●
Blackberries									●	●		
Black/redcurrants						●	●	●				
Crab Apples									●	●		
Cherries						●	●	●				
Chestnuts										●	●	●
Damsons								●	●	●		
Elderberries									●	●		
Gooseberries						●	●	●				
Greengages							●	●				
Loganberries							●	●				
Medlars										●	●	
Mulberries							●	●				
Pears	●	●	●					●	●	●	●	●
Plums						●	●	●	●	●		
Quinces										●	●	
Raspberries						●	●	●	●			
Rhubarb			●	●	●	●						
Strawberries				●	●	●	●	●		●		

INDEX

ACKNOWLEDGEMENTS

The Publishers would like to thank the following for their advice and assistance:

Aberdeen Angus Cattle Society; Adgestone Vineyards; The Apple and Pear Development Council; Aspall Cyder House Products; Bacon and Meat Manufacturers' Association; Beenleigh Manor Farm Foods; Belvoir Fruit Farms; Berwick Glebe Vineyard; Brecon Brewery Ltd; Biddenden Vineyards Ltd; Breaky Bottom Vineyard; Brewers' Society; British Chicken Association; British Egg Information Service; British Food Information Service of Food from Britain; British Frozen Food Association; British Fruit and Vegetable Canners' Association; British Herb Trade Association; British Iceberg Growers' Association; British Poultry Federation; British Quality Vegetables and Salad Association; British Sheep Dairy Association; British Sugar plc; British Tourist Authority; British Trout Association; British Turkey Federation; British United Turkeys; British Watercress Growers' Association; Broadoak Cider Company; Bronte Liqueur Company Ltd; Bruisyard St Peter Vineyard; Butter Information Council; The Campaign for Real Ale; Carmathen Water; Cheddar Farmhouse Cheese Federation; Colman's of Norwich; Colston Bassett and District Dairy Company Ltd; Company of Scottish Cheese Makers Ltd; Copella Fruit Juices; Cornish Scrumpy Company Ltd; Cumbria Tourist Board; Dairy Crest; Delicatessen and Fine Foods Association; Ditchling Vineyards; Dittisham Fruit Farm; Dumfries and Galloway Tourist Board; East Anglia Tourist Board; East Midlands Tourist Board; Elham Park Vineyard; The English Farm Cider Centre; English Hops Ltd; English Vineyards Association; English Wine Centre; F. H. Mann (Bushy Park) Products; Farmhouse English Cheese Bureau; The Farm Shop and Pick Your Own Association; Felstead Vineyards; Flour Advisory Bureau; Food and Drink Federation; Fresh Fruit and Vegetable Information Bureau; Freshly Pressed Juice Association; Frozen Quality Food Ltd; The Game Conservancy Trust; The Goat Producers' Association of Great Britain; Hallgarten Wines Ltd; Hammond & Deacon Ltd; Health Food Manufacturers' Association; Heart of England Tourist Board; Highlands and Islands Development Board; Highlands Spring Ltd; Inch's Cider Company; Industrial Development Board; Infopress; John Murray & Co (Mull) Ltd; Knowle Orchard Produce; Lamberhurst Vineyards; Loch Lomond, Stirling & Trossachs Tourist Board; Meat and Livestock Commission; Meat Promotions Executive; Merrydown Wine and Cider Makers; Milk Marketing Board for England and Wales; Milk Marketing Board for Northern Ireland; Mushroom Growers' Association; National Association of Cider Makers; National Association of Soft Drink Manufacturers; National Dairy Council; The National Farmers' Union; National Farmers' Union – Scotland; National Farmers' Union – Ulster; National Farmers' Union – Wales; National Federation of Fruit and Potato Traders Ltd; National Veal Producers' Association; Norbury's Cider Company; Northern Ireland Tourist Board; Northumbria Tourist Board; North West Tourist Board; Sue Cloke of Paxton & Whitfield; Penshurst Vineyards; Potato Marketing Board; The Processed Vegetable Growers' Association Ltd; Quality British Celery Association; Quality Milk Producers; Royal Agricultural Society of England; Scotch Quality Beef and Lamb Association; Scotch Whisky Association; Scottish Development Agency; Scottish Milk Marketing Board; Scottish Salmon Information Service; Scottish Tourist Board; Seafish Industry Authority; The Shellfish Association of Great Britain; Southern Tourist Board; South East England Tourist Board; Spice Information Bureau; Stilton Cheesemakers' Association; Swiftsden Vineyard; A Taste of Somerset; A Taste of Sussex; Tea Council; Tenterden Vineyards; Thames and Chiltern Tourist Board; Thatcher's Farmhouse Cider; Three Choirs Vineyards Ltd; Torpeek Farm Products; Trofarth Industries; Wales Tourist Board; Welsh Development Agency; Welsh Lamb Enterprise; Westbury Vineyard; West Country Tourist Board; Whitbread Hop Farm; Wye Valley Fruit Farms Ltd; Yorkshire and Humberside Tourist Board.

Cheeses on pages 96–7 supplied by Duff & Trotter, 13 Leadenhall Market, London EC3

With special thanks to Ivan Fagent, Sheelagh Donovan, John Vanner, Geoff Grant, Clare Thomson, Christina Ball and Helen Mott of the Milk Marketing Board; Judith Hodge of British Food & Farming 1989; to David Hellard and Eve Thomson of the National Farmers' Union; and to Emma-lee Gow.

PHOTOGRAPHIC CREDITS

Page 10 Fotobank/England Scene/Andy Gordon; 11 Anthony Blake; 12 (top) Farmers Weekly/P. Allen; 12 (bottom) Stockphotos/Trevor Wood; 13 S & O Mathews; 14 Anthony Blake; 15 (top) Susan Griggs Agency/Simon McBride; 15 (bottom) Colin Molyneux; 16 Colin Molyneux; 17, 20 S & O Mathews; 21 Susan Griggs Agency/Robin Laurence; 22 (top) Andrew Lawson; 22 (bottom) South East England Tourist Board; 23 Daily Telegraph Picture Library/P. Titmuss; 24 (top) Stockphotos/Trevor Wood; 24 (bottom) S & O Mathews; 25 Holt Studios; 28, 29, 30 Colin Molyneux; 31 (top) Neil Holmes; 31 (bottom (2)) Jacqui Hurst; 32 (top) Roger Phillips; 32 (bottom) Colin Molyneux; 33 Susan Griggs Agency/David Beatty; 36 Susan Griggs Agency/Rob Cousins; 37 Daily Telegraph Picture Library/Charles de Jaeger; 38 John Vigurs ; 39 Susan Griggs Agency/Simon McBride; 40 Andrew Lawson; 41, 42, 43 Sefton Photo Library; 46 Stockphotos/Trevor Wood; 47 (top) Susan Griggs Agency/Adam Woolfitt; 47 (bottom) Stockphotos/ Trevor Wood; 48 (top & bottom) Jacqui Hurst; 49 Bruce Coleman Ltd/Eric Crichton; 50 Anthony Blake; 51 Neil Holmes; 52 Frank Lane Picture Agency/Silvestris-Meyers; 53 Susan Griggs Agency/Anthony Howarth; 56 Susan Griggs Agency/Adam Woolfitt; 57 Fotobank/England Scene; 58 (top) Susan Griggs Agency/Simon McBride; 58 (bottom) Fotobank/England Scene; 59 (top) Britain On View (BTA/ETB)/John Melville; 59 John Vigurs; 60 Bruce Coleman Ltd/B & C Alexander; 61 (top) Susan Griggs Agency/Rob Cousins; 61 (bottom) Patrick Thurston; 62 (top) Farmers Weekly; 62 (bottom) Simon Warner; 66 (top) Charles Tait; 66 (bottom) Bruce Coleman Ltd/Gordon Langsbury; 67 Susan Griggs Agency/John Marmara; 68 (top) Susan Griggs Agency/Adam Woolfitt; 68 (bottom) Anthony Blake; 69 (top) The Image Bank/David W. Hamilton; 69 (bottom) Susan Griggs Agency/ Adam Woolfitt; 71 (right) Susan Griggs Agency/Ted Spiegel; 71 (left) Stockphotos/Trevor Wood; 73, 74, 75, 76, 77 John Vigurs.

FURTHER INFORMATION

For further information on dairy products contact:
The Milk Marketing Board
Thames Ditton
Surrey KT7 0EL
01 398 4101

For initial enquiries about any other food produce contact:
British Food Information Service of Food from Britain
5th Floor, 542–544 Market Towers
New Covent Garden Market
London SW8 5NQ
01 720 7551

For a copy of the leaflet 'Vineyards open to the public' send a stamped addressed envelope to:
The English Vineyards Association Information Service
English Wine Centre
Drusilla's Corner
Alfriston
East Sussex BN26 5QS

For a list of PYO farms in your area contact:
Mrs Tessa Crago
The Farm Shop and PYO Association
The National Farmers' Union
Agriculture House
Knightsbridge
London SW1X 7NJ
01 235 5077

Tours of a hop farm can be made at:
Whitbread Hop Farm
Beltring
Paddock Wood
Tonbridge
Kent
TN12 6PY
0622 872 068